This careful study will be very helpful to anyone interested in understanding Christian teaching about what happens after one dies (and how it is based in the Scriptures) and how it compares to some alternative views. It will be especially helpful to those seeking to help others think through this issue and its implications for their own futures.

Dr Roy E. Ciampa
Professor of New Testament,
Chair, Division of Biblical Studies,
Gordon-Conwell Theological Seminary, USA

Bobby Bose's timely book, *Reincarnation, Oblivion, or Heaven?* is well researched and unusual in its content. Very rarely do we find Christian studies on the issue of "State-after-Death," particularly as an alternative voice from the East compared to some well-known perspectives from the West. To theologize effectively in today's multipolar global context, this study follows the old E. Stanley Jones's method of taking the contextual perspectives seriously yet providing an authentic Christian perspective based on the Scriptures and the early church fathers.

I am aware that there are popular books with singular views on life after death and other interrelated topics of great concern to men and women today. But Bose offers us an extensive study considering multiple views, yet keeping its roots grounded in authentic faith.

I commend Bobby Bose for his writing and recommend it as part of any serious thinker's library.

Dr Ken Gnanakan
Founder President of ACTS Group, Bangalore, India

"Why do we die? What happens after we die?" Philosophers as well as theologians suggest various answers to this dilemma. In this book, Bobby Bose investigates Christian as well as Hindu, Muslim, and Modern Secular conceptions of life after death. Make no mistake, however, this is no mere Theology of Death.

Reincarnation, Oblivion, Heaven: three leading words in the title bracket a range of possible explanations clamouring to be heard in today's religiously plural world. Conflicting voices? Through migration the East has come to the West. Also from the South (Latin America, the Pacific Region, and especially

Africa) representative voices of World Christianity are heard. "Mission in reverse" some have called it. One of God's surprises. A Theology of Mission emerging from the Majority World and inter-religious encounter.

Theology of Religions is a critical issue in today's pluralistic world: controversial, difficult, divisive – as Gerald Anderson observes. This is the context in which Bobby Bose addresses the question of "State-after-Death" as understood in Christian, Hindu, Muslim and Secular thought. Rather than an apologetic, polemical, or dialogical approach, Bose has chosen a comparative method. Each religion or ideology thereby gives expression to its response to the "State-after-Death" question. This appears similar to the methodology of the well-known evangelist E. Stanley Jones (1907–1973) who brought the biblical witness to interact with the personal experience of participants at Jones' round-table discussion groups.

Highly recommended for students of world religions, and for all who question, "What happens when I die?"

Dr Roger E. Hedlund
Director Emeritus, Mylapore Institute for Indigenous Studies, Chennai
Managing Editor, *Dharma Deepika: A South Asian Journal of Missiological Research*,
Chief Editor, Oxford Encyclopaedia of South Asian Christianity,
New Delhi, India

The context for Christian missions today is pluralistic, multicultural and multifaith. Bobby Bose provides a great service by addressing a critical area for all people. Because everyone must face death, the "State-after-Death" is an area to which every belief system must attend.

In this scholarly work, Bose overviews how Hinduism, Islam, Secular Humanism and other similar faiths each approach what, if anything, lies beyond death. He explains how Christianity sees the "State-after-Death" by examining contemporary theologians, relevant biblical texts, apostolic fathers and early apologists. Bose believes that a Christian theology of religions must include a response to these various positions. He concludes by proposing points of contact between Christianity and other faith traditions and offers a Christian response.

In the twenty-first century, it is vital that Christians learn to have informed and respectful dialogue with people of other faiths, including Secular Humanists. Bose's *Reincarnation, Oblivion, or Heaven? A Christian*

Exploration goes a long way in equipping Christians to have those conversations and to be able to effectively communicate the hope that is found in Christ.

Paul Sorrentino
Director of Religious Life and Protestant Religious Advisor,
Amherst College, USA

While Christians speak of "the afterlife," their neighbors' preconceptions of the hereafter may diverge widely. In *Reincarnation, Oblivion, or Heaven?*, Bobby Bose examines the "state-after-death" beliefs of Hindus, Muslims, secularists, and others in order to offer insights for sharing the hope of the gospel with greater discernment and clarity. Understanding "state-after-death" perceptions in our conversations matter, he says, because it impacts how others respond to the gospel. Much needed because it is much neglected, Bose's examination of the range of views in comparison to the Bible's teaching is missiologically pivotal and pressing – not to mention overdue. News of Jesus' resurrection made all the difference in the lives of the apostles. As Paul reminded the Corinthian church, the hope of the resurrection is the lynchpin of the gospel. Bose underscores that affirmation and goes on to adeptly offer the help we need for a constructive way forward.

Dr Arthur McPhee
Sundo Kim Professor of Evangelism and Practical Theology,
Asbury Theological Seminary, Wilmore, USA

Bobby Bose in *Reincarnation, Oblivion or Heaven?* invites the reader into a fascinating journey into one of the most crucial questions which every religion must answer: What happens after death? Bose brings us into a vast global and historical survey which can hardly be matched. He surveys the central answer to this question from a Muslim, Hindu and Secularist perspective. He then invites us into a fascinating dialogue with major thinkers such as Dietrich Bonhoefer, Paul Devanandan, Stephen Neill, Hendrick Kraemer, M. M. Thomas, John Hick and Hans Kung. The sheer breath of this holy conversation is truly astonishing. The reader is then invited into a thoughtful study of the biblical response to the question as well as insightful contributions from the early church. This book is a kind of one-stop shop if you want to understand how life after death is understood historically and globally through religious and secular eyes. Throughout this fascinating journey, Bose remains unflinching in his commitment to the biblical proclamation of the power of eternal life through Jesus Christ. If you want to gain a global perspective on life after death, then this is a must read. I joyfully recommend it.

Dr Timothy C. Tennent
President, Professor of World Christianity,
Asbury Theological Seminary, Wilmore, USA

George Bernard Shaw quipped that, "The statistics on death are most impressive: one out of one people die." What then? Allow Dr Bose to take you on a whistle-stop tour through a myriad of scriptures, theologians, saints, secularists and world religions to help answer that question. Biblically faithful, well researched, clearly written, challenging and timely. Highly recommended.

Rev Dr Steve Brady
Principal, Moorlands College,
Christchurch, Chair of the Association of Bible College Principals,
Trustee of the Keswick Convention, UK

This book is a careful exposition of what happens to us in the "State-after-Death," according to Christian, Hindu, Islamic, and modern secular perspectives. As someone who grew up amidst the interaction between these viewpoints in India and has lived and worked as well in the United Kingdom and now in the United States, the author knows his subject matter well and can compare these views on an expert level. The book particularly benefits from his easy movement between western and eastern thinkers, many of whom he can read in the original languages. As a Christian thinker, he has invested the lion's share of discussion into a careful evaluation of conservative to liberal, Protestant to Roman Catholic, theologians across the globe, so readers encounter a breadth of analyses of insights from Athenagoras to Irenaeus to Felix Minucius; Thomas Aquinas to Hans Küng to Kevin Vanhoozer; Antonio Gualtieri to Ajith Fernando to Eliezer Segal; Caroline Walker Bynum to Joyce G. Baldwin to Joanne E. McWilliam Dewart; Mahatma Gandhi to Sunand Sumithra to Swami Adiswarananda; Abdul Qadir Ahmad Zain to Hanna Kassis to Saeed Ali Al-Qahtani - in short, his reading is wide and his mastery of the topic impressive. As a Christian minister, as well as a careful scholar and teacher, he is finally missiological in intent as the book ends on a note of hope, discussing ways to have "effective communication of the gospel to those of other faiths." Readers leave this book equipped to help others grapple with this puzzling and universal topic whose subject matter is essential, as it is the common fate of us all.

Rev Dr William David Spencer
Ranked Adjunct Full Professor of Theology and the Arts, Gordon-Conwell Theological Seminary, Boston Campus/Center for Urban Ministerial Education

The issue of life after death is central to most religions and yet very little is being done to address it from the Christian perspective and use it for mission and evangelism. Dr Bobby Bose in his revised doctoral dissertation entitled, *Reincarnation, Oblivion or Heaven?* has solidly addressed this issue, taking into consideration various religions' views and providing strong biblical as well as theological perspectives of life after death. While acknowledging that all religions discuss this issue and differ drastically from one another, Bose provides a stronger argument to consider the biblical perspective which has strong missional implications. The relevance of this book for the Indian subcontinent where major world religions are practiced is significant. Therefore, it should serve as valuable reading for theology professors as well as students. This book also has a considerable appeal for non-Christians as it provides an extensive and objective treatment of the topic under consideration from various religions' perspectives.

Dr Atul Y. Aghamkar
Professor and Head, Department of Missiology,
South Asia Institute of Advanced Christian Studies, Bangalore,
Chairman, Evangelical Fellowship of India

Reincarnation, Oblivion, or Heaven?

Reincarnation, Oblivion, or Heaven?

A Christian Exploration

Bobby Bose

© 2016 Bobby Bose

Published 2016 by Langham Academic
An imprint of Langham Publishing
www.langhampublishing.org

Langham Publishing and its imprints are a ministry of Langham Partnership

This book is published in cooperation with SAIACS with their permission. First published in 2014 by SAIACS Press.

Indian edition (SAIACS): 978-8-18771-233-6

Langham Partnership
PO Box 296, Carlisle, Cumbria CA3 9WZ, UK
www.langham.org

ISBNs:
978-1-78368-107-5 Print
978-1-78368-166-2 ePub
978-1-78368-168-6 PDF

Bobby Bose has asserted his right under the Copyright, Designs and Patents Act, 1988 to be identified as the Author of this work.

All rights reserved. No part of this publication may be reproduced, stored in a retrieval system or transmitted, in any form or by any means, electronic, mechanical, photocopying, recording or otherwise, without the prior written permission of the publisher or the Copyright Licensing Agency.

British Library Cataloguing in Publication Data
A catalogue record for this book is available from the British Library

ISBN: 978-1-78368-107-5

Cover & Book Design: projectluz.com

Langham Partnership actively supports theological dialogue and an author's right to publish but does not necessarily endorse the views and opinions set forth, and works referenced within this publication or guarantee its technical and grammatical correctness. Langham Partnership does not accept any responsibility or liability to persons or property as a consequence of the reading, use or interpretation of its published content.

To *Supriya Mary* and *Hem Chandra David Bose,* my beloved parents, who went to be in the nearer presence of the Lord in the year 2000.

Contents

Foreword.. xv
Acknowledgements... xix
List of Abbreviations... xxi
Introduction.. 1
1   State-after-Death in Pluralistic Contexts 9
2   The Perspectives of Contemporary Theologians I............. 55
3   The Perspectives of Contemporary Theologians II 93
4   Hermeneutics for Biblical Perspective...................... 131
5   State-after-Death in the Old Testament..................... 171
6   Resurrection from Death in the Old Testament............... 201
7   State-after-Death in the Synoptics and John................ 217
8   State-after-Death in Paul's Epistles and in Revelation...... 245
9   State-after-Death for the Apostolic Fathers 267
10 State-after-Death in the Apologists 291
Conclusions 327
Bibliography.. 333
Index... 345

Foreword

This is an important and unique work. It is important because it deals with a subject that is of profound significance for all humans in all cultures everywhere in the world; yet it has received scant attention in Christian theology, theology of religions and mission theology. Dr Bose deals with the subject of people's thought concerning the "State-after-Death" (SaD) in an irenic, passionate and challenging way. Drawing from his personal background, ministry experience, and missiological research, he is eminently qualified to research, think and write on this topic.

This is a unique work because it deals with such an important topic in a multidisciplinary fashion, drawing from interfaith dialogue, contemporary Christian theology, biblical studies, early Christian thinkers, and Christian missiologists. No stone is left unturned in Dr Bose's careful listening to what others have said or proposed regarding the human being's "state-after-death."

Around the globe, we all live now in a world where people representing different religious perspectives constantly rub shoulders. Dr Bose has chosen to examine four of these religious views: Muslim, Hindu, Secular Humanist and Christian. Everywhere in our world of the twenty-first century, people representing these different religious perspectives work in the same businesses, live in the same neighborhoods, their children attend the same schools, they are members of the same clubs, and they are citizens of the same countries. Yet seldom do we talk to each other about the topic – until a family member, a close friend, or a business associate dies. Then the topic comes to the forefront of our consciousness, yet we find it difficult, even then, to begin such a conversation.

This is an important topic because it deals with a life-transforming question. With the possible exception of the Secular Humanist, the other three views that Dr Bose examines assume the eternality of the soul. This is also true of all ancient worldviews prevalent throughout Africa, Asia and Latin America. I grew up sharing such an assumption living in a Mayan context in southern Mexico. In that context, Christians and Mayan animists are equally convinced that the human soul continues its existence after death, though their paradigms of the "State-after-Death" are quite different. Dr Bose shows how we as Christians may listen carefully in order to take seriously and seek to understand the differing views described in this work. He demonstrates for us all how one's assumptions concerning "state-after-death" influences the way one approaches the life-and-death issues, the deepest values, the most significant priorities of life. Human hope – and Christian hope in particular – flows from, and is deeply influenced by, human perspectives concerning this matter.

This work is unique in the areas of theology of religions and missiological thought. One hundred years ago, a majority of Christian theologians of religion and missiologists alike assumed that all the non-Christian world religions would soon fade into oblivion. And many assumed that even Christianity itself would give way to a pervasive secular humanist perspective that would dominate the global religious scene. One of the surprises of this new century is that the opposite has been true. We have today an explosion of varying religious perspectives, a multiplication of forms of religious affiliation, and a growth of both radically militant and consciously tolerant religious loyalties.

The 1930s and 1940s saw the rise of the comparative religions movement in universities in the West and around the world. This movement presented itself as a quasi-neutral examination of what then were considered varying religious systems: Muslim, Hindu, Secular Humanist, and traditional Christian being examples in relation to this work. Theoretical constructs were created that sought to analyze and explain the similarities and differences between these religious perspectives seen as coherent systems of thought. The comparative religions movement was a scholarly and theoretical enterprise that gave little or no attention to what became known later as the "folk-religious" or "popular-religious" practices of ordinary people in those differing contexts. The significance of the people's assumptions concerning "state-after-death" was given scant attention.

Meanwhile, missionaries and mission thinkers were documenting and reflecting primarily on what they were learning about animism and animist religio-cultural practices around the world. They were concerned about spiritism and the world of the unseen spiritual powers and how to present a Christian gospel that would respond to the deep-level concerns of the people and their cultures to be found in those contexts. The matter of the "state-after-death" was over-shadowed by the missionary concerns regarding the impact of the Christian gospel on the way of life of the living.

The 1960s and 1970s saw the rise of what some would call the "phenomenology of religion" movement. Rather than examine each religious view as an integrated and closed system, this new approach sought to compare and contrast specific practices that could be observed in differing religious perspectives. Thus, some would devote much research to studying, for example, the understanding and role of prayer in Muslim, Hindu, and Christian religious practice. These would be compared and contrasted from a viewpoint that was assumed to be removed and neutral from the groups or cultures being studied.

In the latter part of the twentieth century interest waned in a phenomenological approach to the study of different religious perspectives, giving way to a more "participant-observer," dialogical conversation between people of differing faith traditions who could share with each other their experiences of life as adherents of their faith.

Meanwhile, Christian missiologists and mission practitioners became focused on the impact of the Christian gospel on the differing cultures in various contexts, along with concerns as to how Christians could learn to co-exist with people of other faiths. Gospel-and-culture discussions took center-stage, to be joined by discussions concerning the impact of the gospel in terms of development, compassion, and ministry to the poor.

In the brief summary offered above, the reader can see that the topic of this work was not on anyone's horizon. This work is unique in that it does not follow any of the earlier pathways but rather draws from most of them in seeking to blaze a new methodological trail with regard to a subject that is fundamental in the consciousness of all concerned. The question that this work addresses is essential and crucial in this century of heightened global violence and increased religious persecution. One's assumptions concerning the "state-after-death" influence one's theology, philosophy and missiology – and one's response both to life and to death.

In his irenic and careful listening, Dr Bose maintains throughout a solidly biblical, evangelical and Christian perspective on the topic. This work will be especially helpful for the Christian church and Christian mission as we all learn new ways of interfaith and intrafaith conversation whereby we can "give an answer for the hope that is in us" (1 Pet 3:15).

Charles (Chuck) Van Engen
Pasadena, California

Acknowledgements

First, I thank the Lord Jesus Christ for enabling me to overcome various obstacles in my life to complete this study which I earnestly hope will contribute in some way in his grand endeavor to extend his kingdom in our pluralistic world. Then, I express my heartfelt gratitude to my wife, Margie, for her sacrificial love and support during the several years of study at Fuller Seminary. I acknowledge my debt of gratitude to my mentor, Dr Charles E. Van Engen for his constant encouragement and wise guidance over many years. I also thank other professors: Dr Dean Gilliland and Dr Arthur Glasser for their fatherly counsel, Dr Wilbert Shenk for his advice and insightful comments, Dr Donald Hagner for his help in my study of New Testament perspectives, and Dr Christopher Wright of London, UK, for his helpful corrections.

I am grateful to my parents-in-law, Jack and Peggy Roll, for their enthusiasm and support, to Mrs Barbara Millikan for her generous support, and for others who encouraged and prayed. Of course, I must mention Beulah Wood of SAIACS, whose extensive editorial work has been invaluable. Lastly, but not the least, our daughter, Abigail, has been a great joy and sweetly cheered me up when I felt like quitting.

List of Abbreviations

BDB	*The New Brown-Driver-Briggs-Gesenius Hebrew and English Lexicon* by F. Brown, S. R. Driver and C. A. Briggs, Hendrickson Publishers, 1979.
ILB	*The Interlinear Bible,* ed. Jay P. Green Sr., Hendrickson Publishers, 1986.
NIV	*New International Version*, Zondervan, 1996.
NRSV	*New Revised Standard Version*, Zondervan, 1993.
RSV	*Revised Standard Version*, Oxford University Press, 1963.

Introduction

As millions of people flock to cities all across the globe, many urban centers have become a mixture of diverse ethnic and religious groups. We no longer have what were once considered purely Christian, Muslim, Hindu, or even secular cities, for these cities have become multicultural, multireligious societies, and urban "plurality of faith" has become the norm. In cities, the Christian church is now in close contact with people of many different religious faiths. God's missionary people, the church, must face the theological challenge of multireligious urban contexts around the globe or risk irrelevance.

Once while I was serving in an inner-city church in London, UK, from 1985 to 1992, a Christian schoolteacher asked me to do a memorial service in honor of her Christian mother who had just passed away. I gladly agreed to the request and, assuming my hearers to be broadly Christian, presented a message of hope in the Lord Jesus Christ to comfort the grieving family and friends. However, when I finished the service, a heated discussion arose as to the veracity of the Christian truths I had shared. I soon found out that the schoolteacher's husband, a Hindu, believed in re-incarnation and her two grown sons were Secular Humanists. Some of her friends were Muslims, while others present believed in Purgatory. The universal experience of the death of a loved one had brought together these differing perspectives and I was unprepared.

Time after time this has been my experience in ministry both in the East and in the West, and this is, more than ever, the situation that witnessing Christians must deal with as they encounter people of other faiths in their neighborhoods, workplaces, schools, and in daily social contacts. I have chosen to investigate the views held by Hindu, Muslim, and Modern Secular people on the "State-after-Death"[1] and seek to find a Christian theology that will contribute to Christian conversation in these pluralistic contexts.

---

1. I have created this term "State-after-Death" as a common term in an abbreviated form to refer to the different states or ultimate destiny after death that each of the pluralistic perspectives describes. Some of these perspectives will be developed in later chapters; but, for convenience, from now on I will use the term "State-after-Death" to refer to this complex matter. The issue of what happens after death to humans is a complex, multi-faceted issue with large concepts and assumptions behind it, and a multiplicity of answers offered from numerous perspectives. I have sought to find a way to refer to the issue with a term that would

Since in my view a person's response to questions regarding the "State-after-Death" greatly influences their acceptance or rejection of *God's mission* through Jesus Christ; this study is important for missiological research. Apart from the modern Western or secular culture, all cultures and religious systems have developed ideas on the state of the human "person" after death. Consider the veneration of ancestors in Africa, China and Japan, or the god of the Mayans who holds a limited number of souls for Mayan continuity. Other souls, for Mayans, become planted in animals and then are replanted in new-born humans and so on. A belief in life after death is almost universal yet there is a dearth of missiological literature that deals with the topic, especially needed for interactions with different religions. I find almost no one has examined "State-after-Death" as a missiological topic, yet it is an intriguing possibility for conversations among people of different religious faiths. Death is real and when someone dies in a pluralistic context, people generally set aside their differences to sympathize with those who have lost their loved ones, as we saw in the London reference.

What happens after death is an intriguing yet non-threatening discussion. Yet what happens to the soul after death is an essential part of the gospel, to be communicated thoughtfully in pluralistic contexts as an important task of missiology. Consequently, we will study this issue in relation to three selected religious perspectives in pluralistic contexts, providing basic principles for training for mission and ministry in contemporary multireligious urban contexts.

This study is not primarily about what happens after death as a focus of Christian theology, but, more specifically, it is a study that bears on a Christian theology of religions and therefore mission. In his 1993 essay in honor of Arthur F. Glasser of Fuller Seminary, Gerald H. Anderson observes:

> No issue in missiology is more important, more difficult, more controversial, or more divisive for the days ahead than the theology of religions. This is the arena where conflicting truth claims among world religions challenge Christians to articulate their understanding of the relationship between God's redemptive activity in Jesus Christ and people of other faiths . . .
>
> . . . Christians in the West find themselves immersed in a context of religious pluralism today that they are ill equipped

---

be non-discriminatory towards all perspectives and which would not in the process exclude any possible views of what happens after death.

theologically to deal with . . . The seriousness of the challenge to mission theology is hard to over-estimate . . . This is *the* theological issue for mission in the 1990s and into the twenty-first century.[2]

I would add that the need for a theology of religions is great, not just in the West, but also globally, and I would say further that the issue of "State-after-Death" is one of the crucial issues in the discussion of theology of mission in today's pluralistic contexts.

I have chosen to study Christian beliefs on "State-after-Death" alongside the perspectives of other faiths. What takes place after death is important when the global Christian church (a) engages with the Hindu, Muslim and Secular Humanistic perspectives *inside* and *outside* the church; and (b) communicates the gospel of Jesus Christ as the agent of *God's mission* in these contexts. Harold Netland, summarizing David Bosch's notes in *Transforming Mission*,[3] says:

> If the practice of missions is to be authentically Christian then it *must be shaped by assumptions and values rooted in God's self revelation and the reflection of the church*, and this is what good theology provides. At the same time, if theology is to be faithful to the pattern of the New Testament, *it must be "mission theology," for theological reflection grows out of and responds to the dynamics of the church in its engagement with the world.*[4]

Following Bosch's reference to Thomas Kuhn's idea of a new "paradigm" in science,[5] I want to offer some reflections upon and suggestions for a theoretical structure aimed at a global Christian theology of mission of "State-after-Death" that takes the pluralistic perspectives seriously while also holding faithful to the Bible and early church perspectives. As J. Andrew Kirk affirms:

> Theology of mission . . . has the task of keeping under review and validating best practice in all areas of missionary obedience. It

---

2. Gerald H. Anderson, "Theology of Religions and Missiology: A Time of Testing," in *The Good News of the Kingdom: Mission Theology for the Third Millennium*, eds. Charles Van Engen, Dean S. Gilliland and Paul Pierson (Maryknoll, NY: Orbis Books, 1993), 200–201.
3. Cf. David Bosch, *Transforming Mission: Paradigm Shifts in Theology of Mission* (Maryknoll, NY: Orbis Books, 1991), 15–16, 492–496.
4. Harold Netland, "Theology of Religions, Missiology, and Evangelicals," *Missiology: An International Review* 33, no. 2 (2005): 143 (emphasis added).
5. Bosch, *Transforming Mission*, 184.

tests theory and practice against the apostolic Gospel and history read eschatologically . . . The testing is carried out in the midst of the attempt to implement the new order of relationships, structures and attitudes . . . It is also measured against all known alternatives, be they religious, secular or ideological . . . Theology of mission is a continuous task, as it seeks to point the Christian community in the right direction in its response to the mission to which it has been called.[6]

Christian scholars and theologians have generally failed to recognize that theology of mission is a crucial and continuous task for the church in this day of pluralism. This study seeks to theologize in this new way in order to more effectively communicate the gospel in pluralistic contexts. Thus it will encourage local church leaders to train future church leaders for effective ministry in these contexts.

First, this is an attempt to understand how Hindu, Muslim and Modern Secular thinking perceive the universal experience of death and the hereafter. Second, this study seeks to understand how recent and contemporary Christian theologians deal with the after-death state and their responses to religious pluralism. Third, this study searches biblical and early church perspectives on the State-after-Death and, finally, compares these findings and makes suggestions for communication of the gospel in pluralistic settings.

Questions We Are Asking

- What are the non-Christian views on "State-after-Death" in pluralistic contexts?
- What are the views of contemporary Christian mission theologians' on "State-after-Death" and/or their responses to religious pluralism?
- What are the biblical views of "State-after-Death" in the contexts of religious pluralism?
- What were the perspectives of the pre-Constantinian church on "State-after-Death" in the contexts of religious pluralism of the time?

---

6. J. Andrew Kirk, *What is Mission?: Theological Explorations* (Minneapolis, MN: Fortress, 2000), 21–22.

- What are the implications of this study of "State-after-Death" for a Christian theology of religions (and therefore, mission) for the communication of the gospel in the global pluralistic contexts?

Besides Hindu and Muslim perspectives, there are Buddhist, Jewish, Shinto, Sikh, and so on. I have selected only those that have been major groups within my own ministry in both the West and the East. In fact, most of the other religions have a close affinity to one or the other of the three that I have selected. For example, Buddhism, Jainism and Sikhism are closely related to the Hindu perspective. While Modern Secularism is not usually considered a religion, it has become a major factor in the global pluralistic contexts. A great number of people, even some from the above religious groups, view the ultimate "State-after-Death" through the humanistic lens.

Although I do not agree with the conclusions of John Hick's attempt to construct a global theology of death, I have followed his example of depending on secondary sources due to the enormity of the task. Hick states:

> The notion of a global as distinguished from a one-tradition theology of death requires an inter-cultural as well as an inter-disciplinary approach; and this inevitably involves dealing with a vast amount of material second hand, using work done by experts in the diverse disciplines involved. I have accordingly not hesitated to seek the help of colleagues in other fields.[7]

In providing a definition, I have created the somewhat awkward phrase, "State-after-Death" (see footnote 1), as a neutral term to refer to different states or destinies or what happens after death, according to each of the selected groups. This I will use for convenience and consistency while seeking new directions for a Christian theology of "State-after-Death" which are both biblically authentic and relevant in pluralistic contexts.

Charles E. Van Engen, along with many others[8], has proposed the following method of doing theology of mission,

> Theology of mission encompasses three arenas: biblical and theological presuppositions and values (A) are applied to the

---

7. John Hick, *Death and Eternal Life* (New York, NY: Harper & Row Publishers, 1976), 15.

8. Van Engen notes, "The three-arena nature of missiology is not original with me. A number of others . . . have highlighted something similar" and lists them from Eugene Nida (*Message and Mission* [New York, NY: Harper & Row, 1960]) to Jacobs (1993). Charles E. Van Engen, *Mission on the Way: Issues in Mission Theology* (Grand Rapids, MI: Baker, 1996), 22–23.

enterprise of the ministry and mission of the church (B), and are set in the context of specific activities carried out in particular times and places (C). The ... three circles are brought together by means of an integrating theme that constitutes the central idea interfacing all three circles.⁹

The famous American missionary, E. Stanley Jones, proposed a similar way of doing theology of mission from his sixty-six years of ministry experience (1907–1973) in the pluralistic contexts of India. He combined the interrelation of the biblical text (as the objective reality) with the personal experience in a particular context (as the subjective reality). Jones proposed further that this theology must be then corrected and corroborated by the collective witness of the global church.¹⁰ Following this method of doing theology of mission, this study incorporates the views of "State-after-Death" from the present pluralistic context, from contemporary theologians, and from the biblical and early church perspectives. Finally, this study will suggest a more effective model of theology of "State-after-Death" for global pluralistic contexts.

In chapter 1, I will attempt to show that "State-after-Death" is an intriguing yet important issue for conversations within the Hindu, Muslim and Secular Humanistic perspectives. In chapters 2 and 3, I will show that "State-after-Death" is a much-needed yet ignored subject for discussion within the contemporary Christian church. In these chapters, I will survey contemporary theologians' views of "State-after-Death" and/or religious pluralism. In chapter 2, I will look at Dietrich Bonhoeffer, Paul David Devanandan, Stephen Neill and Hendrik Kraemer. In chapter 3, I will deal with M. M. Thomas, pluralist theologian John Hick and Roman Catholic theologian Hans Küng. This survey will show that "State-after-Death" is a useful area of conversation for the global Christian church as the agents of God's mission in the midst of the pluralistic contexts of the world.

My next task will be to study the primary source of all of our Christian theology, the Scriptures, starting with hermeneutical methodology in chapter 4. In chapters 5 and 6, I will show that "State-after-Death" is a major component of God's mission, that is, God rescues humans from one form of "State-after-

---

9. Van Engen, *Mission on the Way*, 22–23.

10. I have discussed Jones's method of doing theology of mission in more detail in my chapter on "E. Stanley Jones: Doing Theology in a Pluralistic Context" in *Footprints of God: A Narrative Theology of Mission*, eds. Charles Van Engen, Nancy Thomas & Robert Gallagher (Monrovia, CA: MARC, 1999).

Death" to another in the Old Testament. In chapters 7 and 8, I will show that "State-after-Death" is the crucial component of God's mission to rescue humankind from one form of "State-after-Death" to another, accomplished through Jesus Christ by his death and "State-after-Death," resurrection, in the New Testament.

In chapters 9 and 10, I will demonstrate that "State-after-Death" was a central component of conversation by the stalwarts of Christian faith in the early church. As they witnessed for Christ in their religiously pluralistic contexts, they met conflicting pagan views that, "when you are dead that's the end" and "the transmigration of souls." Finally, in Conclusions, I will present suggestions and recommendations for a missiological approach to "State-after-Death" that will communicate the gospel in pluralistic contexts, for "State-after-Death" can prove a positive topic of conversation by Christians with people of other faiths.

1

State-after-Death in Pluralistic Contexts

Humanity is mortal and all humans acknowledge that some day we shall all die, yet we tend to avoid the subject of death. A Yiddish proverb says, "Everyone knows he must die, but no one believes it" and so the whole of humanity lives in conscious denial of death. Whatever religious or sociological backgrounds one may come from and wherever one may travel in this world to live, we all either fear or dislike this seemingly ultimate separation from our loved ones.

Why do we die? What happens after we die? Should we be concerned about it? Or should we just accept it as a passing life-event and ignore it? Should we consider death a taboo topic? Are we not free, in our modern scientific society, to deal with this "fact" in a public way? As a post-modern scientific generation, how are we going to respond to this universal experience?

Philosophers, religious leaders and theologians have proposed personal views but none is universally accepted. Great advances in medical research have only extended life for a limited period. Still the mystery of death and the afterlife need to be treated with importance. Some argue that "death is religion's 'trump card,' for people fear death and religion capitalizes on that fear by claiming to provide answers" but Richard N. Longenecker[1] responds,

---

1. Longenecker, as an editor along with some well-known evangelical scholars, seems to be responding to the same challenge that I am responding to, in this study about "State-after-Death" in pluralistic contexts, in his *Life in the Face of Death: The Resurrection Message of the New Testament*, MNTS, vol. 3 (Grand Rapids, MI: Eerdmans, 1998). In the preface, he notes that the book is attempting to provide "firmer rootage in the biblical materials and better personal application than it usually receives in either scholarly writings or the popular press" (p. ix) and his prayer is that by this book "Christians will be strengthened . . . in their . . . ministries, . . . and witness . . . " (p. x) which is my prayer too.

death is not the invention of religion. Rather, death is religion's greatest challenge. For every religion and every religious philosophy "worth its salt"– or, at least, with any hope of acceptance – must necessarily offer some explanation for death's universal tyranny, some program for alleviating death's effects, and some hope for death's final eradication, thereby providing people with a way of living out their lives in the presence of this ultimate and most vexing human problem.[2]

To that I add that even the secular-humanist must provide some plausible "explanation for death's universal tyranny, some program for alleviating death's effects, and some hope for death's final eradication."

In this chapter I review the literature of the three selected perspectives, Hindu, Muslim and Modern Secular views.

The Hindu Perspective

For the Hindu, tradition is sacred and Hindus look to their tradition for answers over death and "State-after-Death." Hinduism has a storehouse of information about ways of understanding the human conditions here on earth, their plight and methods of deliverance. In all the religious stories, symbols, images and teachings of Hinduism, coded information is transmitted about the nature of reality and how death is to be understood. Longenecker comments,

> In the *Vedas* (Sanskrit for "knowledge"), the oldest writings of Hinduism, little attention is paid to death . . . mostly interested in life . . . speak only vaguely about death and an afterlife . . . have no developed concept of the soul and fear most what is referred to as "re-death" or "the second death" – that is, as Krishna called it, "the terrible wheel of death and rebirth."
>
> The *Upanishads* . . . which is a philosophical collection of teachings on the *Vedas* that dates from the seventh century BC . . . give prominence to *Atman*, the eternal "soul," which is the inmost being of every person and the inmost essence of all that exists . . . And it is Hinduism as defined by the *Upanishads* that

---

2. Longenecker, *Life in the Face of Death*, 2–3.

is most practiced in India today and is the best known form of Hinduism worldwide.[3]

Due to the limited scope of this study, I will only examine the *Upanishads* and later writings such as the *Bhagavad-Gita*.

In the later Hindu tradition, the initial human reaction to death and dying is great anxiety, grief and depression, as in the opening account of the *Bhagavad Gita*. The *Gita* refers to the epic battle between the *Pandavas* and their cousins *Kauravas*. On the eve of the battle, one of the five *Pandava* brothers, *Arjuna* the great Archer, went to survey his cousins on the enemy side and considered the terrible massacre that would take place during battle. He was deeply moved at the prospect of the death of his relatives and decided not to be an accomplice in the bloodshed (*Bhagavad Gita* 1:31–47). This shows that Hinduism acknowledges death to be a painful predicament for both the living and the dead. However, in the above narrative *Arjuna*'s charioteer, *Krishna* (Hindus refer to him as the Lord *Shri Krishna*) soon intervenes in with a message urging *Arjuna* to fight on in spite of the terrible consequences (*Bhagavad Gita* 2:11-18). Nevertheless, in popular practice Hindus dread death as a first reaction and avoid the topic due to the grief and separation it brings upon the living.

Death in the Cycle of Life

"State-after-Death" in Hindu tradition is a cyclic notion of human life and the whole universe. This is in contrast to Semitic religions that move with a linear understanding of human progress from one imperfect life here on earth to a possible perfection in the kingdom of God or heaven after death. In Hinduism, all things move in cycles of birth, death and rebirth, going on endlessly until liberation or salvation from this cycle into the bliss of an abstract *Moksha*. Thus, death is not considered the end of life in humans but simply a passage to rebirth. Death is considered a break in the series of successive events that is called life and so it is a necessary and meaningful passage in the cycle of birth, death and rebirth. Harold Coward[4] notes that the idea that each person

---

3. Ibid., 3.
4. Harold Coward, *Life after Death in World Religions* (Maryknoll, NY: Orbis Books, 1997), 4. Coward has taught religious studies at the University of Calgary, Canada, now teaches philosophy at the University of Victoria, Canada, is its director of the Center for Studies in Religion and Society and has published many books including *Hindu Christian Dialogue* (Maryknoll, NY: Orbis Books, 1989) and *Experiencing Scripture in World Religions* (Maryknoll,

is continually reborn from one life to another is fundamental to the Hindu understanding about life after death. According to Coward, the other basic idea in Hinduism is that this rebirth has been continuing without beginning.

Geoffrey Parrinder says in *Death* edited by John Prickett,[5]

> It seems likely that rebirth was an ancient Indian belief, for it first appears in the philosophical Upanishads (about 800 BC) . . . the traditional belief that when the dead are cremated some pass into the flame of the fire, rise up to heavenly worlds, and never return. Others pass into the smoke and rise up to the sky but eventually they return in the rain, passing into the earth and into plants, becoming food and being born again to women.[6]

This cycle of birth, death and rebirth in Hinduism is due to the principle of *Karma* or deeds. Thus, what a person does or thinks in this life determines what he or she will experience in future lives and what one experiences in this life is the result of one's actions in past lives. In Hinduism, all those who have performed good deeds in this life will probably be born again into a pleasant family of a *Brahmin* (priest), *Kshatriya* (warrior) or *Vaishya* (merchant, trader and farmer). But those who have done much evil in this life will be born as a *Shudra* (menial laborer and servants) or as an animal (e.g. dog or a pig) or even as an *outcaste*. Coward notes that this Hindu concept of the deterministic effect of *Karma* and the cycle of birth-death and rebirth (*Samsara*) was adopted by other later religions of Buddhism, Jainism and Sikhism in India.[7] This cycle of rebirth was slightly modified in these later religions.

According to Coward,[8] the law of *Karma* maintains, when a deed is carried out or a thought is thought, whether good or bad, a memory trace is laid down in the unconscious and when a similar situation is encountered in the future, the previous memory rises up in the consciousness as an impulse. Since humans are supposed to have the freedom of choice, they may go along with this impulse and repeat the same action or they may reject this impulse. If

---

NY: Orbis Books, 2000). Coward edited lectures given by "insider" scholars from various religions at the CSRS and organized "the 1995 Distinguished Speakers Series" on the theme of "Life after Death." Each lecture is given in the form of a chapter for Judaism, Christianity, Islam, Hinduism, Buddhism, and the Chinese religions.

5. Prickett, a former high school headmaster, has been the Honorary Secretary of the Standing Conference on Interfaith Dialogue in Education in UK since its inception in 1973. His book represents "insider" views.

6. John Prickett, ed., *Living Faiths: Death* (London: Lutterworth Educational, 1980), 11.

7. Coward, *Life after Death*, 4.

8. Ibid., 4–5.

this latter is chosen the emergent impulse will wither away leaving no further trace in the unconscious. Coward points out that this Hindu understanding does not assume a blank mind at birth, rather it postulates the mind contains memory traces of all actions from many previous lives going back infinitely.

Coward shows that in this law of *Karma* there is a ladder of existence in which gods are the highest form of existence, with humans in second place on the ladder, animals third, while plants and atoms of matter are at the bottom of the ladder. As humans follow evil impulses and reject the good, at death they are subsequently born a step lower on the ladder of existence. However, if they do good and reject their evil impulses, then at death they are born a step higher. In Hinduism, even humans are supposed to have different levels of existence according to the castes they are born into and the animals too have different levels of existence. As humans look for an escape from this beginningless and endless cycle of birth, death and rebirth, Coward notes that Hinduism presents one solution, one way of escape from this cycle.

Immortality of the Soul or Self

Hindu teaching about the cycle of rebirth and survival after death is based upon teaching in the later tradition that the Self or Soul (*atman*) of human beings is immortal and indestructible. This is taught in both the *Upanishads* and the *Bhagavad Gita*. First, in the *Upanishads*, especially the *Katha Upanishad*, one of the mystical and formative scriptures of Hindu tradition, we find an account of the visit of *Nachiketa* to the land of death and his conversation with the king or god of death, *Yama*.[9]

In the opening account of the *Katha Upanishad*, we find that *Vajasrabasa*, the father of *Nachiketa*, was acting quite stingy in giving only the old, the barren, the blind and the lame of his cattle instead of giving all of his possessions. He was doing this in order to gain some divine favor while he

---

9. Kenneth Kramer, a professor of religious studies at the San Jose State University, CA, described *Yama* in this way: "Hindu scriptures tell us that Yama (to restrain), the King of Death, was the first of the immortals to give up immortality in order to conquer death as a mortal. Yama is presented as the god of the dead, the ruler of the departed, and it is he who prepares a resting place for the dead. As the first man to reach the world beyond, Yama is referred to as the father of fathers, the lord of death who presides over the world of the dead. He is pictured with a fearful dark green skin and with glowing red eyes. Usually he carries an ax, a sword and a dagger. In the *Upanishads*, as in the *Mahabharata*, Yama appears as splendid like the sun, of faultless blackness with beautiful red eyes." Kenneth Kramer, *The Sacred Art of Dying: How World Religions Understand Death* (New York, NY/Mahwah, NJ: Paulist Press, 1988), 28.

performed a ritual of sacrifice. His young son *Nachiketa* noticed this and to provoke his father, he said, "Father, I too belong to you: to whom do you give me?" *Vajasrabasa* did not respond but as his son repeated the question, he replied impatiently, "I give you to Death!" To this reply, *Nachiketa* began to consider the state of those who had died before him and the destiny of those who were still alive and the futility of this world's possessions. Thus, *Nachiketa* decided to visit *Yama*, the king or god of death, to learn about the secret of death. Here is a segment of the conversation between *Nachiketa* and *Yama* from the *Upanishads*:[10]

> And then Nachiketa considered within himself, and said:
>
> "When a man dies, there is this doubt: Some say, he is; others say, he is not. Taught by thee, I would know the truth. This is my third wish."
>
> "Nay," replied Death, "even the gods were once puzzled by this mystery. Subtle indeed is the truth regarding it, not easy to understand. Choose thou some other boon, O Nachiketa." . . .
>
> But Nachiketa stood fast, and said: "These things endure only till the morrow, O Destroyer of Life, and the pleasures they give wear out the senses . . . Nay, only the boon that I have chosen – that only do I ask . . .
>
> "Tell me, O King, the supreme secret regarding which men doubt. No other boon will I ask."[11]

After hearing that *Yama* was deeply pleased and then began to teach the secret of immortality to *Nachiketa* in the *Upanishads*:

> The man who has learned that the Self is separate from the body, the senses, and the mind, and has fully known him, the soul of truth, the subtle principle – such a man verily attains to him, and is exceeding glad, because he has found the source and dwelling place of all felicity. Truly do I believe, O Nachiketa, that for thee the gates of joy stand open.
>
> The Self . . . is the omniscient Lord. He is not born. He does not die. He is neither cause nor effect. This Ancient one is

---

10. I used *The Upanishads: Breath of the Eternal*, the principal texts selected and translated from the original Sanskrit by Swami Prabhavananda and Frederick Manchester (New York, NY: Mentor Books, 1957).

11. Ibid., 15–16.

> unborn, imperishable, eternal: though the body be destroyed, he is not killed.
>
> If the slayer think (sic) that he slays, if the slain think that he is slain, neither of them knows the truth. The Self slays not, nor is he slain.
>
> ... When a man is free from desire, his mind and senses purified, he beholds the glory of the Self and is without sorrow.[12]

Thus, for *Yama*, when death comes, only the body dies, the Self (*Atman*) does not die. So the secret of death is to understand that this Self or Soul is hidden in the heart. According to *Yama*, one who realizes Self actually puts an end to death. This realization is called the *Moksha* or liberation from the *Karma* (deeds) and the *Samsara* (the endless cycle of death and rebirth). As we continue to consider this dialogue between *Nachiketa* and *Yama* from the *Upanishads*, we find that *Yama* goes on to say:

> Know that the Self is the rider, and the body the chariot; that the intellect is the charioteer, and the mind the reins.
>
> The senses, say the wise, are the horses; the roads they travel are the mazes of desire. The wise call the Self the enjoyer when he is united with the body, the senses, and the mind ...
>
> He who knows that the individual soul, enjoyer of the fruits of action, is the Self – ever present within, lord of time, past and future – casts out all fear. For this Self is the immortal Self ...
>
> What is within us is also without. What is without is also within. He who sees difference between what is within and what is without goes evermore from death to death ...
>
> The immortal Self is the sun shining in the sky, he is the breeze blowing in space, he is the fire burning on the alter, he is the guest dwelling in the house; he is in all men, he is in the gods, he is in the ether, he is wherever there is truth; he is the fish that is born in water, he is the plant that grows in the soil, he is the river that gushes from the mountain – he, the changeless reality, the illimitable! ...
>
> What can remain when the dweller in this body leaves the outgrown shell, since he is, verily, the immortal Self?

---

12. Ibid., 18.

Man does not live by breath alone, but by him in whom is the power of breath.

And now, O Nachiketa, will I tell thee of the unseen, the eternal Brahman, and of what befalls the Self after death.

Of those ignorant of the Self, some enter into beings possessed of wombs, (sic) others enter into plants – according to their deeds and the growth of their intelligence. That which is awake in us even while we sleep, shaping in dream the objects of our desire – that indeed is pure, that is Brahman, and that verily is called the Immortal. All the worlds have their being in that, and no one can transcend it. That is the Self.[13]

In these teachings of *Yama*, *Nachiketa* learned the secrets of the meaning of death and immortality of the Self or Soul. Kenneth Kramer, a professor of religious studies at the San Jose State University, CA, sums up these secrets:

1) That death is ever-present within the body and in the world at every moment;

2) That while the gross and the subtle bodies change and die, the True Self of each person is undying;

3) That in order to realize the True Self one must die to fears about living and dying;

4) That the only teacher about death is Death itself;

5) That through the art of wholehearted and disciplined surrender, one attains immortality while yet alive.[14]

Second, as we consider the teachings of the *Bhagavad Gita*, we find a similar note, that the individual Soul or Self changes its body through death. Swami Adiswarananda[15], relates this concept of death to the reference in the *Bhagavad Gita* (2:13) where it says, "Even as the embodied Self passes, in this body, through the stages of childhood, youth, and old age, so does It pass into

---

13. Ibid., 19–22.
14. Kramer, *Sacred Art of Dying*, 31.
15. A Hindu leader and scholar of the *Vedanta* (*Upanishads, Bhagavad Gita, Brahma Sutras* and others) as interpreted by *Sankaracharya*, the exponent of *Advaita* non-dualism Hinduism.

another body."[16] Swami comments, about this Self and how some who do not perceive this Self are deluded, with a quote from *Bhagavad Gita* (15:10),

> A knower of the Self can witness the passing of a soul from one body to another at the time of death: "The deluded do not perceive him when he departs from the body or dwells in it, when he experiences objects or is united with the gunas; but they who have the eye of wisdom perceive him."[17]

If we go back to the incident of the battle between *Pandavas* and *Kauravas* in the *Bhagavad Gita* in which *Arjuna* was reluctant to cause bloodshed, we find the most important teaching of the immortality of the soul given by *Krishna*, the charioteer, who is referred to as Lord *Krishna* in Hinduism. This (lord) *Krishna* in Hinduism is a direct manifestation of *Vishnu* and after listening to *Arjuna's* despair said, "All things born must die and out of death in truth comes life" (*Bhagavad Gita* 2:27).[18] *Krishna* strongly reminds *Arjuna* that there is no alternative but to fight, since that is the *dharma* (duty) of a *Kshatriya* (warrior). *Krishna* goes on to show him that death is merely an illusion, and responding in a similar way as *Yama* in *Katha Upanishad* says the following to *Arjuna*,

> Who believes him [the *atman*] a slayer,
> And who thinks him slain,
> Both these understand not:
> He slays not, is not slain.
>
> He is not born, nor does he ever die;
> Nor having come to be, will he evermore come not to be.
> Unborn, eternal everlasting, this ancient one [the *atman*]
> Is not slain when the body is slain.
>
> Who knows as indestructible and eternal
> This unborn, imperishable one,
> That man son of Prtha, [Arjuna], how
> Can he slay, or cause to slay – whom?

---

16. Swami Adiswarananda, "Hinduism," in *Encounters with Eternity: Religious Views of Death and Life After-Death*, eds. Christopher J. Johnson and Marsha G. McGee (New York, NY: Philosophical Library, 1986), 166.

17. Ibid.

18. This quote and other quotes of *Bhagavad Gita* are from Franklin Edgerton translated copy of *The Bhagavad Gita* (New York, NY: Harper & Row [Torchbooks], 1964), unless mentioned otherwise.

> As leaving aside worn-out garments
> A man takes other, new ones,
> so leaving aside worn-out bodies
> To other, new ones goes the embodied (soul).
>
> Swords cut him not,
> Fire burns him not,
> Water wets him not,
> Wind dries him not.
>
> Not to be cut is he, not to be burnt is he,
> Not to be wet nor yet dried
> Eternal, omnipresent, fixed,
> Immovable, everlasting is he.
>
> Unmanifest he, unthinkable he,
> Unchangeable he is declared to be;
> Therefore knowing him thus
> Thou shouldst not mourn him. (*Bhagavad Gita* 2:19–25)[19]

For *Krishna*, then, death is natural and unavoidable but not real. According to *Krishna*, though everything changes, decays and even dies, the Self or *atman* remains untouched and never changes or dies. It is indestructible and everlasting and is unaffected by whatever changes may take place in the material, historical and social arena. This true Self is completely detached from this world's day-to-day happenings and remains immovable, imperishable, unmanifest and unthinkable. So *Krishna* advises *Arjuna* not to mourn for this Self. Hence, Antonio R. Gualtieri concludes,

> Finally, the self is unthinkable. In the last analysis this kind of language employed to characterize the self is a flimsy and failing effort. Because the self is so different from our ordinary experience it cannot be captured in a conceptual net. Efforts may be made, but the stress in the Indic tradition falls on experiencing the self, not describing the self. Ultimately the self so transcends our routine existence that we cannot adequately conceptualize its nature; hence the stress on directly intuiting the self.[20]

---

19. This quote and other quotes of *Bhagavad Gita* are from Franklin Edgerton translated copy of *The Bhagavad Gita* (New York, NY: Harper & Row, 1964), unless mentioned otherwise.

20. Antonio R. Gualtieri, *The Vulture and the Bull: Religious Responses to Death* (Lanham Way, MD: University Press of America, 1984), 62–63.

Kramer sums up *Krishna*'s teachings on death and the immortality of Self in the *Bhagavad Gita*, like the teachings of *Yama* in the *Katha Upanishad*, in the following four basic attitudes:

1) The death of one's physical body is inevitable and is not to cause prolonged grief;

2) The subtle dimension of the person (jiva) does not die at death, rather takes on a new body;

3) The Eternal Self (Atman) is birthless and deathless, and cannot be destroyed;

4) One who realizes the Eternal Self while yet alive, will not be reborn but, at death, will merge with Brahman.[21]

If the Self is immortal then there is no judgment or punishment for the deeds (*Karma*) on the Self (*Atman*) itself, as it is eternal and cannot be destroyed. A Hindu scholar and professor of Religion at Saint Olaf College in Northfield, MN, Anantanand Rambachan refers to the three major schools of thought in Hinduism and notes,

> For [these] three . . . the self (*atman*) cannot be equated or identified with the time-bound physical body or with the . . . characteristics of the mind . . . Consciousness and bliss constitute its essence. For Śaṅkara, the self is ultimately identical with *brahman*, for Ramanuja it is inseparably related to *brahman* as body to soul or as part to whole, while, for Madhava, it is entirely different from but completely dependent on God.[22]

Thus, the majority view in Hinduism is, either this Self is *Brahman*, or it is a part of *Brahman*, the impersonal ultimate Reality or God. Yet, to the Hindus of Madhava school of thought, the Self is different from but totally dependent on *Brahman*, perhaps a personal God. Perhaps this Self is considered to be of the same essence as *Brahman*.

---

21. Kramer, *Sacred Art of Dying*, 33.
22. Anantanand Rambachan, "Hinduism," in *Life after Death in World Religions*, ed. Harold Coward (Maryknoll, NY: Orbis Books, 1997), 70.

Destiny after Death

Rambachan describes how the Self is reborn in a series of human bodies, from one life to another.[23] He refers to the Hindu scripture *Bhagavad Gita* (2:22) in which the changing of physical bodies at death is like changing from worn-out clothes. He shows that what carries the *Karma*'s memory traces from one life to the next is not the Self but the Subtle Body (*suksma sarira*), "the location of all unique individual personal traits" including the senses, the mind and the intellect, which separates from the physical body at the moment of death.[24] We also see this teaching in the *Brihadaranyaka Upanishad* that describes death as a series of changes through which an individual passes. In *Brihadaranyaka Upanishad*, in the conversation between Janaka and Yagnavalkya regarding liberation of the soul, Yagnavalkya says,

> When a man is about to die, the subtle body, mounted by the intelligent Self, groans – as a heavily laden cart groans under its burden . . .
>
> . . . For all the organs, detaching themselves from his physical body, unite with his subtle body. Then the point of his heart, where the nerves join, is lighted by the light of the Self, and by that light he departs either through some other eye, or through the gate of the skull, or through some other aperture of the body. When he thus departs, life departs; and when life departs, all the functions of the vital principle depart. The Self remains conscious, and, conscious, the dying man goes to his abode. The deeds of this life, and the impressions they leave behind, follow him.
>
> As a leech, having reached the end of a blade of grass, takes hold of another blade and draws itself to it, so the Self, having left this body behind it unconscious, takes hold of another body and draws himself to it.
>
> As a goldsmith, taking an old gold ornament, moulds it into another, newer and more beautiful, so the Self, having given up the body and left it unconscious, takes on a newer and better form, either that of the fathers or that of the celestial singers, or that of the gods, or that of other beings, heavenly or earthly.[25]

---

23. Ibid., 66–86.
24. Ibid., 73–77.
25. I used *The Upanishads: Breath of the Eternal*, the principal texts selected and translated from the original Sanskrit by Swami Prabhavananda and Frederick Manchester, (New York:

According to Swami Adiswarananda,[26] through death the individual soul changes its body just as the embodied Self itself passes through various stages of human life like childhood, youth and old age. Those who know the Self can see the passing of a soul from one body to another at the time of death but those who are deluded without the eye of wisdom do not recognize this. Adiswarananda shows, from the Hindu Puranas, that there are seven upper worlds (including the earth) as parts of heaven and seven nether worlds as parts of hell.[27] For him, heaven and hell are merely different worlds, bound by time, space, and causality in Hinduism and a soul takes on a body determined by its past actions. Those who do righteous deeds enjoy different levels of reward in the upper worlds. After death some fortunate souls even enjoy spiritual communion with a personal god and at the end of the cycle attain liberation (though a few return to earth again). The wicked souls sojourn after death to the *Patala*, the lowest of the seven nether worlds to reap the fruits of their unrighteous works.

According to Adiswarananda, there are four courses that humans follow after death: the way of the gods, the way of the fathers, the way of sub-human species and the way of mosquitoes and fleas.[28] This happens as we saw above in the last reference from *Brihadaranayaka Upanishad*, when the Self gives up the body and takes on a newer or different form. The first course is for those who are spiritually advanced souls and lived an extremely pure life. This course is called *Devayana* meaning, "the way of the gods." All those who followed this course devote themselves to wholehearted meditation on *Brahman* but were not able to achieve complete Self-knowledge before death. They go to *Brahmaloka*, the highest heaven, and from there, in due time, attain *Moksha*, the liberation. The second course is for the ritualists and the philanthropists, that is, those who desire the fruit of their charity, austerity and sacrifice. This second course is called *Pitriyana*, "the way of the fathers." In this path, they go to *Chandraloka*, the lunar sphere, where after enjoying much happiness as the reward of their *Karma*, return back to earth as humans because they still have earthly desires or selfish motives.

The third course is for those who led an impure life and did evil *Karma*. This course leads to what may be called hell, as they are reborn as sub-human species. Then, after they have expiated their evil actions, they are born again

---

Mentor Books, 1957), 108–109.
   26. Adiswarananda, "Hinduism," 166.
   27. Ibid., 167–168.
   28. Ibid., 169–170.

on earth in human bodies. Of course, the fourth course is yet worse than the third course which is for those who are extremely vile in their *Karma* and thoughts. These are reborn again and again as insignificant insects, such as mosquitoes and fleas, and eventually after the expiation of their evil deeds, they too are born again as humans on earth. Finally, for Adiswarananda,

> When a soul assumes a human body, it takes up the thread of spiritual evolution of its previous human birth and continues to evolve toward Self-knowledge. According to Hinduism, all souls will ultimately attain Self-knowledge. The four courses do not apply to those souls who attain Self-knowledge before or at the time of death. For these souls there is no going to any realm. Upon their death, their souls become absorbed in Brahman, and the elements of their body-mind . . . return to their original source.
>
> From the point of view of Hinduism, dying may be compared to falling asleep and after-death experiences to dreams . . . After-death experiences are real to the soul, just as a dream is real to the dreamer, and may continue for ages. Then, when the soul wakes up after this sleep, it finds itself reborn as a human being. According to the Hindu scriptures, some . . . born as human beings without going through the experiences of heaven or hell. There is no real break in the spiritual evolution of the soul toward Self-knowledge. Even the soul's lapse into sub-human birth from human life is a mere detour . . . The path of Self-knowledge . . . alone can confer immortality and eternal peace and happiness.[29]

Rambachan summarizes this Hindu solution to the problem of how someone may escape the cycle of endless birth, death and rebirth in this way.[30] According to Rambachan, Hinduism's solution to the problem of the endless cycle of rebirth has two main options. The first is to be reborn in heaven (*svarga*) with the gods and enjoy a temporary break from the cycle of rebirth. After one's accumulated spiritual merit is used up, one has to be reborn again in the human world. Of course, in this first option, for Rambachan, if the heavenly worlds are temporary, so the unpleasant worlds of *naraka* are transient (mentioned in *Bhagavad Gita*), where people go for their evil actions. But, the best is the second option which is, under the guidance of a teacher (*guru*), one must pursue the spiritual discipline taught in the

---

29. Ibid., 170–171.
30. Rambachan, "Hinduism," 66–86.

Upanishads (knowledge and meditation). In this option, one must continue to pursue the required discipline until one realizes the identity of one's Self with God (*Brahman*), the essence of all things. In this way, one is released from further rebirths, which is called *mokṣa*. In Hinduism, one must achieve this liberation or salvation by one's own hard work in spiritual discipline.

The religious goal of Hinduism is to achieve the release of the soul from *samsara*, the painful cycle of rebirths, and to be united with *Brahman* and thus attain *moksha* or salvation. The *Upanishads* teach complete determinism and the cause-effect relationship between *Karma* (deeds) and the next birth, giving rise to the fundamental principle of *niyati* (fate). According to the *Chandogya Upanishad* of seventh or eighth century BC:

> Those who are of pleasant conduct here – the prospect is, indeed, that they will enter a pleasant womb, either the womb of a "Brahman" [priestly caste], or the womb of a "ksatriya" [warrior] or the womb of a "vaisya" [merchant]. But those who are of stinking conduct here – the prospect is, indeed, that they will enter a stinking womb, either the womb of a dog, or the womb of a swine, or the womb of an outcast.[31]

There are three ways by which one can avoid this painful rebirth and achieve the goal of *moksha*: (a) *Bhakti Marga,* the way of devotion to a personal god through an emotional relationship and experience of this god; (b) *Gnana Marga,* the way of true knowledge that the world is an illusion (*maya*) and the soul is drawn through ignorance (*avidya*); and (c) *Karma Marga,* the way of good deeds by either becoming a hermit (*sanyasin*) or by engaging in good works while renouncing (*tyaga*) their fruit. A Hindu scholar K. M. Sen observes that each of these ways is effective and legitimate in its own way, and states,

> As the age-old Mahimna-Stotra puts it: "All these paths, O Lord, Veda, Samkhya, Yoga, Pasupata, Vaishnava, lead but to Thee, like the winding river that at last merges into the sea." This, in fact, is the message of Hinduism, if it has one.[32]

In all these three above efforts, the cycle of birth and rebirth (*samsara*) is something to be shunned and overcome and liberation or *moksha* has to be achieved.

---

31. Harold Netland, *Dissonant Voices* (Grand Rapids, MI: Eerdmans, 1991), 46.
32. Ibid., 56.

The Muslim Perspective

The Muslim perspective of "State-after-Death" is in many ways similar to Judaism and Christianity, the other major faiths of Semitic origin, just as the Hindu perspective is similar to Buddhist and other faiths of South and East Asian origin. In contrast to others'[33] presentation of Semitic faiths as Western religions, Parrinder notes,

> For convenience living religions may be roughly divided into prophetic and wisdom religions, but this division is only approximate, for prophecy and wisdom may appear in both areas. However, it is better to make such a division than to speak of western and eastern, or monotheistic and pantheistic, for that would cause even more confusion and overlapping. The prophetic religions . . . are the Jewish, Islamic and Christian religions, and the wisdom religions are the Hindu, Buddhist and far-eastern faiths, with smaller traditions in both areas.[34]

With regards to the place of origin, the Greco-Roman religions with their many gods and goddesses would truly be Western religions. The Semitic religions are more of Middle-Eastern origin if anything, yet now followers of most of these religions can be found in both the East and the West. Hence, each of these religions has become more global instead of being only Eastern or Western. However, that fact does not cancel out the similarities of views that are found within the religions of Semitic origin. Contrary to Hinduism or Greco-Roman religions, the dead in Islam have neither a way to return to earth nor a way to be reincarnated. Referring to the Qur'an (Sura 7:34), Muslim author Abdul Qadir Ahmad Zain, from Saudi Arabia, comments, "Death is the passing of the human being from '*Ad-Dunya*'; the temporary life of this world to the Hereafter '*Al-Aakhirah*'; that is the life of retribution and eternity. The life of every human being is limited. Man cannot transcend his appointed and limited term."[35] Thus, for Muslims, there is only one life on

---

33. E.g. Kramer, *Sacred Art of Dying*, 22; Hiroshi Obayashi, *Death and Afterlife: Perspectives of World Religions* (Westport, CT: Greenwood Press, 1992), v-vi, xxii; Coward, *Life after Death*, v, 2; etc. I have footnoted before that Parrinder wrote this in John Prickett's book *Death* which represent "insider" views.

34. Geoffrey Parrinder, "Death in the World Faiths: Introduction," in *Living Faiths: Death*, ed. John Prickett (London: Lutterworth Educational, 1980), 3–4.

35. Abdul Qadir Ahmad Zain, *Save from Hell-Fire* (Buraydah, Kingdom of Saudi Arabia: Foreigners Guidance Center in Al-Qasseem, 1995), 23.

earth and after death they must await God's judgment in the future, for the righteous to be rewarded and the unrighteous to be punished.

Following the details given in the Qur'an and the *Hadith* (sayings of Prophet Muhammad), William C. Chittick briefly shows the events that will occur after death.[36] Chittick notes that on the first night in the grave, all persons will be questioned by two angels about their beliefs and as a result will be placed in a pleasant or unpleasant situation depending on their response. The dead will remain in the grave until the day of resurrection, when God will judge each person according to their good or bad deeds, however minute these may be. After judgment they will be sent to everlasting paradise or hell. Chittick notes, "Belief in the afterlife is so basic to Islam that the whole of Islamic thought has been divided into three basic 'principles' from the early times: the Unity of God (*tawhid*), prophecy (*nubuuwa*), and eschatology (*ma'ad*), or questions pertaining to the next world."[37] Chittick emphasizes that we have to understand the first two to some extent in order to understand eschatology in Islam.

In eschatology, Chittick shows from the Qur'an that all things come from God and *return* to him and that God has created human beings for a specific purpose.[38] He notes that the degree to which humans succeed in fulfilling this purpose shapes their own self-nature, which in turn, determines the mode in which they return to God after death. If they love God and sincerely strive to the fullest of their own human nature, they will return to God and find him loving and compassionate. However, if they forget God and ignore their human responsibilities, they will return to God and find him severe and wrathful.[39] Thus, for Muslims, after death all people must await God's Judgment Day to determine their ultimate destiny.

---

36. William C. Chittick, "'Your Sight Today is Piercing': The Muslim Understanding of Death And Afterlife," in *Death and Afterlife: Perspectives of World Religions*, ed. Hiroshi Obayashi (Westport, CT: Greenwood Press, 1992), 125. He is a well-known scholar on Islam, teaches religious studies at the State University of New York at Stony Brook and has published quite a few books on Islam.
37. Ibid.
38. Ibid., 126.
39. Ibid.

God's Judgment Day

According to Parrinder, "The doctrine of the Last Judgement (sic) has been reckoned as the second great tenet of the Qur'an, after the unity of God."[40] He notes that this means after death humankind will be raised from the dead in the future to be judged before God. They will be sent either to Paradise or Hell based on their deeds. Kramer, noting the parallels to the biblical creation account, shows that the creation account in the Qur'an also declares death's inevitability and resurrection on the day of judgment.[41] Thus Kramer shows that in Islam, creation, death and resurrection (so judgment) are inexorably linked right from the outset. With regard to a possible link between the qur'anic accounts and the biblical accounts, it is worth noting, Roman Catholic scholar on Islam, Thomas O'Shaughnessy's comments:

> The commentators and orthodox Islam in general believe that the Qur'ān is the eternal word of God of which Muhammad was the passive recipient through the intermediary of the holy spirit, the angel Jibrīl. But to a non-Muslim studying the same work it seems clear that Muhammad's knowledge of biblical accounts was constantly growing and that he was receiving information from others which he incorporated into his preaching to his followers. A Muslim might perhaps admit that God was phrasing the verses of the Qur'ān in a way comprehensible to the preacher and those to whom he spoke and so was revealing to them the inner meaning and the doctrines contained in biblical material obtained from human sources.[42]

Like the biblical account, the qur'anic account of creation, temptation, and the fall of Adam explains the origins of death.[43] Under God's judgment, one's soul will receive God's mercy or will be consigned to spiritual fire; so the choice is between eternal life for following the will of Allah or eternal death for not following.[44] Thus, death is a transition from this world to eternity and, according to the Qur'an, the purpose of this life is to prepare for eternal life.[45]

---

40. Parrinder, "Death in the World Faith," 6.
41. Kramer, *Sacred Art of Dying*, 157–158.
42. Thomas O'Shaughnessy, *Muhammad's Thoughts on Death* (Leiden, Holland: E. J. Brill, 1969), 5.
43. Kramer, *Sacred Art of Dying*, 159.
44. Ibid.
45. Ibid., 160.

Based on the descriptions given in the Qur'an, Parrinder notes, "The Day of Resurrection is also the Day of Judgement (sic), Distinction or Gathering, or simply the Last Day, Hour or Event" and that Day will come suddenly, "preceded by a thunderclap or a blast of trumpet."[46] "There will be a cosmic upheaval, the mountains dissolve, the seas boil, the sun is darkened, the stars fall and the sky is rolled up," "God appears on a throne, surrounded by angels" and all the dead are raised up for the judgment of all nations.[47] Following the qur'anic view on judgment day (e.g. Sura 56:8–10, 101:5–6), Parrinder also notes,

> At the Judgement (sic), every man will have a book handed to him which records his deeds on earth; the good man receives it in his right hand and the bad man in his left and behind his back. False gods will be invoked in vain by unbelievers, and a light or heavy balance of good or evil deeds will decide the future lot.[48]

The consequence of the judgment is that some will go to everlasting Paradise and others to everlasting punishment in Hell.[49] Chittick shows from the Qur'an that, on the resurrection day secrets will be divulged (Sura 86:9) and all will be exposed.[50] Not one of humanity's secret will be concealed on that day (Sura 69:18).

Kramer also gives a description of the day of judgment from the references in the Qur'an, noting: "the dead will rise from their graves amidst cataclysmic events which will disrupt the natural order;" their judgment will be based on "the number of good and bad entries that have been recorded into a set of heavenly books by secretary angels;" "When the earth shakes and mountains crumble into atoms, the resurrected shall be sorted out into three classes," the righteous, the unrighteous and the spiritually advanced persons.[51] According to Jane Idleman Smith,[52] for Muslims "life on this earth has no purpose if it is not to prepare oneself specifically for life in the next" and to "live ethically in recognition of God's oneness is virtually to assure a felicitous hereafter in the gardens of paradise."[53] However, Smith also notes that along with this

---

46. Parrinder, "Death in the World Faiths," 7.
47. Ibid.
48. Ibid.
49. Ibid.
50. Chittick, "Your Sight Today is Piercing," 134.
51. Kramer, *Sacred Art of Dying*, 161–162.
52. Jane Idleman Smith, formerly a professor of Comparative Religion at Harvard University, is considered a scholar on Islam by the wider academic community.
53. Jane Idleman Smith, "Islam," in *Encounters with Eternity: Religious Views of Death and*

ethical obligation for life is the qur'anic understanding that "as humans we will err" and that God's mercy is abundant.[54] Smith notes that "Humans are not described in Islam as inherently evil or misguided," in spite of Adam and Eve's first sin. Further, in Islam, "We are often subject to error, but always have the potential to recognize the truth and to act accordingly."[55] Later on, Smith notes that according to the Qur'an, "each individual alone is responsible for his or her past deeds" and that each person will have to face the consequences on the day of judgment.[56]

Linked with the day of judgment, Smith refers to the *mizan* or balance, from the Qur'an, which means "the principle of justice;" and "the bridge (*sirat*), adopted into Islamic tradition to signify the span over Gehenna, the top layer of the Fire."[57] Smith notes that "both the saved and the condemned must pass over the bridge, although the judgment process actually has been completed at the point at which the bridge is mentioned in most narratives."[58] Referring to the Qur'an (Sura 37:23) and the Islamic tradition, M. S. Seale notes,

> The bridge that stretches across the fiery Pit is sharper than a sword's edge and finer than a hair. The upright will run across in safety. Some will walk across, others will just manage to crawl across, still others . . . under a load of guilt, will slip and fall into the Pit. The Prophet will be the first to reach the other side. His prayer will be: "Preserve us, Oh Lord!" Angels will rescue believers who are too frightened to step onto the bridge, and will help them make their way across through the leaping flames.[59]

As an interesting aside, Hanna Kassis[60] notes that a belief has evolved among Muslims that judgment begins in the tomb itself soon after death

---

Life After-Death, eds. Christopher J. Johnson and Marsha G. McGee (New York: Philosophical Library, 1986), 189.

54. Ibid.
55. Ibid., 190.
56. Ibid., 198.
57. Ibid., 198.
58. Ibid.
59. M. S. Seale, "Islamic Society," in *Life after Death*, eds. Arnold Toynbee and Arthur Koestler (New York: McGraw-Hill Book Co, 1976), 128.
60. Hanna Kassis, a non-Muslim Arab, is a professor of Near Eastern and Islamic Studies at the University of British Columbia. He is an expert on Islam and received his PhD in Near Eastern Languages and Civilization from Harvard University. He published his *Concordance of the Qur'an* (Berkeley, CA: University of California Press, 1983) and a Spanish equivalent *Las Concordancias del Corán* (Madrid: Instituto Hispano-Arabe de Cultura, 1987).

when the deceased are visited by two angels, Munkar and Nakīr.⁶¹ These angels make dead persons sit up in the grave in order to ask them questions of faith. Kassis notes that this is why during burial the dirt is placed loosely over the dead body. In the questioning of faith, the deceased are asked about the uniqueness of God and the identity of Muhammad. Incorrect responses mean that the punishment of burning will begin in the grave itself, known as *'adhāb al-qabr* (torment in the tomb).⁶² Muslim scholar Abdul Qadir Ahmad Zain notes, "Peace and torture in the grave are facts. Those who are going to dwell in Heaven (*Jannah*) shall be at peace in their graves and those who are going to be among the inmates of Hell shall be tortured in their graves."⁶³

Kassis refers to the fact that Muslims turn to the Traditions (*Hadith*) for guidance when there are no clear details in the Qur'an about something and the formulations arrived at by the scholars or jurisconsults (*fuqahā'*) are generally accepted.⁶⁴ With regard to punishment in the grave, Kassis notes,

> While such a concept has no evident mention in the Qur'ān, the *fuqahā'* found support for the notion in the interpretation of certain verses . . . for the notion of a twofold chastisement, the first of which is in the tomb, was found in the passage, "We [God is speaking] will chastise them twice, then they shall be turned back to a grievous chastisement" (Qur'ān 9:101), as well as in the passage, "And most certainly We [God is speaking] will make them taste of the nearer chastisement before the greater chastisement that haply they may turn" (Qur'ān 32:21).⁶⁵

If the responses given by the deceased are correct then the deceased is left to rest in peace until the day of resurrection (*yawm al-qiyāma*) or the day of judgment (*yawm al-dīn*).

Kassis notes that, according to the Qur'an (Sura 33:63), only God knows when that day or that hour will be when life on earth will end and the resurrection will take place.⁶⁶ According to Kassis, like its predecessor and sister religion Christianity, that day or hour will be announced by terrible portents such as splitting of the moon, earthquakes, fire, and the sun will rise

---

61. Hanna Kassis, "Islam," in *Life after Death in World Religions*, ed. Harold Coward (Maryknoll, NY: Orbis Books, 1997), 54–55.
62. Ibid., 55.
63. Zain, *Save from Hell-Fire*, 23.
64. Kassis, "Islam," 52.
65. Ibid., 55.
66. Ibid., 57.

in the west instead of east. According to the Qur'an, on that day, at the sound of the trumpet, all the dead will rise and individually stand before God to be judged according to the record of their own actions. The righteous will enter Paradise and the wicked will suffer a second punishment by being sent to the fires of Hell (*jahannam*).[67] There seems to be an intermediate state from death to the day of resurrection for Muslims and death marks the demarcation line between this world (*al-dunyā*) and the next world (*al-'ākhirah*).

Intermediate State

Jane I. Smith notes, "Essential to an understanding of the Islamic view of the afterlife is a consideration of the flow of time and history."[68] This sequence of time and history for a Muslim runs "from birth to death, followed by existence of the soul in the grave (or elsewhere) awaiting the resurrection" and the impending judgment, then the final passing into eternity.[69] As we consider the existence of the soul after death in the grave (or elsewhere) awaiting the resurrection and the final judgment in Islam, we will call it the Intermediate State, the first stage of "State-after-Death." Muslims believe that souls of the dead are taken into the charge of the angel of death and held until the resurrection.[70] However, Parrinder adds without any explanation that "the interval seems to them only like one day" and perhaps this is why later on he notes that, "there is no intermediate state."[71] Although, Parrinder notes that this interval seems to be short in Islam, he also notes that prayers may be said for the benefit of the dead persons during this interval. However, Muslim writer R. El-Droubie gives evidence that seems to corroborate the idea of longer duration of Intermediate State for the deceased by referring to funeral prayers including a prayer that the deceased person will receive God's forgiveness and mercy.[72] He also notes that alms may be given on behalf of the

---

67. Ibid., 58–60. According to Kassis (Ibid., 57–58), in eschatology Islam may have borrowed many ideas from Christianity and Judaism. One of the ideas is the return of Jesus, the son of Mary, to do battle on the anti-Christ (*al-Dajjal*, the false one), a manifestation of Satan or one of his allies, who appears prior to the day of resurrection. Kassis shows from this eschatology that the anti-Christ will at first entice many Muslims to follow him because of his resemblance to Christ. But then Jesus, the Messiah, will appear to do battle and defeat Satan, the anti-Christ, restoring the reign of faith, justice, and peace until the day of judgment.
68. Smith, "Islam," 190.
69. Ibid.
70. Parrinder, "Death in the World Faiths," 7.
71. Ibid.
72. R. El-Droubie, "Statements and Extracts: Islam," in *Living Faiths: Death*, ed. John

dead and quotes from Prophet Muhammad, "When a man dies his actions cease except for three: continuous charity (paid on his behalf), knowledge he leaves behind (for the benefit of the people), and a pious son (or daughter) who prays for him."[73] Finally, El-Droubie adds that, in the interim life in the grave until resurrection, some may feel pain in separation from the world while others may feel pleasure, and while sinners will live in continual agony, virtuous persons will live in a state of happiness in the grave.[74] Muslim convert and Islamic scholar Abu Ameenah Bilal Philips asserts that a person's reward or punishment after death is primarily determined by deeds done by that person and that sins cannot be transferred to another.[75] However, Philips also concurs with El-Droubie that prayers, fasting, payment of outstanding debt, and charity by others may somehow benefit the deceased.[76]

In considering the state of the soul after death in Islam, we also need to understand the inter-relationship between body, soul and spirit. To illustrate that relationship, Chittick explains from the Qur'an that God shaped Adam's outer shell or body out of clay then breathed his own Spirit into Adam.[77] The Spirit of God, made of pure light, is Adam's center. Thus humans are compounded of spirit and body. The spirit is pure light and the body is almost pure darkness. Similar to the macrocosm, which has many degrees of mixed light and darkness, is the microcosm, and the human "soul" (*nafs*) which is an intermediary realm of mixed light and darkness. All humans are essentially the same in their spirits and in their bodies but they differ in their souls, with each soul showing a unique mix of light and clay or spirit and body. Below the surface, each and every human being displays a different intensity of the light of the spirit so that no two persons are the same.[78] Thus, one of the keys to Islamic eschatology is that when the veil of the body is removed at death, the soul manifests its true form and nature for everyone to see.[79] Addressing the human soul at death, the Qur'an says that, "We have now removed from thee thy covering, so thy sight today is piercing" (Sura 50:22).

Prickett (London: Lutterworth Educational, 1980), 94.
    73. Ibid., 95. Parrinder ("Death in the World Faiths," 7) also notes that prayers may be said for the deceased only if they have died in the faith, as Muhammad himself was unable to pray for his own father who had died a pagan.
    74. El-Droubie, "Statements and Extracts," 95.
    75. Abu Ameenah Bilal Philips, *Funeral Rites in Islam* (Sharjah, UAE: Dar Al Fatah, 1996), 131.
    76. Ibid., 131–136.
    77. Chittick, "Your Sight Today is Piercing," 132.
    78. Ibid.
    79. Ibid., 134.

Moreover, Chittick[80] notes that, of the three major stages of "State-after-Death" in the Islamic perspective, the first (the Intermediate State) is from death until the day of resurrection. This state is called the "grave" (*gabr*) or the "interworld" (*barzakh*). This is "an imaginal realm in which the actual attributes of the soul display themselves in appropriate forms," just like a dream-state during sleep. The exception is that humans can awaken from their dreams to forget them but no one can awaken from the interworld or *barzakh* until the distant event of the day of resurrection. Furthermore, the interworld represents a kind of awakening in relationship to life in this world, so that the soul is more aware of itself and its surroundings than when in the world. As a result, the Qur'an says that a person's sight at death is "piercing" because now the soul sees clearly at death what it had seen only dimly before when it was incased in the body of clay. Thus, in Islam the soul receives at death a foretaste of its ultimate and permanent state. Chittick notes that, for the Prophet Muhammad, death is the "lesser resurrection" and the grave is "either one of the pits of hell or one of the gardens of paradise."[81]

Whereas Chittick sees *barzakh* as "interworld" (the Intermediate State of the soul from death to the day of resurrection),[82] J. I. Smith[83] and Kramer[84] in referring to the Qur'an (Sura 23:100) see *barzakh* as a description of a partition or a barrier separating the land of the living from the dead. They interpret this to mean that the deceased will never be able to return to earth. Smith and Kramer use this interpretation to show that the Qur'an does not support the idea of reincarnation or multiple births in any way. In Islam, there is only one life on earth and the hereafter will be determined on the basis of the quality of life here. Smith notes that, except for a few splinter sectarian groups, Islam has consistently rejected the notion of reincarnation in different bodies for the purpose of restitution or earning more merit.[85]

However, both Smith[86] and Kramer[87] recognize that there is an intermediate waiting period for the soul until the day of resurrection and Smith notes that "The term *barzakh* has also come to be applied to the place/time in

---

80. Ibid., 136.
81. Ibid., 137.
82. Ibid., 136.
83. Smith, "Islam," 193.
84. Kramer, *Sacred Art of Dying*, 160.
85. Smith, "Islam," 193.
86. Ibid.
87. Kramer, *Sacred Art of Dying*, 160.

which the dead wait for the day of resurrection in a variety of conditions."[88] But, according to Smith, precisely what happens to the soul in *Barzakh* where the dead wait for the resurrection is not discussed in the Quran and, as a result, there is much speculation about it.[89] The Islamic tradition has filled this gap with many details with varying degrees of authenticity and reliability. The theme of joys or torments to be experienced at the final judgment by the righteous or the faithless is repeated and prefigured in a variety of ways as one follows the sequence of after-death events.[90] This foreshadowing can be seen from the very beginning with the kind of welcome that will be given by the grave to the deceased, based on the relative virtue of the deceased.

Smith[91] and Kramer[92] describe one of the most commonly accepted narratives in which the soul, separated from the body, embarks on a journey. This is modeled on the mystical journey (*miraj*) of Prophet Muhammad (from Mecca to Jerusalem to heaven) in which he ascended to the heavens and was able to look down into the layers of hell. In this journey, a good soul supposedly slips easily and painlessly from the body and, wrapped in perfumed coverings, is escorted by the angel Gabriel through the seven layers of heaven to see what will ultimately be that soul's abode. At the end of the journey there is a vision of God and then the soul returns to the grave. However, the wicked souls or those who did not follow God's command in life will leave the body in pain and torment. These souls are foulsmelling and are rejected from even the lowest levels of heavens. Having seen the vision of what awaits them on the day of judgment, by glimpses into the fires of punishment, these souls return to the grave.

Smith reminds us about the other commonly accepted event, as mentioned previously, that is, the visit of questioning angels (Munkar and Nakir).[93] These are generally considered fearsome to look at, black in appearance with green eyes, with voices like thunder and lightning, and with long fangs that rend the ground. These angels ask the deceased about their knowledge of God, Prophet Muhammad and Islam and their responses (easy for the righteous and impossible for the faithless) determine the quality of their Intermediate State until the day of judgment. Smith notes that, "Sometimes it is said that,

---

88. Smith, "Islam," 193.
89. Ibid.
90. Ibid.
91. Ibid., 194.
92. Kramer, *Sacred Art of Dying*, 160.
93. Smith, "Islam," 194.

for the good soul, windows will be opened in the top of the tomb so that one can feel the sweet breezes from the Garden, and that for the evil soul a similar opening on the bottom will allow the hot stench of hell to penetrate."[94] To this Smith adds, "Respectively, graves will be expanded for greater comfort or straightened so that the suffering soul will shriek in agony." Smith notes that, according to Muslim superstition, "animals passing through graveyards can sometimes hear the piercing cries of the tormented damned" and one of the particular sins for which there is punishment in the grave is suicide.[95]

Smith points out that more attention has been given in the Islamic theological writings and folk traditions about punishment than rewards in the grave.[96] Smith also notes that apart from the narratives that suggest that the soul is experiencing joy or pain in the grave, there are other narratives that show that the soul is separated from the tomb and going through appropriate pleasure or purgation elsewhere. She notes that the souls of the damned are sometimes considered to be already in the fire, or suffering somewhere in pits of snakes and other loathsome creatures.[97] In contrast, the souls of the righteous are sometimes considered free to wander through the spheres at will, or rest at the right hand of Adam, or wait at the gates of the Garden of Paradise.[98] Some Islamic traditions suggest that the righteous are very much aware of life on earth while waiting for the resurrection and that sometimes the righteous pray for the living or even attempt to greet us.[99] Smith concludes that afterlife-beliefs in Islam are a blend of qur'anic description, traditional elaboration, theological speculations and popular beliefs.[100]

M. S. Seale shows how historically Islamic society passed through three well-defined stages in their views about "State-after-Death."[101] In the earliest pre-Islamic pagan period, they grieved at the loss of the deceased yet sought comfort in the thought that the deceased were not really far away. They believed that the departed lived a separate life and enjoyed a conscious existence in the grave. Seale notes that, though the pre-Islamic pagan Arabs believed in existence beyond death, they knew nothing about the resurrection of the

---

94. Ibid., 194–195.
95. Ibid., 195.
96. Ibid.
97. Ibid.
98. Ibid.
99. Ibid.
100. Ibid., 201.
101. M. S. Seale, "Islamic Society," in *Life after Death*, eds. Arnold Toynbee and Arthur Koestler (New York: McGraw-Hill Book Co, 1976), 123.

body.¹⁰² In the second stage, after the emergence of Islam, they continued to believe that the departed lived their own life in the tomb but now the interest centered more on human destiny and ultimate condition. Muhammad tried to convince them about the coming day of resurrection and about the day of judgment when the human beings will have to give an account to a sovereign creator.¹⁰³

Seale notes that the Qur'an reveals that the underworld is no longer a refuge of beings which are mere shadows of their former selves, but is now a place full of life and movement.¹⁰⁴ For some it is a sad place and for others it is a happy one, depending on the life they lived before and the God they believed in or denied. According to Seale,¹⁰⁵ the Qur'an is the best source for the second stage, and that after Muhammad's death, Islamic *sunna* (tradition) grew and expanded into the third stage of Islamic understanding of death and hereafter. The tradition added now that there are two trials, one in the grave and the other at the end of the world. It shows also that the underworld is occupied with angels and demons. Munker and Nakir, the two black angels, interrogate the dead both the believers and the infidels regarding their faith and works, and the angel of death which extracts the soul from the dead body has two eyes: one in the face and the other in the nape of the neck.

Seale notes that, according to Islamic tradition, the righteous are welcomed by angels "with faces like the sun" but the unbelievers are greeted by the ugly and horrendous angels.¹⁰⁶ There are silk and musk for the believers but sackcloth and burning coals for the unbelievers. The believers' graves become luxuriant gardens but unbelievers' graves are filled with seven-headed snakes. Seale notes further that believers' responses work miracles by changing dark graves into a spacious place full of light, but unbelievers' responses make the graves close-in to bruise their ribs, and iron whips are struck with no pity on the victims.¹⁰⁷ Previously, we have noted that the bridge mentioned in the Islamic tradition linked with judgment may be a description of a time between the final judgment after the resurrection and the final punishment into everlasting heaven or hell. Or it may be a description of the intermediate

---

102. Ibid., 124.
103. This accountability to God along with the alms tax prescribed by the Qur'an was imposed on the immediate Islamic society by force of arms after the prophet's death (Seale, "Islamic Society," 124).
104. Seale, "Islamic Society," 124.
105. Ibid., 125–126.
106. Ibid., 126.
107. Ibid., 127.

state between the death and the resurrection until the final judgment. However, one thing is clear: this bridge will ultimately lead one to heaven or if one falls from it, to hell. Next we will consider the final stage of "State-after-Death" in Islam, the ultimate destiny of humans in heaven or in hell.

Heaven and Hell

While showing what happens at the day of judgment, the second stage of "State-after-Death," separation of "the companions of the right hand," the righteous, the believers, and "the companions of the left hand," the unrighteous, the unbelievers, Kramer[108] also gives a description of heaven and hell, the final stage of "State-after-Death," with references from the Qur'an[109] (Sura 56:8–9). The Qur'an describes a difficult existence for the unbelievers who will be thrown into a roaring blaze, chained together, and will burn in hell in a blast of fire and in boiling water (Sura 14:28–30; 56:41–56). But the believers, those who do good work, will inherit paradise (*al-janat*) dwelling forever among flowers and trees in shade by flowing waters with pure virgins equal in age (Sura 9:72; 16:30–31; 56:8–38). Referring to Muhammad's sayings in the *Hadith* that hell is screened with allurements and paradise with loathsome objects, Muslim scholar Saeed Ali Al-Qahtani comments,

> It means that Paradise cannot be reached unless by striving for good, and Hell-Fire unless by striving for allurements, and so both are screened. Whenever one rips apart the screen he can reach the thing concealed behind it. Thus the screen of the Paradise is ripped apart by doing good deeds such as: striving in worship with persistence on it, patience on its hardship, quenching of anger, pardoning, forbearance, charity, dealing generously with the one who does wrong and forbearance against lustful things that surround Hell-Fire and screen it are-as it seems, the forbidden things such as alcohol, fornication, glancing at other women, back-biting, slandering, using night clubs, etc. Although lustful things which are permitted are not included in this, yet one should not over use them so that they should not lead him to those forbidden or to things which harden the heart or take off

---

108. Kramer, *Sacred Art of Dying*, 161–162.
109. Seale ("Islamic Society," 125) refers to the qur'anic view of the great divide between the 'people of the right hand' and the 'people of the left' from Sura 90:10–20, very similar to the biblical view of sheep and goats.

one's attention from Allāh's obedience or make one in constant need to achieve this world.[110]

Seale reminds us that the last day, or the day of resurrection and judgment, was always in Muhammad's mind and speech, and the term *"al-'akhira"* or "hereafter" occurs 113 times in the Qur'an.[111] Seale also notes that in Islam the summons to judgment will bring together not only human beings but also *jinns* and the animal creation. Every creature's deeds will then be placed on the scales to be weighed and those who have more good deeds will go to the Garden or Heaven and those with less good deeds will be sent to the Pit or Hell. Referring to *Kauthar* in the Qur'an (Sura 108), Seale describes it as a river of paradise:

> Kawthar is a river of Paradise, its water is whiter than milk, sweeter than honey and more fragrant than musk. Its banks are of gold, the river bed is of pearls and coral. One tradition says that the domes on each side of the river are of hollow pearls. The Prophet's pool, which is a part of the river, is supplied with water from Paradise. To drink of this water is never to thirst again.[112]

Parrinder notes that, in Islam Paradise (*Firdaus*) or the Garden (*Jannat*) is the Garden of Eden or place of delight through which rivers flow.[113] *Firdaus* is for the blessed for their enjoyment of rich clothing, food and celestial wine served by youthful boys. There are also the *houris* or wide-eyed damsels, perhaps like angels, for companionship. While everyone, men, women and children, may enter Paradise and seek the vision of God, only those who have been prayerful and charitable or have died for their faith can actually achieve Paradise. Muslim scholar Al-Qahtani points out from the *Hadith*, narrated by Abdullah Ibn 'Omar and by Imran Ibn Husain, that Muhammad had said that he found most of the inhabitants of hell are women.[114]

According to Parrinder, in Islam Hell or Gehenna (*Jahannam*) also called the Fire and the Pit has seven gates, guarded by nineteen angels.[115] Spiritual beings are sent to execute punishment. In the Fire, inmates are given hot water to drink and bitter fruit from a tree, which seems peculiarly Arabian,

---

110. Saeed Ali Al-Qahtani, *The Supreme Triumph and the Evident Loss* (Riyadh, Saudi Arabia: IIPH, 1999), 48.
111. Seale, "Islamic Society," 125.
112. Ibid., 128.
113. Parrinder, "Death in the World Faiths," 7–8.
114. Al-Qahtani, *Supreme Triumph*, 58.
115. Parrinder, "Death in the World Faiths," 8.

but other descriptions look like those of Zoroastrian, Jewish and Christian mythology. Those in the Fire call to those in the Garden for water but God forbids it to unbelievers. Hell is full of humans and evil spirits (*jinn*), but is always thirsting and hungering for more humans. Parrinder also notes that these pictures of "State-after-Death" in Islam, like other religions, are exhortations to Muslims to lead a good life with the warning of consequent punishment for sin. Parrinder wonders how literally these are taken by the Muslims and points out that the great theologian Al-Ghazali in the twelfth century considered some of the descriptions of the future life to have chiefly moral meaning in order to emphasize the importance of the 'straight path' by which God conducts the faithful.[116]

Chittick shows that the next two stages after the "grave" (*gabr*) or the "interworld" (*barzakh*) are the day of resurrection and the final destiny.[117] He notes that in some of Prophet Muhammad's sayings, the day of resurrection is referred to in terms of thousands of years during which many events occur that are perceived in accordance with the state of the soul and the laws of the imaginal existence. Those who are destined for paradise, the happy souls, experience these events as easy and pleasant, but the wretched souls experience terrible trials and tribulation. After these events of the day of resurrection, one group is taken into the Garden and the other into the Fire and there they will abide eternally. Chittick notes that both Garden and Fire are imaginal modes of existence.[118] The difference between them is: "Garden" is close to the source of light but "Fire" dwells in relative darkness. According to a prophetic saying, after the resurrection, light from the Fire will go to heaven but its heat will remain in hell.

While the Qur'an clearly gives two alternatives of ultimate destiny, the Garden or the Fire, for all on the Day of God's Judgment, Smith refers to one verse in the Qur'an (Sura 7:46) that mentions "the Heights" (*al-a' raf*) and which has helped develop a "limbo" theory of Islam.[119] The assumption is that there is a place for an intermediate group of people who are sent to neither heaven nor hell. Although this verse is interpreted in a number of ways, according to Smith, "most exegetes have said those on the heights are persons whose good deeds keep them from the fire and whose evil deeds keep them from the Garden – i.e. those whose actions balance in terms of merit and

---

116. Ibid.
117. Chittick, "Your Sight Today is Piercing," 137.
118. Ibid.
119. Smith, "Islam," 199.

demerit, and who are therefore the last to enter the Garden."[120] Thus, those who have equal merits and demerits may either remain in an intermediate place or are the last to enter heaven. Smith also notes that while the eternal nature of the Garden is not questioned, the majority of Muslims hold the view that "it is not only possible but even likely that at some future time all sinners will be pardoned and the Fires of judgment will be extinguished forever."[121]

Chittick notes that the Garden has eight basic levels and the Fire has seven levels, with many subsections in each level, and that for some Islamic authorities the degrees of heaven and hell are as numerous as human souls.[122] Chittick argues that if in Islam highest bliss is the vision of God and the worst punishment is to be veiled from God then (quoting Ibn al-Arabi) the next world has two abodes: vision and veil. According to Chittick, Islam teaches that human beings, created in the image of God, have the potential to become semi-divine. But, by failing to live up to the divine qualities human beings cut themselves off from God, become less than human and suffer in hell by being torn this way and that, by conflicting forces within themselves. Chittick also notes that most Muslim authorities believe that the fires of hell will eventually abate and after many aeons those who exist in them will become so used to the veil that they will not be able to bear entering into paradise. Thus, in Islam, God's all-embracing mercy gives solace even to the damned in hell.[123]

Referring to the Qur'an (Sura 19:71–72; 4:56) and the Traditions, Seale describes hell in Islam in this way:

> The condemned will cry out to Malik, their keeper, but in vain. There they will lie, manacled, with fire above them and fire below them, fire on their right and fire on their left; their clothing is fire and so is their bedding. Pierced by many sword thrusts, their foreheads broken, their livers ruined, their flesh, skin and hair gone, they will be given new skins periodically for their torments to begin all over again . . .

---

120. Ibid.
121. Ibid., 201.
122. Chittick, "Your Sight Today Is Piercing," 138. For Smith ("Islam," 200), "In the Qur'an (15:43–44), Gehenna is described as having seven gates; this led to the popular notion that the Fire consists of seven descending layers of increasing torment . . . In some ways the divisions of the Fire directly parallel those of the Garden, although the Garden is sometimes said to have eight rather than seven layers (and at other times is described as being of four portions)."
123. Chittick, "Your Sight Today Is Piercing," 138.

> Gehenna is the highest of Hell's several compartments; the others follow in descending order: Hell-Fire, the Flame, the Scorcher, the Blazes, the Inferno and the Abyss, which is bottomless...
>
> The vehemence of the fire is described in these words: God, the Most High, ordered the fire to burn for a thousand years till it turned red, then another thousand till it turned white, and yet another thousand till it turned black, its present colour. When the fire complained that it was being consumed, the Lord gave it two natures: in the summer it is boiling hot, in the winter it is freezing cold.[124]

Seale also refers to Sura 14:15–17 for the drink that will be offered to the wicked which cannot be swallowed. This passage of the Qur'an also says that though death may come from every side to the wicked yet they will not die and the torments of hell will continue relentlessly without annihilation. However, Seale refers to Sura 4:40a and notes that God's punishment will be in proportion to the person's wrongdoing.[125] In his description of heaven, Seale refers to the Traditions and notes,

> A Tradition traced back to the Prophet says: "If you want to enjoy wine in the hereafter, abstain here and now. This applies equally to gold and silver ornaments and silk garments: shun them in this life and you will have them in abundance in your eternal home. The clothes of the citizens of Heaven never wear out and the person himself never grows old. We shall experience what eye has not seen, what ear has not heard and what has not entered the mind of man."...
>
> A Tradition found in both Al-Bukhari and Muslim declares that the greatest delight awaiting the citizens of Heaven will be to look on the face of God. This is named the "surplus" (Qur'an 10:26)...
>
> The Qur'an refers to "charming abodes in the Gardens of Eden" (61:12). These abodes, Tradition affirms, are pearly palaces: each palace contains seventy courts, each court seventy houses, and each house seventy couches, with a houri on each couch. There is a tree in the Garden through whose shade one

---

124. Seale, "Islamic Society," 129.
125. Ibid., 130.

may ride for a hundred years without crossing it. The smallest house in the Garden has a thousand servants, each going about his appointed task. Finally, everyone in the Garden will marry five hundred houris, four thousand virgins and eight thousand non-virgins.[126]

Finally, from the Traditions, Seale shows the power of intercession especially that of Prophet Muhammad to help those who might be bound for hell in order to rescue them:

> In one Tradition, the Prophet is reported to have said: 'Five things were given to me alone out of all God's prophets: I was feared by people who lived as far as a month's journey from where I was. I was allowed to keep the spoils when others were not. My people were allowed to worship anywhere and everywhere. I was sent not to one people but all peoples. I was given the prerogative of interceding for others." When all intercessors fail them, they will come to Muhammad and ask him to intercede for them in their plight. The Prophet will approach the throne and bow down before the Most High. God will then say what he has not said to anyone before. "Rise, Oh Muhammad, ask and you will receive, plead and your pleading will be accepted." The Prophet will say: "My people, I pray for them" . . . The good folk and the learned will be allowed to intercede for their own tribe . . . If one of God's people was in life given a cup of cold water, he will be allowed to plead for his benefactor, rescuing him from Hell. Another Tradition runs: some of the Prophet's companions spoke with admiration of Abraham, the friend of God, of Moses, who conversed with God, of Jesus, God's Word and spirit. Muhammad said: "All you say is true, and I, without boasting, am the beloved of God whose intercession will be accepted on the Day of Judgment."[127]

Here, the inference is that the Islamic Traditions show that the Prophet Muhammad and his power of intercession are unique when compared to other prophets before him. In addition, the Islamic Traditions suggest that only Muhammad's intercession will be accepted by God on the day of

---

126. Ibid., 130–131.
127. Ibid., 128.

judgment. Perhaps Muhammad's power of intercession provides Muslims with a general sense of assurance that all will be well in the end because of their faith in God and Muhammad, the last of the prophets.

The Modern Secular Perspective

Having looked at Hindu and Muslim perspectives, two of the major religious perspectives of "State-after-Death" in the world today with nearly a billion each as their followers, we now consider the post-Enlightenment Modern Secular perspective which has been the predominant perspective in the Western world for a long time. This Western perspective has spread quite widely into the urban pluralistic contexts of the two-thirds world under the impact of globalization. Of course, here we are specifically looking at the classical or traditional Modern Secular perspective as opposed to the more current Post-Modern perspective of the Western world, which itself seems to be an off-shoot of Modern Secular perspective. This classical Modern Secular perspective also permeates the urban centers of Latin America, Asia and Africa today, and is especially popular among those who have rejected their indigenous religious systems and have embraced Secularism as a kind of intellectual elitism. We examine this Modern Secular perspective only because of its global influence. It lays the broad foundation, out of which arise the threads of more recent Western Post-Modernity and some forms of eclectic spirituality.

I will not consider here the more recent Post-Modern perspective, which denies the so-called "absolute" or "objective" truth, contends all claims of truth are "subjective" opinion and hence considers them "true" only as they fit into the particular paradigm. In light of this, the question needs to be asked, is Post-Modernity a reverse influence of globalization from the Eastern world to the West? That is, has the Post-Modern perspective developed due to the influence of the broad Eastern Hindu-Buddhist-New Age perspective which sees truth as unknowable and considers all religious paths as equally true and salvific? Be that as it may, my main interest here is the Secularism that is spreading into the global pluralistic contexts.

Though the classical Modern Secular perspective is not usually considered a religion, as such, it has become a major perspective in the global pluralistic contexts through which a great number of people, even of some from the above religious groups, perceive the ultimate reality of "State-after-Death."[128] Harvey Cox in his popular book, *The Secular City*, helps us understand the Modern Secular perspective (which he calls Secularism) as a religious perspective by distinguishing it from the Secularization process, which is taking place in all the major cities of the World. Cox notes,

> Secularization implies a historical process, almost certainly irreversible, in which society and culture are delivered from tutelage to religious control and closed metaphysical world views . . . Secularism, on the other hand, is the name for an ideology, a new closed world view which functions very much like a new religion . . . It is a closed ism. It menaces the openness and freedom secularization has produced; it must therefore be watched carefully to prevent its becoming the ideology of a new establishment. It must be especially checked where it pretends not to be a world view but nonetheless seeks to impose its ideology through the organs of the state.[129]

Now whether or not one accepts the Secularization process going on in the global cities as a good thing, it is clear from Cox's above clarification that the Modern Secular perspective must be recognized for what it is, a religious perspective, which has become equally influential and controlling as has any other religious way of life. Many who hold the Modern Secular viewpoint argue that "death is religion's 'trump card,' for people fear death and religion capitalizes on that fear by claiming to provide answers" but, as we have noted before, Longenecker has said that, every religious perspective "worth its salt" must provide answers for the universal problem of death.[130] Obviously, the Modern Secular Humanist perspective, as a religious perspective, also must provide some kind of hope "for death's final eradication." However, "The modern secularized mind" says "When you're dead you're dead."[131] Also, it sees one's life from the perspective of one's "ultimate death and ceasing to be is the foundation of all courage and clear vision of life's possibilities" and "For

---

128. Many Hindus and even some Muslims in the urban world have been strongly influenced by this Modern Secular perspective and even if they may not publicly confess it, they follow it in practice.
129. Harvey Cox, *The Secular City: Secularization and Urbanization*. Rev. ed. (New York: Macmillan, 1966), 18.
130. Longenecker, *Life in the Face of Death*, 2–3.
131. Hick, *Death and Eternal Life*, 11.

Sartre, human freedom must be exercised in a world where God is dead and death for man is the final end."[132]

Russell Aldwinckle, in *Death in the Secular City*, acknowledges the influence of this perspective even within the Christian church, particularly in the West, where many tend to downplay the importance of a life after death as far as their behavior in this life is concerned.[133] Aldwinckle wonders "whether this comparative indifference to personal survival [among Christians] is not bound up with deep and gnawing doubts about God and His purpose for men's future."[134] This he attributes partly to the post-Enlightenment denial of any personal existence beyond death. This view came from "skeptical philosophers, materialistic scientists . . . humanists, naturalists, and Marxists" from the Eighteenth Century onwards due to their naturalistic view of the world and human beings.[135] Aldwinckle finds quite striking "the degree to which thinkers who claim to be Christian have capitulated to this modern mood and seek to interpret the gospel in purely this-worldly terms."[136]

Aldwinckle sees present "Western culture is a curious mixture of sophistication, sentimentality and sheer superstition," resembling in many ways "the Greco-Roman world in which the Christian faith had to win its way in the early centuries of our era."[137] In an "attempt to redress the balance," he responds to those who promote "an exclusively this-worldly version of the Christian faith" that it is not a case of "either-or" but "both-and" and continues to note:

> Yet human aspirations and yearnings can never be satisfied for ever with crusades against pollution and social injustice, necessary as these are and in their true perspective, the proper objects of Christian sacrificial concern here and now. It is part of our contention that a superficial 'either-or' is not the only option of the Christian for the future. It does not follow that the hope of heaven necessarily means that one is against earth . . . The present world, with all its possibilities, is after all God's world.

---

132. Russell Aldwinckle, *Death in the Secular City* (London: George Allen & Unwin Ltd, 1972), 21.
133. Ibid., 19.
134. Ibid.
135. Ibid.
136. Ibid., 20.
137. Ibid., 21.

What comes after death is also in His hands. The Christian hope spans both time and eternity and we should not opt for less.[138]

It is clear that there has been a shift of perspective towards naturalism, positivism and Marxism in the Western world that has led many to ignore any discussion of "State-after-Death," but to accept death as the final end of a human being in this Modern Secular West. Aldwinckle has pointed to the late Bertrand Russell as the prime agent who brought about this paradigm shift in the English-speaking countries and generated a philosophy of despair and modern distrust of human desires.[139] He thinks that Russell (along with Freud) has implanted a bizarre anxiety among people that they are becoming prey to some wishful thinking about "State-after-Death" and, as a result, for many of them, the Christian hope has really become a "pie in the sky."[140] Arnold Toynbee traces the roots of this thinking back to the Epicurean school of Greek philosophers and considers it the most logical ("commonsense") conclusion about what happens after death. Toynbee notes,

> The most logical guess about the fate of a human personality after death is to suppose that it is analogous to the fate of a corpse . . . and, if we assume that the analogy is valid, we should conclude that, at death, a human being's personality becomes extinct. This guess . . . was held to be the truth by the Epicurean school of Greek philosophers. Its most earnest, and most distinguished, spokesman is the Roman Epicurean poet Lucretius; Lucretius's doctrine has had an echo in the poetry of a modern English poet, A. E. Houseman. This Epicurean answer to the question of the sequel to death for a human personality may look like the obvious answer. It is, indeed, a "commonsense" inference . . . to the unknown from what was believed to be known for certain till recently.[141]

So it is that in the Modern Secular mind, death is considered to be a total extinction of life and the only hope is to live "in the now" without fear for "the

---

138. Ibid., 23.
139. Ibid., 24.
140. Ibid.
141. Arnold Toynbee and Arthur Koestler, eds., *Life after Death* (New York: McGraw-Hill Book Company, 1976), 6. Later on Toynbee notes, "One alternative guess is still more logical than" this one (Ibid., 7).

beyond," that is, having no concern for what happens after death. Yet, this way of thinking has failed to bring relief from the fear of death among humans.

Longenecker notes that naturalistic humanism developed in the Renaissance due to the sole focus on humanity and the exclusion of the supernatural.[142] Death, therefore, was accepted as a purely natural phenomenon. While some Renaissance thinkers believed that the essential personality of humankind continued to exist in some form after death, yet most of them believed that personality ended at death and "immortality [can be] attributed only to a person's ideals as passed on to his or her posterity."[143] Thus, the only hope for the naturalistic humanists was to be remembered by others for their achievements and ideals after they were gone and finished in death. Longenecker sums up the Modern Secular Humanistic perspective of death in this way:

> that death is perfectly natural phenomenon, which is to be accepted with as much tranquility as possible. This attitude stems from a number of sources: from Buddhism or Confucianism (its Eastern heritage); from Stoicism or the Epicureans (its Classical heritage); and/or from naturalistic or religious humanism (its Western heritage). In this view, (1) resignation in the face of the natural and inevitable is stressed, (2) training the mind to accept death as only part of the world process of change and decay – and so, not to think of death in personal terms – is advocated, (3) making the most of our human lives, both personally and on behalf of others, is strongly urged – with the hope that hereby one will be remembered, even though faced with the sure prospect of personal oblivion, and (4) working for the continuance and well-being of the human race generally, as well for the continuance and development of one's own ideals in the lives of one's posterity in particular, are taught as humanity's only hope.[144]

According to John Hick, Modern Secular humanism mainly based in the West tends to present "an optimistic view of life." Hick also suggests that it is "an elitist doctrine for the fortunate few," who belong to "the small educated and affluent minority of mankind."[145] Hick notes that an affluent

---

142. Longenecker, *Life in the Face of Death*, 11.
143. Ibid., 11–12.
144. Ibid., 14.
145. Hick, *Death and Eternal Life*, 152.

Western society person's life can be positively good and acceptable without any reference to the idea of an afterlife, because in Western societies "work can be purposeful and satisfying, in which the family can flourish, and to which we can hope to make our own small contribution."[146] But Hick also points out that "the majority of the human race unhappily lacks and has always lacked" these things that the Western societies enjoy and, hence, in essence, the Modern Secular perspective with no life after death does not provide any hope for a large majority of human race of both the past and the present world.[147]

Aldwinckle shows another weakness of this Secular humanistic perspective:

> There is another aspect to this question which has been well expressed by Bonhoeffer, and that is the psychological effect upon men of the conviction that death is really the end. It is often considered to be a libel to assert that if men do not believe in a life after death, they will eat, drink and be merry, for tomorrow they die. The fact remains, however, that the finality of death can also evoke a frantic attempt to squeeze as much as out of this life as possible in the shortest period of time, since no man knows when the bell will toll for him.[148]

This remark by Aldwinckle does explain why life and society at large, deeply influenced by the Modern Secular perspective, are so fast-paced, even frantic in Western countries and also in some of the urban centers of the rest of the world. On one hand, it would seem that those who are persuaded by the Modern Secular perspective have only a limited time in this life to work for and enjoy all that this life can provide with no hope of life beyond death to look forward to, in addition to which, no one knows how limited life on this earth might be. On the other hand, many who adhere to this perspective for day-to-day living, rather than the despair and denial of death, do believe in some kind of existence beyond death, even in a form of reincarnation[149] or a general heaven. This is because some of them believe that indeed, if there is a god and this god is a benevolent god, then this god will accept everyone without judgment or accountability.

---

146. Ibid., 152–153.
147. Ibid., 153.
148. Aldwinckle, *Death in the Secular City*, 23–24.
149. Reincarnation is also widely accepted because it seems quite a fascinating new idea along with its association with occult practices, out of body experiences, and other kinds of psychic experiences.

Summary and Implications

Although there is no single, universally accepted view on what happens after death, all must recognize that death itself is not an invention of religion but an existential reality and therefore the greatest challenge to all religious and philosophical viewpoints. In this chapter, I have studied three predominant non-Christian perspectives (Hindu, Muslim and Modern Secular) to investigate their relationship with each other and clarify the implications they may have for a relevant Christian theology of the "State-after-Death" in pluralistic contexts.

In *the Hindu perspective,* following the tradition of the *Upanishads* and later writings, the predominant view about "State-after-Death" is reincarnation, with some variances of interpretation. In Hinduism, death is a painful predicament for both the victims of death and the surviving community. Death is dreaded by Hindus as a first reaction and is generally abhorred because it causes grief and separation. However, death is not considered the end of life but a passage to rebirth. Death is considered a break in the series of events called *life*, necessary and meaningful in the cycle of birth, death and rebirth. The Hindu rebirth cycle is based on the principle of *Karma* (deeds). Good deeds help one to be re-born into a higher caste, *Brahmin* (priest), *Kshatriya* (warrior) or *Vaishya* (merchant or farmer), while evil deeds lead to rebirth as a *Shudra* (menial laborer or servant) or even as an animal. This follows the *Karmic* view that gods are the highest form of existence, followed in order by humans, animals, and plants and atoms of matter are the lowest.

According to Hinduism, the Self or Soul (*atman*) of humans is immortal and indestructible and when death comes, only the physical body dies. This Self is eternal, and is generally considered either a part of or the same as *Brahman*, the impersonal ultimate Reality; and if different from *Brahman*, possibly of the same essence as *Brahman*. While the physical body dies, Rambachan shows that the so-called Subtle Body (*suksma sarira*), and not the Self, carries the memory traces of *Karma* from one life to the next as the Subtle Body separates from the physical body at the moment of death. The way of salvation from this seemingly endless cycle of birth and rebirth is through Self-Realization, that is, the discovery of the Self that is hidden in the heart, through the process of spiritual discipline in the present life. There are three main paths of spiritual discipline to escape from this cycle of rebirth:

the way of good deeds (*Karma Marga*), the way of knowledge (*Jnana Marga*) and the way of devotion (*Bhakti Marga*).

If there is no judgment or punishment/reward of the eternal Soul or Self itself for the deeds done in this life, then what particular aspect of an individual human person is being judged? Perhaps the Hindu way of asking this question would be: Exactly what dimension of an individual's human person is subject to the deterministic consequences of *Karma*? Is it only the so-called "subtle body" that faces the consequence of actions of the previous life to the next in the cycle of rebirth? It would seem that this is what the later Hindu scriptures teach. However, Adiswarananda notes that according to Hinduism all people will attain Self-Knowledge ultimately, even though they may take many detours of multiple births in the process, whether higher or lower on the ladder of existence.[150] Perhaps, this is why many urban Hindus, vying to succeed in the fast pace of today's world, leave very little time for practising the three religious ways of escape from the cycle of rebirth. These Hindus have more or less accepted, in practice, the Modern Secular notion that death is the end of all existence.

There are two main implications of the Hindu perspective in connection with what ultimately happens after death. The first is that somehow, after-death, the whole being of an individual person does not face the full consequence of actions done in one's life. The result is that the whole being of an individual person is not considered responsible for those actions. If, on one hand, the Self is the primary "I" of a person and the Self does not face the consequence of that person's actions, then, in essence, the responsibility of the primary "I" for every action is being ignored or excused. If, on the other hand, the Self is not the primary "I" of a person but is a part of or is *Brahman* present in a human being, then what is the primary "I" of a person that is responsible for and must face the consequences of that person's action? Is it the physical body that is destroyed at death and/or the subtle body that includes the senses, the mind and the intellect? If the Self is not the primary "I" of a person, then why did *Krishna* advise *Arjuna* not to mourn for the Self, since the Self is not killed when the body is killed, but is "leaving aside worn-out bodies, To other, new ones goes the embodied (soul)" (*Bhagavad Gita* 2:17–22)?

The second implication of the Hindu perspective of "State-after-Death" is that, whatever the primary "I" of a person is, the Self or some aspect of the

---

150. Adiswarananda, "Hinduism," 170–171.

body (such as the subtle body), the succession of lives resulting from multiple births minimizes responsibility for actions, and promotes a lackadaisical attitude towards this life. Even further, it obliterates a sense of accountability in the present life because of the option that the consequences of human actions can be faced in the next life. The Hindu understanding that ultimately all will attain Self-knowledge and salvation in the end (through the detours of many lives) may give people the idea that ultimately it does not really matter how unrighteously one lives in the present life.

The Muslim perspective of "State-after-Death" is in many ways similar to Judeo-Christian views, with one life here on earth, then death and finally resurrection on the Judgment Day, a day of cosmic upheaval. The dead from all nations will be judged according to their deeds during life on earth, however minute these may be, and then sent to either an everlasting Paradise of pleasures or a Hell of continuous affliction and suffering. In Islam there is no way for the dead to return to earth and no concept of reincarnation. Although human beings are not considered inherently evil or misguided, Islam recognizes that all people err and that each individual alone is responsible and accountable for one's own deeds at the Judgment. A traditional belief has evolved among Muslims that judgment really begins on the first night in the grave after death itself. At this time all are questioned by two angels about their beliefs and depending on their response are placed in a pleasant state or a situation of torment in the grave itself.

Muslims believe the deceased remain in the grave until the day of resurrection in an Intermediate State, the first after-death stage. During this period, prayers are said and alms given on behalf of the dead to add to their tally of good deeds. The concept of *Barzakh* in popular Muslim understanding is, perhaps, this loosely defined Intermediate State. Exactly what happens to the soul in *Barzakh*, where the dead wait, is not discussed much in the Qur'an and there is a lot of speculation about it in the *Traditions*, with varying degrees of authenticity and reliability. The themes of joy and torment to be experienced at the time of final judgment is prefigured and repeated in a variety of ways from the very beginning, as one follows the sequence of death and after-death events, beginning with the kind of welcome the grave will offer to the deceased.

For a Muslim, faithfulness in religious duties will be rewarded on the Judgment Day in the Garden, a place of beauty and physical satisfaction. However, delinquency in religious duties and unrighteous acts will be punished on Judgment Day in the Fire, a place of roaring flames and torment.

Muslims believe that varying levels of the Garden and the Fire exist for varying degrees of success or failure in one's deeds in life. They also believe in some poorly defined interventions, including prayers and alms-giving for the dead, which will favorably assist them on Judgment Day. As there is no sure means of forgiveness in Islam, there is also no clear assurance of salvation after death, though there is a vague hope for Allah's mercy because of allegiance to Prophet Muhammad.

It seems the *Hadith* (Traditions) consider the Prophet Muhammad and his power of intercession quite unique compared to the other prophets in that only his intercession will be accepted by God on the day of judgment. Perhaps this power of intercession of Muhammad provides Muslims with a general sense of assurance that all will be well in the end because of their faith in Allah and his last Prophet. Of course, in the twelfth century, the great Islamic theologian, Al-Ghazali, thought that some of the descriptions of heaven or hell seem to have chiefly moral meaning in order to emphasize the importance of the 'straight path' by which Allah guides the faithful. Moreover, while the Qur'an affirms the eternality of both heaven and hell, most Muslims, without doubting the eternality of the Garden, seem to think that "it is not only possible but even likely that at some future time all sinners will be pardoned and the Fires of judgment will be extinguished forever."[151] Thus, like many urban Hindus in the fast pace of today's world, some urban Muslims also have little time for keeping religious ways to escape from the punishment of the day of judgment. They too have, in practice at least, bought into the Modern Secular perspective of death. Even these Muslims still have some hope of Allah's mercy because of their allegiance to the Prophet Muhammad, provided they live a good life and practice some of their religious duties.

There are two main implications of the Muslim perspective of "State-after-Death." The first is a positive one, in that, Muslims, in general, have some fear about the judgment of God after death, be it immediately after death or at the final day of judgment. This fear of judgment of God after death motivates them to live a religious life (praying five times a day, fasting in the month of Ramadan, giving alms, etc.) and avoiding evil deeds, according to the standards of Islam. The second implication is that they have to depend entirely on their individual good works for a blessed hereafter. In addition, no one can be sure whether his or her good deeds will be good enough in God's sight for paradise. Due to this ambiguity, Islamic Traditions have tried

---

151. Smith, "Islam," 201.

to strengthen the hope of Muslims by emphasizing the unique power of Muhammad's intercession for them to assure them all will be well in the end.

In *the Modern Secular perspective*, death is denied or ignored, controlled and managed. "Here and now" is what matters and any thought about an existence after death is totally shunned and rejected as "pie in the sky." The common refrain of this humanistic, naturalistic perspective is that when you are dead, that's the end. Our biological life is what matters and any concept of human essence beyond the physical realm is considered absurd and outside the public arena of inquiry. Though this notion is not usually considered a religious perspective, it has become a primary idea in pluralistic contexts. This is embraced by a great number of people, even by some religious groups. Thus, the Modern Secular perspective must be recognized as a religious position that is equally influential and controlling as is any other religious perspective.

Aldwinckle shows us how strong the influence of this Modern Secular perspective is, even within the Christian church, particularly in the West, where many tend to downplay the importance of a life after death.[152] This neglect is reflected in their day-to-day behavior with a narrow concern only for this earthly life. While Aldwinckle sees Bertrand Russell, along with Freud, as primarily responsible for bringing about this perspective,[153] Toynbee traces the roots of this thinking to the Epicurean school of Greek philosophers.[154] However, Longenecker derives this Secular perspective from three sources: "Buddhism or Confucianism (its Eastern heritage); from Stoicism or the Epicureans (its Classical heritage); and/or from naturalistic or religious humanism (its Western heritage)."[155]

Hick shows the weakness of the Modern Secular perspective in that with no life after death, it does not provide any hope for a large majority of the human race, of both past and present worlds, who have not enjoyed or do not enjoy the basic amenities of life that the people of the affluent Western societies enjoy.[156]

Aldwinckle, following Bonhoeffer, shows another weakness in that life is fast and frantic in the Western countries and in the urban centers of the world, because Modern Secularists have only a limited time to work for and enjoy everything life provides. They lack hope of life beyond death and, with only

---

152. Aldwinckle, *Death in the Secular City*, 19.
153. Ibid., 24.
154. Toynbee and Koestler, *Life after Death*, 6.
155. Longenecker, *Life in the Face of Death*, 14.
156. Hick, *Death and Eternal Life*, 152–153.

this limited life are frantic to make the best use of their short time. There are, however, some who, instead of a philosophy of despair and denial of death, believe in an existence beyond death, even in some form of reincarnation or a general heaven.

2

The Perspectives of Contemporary Theologians I

In following this survey of thinking on "State-after-Death" from the three perspectives, I reiterate that this study is a search for the meaning of death and after-death because it is a major component of a Christian theology of religions and, therefore, mission. Gerald H. Anderson's insight bears repeating, that, the challenge of religious pluralism to mission cannot be overstated; and that, "This is the theological issue for mission . . . [going] into the twenty-first century."[1] Yet, my broad survey of mission theologians shows that very few have touched on the issue of "State-after-Death" in their response to the challenge of religious pluralism. I will address this problem in this and the following chapter.

In response to my second research question, these chapters will look at the views of contemporary Christian theologians on "State-after-Death" including their responses to religious pluralism, selecting only highly influential theologians who were globally recognized in twentieth century mission theology. Some of these have touched on "State-after-Death," while others, who have not considered this issue I have retained to highlight their omission. Some of these theologians broadly relate to religious pluralism, but these are minimal, as Harold Netland observes, confirming my own findings:

> Although Roman Catholic and mainline Protestant thinkers have been engaged in theology of religions for much of the past century, evangelical interest in the subject is quite recent, emerging only in 1980s and 90s. Evangelical missiologists'

---

1. Anderson, "Theology of Religions," 201.

contributions have been largely limited to responding to the more open and inclusive soteriological perspectives of theologians.[2]

In this chapter I deal with four very influential Christian thinkers in global mission theology: German theologian Dietrich Bonhoeffer, Indian theologian Paul David Devanandan, British missiologist Stephen Neill and Dutch missiologist Hendrik Kraemer. In the next chapter, I will deal with three additional Christian thinkers of the twentieth century: the ecumenical theologian of India M. M. Thomas, British pluralist theologian John Hick and the German Roman Catholic theologian Hans Küng. I have selected these well-known theologians because they have either specifically dealt with the issue of death and after-death in some form or have engaged with the perspectives of other religions. I was unable to find others who have dealt with the "State-after-Death" problem in global contexts. I will look into how they approach the challenge of pluralistic religious beliefs for a Christian theology of mission and how they have touched on the issues of death and after-death.

Dietrich Bonhoeffer

Bonhoeffer was born on 4 February 1906 in Breslau, Germany (now Poland) but his family of eleven moved to Berlin in 1912.[3] Bonhoeffer's extended family was quite well off and highly educated. His father was a professor of psychiatry and neurology. Quite a few of the previous Bonhoeffer generations, from both sides had a theological background.[4] This may have led him to study theology after high school. He first entered Tübingen at the age of seventeen and joined Berlin University the next year, studying under Adolf von Harnack and others. As he began to work toward his doctoral dissertation, *Sanctorum Communio* in 1925, he was influenced by Karl Barth's theology.[5] After studies at Berlin, he became a curate of a German church in Barcelona in 1928 and then in 1930 a lecturer in Systematic Theology at

---

2. Netland, "Theology of Religions," 142.
3. G. Leibholz, "Memoir," in *The Cost of Discipleship*, ed. Dietrich Bonhoeffer, trans. R. H. Fuller (New York: Macmillan, 1963), 11; Ed L. Miller and Stanley J. Grenz, *Fortress Introduction to Contemporary Theologies* (Minneapolis, MN: Fortress Press, 1998), 69.
4. Leibholz, "Memoir," 12.
5. Charles Marsh, "Dietrich Bonhoeffer," in *The Modern Theologians: An introduction to Christian theology in the twentieth century*, ed. David F. Ford. Second edition. (Oxford, UK: Blackwell Publishers, 1997), 38.

Berlin University.⁶ He also did post-doctoral studies at Union Theological Seminary, New York in 1930–31.

Unfortunately, his career as a professor of theology was disrupted by Adolf Hitler's rise to power in 1933. He strongly opposed Hitler's policy called the "Aryan Clause" in which people of Jewish origins were excluded from government service. And once this exclusion was adopted by the Reich Church, they were excluded from church ministry. Charles Marsh notes that in August of 1933 "Bonhoeffer criticized the Nazi theologians' 'disinheritance theory,' which promoted *the world mission of a master race* to replace the Jewish people."⁷ Bonhoeffer said, "We oppose the attempt to deprive the German Evangelical Church of its promise by the attempt to change it into a national church of Christians by Aryan descent."⁸ In October 1933, he left for London and served as a pastor in two German congregations and tried to inform the British Church, especially the Bishop of Chichester, G. K. A. Bell, of the real nature of the conflict in the German church.⁹

When he returned from London in 1935, he began an illegal seminary in Finkenwalde for the Confessional Church. This church was formed at Barmen in 1934 opposing the Reich Church's adoption of the Aryan Clause. But soon the Gestapo found out and closed the seminary down in 1940. While at Finkenwalde, he met Maria von Wede and later got engaged to her. There, he wrote his well-known books on spirituality, *The Cost of Discipleship* (1948) and *Life Together* (1954).¹⁰ He left for the USA in June 1939 but felt he had to return to Germany. He wrote to Reinhold Niebuhr, "I shall have no right to participate in the reconstruction of Christian life in Germany after the war if I do not share the trials of this time with my people."¹¹ When he returned, he was forbidden to speak anywhere in the Reich. He joined the resistance movement and worked as a civilian in the counter-intelligence agency. But the Gestapo arrested him on 5 April 1943 shortly before his marriage.

By then he had finished *Ethics* which was published posthumously. His *Letters and Papers from Prison* is an influential theological document of the

---

6. Leibholz, "Memoir," 13.
7. Marsh, "Dietrich Bonhoeffer," 38 (emphasis added).
8. Ibid. Marsh (Ibid., note 2, 49–50) quotes from Bonhoeffer's "The Barmen Confession," in *A Testament to Freedom: The Essential Writings of Dietrich Bonhoeffer*, eds. G. B. Kelly and F. B. Nelson (San Francisco: HarperSanFrancisco, 1990), 143.
9. Leibholz, "Memoir," 14.
10. Stanley J. Grenz and Roger E. Olson, *20th-Century Theology: God & the World in a Transitional Age* (Downers Grove, IL: InterVarsity, 1992), 148.
11. Leibholz, "Memoir," 16.

twentieth century dealing with the relationship between Christianity and the apparatus of human religion.[12] In prison, he was involved in the 20 July 1944 plot to assassinate Hitler. As a result, he was executed in the morning of 9 April 1945 at Flossenburg, a week before the Allies liberated the camp.[13] Here, I briefly survey his theology to find whether he touched on "State-after Death" with any implications for a pluralistic context.

Christ-Centered Theology of Mission

While the German Reich Church cooperated with Nazism, Bonhoeffer called on the church to *not* cooperate but stand against these forces and follow the biblical teaching. However, in his short and turbulent life, he did not have much opportunity to systematize his theological reflections. He attempted to grow, develop and change personally within his mission context in Germany as he reflected on his own experience and theology. One example of his change can be seen in that, while he was a pacifist earlier, he became involved in the plot to assassinate Hitler while in prison.[14] But in his growth and change, Bonhoeffer remained rooted in a Christ-centered theology of mission.

Therefore Marsh notes, "The whole of Bonhoeffer's theology can be understood as an account of the continuities of God's identity, as well as human identities, interpreted through the reconciling work of Jesus Christ."[15] Marsh continues, "Bonhoeffer's formulations, 'Christ existing as community,' 'Christ the center,' 'Christ as reality,' and 'Jesus as the one for others' are all ways of demonstrating how a christological description of human sociality affirms genuine relationship."[16] These formulations highlight Bonhoeffer's Christ-centered theology of mission and show us how he would have stood for the uniqueness of Christ if he did face the challenge of religious pluralism. His personal conviction about *mission to others*, including the people of other faiths, was primarily centered on Christ. He believed that the church's most important task of mission must be first and foremost based on Christ.

In spite of the Nazi repression, he did not cease to emphasize Christ as the starting point for all mission of the church. In his Christology lectures

---

12. John B. Webster, "Bonhoeffer, Dietrich," in *New Dictionary of Theology*, eds. Sinclair B. Ferguson, David F. Wright and J. I. Packer (Downers Grove, IL: InterVarsity, 1988), 107.
13. Marsh, "Dietrich Bonhoeffer," 38.
14. Grenz and Olson, *20th-Century Theology*, 149.
15. Marsh, "Dietrich Bonhoeffer," 42.
16. Ibid.

he argued that Christ is at the center of human existence, of history and of nature.[17] For Bonhoeffer, Christology starts from the historical Jesus of Nazareth, his death and resurrection, rather than the abstract notions like *logos* or Being.[18] Earlier in his life, he primarily stressed the presence of Christ in the church as a community; so the church discloses and reveals Jesus Christ as the center of the church's mission for others in the world. However, later on, while in prison, he was more concerned about the presence of Christ and his movement in the world, outside the church.[19]

Secular Humanism, Liberalism and Pluralism

Aldwinckle shows how Bonhoeffer responded to the secular humanistic perspective of "State-after-Death" from his *Ethics*,[20]

> There is another aspect . . . well expressed by Bonhoeffer, and that is the psychological effect upon men of the conviction that death is really the end . . . The fact remains . . . the finality of death can also evoke a frantic attempt to squeeze as much out of life as possible in the shortest period of time, since no man knows when the bell will toll for him. This has been powerfully stated by Bonhoeffer in his *Ethics* in a passage . . .
> "The miracle of Christ's resurrection makes nonsense of that idolization of death which is prevalent among us today. Where death is the last thing, fear of death is combined with defiance. Where death is the last thing, earthly life is all or nothing. Boastful reliance on earthly eternities goes side by side with a frivolous playing with life. A convulsive acceptance and seizing hold of life stands cheek by jowl with indifference and contempt for life."[21]

Here Bonhoeffer affirmed not only the miracle of Christ's resurrection but by it the sure and certain reality of "State-after-Death." He showed the futility of the Modern Secular perspective notion that there is no form of life after death and "death as the final end." Aldwinckle points out that the current

---

17. Grenz and Olson, *20th-Century Theology*, 342.
18. Marsh, "Dietrich Bonhoeffer," 45.
19. Grenz and Olson, *20th-Century Theology*, 150, 342.
20. Dietrich Bonhoeffer, *Ethics*, ed. E. Bethge (London: SCM, 1955), 16.
21. Aldwinckle, *Death in the Secular City*, 23–24.

human search for intense experiences in this present life corroborates with Bonhoeffer's analysis of secular humanists, in that the secular humanists have nothing to look forward to after death.

> It is not enough to dismiss this with contempt as a Christian distortion or to say that men ought to accept death as perfectly natural and die with quiet and serene acquiescence. Bonhoeffer has put his finger on a sensitive spot which contemporary man may consciously refuse to face. There is much, however, in the feverish modern search for intense experiences in this present life which gives impressive support to his analysis of our situation.[22]

Bonhoeffer recognized the invasion of secularism into society and realized even before Hitler's rise to power that there was an attempt on the part of National Socialism to base history on humankind without acknowledging God. He also recognized that the churches in the world situation of the thirties were not going to gain much by merely citing old creedal statements. Instead, he felt the dire need of the day was for churches and denominations to unite as members of one body of Christ through the worldwide ecumenical movement in order to make a united impact on the world at large.[23] Leibholz notes that, "Bonhoeffer considered it the duty of the Churches to listen anew to the message of the Bible and to put themselves in the context of the whole Church."[24] Hence Bonhoeffer played a significant role in the ecumenical movement and motivated students in Germany to get to know the life, the history and development of non-Lutheran churches. He stressed the unity of the churches in the world in order to keep the German Church from strictly Nazi control. He believed that the church's mission would be more effective in the world through that unity. His effort for the unity of the church, based on the Bible, shows his interest in seeking a global theological perspective based on the Scriptures rather than an ethnocentric one.

Influenced by Karl Barth's theology, Bonhoeffer resisted liberalism and tried to make a complete break with the liberal teaching of his former professors. Grenz and Olson note that, "Liberalism had employed the assumption of an innate human ability to sense the infinite in order to develop a point of contact between God and humanity and thereby to establish natural

---

22. Ibid., 24.
23. Leibholz, "Memoir," 14–15.
24. Ibid., 15.

theology."[25] But, for Bonhoeffer, God's revelation comes only in and through Jesus Christ, which, for him, is the heart of Christian theology and ethics. This conviction shows how Bonhoeffer would have responded to religious pluralism in the world.

In contrast to God's revelation through Jesus Christ, Bonhoeffer considered all religions as human attempts to reach God. In this we see the seeds of his later summons to the church for a "religionless Christianity." In the earlier part of his ministry, he followed the traditional view that politics should not be mixed with Christian faith. Later, however, he changed his mind as he saw that, indeed, the political authority in Germany had become totally corrupt. He felt "it is not only a Christian right but a Christian duty towards God to oppose tyranny . . . a government which is no longer based on natural law and the law of God."[26]

He drew a closer link between Christ and the church than Barth, because, for him, the revelation of God in Christ is an ecclesiological reality. Yet he rejected liberalism's concept of the church as a religious community.[27] In his *The Cost of Discipleship*, he contrasts 'cheap grace' with 'costly grace' by showing that cheap grace is preaching easy believism without repentance, whereas costly grace requires obedience.[28] As far as mission and evangelism is concerned, this theological perspective shows that he was more interested in "making disciples" of Christ than merely making them nominal members of the church.

Compared to the immanental theology of liberalism, Bonhoeffer emphasized the transcendence of God in all aspects of life. Bonhoeffer believed the transcendent God is "the Beyond in the midst of the world," shown clearly by the following observation:

> Transcendence consists not in tasks beyond our scope and power, but in the nearest Thou to hand. God in human form, not, as in other religions, in animal form . . . nor yet in abstract form – the absolute, metaphysical, infinite, etc., – nor yet in the Greek divine-human of autonomous man, but man existing for others, and hence the Crucified.[29]

---

25. Grenz and Olson, *20th-Century Theology*, 150.
26. Leibholz, "Memoir," 30.
27. Grenz and Olson, *20th-Century Theology*, 150.
28. Dietrich Bonhoeffer, *The Cost of Discipleship*, trans. R. H. Fuller (New York, NY: Macmillan, 1963), 45f.
29. Grenz and Olson, *20th-Century Theology*, 155. Grenz and Olson quote from

In this note about the transcendence of God, Bonhoeffer shows the uniqueness of God in contrast to, not only liberalism's view of God, but also to the views of God (or the so-called Ultimate Reality) in pluralistic perspectives. In his view, the transcendent God is active at the center of human life, breaking down all injustice, disparity, distinction and so on. According to Grenz and Olson, in Bonhoeffer's view of God "the reality of ultimate . . . gives meaning to the penultimate, the presence tapped by means of the secret discipline . . . gives sustenance to the believer and the church in their task of being in the world."[30] The churches must understand and know this transcendence of God in the midst of the secular world. True believers, while living in the secular world, through the sustenance of this transcendence must share in the suffering of God. It was his strong conviction that this is the mission of the church; so the church is not to be preoccupied with its own religious concerns but be committed to serve others.

State-after-Death

In his response to secular humanism, Bonhoeffer affirmed not only the miracle of Christ's resurrection but by it the sure and certain reality of life after death. For him, obedience to God in self-sacrifice is the key to fulfilling God's mission on earth.[31] In order to obey God, to do his bidding in his mission, a Christian must be willing to suffer and die and Bonhoeffer followed that example like so many of the early church martyrs. But his willingness to obey God even at the price of physical death, was based on the foundation of Christ's resurrection which assures the future resurrection and eternal life for the believer. He wrote this in a poem about death from prison as he was awaiting his own execution:

> *Come now solemnest feast on the road to eternal freedom,*
> *Death, and destroy those fetters that bow, those walls that imprison*
> *this our transient life, these souls that linger in darkness,*
> *so that at last we see what is here withheld from our vision.*

Bonhoeffer's *Letters and Papers from Prison*, trans. Eberhard Bethge (London: Collins, Fontana, 1953), 165. Here "Thou" is used instead of "thing" in Bonhoeffer's definition of transcendence. See also Grenz and Olson, *20th-Century Theology*, 343, endnote 58.

30. Grenz and Olson, *20th-Century Theology*, 155.

31. For Bonhoeffer, it was not enough to just seek and suffer for truth, justice and goodness for their own sake but we need to do this in loyal obedience to God.

Long did we seek you, freedom, in discipline, action and suffering.
Now that we die, in the face of God himself we behold you.[32]

These words reveal a clear concept of true freedom and eternal life after death in the presence of God. For him, self-sacrifice in death for God is the highest fulfillment of life, for it is through obedience, even to death, that we show our love to God and our responsibility in God's mission. Thus, Bonhoeffer accepted his own death with full assurance of eternal life in God's presence after death, yet he struggled within himself to know the deeper meaning of life. He also felt that sometimes he was disconnected from God and so, initially, he refused to suffer for God's sake. But later on, his life was full of suffering as he was being harassed by the Nazi authority in whatever he did for the extension of the church. Leibholz highlights Bonhoeffer's example of love for his fellow human beings, which was rooted in the Christian faith:

> It was his brotherly love of his fellow-men which also caused Bonhoeffer to believe that it was not enough to follow Christ by preaching, teaching and writing. No, he was deadly earnest when he called for Christian action and self-sacrifice . . . he offered his life for a new understanding of the personal life which has its root in the Christian faith.[33]

His suffering and death in a dark time left to the church a remarkable example for future mission. His life-style reflects Christ's life and is a true model for the mission of the church. Alfred A. Glenn, Professor of Theology at Bethel Seminary-West, CA notes,

> He is the inspiration for Christians today, both in North America and the Third world, who are either opposed to or suffering under oppressive political regimes. Ultimately it is Bonhoeffer's life that has so pervasively challenged Christians. He did what he said; he was a person of intense Christological piety who died as a martyr for his Lord.[34]

Bonhoeffer's example is, indeed, an inspiration for Christians today, especially those who are being persecuted and physically tortured for their faith and Christian witness. Bonhoeffer followed the example of his Lord, as well as

---

32. Leibholz, "Memoir," 23.
33. Ibid.
34. Alfred A. Glenn, "Bonhoeffer, Dietrich," in *Dictionary of Christianity in America*, eds. Daniel G. Reid, Robert D. Linder, Bruce L. Shelley and Harry S. Stout (Downers Grove, IL: InterVarsity, 1990), 173.

numerous disciples from the early church onwards, by his obedience in becoming a martyr for his Lord. Bonhoeffer was able to do this because he believed in Christ's resurrection and was fully assured that his "State-after-Death" would be eternal life with Christ and God.

Bonhoeffer's last words to his friend as he was called to Flossenburg to be executed were, "this is the end – for me the beginning of life."[35] How clearly and succinctly this expressed his view of "State-after-Death." He felt fully assured of eternal life after death in Christ and so was not afraid to go through physical death, even by execution. Death for him was, "the beginning of life," and that life was possible because of his faith in Christ, who is the Resurrection and the Life.

Paul David Devanandan

Paul David Devanandan, born 8 July 1901 in Madras, India in an ordained pastor's family, studied in Madras, Tiruchirapalli and Hyderabad, before graduating from Madras University in 1924. He was greatly influenced by a famous Indian Christian leader, K. T. Paul and subsequently traveled to the USA with Paul as his secretary in 1924–25. Remaining in the USA for seven more years, he studied for a Bachelor of Divinity at the Pacific School of Religion in Berkeley, CA; and completed a doctorate in Christian Theology on "The Concept of *Maya*" at Yale University.[36] Later he married K. T. Paul's daughter.[37]

When Devanandan returned to India in 1932, he joined the faculty of United Theological College, Bangalore, and taught philosophy and history of religions for seventeen years, after which he served for eight years as the literature secretary of YMCA in India. Then the National Council of Churches in India (World Council of Churches' constituent in India) asked him to lead the newly formed CISS – Christian Institute for the Study of Society. Later the CISS merged with the Christian Institute for the Study of Hinduism and became CISRS – the Christian Institute for the Study of Religion and Society at Bangalore, India. He served as CISRS Director until his untimely death

---

35. Grenz and Olson, *20th-Century Theology*, 149.
36. Robin Boyd, *An Introduction to Indian Christian Theology*, second edition (New Delhi, India: ISPCK, 1975), 186.
37. Sunand Sumithra, *Christian Theologies from an Indian Perspective* (Bangalore, India: Theological Book Trust, 1995), 142.

from a heart attack on 10 August 1962.[38] While Director at CISRS, he traveled all over the world, lecturing and teaching at places like Selly Oak Colleges in Birmingham, UK, and Union Theological Seminary in New York, USA.

One of his major roles was his involvement from its beginning in WCC's theological and evangelistic studies. In December 1961, he gave his world famous message under the title "Called to Witness" at the Third Assembly of WCC at New Delhi, India.[39] Apart from his dissertation on *Maya* (a philosophical concept in Hinduism meaning illusion, creative power, etc.), his writings are mainly papers and sermons collected and printed by CISRS, some after his death.

Inspired by his mentor, K. T. Paul's lead in the Indian nationalist movement and friendship with Mahatma Gandhi, Devanandan determined as a Christian to be fully involved in nation-building.[40] Although Devanandan's theology did not specifically touch on "State-after Death," I will discuss his views in relation to pluralistic religious perspectives.

Liberalism and Religious Pluralism

In his younger days, Devanandan opposed the theological liberalism that was rife in the established church. As he studied the works of Hendrik Kraemer and Karl Barth, he was impressed by them and that their approaches were a good basis for dealing with theological liberalism. In his understanding of God as a "personal" being as well as "the wholly other," we see traces of Kraemer and Barth. Later on, however, he reacted against Kraemer's negative attitude towards the 'non-Christian world'.[41] Kraemer postulated the discontinuity thesis, which affirmed that there is little, if any, point of contact between Christianity and other religions and rejected the validity of all so-called natural revelation.[42] Likewise, Barth considered all non-Christian religions as products of human endeavors.

Kraemer and Barth's position on other religions greatly disturbed Devanandan. Brought up among people of other faiths, he felt he could not

---

38. Boyd, *An Introduction to Indian Christian Theology*, 187; Sumithra, *Christian Theologies*, 142; Paul David Devanandan, *Christian Issues in Southern Asia* (New York: Friendship Press, 1963), 9.
39. Paul David Devanandan, *Preparation for Dialogue* (Bangalore, India: Christian Institute for the Study of Religion and Society, 1964), 179.
40. Boyd, *An Introduction to Indian Christian Theology*, 186.
41. Ibid., 187.
42. Sumithra, *Christian Theologies*, 143.

reject these faiths as demonic and containing no elements of truth. For him, Barth and Kraemer overly emphasized that "revelation is *from God* at the expense of the fact it is *to and for the world of men*," and he tried to balance that by doing a detailed sympathetic study of society in modern India.[43]

Boyd points out that Devanandan was "not seeking to 'adapt' the Christian message to Hinduism but rather so to understand the inner workings of Hinduism that he may be able to show his Hindu friends the points at which their beliefs can find true meaning only in Christ."[44] Devanandan in his *Christian Concern in Hinduism* notes,

> All this will point to the fact that one of the functions of the Christian evangelist in India is not so much to counter forces of secularism and irreligion, but to help Hindus, in city and in village, at all levels of culture, to redefine the very nature of what is called religion . . . It means that the preaching of the gospel would not only consist in the formulation of valid religious truths, but in the endeavour to harness the forces of faith to creative action to fulfill God's purpose. To believe in Jesus Christ is to trust in a *God that is redemptively at work in the world* for man's good.[45]

After long and careful research, Devanandan came up with the idea on which many later theologians built their theology of religions and which is quite often called the "Devanandan discovery,"[46] which we will deal with next.

Theology of Religions

Sunand Sumithra thinks that, "the very decision of Devanandan to study Hinduism (the concept of *maya*) shows his entry into theology was through the study of religions."[47] Below is the summary of Devanandan's innovative and insightful description of the characteristics of religions,

> Every historic religion is characterized by a creed, a cultus and a culture . . . a series of concentric circles. Each . . . takes years to

---

43. Boyd, *An Introduction to Indian Christian Theology*, 187.
44. Ibid., 187-188.
45. Paul David Devanandan, *Christian Concern in Hinduism* (Bangalore, India: Christian Institute for the Study of Religion and Society, 1961), 91-92 (emphasis added).
46. Sumithra, *Christian Theologies*, 143.
47. Ibid.

gather form and content, and together they constitute . . . "the religion of a people" . . . [It is] misleading to regard any one of them as independent or unrelated . . .

At the core is a body of beliefs, . . . "creeds" . . . basic fundamentals of the religion . . . may . . . be abstracted and examined, but always as parts of a whole, never as independent units, . . . accepted together as an entirety . . .

Beyond the innermost circles of affirmations, whether implicitly taken for granted by simple minds, or indifferently conceded by nominal adherents, or deliberately adopted by learned theologians, there tends to grow an outer circle of religious practices, constituting . . . the cultus.

The third and outermost circle represents what is generally described as the culture characteristic of a people . . . nurtured for centuries on the creed and cultus of a historic faith.[48]

This description is quite insightful because it helps us to understand that every human culture (or cultural practice) is deeply related to a particular religious creed (or belief system). Similarly, in our task of cross-cultural communication of the gospel in pluralistic contexts it is important to recognize the difficulty of separating the culture and the cultus (or the rituals) from the religious creed. Devanandan contends that "when a religion interacts with its environment, the impact is first felt in the area of culture. Only later in the process is the effect felt upon the cultus; and later still on the creedal core itself, if at all."[49] Thus the theological core of a religion changes quite rarely, and only with great difficulty. But the goal of Christian mission is to effect a change at this core assumption level. In pluralistic contexts, a person's acceptance or rejection of the eternal life in Jesus Christ is intrinsically linked with that person's core beliefs about "State-after-Death."

According to Devanandan,[50] four types of resurgent or renewal movements are taking place in Asian religions: On one hand, *Reform Movements* occur when the effects coming from the outside lead to an emphasis on the *new* rather than on the *old* and sometimes an emphasis on the *new* against the *old*. *Revival Movements*, on the other hand, are generated from within rather than from without and the response to the environment is quite dynamic. Here

---

48. Devanandan, *Christian Concern in Hinduism*, 10–12.
49. Ibid., 13.
50. Ibid., 15–16.

the emphasis is on the *old* rather than the *new*. The new environment will be questioned based on old principles. *Renascent Movements* occur through internal and external forces interacting rather than reacting and all the "basic fundamentals of the religion" are shaken up. In *Revolt Movements*, the ancestral faith is shaken up so much that the change leads to the repudiation of its fundamentals. The old is outmoded and the new elements are built up. Devanandan felt that a new *Renascent Movement* was taking place in Hinduism and new values of person, society and history were being accepted instead of the ancient caste system and the deterministic effect of *Karma*.

According to Sumithra, the "Devanandan discovery" is that this *new* Hinduism is the result of the Christian message and influence.[51] Thus, to Devanandan, the arrival of *new* human values in Hinduism, are a change brought about by the gospel of Jesus Christ, and as we enter into dialogue with Hindus, we will recognize that the hidden Christ is already at work in Hinduism. This is Devanandan's response to Barth and Kraemer's views on non-Christian religions. One wonders if Devanandan would have changed his views if he were still alive, facing the resurgence of hostilities from the Hindu fundamentalists against Christians. These developments would bring us closer to Barth and Kraemer's views on other religions, even if we accept Devanandan's position that elements of truth are present in non-Christian religions.

Devanandan[52] was partly right in that some of the newer developments in the Asian religions in India were due to the influence of Christianity. Some evidence for this is the reformation of Hinduism, led by Raja Ram Mohan Roy (1772–1833), who was influenced by Christianity and was a contemporary of William Carey and Alexander Duff in Calcutta. In addition, Sir Syed Ahmad Khan (1817–1898) pleaded for the modernization of Islam and the importance of reason in the interpretation of Koran because of Christian influence. However, Devanandan also recognized that, even though Hinduism adopted some of the teachings of Christianity, their religious leaders felt that their ancestral faiths should not be *totally* rejected.[53] The *Vedas* and the *Upanishads* of classical Hinduism teach that God, as the Absolute Self, is only apprehended in the mystical realization of unity (of God and humans) by the real Self in human beings. Still, there is also the popular belief in personal gods among Hindus who supposedly become manifest in many forms, even

---

51. Sumithra, *Christian Theologies*, 144.
52. Devanandan, *Christian Issues in Southern Asia*, 72.
53. Ibid., 73.

as humans.⁵⁴ These wide varieties in Hindu beliefs and practices led to the Hindu doctrine that all paths lead to the same goal.

Thus, realistically speaking, what has happened in the Asian religions, due to interaction with Christianity, is that there is some kind of mixture of the *new* with the *old*. Of course, immediately what comes to mind is Jesus' saying that "new wine is not put into old wineskins, for if it is, the skins burst and the wine is spilled" (Matt 9:17; also Mark 2:22 and Luke 5:37). Devanandan is correct in noting that, "The tolerance of Hinduism, its spirit of accommodation to different doctrines and observances, is based on the conviction that the essential nature of the Ultimate reality is unknowable."⁵⁵ The Christian gospel, however, proclaims that God has made himself known to humanity once for all through his Son, Jesus Christ, who is Immanuel (God-with-us) in human form. This is where the real clash is between the *Old* and the *New* so that both cannot co-exist. Devanandan may be right that the hidden Christ is at work in other religions. Yet once that Christ is revealed to the people of other faiths, they will have to either accept him or reject him, but they should not syncretize the *New* with the *Old*.

Theology of Mission

Devanandan's theology of mission is primarily a theology of Christian participation in nation building and of dialogue with other religious and secular faiths. From the time he was working on his dissertation on "the Concept of *Maya*," the question he raised was whether traditional Hinduism was able to provide an adequate cultural and spiritual foundation for India's national self-awakening and nation-building. It was his conviction that the mission of the church, especially the task of evangelism, is to be carried out through "dialogue" with the spiritual quest already going on in modern India.⁵⁶ His perspective of mission is that the church should witness to the Christian faith through active participation in the struggle for a new society, and through a life of spiritual dialogue with the other religious and secular faiths as to the meaning and basis of being human. According to Devanandan,⁵⁷ when we are convinced of God's redemptive purpose in our lives we discover our calling as "witnesses" to work together with God and

---
54. Ibid., 74.
55. Ibid., 77.
56. Boyd, *An Introduction to Indian Christian Theology*, 202f.
57. Devanandan, *Christian Issues in Southern Asia*, 141.

with fellow humans in the fellowship of the church to fulfill God's purpose for his creation. For him, witnessing to the faith is a peculiar characteristic of Christian belief and as a Christian believer one must bear living testimony to the redemptive work of God in Christ Jesus as a present reality in one's life, for the benefit of the society.

For Devanandan, "The crucified and risen Christ points to the emergence of a new creation which has personal, social and cosmic dimensions."[58] He believed that just as the Cross and the Divine forgiveness mediated by it destroyed the Jew/Gentile religious hostility, so also today the Cross is able to destroy the hostility between Christianity, Hinduism and Secularism and build a spiritual basis for a community of persons transcending religion and ideology. According to him, this would be the true beginning of the New Creation. Devanandan notes that, "Thus evangelistic witness, which is at the same time, and for all times, a cosmic process, a divine activity, a historic reality and a people's movement, is missionary in origin and intention, and congregational in purpose and design. It is both a going forth and a gathering in."[59] Responding sympathetically to the general concerns of Hindus about conversion and proselytism, he differentiated between 'propagation' and "propaganda,"

> when we talk about "propagating" the Christian faith we are not thinking of a "propaganda" for the Christian religion. It may be that in some cases, a previous generation of ... missionaries had given the impression that all they were anxious for was to win over people of other faiths, and add them to the membership of the Church. Perhaps some evangelists still do so. In such propaganda, methods of persuasion are sometimes employed which may be questionable, and the intention may also be the wrong one of getting people to our side because we have a feeling that we are in some way a better and a superior group of people. Also, in our anxiety to produce results we may give the impression that all we want is for people to join us, whatever their motives. This is partisan propaganda, which certainly is not Christian.[60]

---

58. M. M. Thomas and P. T. Thomas, *Towards an Indian Christian Theology* (Tiruvalla, India: Christava Sahitya Samithi, 1998), 212.
59. Devanandan, *Christian Issues in Southern Asia*, 142.
60. Devanandan, *Preparation for Dialogue*, 104–105.

However, Devanandan did not negate the importance of the task of the propagation of the gospel and saw it as the mission of every Christian believer, as he notes,

> the propagation of the Gospel, which is the mission of every Christian believer, is primarily to spread abroad the good news that God has initiated a movement in the history of mankind by Himself entering into this very world of want and violence, of disease and death, of human sin and willfulness, in order that this whole realm of world-life may be transformed into a veritable new creation in which will be acknowledged the sovereignty of God. The Christian believes that in the Person and Work of Jesus Christ, God Himself has begun this process of renewing the whole creation. The Christian message is thus no mere exposition of a body of teachings about the nature of God, the world and salvation. It is really transmitting a communication which is the result of a personal conviction of faith that something tremendous and revolutionary has happened, and is happening in the whole cosmic process.[61]

Thus, it seems that Devanandan did not eschew the task of spreading the gospel (for him, the good news of transformation here and now) when executed with correct methods and right motivation and he felt that every Christian believer must share that good news. For him, "Effective communication of the gospel to the non-Christian man of faith depends on the effective use made of the religious vocabulary with which he is familiar, and of the cultural pattern of life in which he finds self-expression and community being."[62] Thus, it seems, he was deeply concerned about the importance of contextualization of the gospel to the people of other faiths and aware of its effectiveness in the communication of the gospel to the people of other faiths.

Devanandan greatly desired to see that different Christian denominations of the church work together in mission and evangelism. He noted that, "the confusion created by denominationalism has been a great hindrance to evangelism."[63] In the 19th century, missionaries felt that it was good to have some kind of agreement on regions where different denominations

---

61. Ibid., 105.
62. Ibid., 191.
63. Devanandan, *Christian Issues in Southern Asia*, 98.

were serving. However, later on this agreement only helped perpetuate the problem of denominationalism and regionalism. He noted that,

> What really pricked was the question whether people of other faiths should become Christians – or Baptists, Anglicans, Congregationalists, and so forth. Moreover, it became increasingly apparent that wastage in men and money could be avoided if denominational forces were persuaded to co-operate; this would certainly make for more effective witness, too, especially in service projects.[64]

Devanandan pleaded for unity in the churches of India and on 27 September 1947, the South India United Church was formed, and this unity continued further with the Anglicans joining the church of South India later. Devanandan hoped that it would continue further and after his death in November 1970 many denominations joined to form the United Church of North India.[65] However, it needs to be noted that some of the leadership of both Church of South and North India, instead of facilitating evangelism, which was Devanandan's primary concern in his desire to see the unity of the church, now forbid it.

For Devanandan, the primary responsibility of the church is to gather around and be vitally connected to its Center, Christ, from whom it draws the power to be the transforming community in the midst of this world. Devanandan noted,

> True community is created by the conscious sense which each one in the group has of being vitally connected with a living Centre. And because of this living relationship to the Centre, they are all bound to one another. That is the real difference between the communion of saints and association of people.[66]

For him, as everyone within the church has a vital relationship with Christ, the church becomes the new creation and lives the kingdom life. Then this new community desires to do God's will sincerely and accomplish his purpose. "The Church is therefore the fellowship of those who endeavour in community as well as in their own personal lives to 'do the will of the

---

64. Ibid., 99.
65. Boyd, *An Introduction to Indian Christian Theology*, 206.
66. Ibid., 200. Robin Boyd quotes from Devanandan's *I will lift up mine Eyes unto the Hills: Sermons and Bible Studies*, eds. S. J. Samartha and Nalini Devanandan (Bangalore: Christian Institute for the Study of Religion and Society, 1963).

Father.'"⁶⁷ For him, the church does the will of the Father by doing wholistic mission through proclamation (*kerygma*), service (*diakonia*) and through the living witness of fellowship (*koinonia*).⁶⁸

For Devanandan,⁶⁹ while the underlying motive in all of our service is to point human beings to Christ, yet serving their physical needs is an integral part of the Christian mission. For him, social service should not be separated from the proclamation of Christ with the expectation that people will come to Christ and become his disciples and be active members of the church. However, he cautioned that social concern should not be treated as a means to an end to induce people to become Christians and added,

> The social concern for the liberation of man from prevailing conditions that make it difficult for him to fulfill his destiny is integral to Christian evangelism. It has been well said that, "No theology can be true which is intrinsically inhuman and, in this sense the highest religion is necessarily and rightly anthropomorphic."⁷⁰

Devanandan considers the crucial need in many parts of India is for literacy and education which will help the people not only to learn to read and write but also to acquire modern skills to earn a living in both urban and rural contexts. For him, the witness of Christian faith can be demonstrated only if Christian teachers, welfare workers, doctors and nurses choose to live as Christians not just as employees. But his advice to the church is, "The church, as the church, should not identify itself with any political party or program . . . but individual Christians should be free to take a stand."⁷¹ He further says, "The issues that Christians need to watch most closely are those concerning rights of minorities, religious freedom and undue governmental regulation of the lives of citizens."⁷²

Like all others, Devanandan's theology of mission has both strengths and weaknesses. The main thrust of his mission theology was that the gospel must be spread among the non-Christians through word and deed. Devanandan held a balanced perspective of mission in which evangelism and social action go together. He wanted the church in India to be united

---

67. Devanandan, *Preparation for Dialogue*, 116.
68. Boyd, *An Introduction to Indian Christian Theology*, 200.
69. Devanandan, *Christian Issues in Southern Asia*, 116.
70. Devanandan, *Christian Concern in Hinduism*, 92.
71. Devanandan, *Christian Issues in Southern Asia*, 120.
72. Ibid., 121.

and to be effective cross-cultural communicators of the gospel to people of other faiths, using their religious vocabulary and their cultural patterns of life. This is an acceptable endeavor except that in pluralistic contexts it usually ends up meaning different things to different people. Furthermore, though Devanandan did not explicitly deny the importance of the hope of eternal life beyond death through Jesus Christ, neither did he deal with it as an essential issue as the motivation for mission. He did not emphasize enough this hope of the gospel to the people of other faiths in Indian pluralistic contexts who believe in reincarnation. He was more interested in seeing how the gospel can transform present-day society in India, rather than presenting them the assurance of eternal life beyond death through the gospel.

Perhaps he went too far in looking for elements of truth in other religions of India. He was correct in his assessment that every religion has a creed, a cultus and a culture, and that the creedal core of a religion changes quite rarely and with great difficulty. But it is not obvious whether he realized that the ultimate task of the communication of the gospel is to see a change in the hearts of the hearers at the creedal core level or, if he did realize it, what he intended to do about it among people of other faiths. For this study we seek a suitable theology of "State-after-Death" in pluralistic contexts and how to communicate it to bring a change at a person's core assumption level, as acceptance or rejection of eternal life in Jesus Christ is intrinsically linked with that person's core assumptions about "State-after-Death." Devanandan's idea of dialogue with the people of other faiths is the first step towards that effective communication, but we need to go beyond that to discern how best to carry on that dialogue in a hostile pluralistic situation.

Stephen Charles Neill

Stephen Charles Neill was born in Edinburgh, Scotland on 31 December 1900, third of six children born to a medical doctor Charles Neill. Stephen Neill's missionary parents served in Ranaghat, Bengal under his maternal grandfather James Monro, a missionary doctor himself. James Monro took care of Stephen and his siblings when their parents were away. Monro's "strong sense of duty, evangelical convictions, and Victorian view of personal discipline seem to have made a deep impression on Stephen."[73] Stephen Neill

---

73. Eleanor M. Jackson, "The Continuing Legacy of Stephen Neill," *International Bulletin of Missionary Research* 19, no. 2 (1995): 77.

was converted in 1914 as he was recovering from mumps at a boarding school. He wrote about his conversion (edited by Eleanor Jackson after his death),

> It occurred to me that, if it was true, as I had every reason to believe, that Christ died for my sins, the rest of my life could not be spent in any other way than in grateful and adoring service of the One who had wrought that inestimable benefit. Even now I can see no way of improving on that discovery. I can recall no emotional accompaniment. All that happened was that I got out of bed and said my prayers.[74]

In 1919 Neill entered Trinity College, Cambridge and joined the Cambridge Inter-Collegiate Christian Union (CICCU), that is, the InterVarsity Christian Fellowship in UK. Soon, however, he was asked to become the chairman of the Cambridge Student Christian Movement, the more liberal student body for 1922–1923.[75] Not wholeheartedly loyal to either group, for he felt both groups were corrupting each other,[76] Neill began to organize University missions, student missions to towns and villages and Bible study programs. Thus began his important career as a missionary and evangelist, which tended to overshadow his work as a scholar and teacher.[77] At Trinity College, he compared the writings of Plotinus with those of the Cappadocians, particularly Gregory of Nazianzus and Gregory of Nyssa in his dissertation. Christopher Lamb notes,

> The choice reveals the missionary in the making . . . calculated to focus on the distinction between Hellenism and Christianity in the European intellectual tradition. The mysticism of Plotinus had many uses too as an introduction to Hindu monism, and served as a foundation and model for all Neill's writing on Christianity and other faiths.[78]

After Trinity, Neill decided to serve as a missionary and wrote this about his decision:

---

74. Ibid., 79. Jackson quoted from her edited version of *God's Apprentice: The Autobiography of Bishop Stephen Neill* (London: Hodder & Stoughton, 1991), 35–36.
75. Jackson, "Continuing Legacy," 77.
76. Christopher Lamb, "The Legacy of Stephen Neill," *International Bulletin of Missionary Research* 11, no. 2 (1987): 62.
77. Jackson, "Continuing Legacy," 77.
78. Lamb, "Legacy of Stephen Neill," 62.

> There can never have been anything less emotional than my acceptance of the vocation of a missionary. For years I had been convinced that, since Christ died for all men, no less than for me, this Gospel of Christ must be preached to all men, whether they will hear or forbear; that this Gospel will not be preached unless a sufficient numbers of those who are young, free and in reasonable health, are prepared to forgo all worldly ambition and accept the call to become Christ's witnesses and stewards.[79]

Neill understood the importance and urgency of preaching the gospel to all people on earth and that it requires some sacrifice on the part of those who are young and willing to respond to the call of Christ to missions.

In 1926, he traveled to India to teach and to learn the local language as a layman, but was soon ordained in the Tirunelvelly diocese of the Anglican Church in South India. He served there for about twenty years, becoming Bishop of Tirunelvelly in 1939. He spent most of his time in small remote villages of South India as an evangelist, pastor and theological teacher. In 1945, due to a physical breakdown, he resigned his bishopric and left India for good. He became the associate general secretary of International Missionary Council from 1948 to 1951, and general editor of World Christian Books from 1952 to 1962. From 1962 to 1967, he served as a professor of mission and ecumenical theology at Hamburg University and as a professor of philosophy and religious studies at Nairobi University from 1969 to 1973. He also held numerous visiting professorships. Neill died on July 20, 1984. Thus, after India and a short time of chaplaincy at Trinity, Cambridge, his main impact was in the area of writing, speaking and leadership in the WCC, IMC and Third World theological education.[80]

Serving as a missionary in India, a leader of the International Missionary Council, and a professor of mission and ecumenical theology, Neill contributed much to world mission and mission theology. We will briefly survey Neill's theology, with an interest in what he might have thought on the issue of "State-after Death," and what his response on the topic would be in the context of religious pluralism of his day.

---

79. Jackson, *God's Apprentice*, 70.
80. Lamb, "Legacy of Stephen Neill," 64; Jackson, "Continuing Legacy," 79.

Theology of Mission and Evangelism

Neill's most quoted contribution to mission theology is "his famous adage" of 1959: "If everything is mission, nothing is mission."[81] During that time the term "mission" was being used too broadly to describe any or every activity both within the Christian churches and in the secular world and so he made this observation:

> There is a great deal of talk to-day about the "theology of mission." This may be good thing; but I apprehend certain dangers in both of two contrary directions. The first is that we may cast our net too wide and so make the enquiry almost meaningless. If everything is mission, nothing is mission. If everything that the Church does is to be classed as "mission," we shall have to find another term for the Church's particular responsibility for "the heathen," those who have never yet heard the Name of Christ; and that, in 1959, means half the people now living on the earth. By reaction against this too general formulation, we are in danger of thinking really in terms of a theology of *missionary societies* and of *missionaries*, of a theological justification of what we have done in the past and what we are trying to do in the present. And this, in my judgment, is exactly what cannot be done.[82]

Here, Neill argues that mission is primarily the task of communicating the gospel to those who have not yet heard the Name of Christ and these are mainly the people of other religious faiths.[83] For Neill, "'Missionary' does not signify status; it has reference to an activity and a relationship" and he continues,

> A correct theology of *the Church* would include everything that we now regard as the special and separate problems of "missions"; and a correct theology of *ministry* would include everything that now perplexes us as the special problem of the "foreign" missionary. Yet in fact, "foreign missions" have come to

---

81. Bosch, *Transforming Mission*, 511.
82. Stephen Charles Neill, *Creative Tension* (London: Edinburgh House Press, 1959), 81–82.
83. In the past, Neill and other Western missionaries used the offensive term "the heathen" to refer to the people of other faiths which needlessly may have caused much harm for the primary task of the communication of the gospel among these people, however well-intentioned those missionaries were.

be largely divorced from the general life of the Church, and 'the missionary' tends to be regarded as a man who holds a special office in the Church, to which this special title has been assigned.

How has this separation come about, and why are we perplexed by problems of which the early Church in the great days of its expansion seems to have been wholly unaware?[84]

Neill's conviction is that the "one central purpose for which the Church" exists is to "preach the Gospel to every creature," and other aspects, such as "ministry, sacraments, doctrine, worship," etc. are additional to this purpose.[85] He laments that in most books on doctrine, "mission" is covered only briefly under practical theology. He contends that "if the doctrine of the Church came to be thought out in its true content and splendour," there would be rethinking and rewriting of every aspect of Christian theology in terms of its missionary character and purpose.[86] Thus, for Neill, all true theology in its essence and its totality is missionary (or mission) theology.

In the seventies, Neill in his Chavesse Lectures[87] at Wycliffe Hall, Oxford on evangelism complained about the nondescript use of the term "mission" and felt that "witness" is the more comprehensive term which includes every form of Christian activity bearing witness to Christ as Lord.[88] Neill held that, "witness" is a broader term than "mission" and can function in different forms "as it is directed to the sophisticated society of the post-Christian world, to half-Christianized young people, or to those who have never heard a word of the gospel of Jesus Christ."[89] In this sense, "mission" really means "evangelism" or the work of extension of the church to the outside world.[90] From the New Testament, he sees two distinct parts in this work of mission, first the mission to Israel and then the mission to the Gentiles (*ta ethne*). Referring to the Holocaust, Neill notes, "The mission to Israel has to be carried out with the utmost prudence and delicacy."[91] In "mission to the

---

84. Neill, *Creative Tension*, 82.
85. Ibid., 111–112.
86. Ibid., 112.
87. These lectures were rewritten by Neil in the light of then world events and the Fifth Assembly of WCC at Nairobi in 1975 and published as *Salvation Tomorrow* (London: Lutterworth Press, 1976).
88. Stephen Charles Neill, *Salvation Tomorrow* (London: Lutterworth Press, 1976), 57.
89. Ibid., 57–58.
90. Ibid., 58. Neill's view of "mission" only as evangelism has been critiqued by many evangelicals from the perspective of post-Lausanne Congress of World Evangelization, 1974 which views "mission" as holistic.
91. Ibid.

Gentiles," he notes, there should not be a sense of western superiority as they themselves were gentiles before, "practicing human sacrifice and other not very edifying rites."[92] Neill continues,

> This mission does not deny the working of God among all those nations whom he has held in the hollow of his hand and whom he has kept within his covenants of creation and providence. It simply takes the New Testament seriously, basing itself on the affirmation that Christ died for all in order that all men may die to themselves to live in him in the light of the new covenant that he has made with them in his death and resurrection. That mission will remain an obligation resting on the Church until time as we now know it comes to an end and the new age begins. It is mission "to the ends of the earth and ends of the time."[93]

Here Neill argues that the New Testament's call to "mission" is to be followed seriously in order to avoid confusion and dilute the church's obligation in the task of mission to all people. Perhaps Neill's view of "State-after-Death" becomes apparent here, as he affirms Christ's death and resurrection is for all, and through that "all men may die to themselves to live in him," and that "time" will end and "new age" will begin.

Thus, for Stephen Neill, "mission" is a very specific term to be used carefully in that, all the activities the church may be involved in is not necessarily "mission." Only the communication of the gospel to those who have not yet heard ought to be classed as "mission." All theology to be true theology in its essence and in its totality, ought to be mission theology. This, then, calls for the rethinking and rewriting of every aspect of Christian theology in terms of its missionary character and purpose.[94] For him, mission is the task in which God the Father is the sender of the Son, the Son the sender of the Holy Spirit and the Holy Spirit, working through the church, sends out the church. Thus mission should be continued by the church, through the believers, to the ends of the earth and to the end of the time.[95]

---

92. Ibid., 59. In footnote 83, I noted how the use of the term "the heathen" for the people of other faiths by Neill and others may have caused much harm for the communication of the gospel. It is good to see here Neill's later recognition that Western people were not any better than the people of other faiths in the past.
93. Ibid.
94. Neill, *Creative Tension*, 112.
95. Neill, *Salvation Tomorrow*, 57–59; Stephen Charles Neill, *Men of Unity* (London: SCM Press Ltd, 1960), 190.

Challenge of Religious Pluralism

Neill, as we have seen, takes very seriously the New Testament's call to mission to preach the gospel to the people of all nations, hence to the people of other faiths. But we also see Neill's recognition, in some ways like Devanandan, of God's general revelation to peoples of other faiths. Neill says, "This mission does not deny the working of God among all those nations whom he has held in the hollow of his hand and whom he has kept within his covenants of creation and providence."[96] Earlier, Neill had asked, "How should a Christian regard non-Christians, and the systems of belief of which they are the sincere adherents? This question has been before the Church from the time of the apostles till to-day."[97] Neill finds that through history the answers have ranged, "from the unquestioning 'Nay', which refuses to see any ray of light in the darkness of heathendom, to the enthusiastic 'Yea', which . . . reject[s] as sectarian narrowness any Christian affirmation concerning Christ as the only Saviour of the world."[98]

Neill finds his clue for his response to the challenge of religious pluralism, by looking at the relationship of Christian faith to Judaism, and how Christ fulfilled Judaism. He notes, "we can now look back on them Christologically; we see them as part of that historical preparation which found its culmination in Christ."[99] In comparative study of religions, Neil felt, the tendency has been to begin by looking at similarities with other faiths, by comparing these faiths at their highest to the biblical teachings of Christ, and then, quite regretfully, deal with the dissimilarities, in order to show that these faiths are fulfilled in Christ. For Neill, from his personal life experience, the response to other faiths should not first be "Yea" but "Nay," to show that "Christ is the Destroyer before he can be the Saviour"[100] and then go to the possible "Yea" part. However, in relating to Judaism, it seems he begins with "Yea" first and then deals with the "Nay." In any case, Neill concludes by trusting in God to take care of the "Yea" part:

> We may be sure that God, who has worked so long and so patiently among the nations, will see to it that if the nations and their faiths in the end turn to Christ nothing of value will be lost,

---

96. Neill, *Salvation Tomorrow*, 59.
97. Neill, *Creative Tension*, 9.
98. Ibid.
99. Ibid., 29.
100. Ibid.

and that whatever of worth the other religions have gathered in the course of their separate pilgrimage will in some way be brought into the riches of his everlasting city.[101]

Neill is perceptive in his discernment of the church's range of responses from "Nay" to "Yea" to religious pluralism down through the history. However, it is arguable whether Christianity can relate to all the other faiths in the same way it related to Judaism. This is because, traditionally, both Judaism and Christianity accept the Old Testament as God's revealed word whereas other faiths generally do not. Also, it is difficult to begin a conversation with people of other faiths with his response of "Nay" first and then "Yea."

Neill also points out, that those who propose dialogue as the ideal method to relate to people of other faiths are not aware of the difficulty of finding those of other faiths who will be willing to dialogue on terms acceptable to Christians.[102] Neill points out, "The fact is that the attitude of the leaders in the non-Christian world towards Christianity is so contemptuous that it is hard for them to consider that that faith might be a worthy subject of serious study."[103] Thus, for Neill, Christians are unlikely to find a partner in dialogue from other faiths who are sincere, open-minded and willing, but if a partner is found a Christian's faith in Christ will be severely tested, purified, modified and strengthened.[104] For Neill, the purpose of dialogue is that,

> truth may appear in all its majesty. The Christian is committed to the view that all truth . . . is from God. He is free to recognize truth which is not evidently and clearly related to . . . Jesus Christ; but he is not likely to give up his conviction that every such truth . . . is related to that supreme manifestation of the truth.[105]

Neill points out the difficulties of dialogue as a method to relate to people of other faiths, especially in modern hostile India. He also shows how enriching the experience of dialogue can be when the partners are open-minded and willing. In the task of mission to communicate the gospel in pluralistic contexts, our hope is that we will find partners for dialogue who are open-minded and willing. But we will only find out how willing they are when we have taken the first step of starting the conversation. Neill correctly

---

101. Ibid.
102. Neill, *Salvation Tomorrow*, 40.
103. Ibid., 41.
104. Ibid., 42.
105. Ibid., 43.

recognizes that the purpose of dialogue with the people of other faiths is to seek the truth, yet not at the expense of denying the Truth, Jesus Christ.

Neill was much concerned about the importance of unity among the churches, for the fulfilling of the task of mission in pluralistic contexts. He felt that though in the West people may accept many churches on a single street, these multiple churches become an obstacle for those in India who belong to other religions and want to join a Christian church. Neill notes, "The arguments in favour of having just one Christian Church in such a region would seem to be strong."[106] Neill argued that in the New Testament, he finds the strongest reason for unity in the will of God himself. He notes, "In Christ, we are told, there is neither Jew nor Greek, barbarian, Scythian, bond nor free, but altogether have been made one new man in Jesus Christ. The Church is meant to be the great international society, in which at last all men will find a home."[107]

However, even as he wants the church to be united, Neil does not expect this unity to be absolute uniformity among the churches. For Neill, as all the churches are able to come together, there must be "room for a great variety of national expressions of the faith, of types, and forms of worship and so on."[108] But, according to him, in such a united church, anyone who is a minister in one place in the church would be recognized as a minister everywhere else, and anyone who is a communicant in one of the churches would be a communicant in all of them.[109] Neill's concern for the unity of the church to be an effective agent for mission in a pluralistic context like India, especially during contemporary hostility and opposition from the fundamentalists, is an important one. There is much disunity among the Christian churches due to the denominational differences in India and the world at large and this definitely hinders the fulfillment of the task of mission and evangelism in pluralistic contexts.

Neill argues that sometimes churches are inward looking, only concerned for the guidance and sanctification of their own members, with no concern for the world.

> In that case they have not really been Churches of Jesus Christ, the good Shepherd who gave his life for the sheep. His Church exists only as it is mission, only as it lives related to the ends of

---

106. Neill, *Men of Unity*, 8.
107. Ibid., 9.
108. Ibid.
109. Ibid.

the world and the end of time, only as it is turned outward to men and women in all the needs and tragedies and darkness of their daily lives, and also at their highest point of human achievement and natural delight.[110]

However, if the churches really began to live outward-looking lives for mission, with a concern for the world outside, they would soon discover that they need the help of other churches. Neill argues, "Take any area of the world you like; all the Churches together are far less than adequate to deal with the social needs of that area."[111] Neill laments that a great deal of the work of the church does not get done because the churches do not know how to work together. He concludes that,

> Every Church should live all the time in awareness of its membership in the great fellowship of all those who call on the name of our Lord Jesus Christ as God and Saviour; and at the same time in awareness of the unfinished task that lies before it. If all the Churches were to work together to an intelligent and planned strategy, and were to multiply five-fold their giving in money and in man-power, they would still be inadequate to the task of preaching the Gospel of Jesus Christ to every creature.[112]

Neill is convinced that we have no choice but to live and work in unity in the church in order to fulfill the great task of the mission of our Lord Jesus Christ to the whole world. In my study of Neill, I did not find him dealing with the specific issue of "State-after-Death" at length, but his primary concern in life has always been to see the unfinished task of preaching the gospel of Jesus Christ to every creature accomplished. No one can have this sincere heartfelt concern for all those, who have not heard the gospel of Jesus Christ, without a deep conviction that Jesus Christ offers eternal life beyond death.

Hendrik Kraemer

Hendrik Kraemer was born in 1888 in one of the slum quarters of Amsterdam. Kraemer's father died when he was six and two years later his mother died.[113]

---

110. Ibid., 190.
111. Ibid., 191.
112. Ibid.
113. Johannes Verkuyl, *Contemporary Missiology*, trans. and ed. Dale Cooper (Grand Rapids, MI: Eerdmans, 1978), 41. However Hoedemaker ("The Legacy of Hendrik Kraemer,"

After his parents' death, orphan Kraemer lived in a family with strong links with the pioneers of socialist movement, and thus had a lifelong interest in political and social issues and was a supporter of the Christian Socialists until his death. Later he also lived with a family with church connections, and then was moved to a Reformed (*Hervormd*) church orphanage at age thirteen, where he experienced a conversion to the Lord Jesus Christ at age fifteen through his personal reading of the Bible. Instead of a cold, hard and routine reading of the Bible by an orphanage supervisor, his personal reading of the Bible became the word of the living God to him.[114]

At age sixteen, he decided to become a missionary,[115] mainly through his interaction with missionaries and by reading missionary literature. While at Rotterdam school of missions, Kraemer got a renewed vision of world mission through his meeting with J. H. Oldham, a famous leader of IMC.[116] In 1911, supported by the Dutch Bible Society, he went to Leiden University and studied Eastern philology and cultural history for ten years and received a doctorate under the famous Islamics Scholar, Snouck Hurgronje.[117] For many of his student years, Kraemer was the chairman of the Dutch SCM and had very close links with John R. Mott, leader of the World Federation of Christian Students.[118] Prior to finishing at Leiden, Kraemer was personally challenged by Prof. P. D. Chantepie de la Saussaye, chairman of the Dutch Bible Society, to become an advisor to the Dutch-Indonesian churches to guide them through the process of becoming independent churches.[119] Kraemer accepted that challenge. These links with Oldham, Mott and Saussaye greatly influenced the making of the missionary Kraemer.

In 1919, Kraemer married Hyke van Gameran, whom he had met as a Liberal opponent in a debate during his student years. They were a great support to each other during the difficult periods of their marriage. They had two daughters and two sons, one of which died at age seven in 1931.[120] Kraemer's health was weak physically and he suffered psychologically due to the excessive tensions in his life. He struggled with insomnia throughout

---

Occasional Bulletin from the Missionary Research Library 4, no. 2 [1980]: 60) notes that his mother died when he was twelve. As Kraemer lost both of his parents early, some uncertainties arise about his childhood, e.g. day/month of his birth etc.
114. Verkuyl, *Contemporary Missiology*, 41.
115. Hoedemaker, "Legacy of Hendrik Kraemer," 60.
116. Verkuyl, *Contemporary Missiology*, 41–42.
117. Ibid., 42.
118. Ibid.
119. Ibid., 42–43.
120. Hoedemaker, "Legacy of Hendrik Kraemer," 60.

his life and the famous Swiss psychiatrist Maeder helped him cope with this problem. Verkuyl notes, "It is remarkable that a man . . . so fragile could . . . achieve so much through God's strength."[121]

Kraemer served in Dutch controlled Indonesia 1922–1928 and 1930–1935 and for short recurring periods later. He did missionary work among Muslims and encouraged others to do the same through friendly contacts with both simple and highly learned Muslims. He also did linguistic work for the Dutch Bible Society in Indonesia and served as an advisor for churches and mission in Indonesia.[122] After that, he became a Professor at Leiden University in 1937 until the Second World War, was active in the work of church-building in Holland and participated in building up Dutch ecclesiastical and political life after the war. Kraemer became the director of the Ecumenical Institute in Bossey, Switzerland from 1948–1957.[123] He traveled extensively to Asia, Middle East and USA and was a guest lecturer at Union Theological Seminary in New York (1956–57). Kraemer died in 1965.

I will briefly survey Kraemer's mission theology, with the special interest of "State-after Death," and what his perspectives on this topic were through discussions he carried out in pluralistic religious contexts.

Theology of Mission

Hoedemaker notes that Kraemer's "legacy is the legacy of a missionary, and of a missionary theologian whose awareness of the problematic of the present and future of Christian missions was sharper than that of many of his contemporaries."[124] In the recent history of missions and missiology in general, Kraemer is remembered most for his book, *The Christian Message in a Non-Christian World*, published in 1938. This book was a response to the Jerusalem conference of IMC in 1928, in which there was a tendency towards relativism in mission and along with W. Hocking's effort to encourage syncretism with other religions against materialism.[125] This book became the central point of discussion at the IMC conference held at Tambaram, Madras in India in 1938. In it, Kraemer begins by discussing the world in transition

---

121. Verkuyl, *Contemporary Missiology*, 49–50.
122. Ibid., 43–44.
123. Ibid., 49.
124. Hoedemaker, "Legacy of Hendrik Kraemer," 60.
125. Verkuyl, *Contemporary Missiology*, 48; Roger E. Hedlund, *Roots of the Great Debate in Mission: Mission in Historical and Theological Perspective* (Bangalore, India: Theological Book Trust, 1993), 61–94.

by dealing with a number of issues which are still relevant for us today. The Jerusalem conference met in this kind of world situation and reflected on "the trouble, change and uncertainty of the church in the midst of an insecure world."[126] And the world had become even less secure by 1938. In the midst of this transition, Kraemer argued for a firm and positive response to the issue of "whither missions?"

According to Kraemer, the Christian Mission must be continued no matter what happens in the world and world systems. Kraemer noted,

> The transitional character of the present time is particularly evident in the fact that, as never before, new extraordinarily militant world-conceptions, all deeply tinged with religious quality, force millions . . . under their sway, claiming their absolute allegiance . . . They are the clearest symptoms of turbulent transition. It is quite natural that the missionary enterprise should also be affected by the storm, and that in its ranks, at home as well as abroad, there should be confusion and a manifold cry for re-orientation and clarification. The coming World Conference at Madras in December 1938 will not achieve anything worth-while unless it achieves a deepened sense of direction and a renewed consciousness of the meaning and purpose of the Christian Mission in the world under *any* circumstances, whether quiet and evolutionary or turbulent and revolutionary.[127]

Kraemer concluded in a positive note, showing that instead of a moratorium on missionary activity, through the cooperation of younger and older churches, in the global church community, increased activity of mission work would be possible:

> The Christian Church is not at the end of its missionary enterprise in the non-Christian world, but just at the beginning. The independence and autonomy of the daughter-churches in the non-Christian world does not mean a gradual withdrawal of the missionary activity of the parent Churches. On the contrary, the fact that the Christian Church actually has become a world-wide community, the responsibility this involves, and the solidarity in

---

126. Hedlund, *Roots of the Great Debate*, 87.
127. Hendrik Kraemer, *The Christian Message in a Non-Christian World* (Grand Rapids, MI: Kregel Publications, 1938), 31.

faith and love and hope in which the older and younger Churches have been thereby bound together, point to the obligation of renewed missionary consecration and activity.[128]

Instead of presenting Christianity to the non-Christian world for the wrong reasons (that is, for introducing Western culture or only for improving people socially, economically and morally) Kraemer strongly urged a return to the biblical basis of mission. For him, "a crisis of missions is a crisis of faith."[129] Thus he recommended to the church first to have a clear grasp of the Christian faith and then translate the rich contents of this faith to the present conditions of the world.[130]

Kraemer believed that the true biblical purpose of mission is that the Christian message be communicated to the non-Christian world and the gospel be expressed within the framework of the culture of the place and people so that they can understand the message.[131] Thus, for Kraemer, the church should know its original faith, and that faith must be translated meaningfully to the non-Christian world. Kraemer's biblical realism meant that, "the only legitimate source from which to take our knowledge of the Christian faith in its real substance is the Bible."[132] Like Barth, he rejected the views of "natural" theology and "general" revelation and stressed biblical realism as the fundamental starting point for all theological thinking.[133] Perhaps, later on, he was willing to accept the possibility of "general" revelation in other faiths but insisted that such truths can only be correctly interpreted and understood through the "special" revelation of Christ and hence the Bible.[134] This "biblical realism" clearly shows what Kraemer believed as far as his perspective of "State-after-Death" is concerned in relation to other faiths.

Religious Pluralism and Relativism

According to Kraemer, "The Christian religion in its real sense, that is, as the revelation in Christ . . . revolves around two poles" of knowledge of God and knowledge of humans.[135] In the light of the revelation in Christ, the Christian

---

128. Ibid., 40.
129. Ibid., 60.
130. Ibid., 61.
131. Hedlund, *Roots of the Great Debate*, 89.
132. Kraemer, *Christian Message*, 61.
133. Ibid., 66.
134. Ibid., 110.
135. Ibid., 101.

knowledge of God "upsets all other conceptions of God or of the Divine" and the Christian knowledge of humans is "revolutionary in comparison with any other conception of man."[136] Thus, Kraemer's attitude towards non-Christian religions is based on the revelation in Christ and he views everything (including other perspectives on "State-after-Death") from the point of view of this revelation, an entirely different basis compared to William Hocking.[137] In terms of how to relate to religious pluralism, Kraemer noted,

> To define our attitude towards these religions virtually means to affirm our conception of man and his faculties, to pass judgment on our fellow-man and his aspirations, attainments and aberrations . . . Christ, as the ultimate standard of reference, is the crisis of all religions, of the non-Christian religions and of empirical Christianity too. This implies that the most fruitful and legitimate way to analyze and evaluate all religions is to investigate them in the light of the revelation of Christ.[138]

However, he also adds that there can be no arrogance or sense of superiority on the part of Christians in relation to the people of other faiths. Kraemer noted,

> A missionary or a Christian who harbours the tiniest spark of spiritual arrogance and boasts of "his" superiority by being a Christian and "having" the truth, grieves the Spirit of Christ and obscures his message, because the foundation of the Christian life is to "boast in the Lord" and to rejoice gratefully and humbly in *His* mercy.[139]

To the question, whether God reveals himself in the religious life of non-Christian religions, Kraemer's response is that though there is a universal religious consciousness among people of all races and ages, which produces different great religions and ethical systems, there is a problem in human nature. "Man's dangerous condition is that he is a dual being. He is of divine origin, and he is corrupted by sin and constantly prone to assert his self-centered and disordered will against the divine will."[140] Thus there is a condition of disharmony in humans. Kraemer added,

---

136. Ibid.
137. Hedlund, *Roots of the Great Debate*, 91.
138. Kraemer, *Christian Message*, 110.
139. Ibid., 110–111.
140. Ibid., 112.

This fundamental and horrid disharmony, this dialectical condition of man is called by the Christian revelation, as contained in biblical realism, sin, guilt, lostness past recovery except by God Himself; and no other religion does this in such unmistakable and consistent terms. The universal religious consciousness of man itself nowhere speaks this clear language, because it is confused and blinded by its inherent disharmony.[141]

Kraemer shows from Romans 1 and 2, that "Man seeks God and at the same time flees from Him in his seeking."[142] Even spiritual representatives of non-Christian religions who show "an extraordinary degree of devotion to the reality of the world of the spiritual and eternal," quite "often do not show the least comprehension of the greatest gift of Christ – forgiveness of sins."[143] Therefore, with Kraemer, the correct attitude of the church towards non-Christian religions "is essentially a missionary one, the church being sent by God in the world as ambassador of His reconciliation, which is the truth that outshines all truth and the grace that works faithful love."[144] He deals with non-Christian systems of life and thought such as Hinduism, Buddhism and notes some similarities with Christianity. Yet, he contends that these religions "are radically different from the prophetic religion of biblical realism."[145]

Kraemer shows that the phenomenon of "syncretism and religious pragmatism" is considered necessary and a normal trait in all the ancient and naturalist non-Christian religions.[146] He perceives that there is an "underlying inherent unity" in all these religions and this is because of "their being products of the primitive apprehension of existence and their naturalistic monistic framework."[147] He points out that while the term "syncretism" usually means the *illegitimate* mingling of elements of different religions in Christian circles, for naturalistic religions "syncretism" is *legitimate* and expected and is called "amalgamation."[148] He says, "This amalgamation, the universal pragmatic attitude, the typical tolerance, the aversion to doctrinal borderlines, the relativist and . . . very subjectivist . . . conception of religion,

---

141. Ibid., 113.
142. Ibid., 126.
143. Ibid., 129.
144. Ibid., 129–130.
145. Ibid., 170.
146. Ibid., 201–203.
147. Ibid., 203.
148. Ibid.

are all the natural products of the naturalistic monism in these religions."[149] According to Kraemer, though RadhaKrishnan and Gandhi stressed relativism and considered "Truth Itself is unattainable. Yet, in practice, this fundamental relativism behaves itself as a militant absolutism."[150]

Kraemer found that fundamentally there is little difference between the eastern "religionist" and the western "secularist," "because under the thick veneer of religion he often is already an outright secularist."[151] He notes, "man's cardinal and elementary need is not to be religious, but to be *sincerely religious*" and "this radical sincerity is born from the prophetic theocentric religion of biblical realism."[152] Hedlund notes that, for Kraemer, "Syncretism has no place in the revealed religion of the Bible in which 'God solely and really creates a way where there is no way.'"[153]

In the midst of the theological crisis that arose at the IMC Jerusalem Conference in 1928, Kraemer, the missionary theologian, strongly defended the uniqueness of the historic Christian faith and highlighted its discontinuity with the non-Christian religions. He continued this defense explicitly in the IMC Madras Conference of 1938 and beyond, emphasizing the importance of continuing Christian mission among people of other faiths and Secularists. This issue to which Kraemer responded is still very crucial and continues to be debated presently within the mainline churches in Asia and rest of the world. Kraemer's convictions are important for this study as we seek fruitful conversation with the people of other faiths in today's pluralistic contexts. Though Kraemer did not look into the issue of "State-after-Death" specifically, yet he shows us how he would have responded to the pluralistic perspectives of the same.

Kraemer's theology of mission took the biblical basis and mandate for mission seriously. The IMC Madras Conference of 1938 was greatly influenced by his Bible-centered theology of mission, even though some vigorously opposed his uncompromising response to non-Christian religions. He provided a strong response to relativism and syncretism debates with sound biblical grounding or, as he called it, biblical realism. His efforts contributed greatly towards the continuing advance of missions among people of other faiths. Today's world faces the same transition of

---

149. Ibid., 204.
150. Ibid., 205–206.
151. Ibid., 215.
152. Ibid.
153. Hedlund, *Roots of the Great Debate*, 93.

trouble, change and uncertainty and his biblical response can help us hold solid ground with which to address this transition. His call for responsibility toward the daughter churches applies today. The older churches cannot wash their hands of the problems of the newer churches, nor leave the missionary task to be completed only by them. The newer churches also need to take up their own responsibility in the missionary task and partner with the older churches to finish the task of making Christ known to the whole world. This was Kraemer's vision of the church.

Summary and Implications

In this chapter I have surveyed the life and perspectives of four mission theologians of the twentieth century and I will look at three more in the next chapter. I have only considered those who have either dealt with or contributed in some way to the question of "State-after-Death" and/or have responded to the challenge of religious pluralism in their mission contexts. Dietrich Bonhoeffer, Paul David Devanandan, Stephen Neill and Hendrik Kraemer did not deal with "State-after-Death" at great length, yet all faced the challenge of religious pluralism in their mission contexts.

Bonhoeffer and Kraemer stand out as biblical theologians who refused to compromise on the uniqueness of the gospel in the public square. Insisting on the continued proclamation of the uniqueness of the gospel and standing for biblical values in the face of opposition from the Nazis, Bonhoeffer suffered and died willingly, believing he suffered out of obedience to God. His assurance that death was "the beginning of life" helped him live his brief earthly life in service to humans and uncompromising obedience to God. Kraemer distinguished himself by his public defence of the historic Christian faith and its discontinuity with other faiths. He presented *biblical realism* as an answer to the liberal relativism and syncretism debates of his day. Within the church, Kraemer pressed for renewed emphasis on mission among people of other faiths and interdependence within the family of faith to complete the task of world evangelization.

Devanandan, in his desire to be sensitive towards people of other faiths, allowed a level of theological laxity, perhaps leading to some compromise in his responses to people of other faiths. Though Devanandan himself held a balanced view of evangelism, social action and contextualization, his teachings were often portrayed within the church without that balance. Though relatively more orthodox than many other Indian theologians, he still favored the idea of formal dialogue as a response to people of other faiths and may have gone too far in looking for elements of truth in other religions. Yet, his idea of dialogue, especially interpersonal conversation, is definitely the first step one must take to communicate the gospel of Jesus Christ to people of other faiths.

Neill was most instrumental in defining mission for the modern church as the preaching of the gospel among those who have yet to hear the gospel. He highlighted the importance of church unity for witness to those of other faiths and suggested the church's response among them should be "Nay" first and then "Yea." However in practice, this order of speaking may not work well to communicate the gospel to people of other faiths. For Neill, dialogue with those of other faiths, though difficult in a hostile environment, may be enriching if open and willing individuals actively seek the truth. From his first hand experience in India, Neill recognizes this is rarely the case. Though he did not deal with "State-after-Death" at length, Neill certainly believed that Jesus Christ makes his death and resurrection the gateway to eternal life.

3

The Perspectives of Contemporary Theologians II

In this chapter, we shall examine the work of three additional and equally influential Christian scholars in global mission theology of the twentieth century: Indian theologian M. M. Thomas, British Pluralist theologian John Hick and German Roman Catholic theologian Hans Küng. Hick and Küng deal with "State-after-Death" at length in relation to pluralistic religious perspectives. Though M. M. Thomas did not specifically touch on this, he broadly addressed religious pluralism and engagement with other faith perspectives in India. Here we continue to consider how these thinkers approach the challenge of pluralistic religious beliefs for a Christian theology of mission and how they touch on death and after-death.

M. M. Thomas

Madathilaparampil Mammen Thomas, known as M. M. Thomas, was born in Panavila, Kerala, India on 15 May 1916. His father, a member of Syrian Orthodox Church, was a renowned evangelist. After he finished school, M. M. Thomas went to study Chemistry at a college in Trivandrum, Kerala in 1931. In the first year there, he had a personal experience of Christ and dedicated his life to Christ.[1] He became actively involved in the Mar Thoma Youth Union and Student Christian Movement and began to witness for Christ among his friends. After college, he taught at a school at Perumpavoor Ashram while trying to create an international and inter-religious fellowship of students. Sunand Sumithra notes that, while at this Ashram, Thomas "rejected both evangelism and the exclusive claims of Christianity, arguing

---

1. Sumithra, *Christian Theologies*, 169.

'love is at the heart of universe' and in love we need not pressurize one another to change one's convictions."[2] During his student activities, Thomas met Pennamma, whom he married after ten years of engagement. Sumithra notes that Thomas acknowledged in some of his books that his wife helped him to remain Christ-centered.[3]

In 1938, Thomas cofounded the Youth Christian Council of Action, which stressed the social implications of the gospel. In 1942, he came out of YCCA because he rejected non-violence. He started a new National Christian Youth Council which did not last very long. At that point in his life, he sought ordination in the Mar Thoma Church and also wanted to become a member of the Communist Party of India but both organizations refused him. Sumithra notes that, "This . . . attempt of Thomas to reconcile the spirit of Christ to the Marxist-Leninist ideology has remained the most dominant characteristic of his life and thought throughout."[4] He worked briefly at a hostel for street boys and then went for further study in Bangalore. During 1943–45 he joined the Student Christian Movement and then moved to Geneva to work as political secretary of the World Students' Christian Federation. In that role, he organized the World Youth Conference in Kottayam in 1947 and the Asian Leader's Conference at Kandy in 1948. In 1947, he attended the Oslo Youth Conference and while in Geneva was involved in preparations for the first WCC Assembly at Amsterdam.

In 1953, Thomas went to study at Union Theological Seminary, New York, for a year and returned to India to serve as the Associate Director of CISRS (Christian Institute for the Study of Religion and Society) in Bangalore with P. D. Devanandan as its Director. After Devanandan's death in 1962, Thomas became the Director until his retirement. In 1966–67 he taught at Union Theological Seminary, New York, as a visiting professor and also became the chairman of World Conference on Church and Society, Geneva, in 1966. In 1968, he was elected moderator of the central committee of the World Council of Churches, the highest position ever given to an Indian Christian leader. He became a renowned leader of the ecumenical movement in WCC and East Asia Christian Conference. In 1969, his wife Penamma died of cancer after suffering for a long period. Without her guidance, Thomas acknowledged, he became somewhat directionless in his theology.[5] He continued to travel

---

2. Ibid., 170.
3. Ibid.
4. Ibid., 171.
5. Ibid., 173.

to Europe, USA and other places in the world every year to lecture and teach until his death in 1996.

M. M. Thomas is widely accepted as the most experienced Indian Christian theologian and the most prolific reader and writer of theology among all Indians, making significant contributions to the development of Indian Christian Theology. Sumithra notes, "In the years to come he may also have the greatest influence for Indian Christian theology. Along with Raymondo Panikkar and Stanley Samartha, M. M. Thomas makes up the modern trio of Indian theologians, comparable to the classical trio of Chakkarai, Chenchiah and Devanandan."[6] Robin Boyd notes, "Thomas is the leading representative of those who advocate a theology much more closely related to modern, secular India and to the world of the Asian revolution."[7] Johannes Verkuyl noted, "two figures who in my judgment have contributed most profoundly to the development of Indian theology – Paul Devanandan and M. M. Thomas."[8] Though Thomas did not discuss "State-after-Death," his theology is relevant to pluralistic perspectives.

Theology of Mission

Apart from his nearly one thousand articles, Thomas produced, contributed to and edited several books, which led Verkuyl to attest that "M. M. Thomas is one of the most productive Christian thinkers in all of India."[9] Some of his books are: *The Christian Response to the Asian Revolution, Christian Participation in Nation Building, The Acknowledged Christ of the Indian Renaissance, Man and the Universe of Faiths, Salvation and Humanization, Towards a Theology of Contemporary Ecumenism* and *Risking Christ for Christ's Sake*. His theological methodology may be understood in the light of his life-long sincere quest for a *Christian Dharma* (Hindu Sanskrit term for Religion), which he expounded in his autobiography, *The Story of My Spiritual and Theological Pilgrimage*. Boyd sums up how Thomas tried to follow through with Devanandan's ideas of dialogue with Hinduism in India:

> In carrying forward Devanandan's experiments in dialogue, Thomas speaks of three different levels at which dialogue with Hinduism must first be carried on. First, there is the dialogue

---

6. Ibid., 169.
7. Boyd, *Introduction to Indian Christian Theology*, 311.
8. Verkuyl, *Contemporary Missiology*, 266.
9. Ibid.

which studies the contribution of each faith to man and society – a secular conversation which should, he believes, lead on to the possibility of a common culture – not a "Christian" culture, but an "open" culture based on a common humanity. Secondly there is the type of dialogue which seeks to come to grips with central theological issues of each faith. And thirdly there is dialogue at the level of interiority – the dialogue "in the cave of the heart" ... All of these are necessary, but Thomas' own special interest is in the first type, where Christian and Hindu meet together in the context of modern, secular India in order to find common fields of action and service for the good of the nation as a whole and of individual "persons."[10]

In the Appendix of his book, *The Acknowledged Christ of the Indian Renaissance*, Thomas gives his contextual approach to doing theology in which he begins with the condition of the world or humans first and so his theology is human-centered (anthropocentric). Sumithra notes, "since the human situation is the starting point, his theology asks for pluralistic answers."[11] Sumithra sees Thomas' theology as action-oriented like the Liberation Theology of Latin America[12] and Boyd called Thomas' theology "The Way of Action," "perhaps indeed a form of *karma mārga*."[13] Thomas stressed *praxis* before or instead of *orthodoxy*. Boyd noted, "Thomas, like Devanandan, is constantly on the lookout for the emergence of a theology which will prove an effective spring for action – action in the four spheres of the created world, the person, the community and history."[14] In spite of his significant contribution, it is not quite apparent how effective Thomas' theology was as a spring for action within the church in India and the world for the task of mission.

J. Russell Chandran sees Thomas' theology as a theology of liberation and humanization and sums up Thomas' views on sin and salvation in this way:

> [Thomas'] faith is deeply rooted in the affirmation of Christ crucified and risen as the basis for the hope of salvation for the sinner. He is critical of religious as well as secular systems of

---

10. Boyd, *Introduction to Indian Christian Theology*, 311–312.
11. Sumithra, *Christian Theologies*, 175.
12. Ibid.
13. Boyd, *Introduction to Indian Christian Theology*, 311, 313.
14. Ibid., 313.

thought that fail to recognize the tragic character of sin. But *he understands sin and salvation in terms of the loss and restoration of true humanity*. He rejects the separation of theology from anthropology and interprets salvation as essentially humanization. The Christological affirmation of Christ as the true man is the basis for his interpretation of the work of Christ as humanization. *He says that 'the mission of salvation and the task of humanization are integrally related to each other, even if they cannot be considered identical.'*[15]

Thomas used the phrases "the mission of salvation" and "the task of humanization" instead of "evangelism" and "social action" and, although he recognized that these two are not identical, he strongly supported the importance of the latter. Thomas' understanding of "sin and salvation in terms of the loss and restoration of true humanity" may be sound. However, he was more concerned about the loss and restoration of true humanity in this life on earth than in the overall eternal life, including the "State-after-Death." Thomas' concern to help people to restoration in this life is essential because the gospel does have social implications. However, we also recognize a strong influence of the liberal ecumenical movement and Secular Marxist philosophy on Thomas' thinking and actions, in that his idea of liberation is primarily tied to this world. Perhaps this was one step away from helping people of other faiths become "better Hindus," "better Buddhists," "better Muslims," and so forth, which has become the main goal of many WCC churches, with little or no concern for the hereafter.

Here we must note Thomas' view on sin in his response to Gandhi's view on sin. According to Thomas, Gandhi considered only the physical body as the source of sin; hence, he tried to control sin through celibacy and asceticism. For Thomas, Gandhi did not recognize the spiritual sin of pride and self-righteousness and so failed to understand Christianity correctly. Gandhi did not go beyond the principles of ethics in the Sermon on the Mount of Jesus Christ to recognize the Person of Jesus Christ.[16] For Thomas, the sins of pride, selfishness and rebellion against God cannot be dealt with by asceticism but by the grace of God and forgiveness through the Person of Christ. Here it

---

15. J. Russell Chandran, "Development of Christian Theology in India," in *Readings in Indian Christian Theology*, vol. 1., eds. R. S. Sugirtharajah and Cecil Hargreaves (Delhi, India: ISPCK, 1993), 12 (emphasis added).

16. M. M. Thomas, *The Acknowledged Christ of the Indian Renaissance* (London: SCM, 1969), 226.

seems Thomas was quite orthodox in his views of sin and forgiveness, as he noted,

> Lacking the awareness of this dimension of sin and the need of divine forgiveness, Gandhi does not move through the principles to the Person. Probably the basic theological issue in the debate between Gandhism and Christianity lies precisely in the concept of human selfhood. The Christian message of the centrality of the divine act in the Person of Christ for reconciliation stands or falls with its view of the tragedy inherent in man's pursuit of a righteousness of the law, and of the need of divine initiative from beyond the tragedy.[17]

Though Thomas appreciated Gandhi's service and agreed with him with regard to social and political action, he felt Gandhi's view of humanity and God was too limited to deal with the real problems of human existence.[18] Thomas argues, "One of the most important tasks of the Church is to reconstruct the Gandhian insights about the ethics of Christ within the framework of its doctrine of redemption in Christ."[19]

However, later we find that in dealing with sin, Thomas over-emphasized the corporate nature of sin as against personal sin, leading him to look for corporate remedies rather than to stress the preaching of the gospel for the personal salvation of souls. We see this in his address, "Spirituality for Combat," as the moderator of the Central Committee of WCC at the Nairobi Assembly in 1975. Thomas noted, "It is the salvation of soul and body, persons and structures, human kind and creation. Just as sin has both individual and corporate dimension, so too has salvation."[20] But then he argued for corporate solutions/social action instead of evangelism,

> *Oppressive structures of corporate life are the result of the accumulated sins of generations,* and they develop an anonymity and a momentum *almost independent of persons now living.* The gospel is that, through the Cross and the Resurrection, Jesus Christ has triumphed over the demonic powers which dehumanize our

---

17. Ibid., 236.
18. Boyd, *Introduction to Indian Christian Theology*, 316.
19. Thomas, *Acknowledged Christ*, 236.
20. M. M. Thomas, "Spirituality for Combat," in *Roots of the Great Debate in Mission: Mission in Historical and Theological Perspective*, ed. Roger Hedlund (Bangalore, India: Theological Book Trust, 1993), 361.

culture, technology, politics and social structures, and that in Him we can resist these powers and renew these realms of life.[21]

Thomas understood the doctrines of sin and salvation in the light of his theological understanding of human history. These doctrines for him are the basic elements that clarify the relationship of people to their community in each particular historical context. Thus, Thomas was more interested in this-worldly salvation/liberation of humanity as a whole, corporately, than every human individual's hope of "State-after-Death" and it seems Thomas did not take seriously the inevitability and reality of natural human death.

Finally, M. M. Thomas' theology of mission begins with humanity instead of with God and is action-oriented. He encouraged Christians to participate in national, political and social life and the church to be involved in the struggles of contemporary society. He sees the mission of the church as humanization and attempted to do his theologizing by becoming involved in the interaction between the church and the world and by searching for contacts to make faith work for the betterment of the immediate society. Thomas felt that theology could not meet basic human problems and needs without first dealing with the corporate issues of power structures, dehumanization and injustices, and their historic connections with contemporary problems. Hence, his theology is less of a classic theology, as such, and is more a political ideology or sociological history of humankind.

While he contributed much towards the church's involvement in the social and political struggle of the people in society, M. M. Thomas failed to see that without the transformation of each individual in Christ, the social structures cannot be effectively reformed.

Creation and Mission

Reflecting on the biblical story of creation (Gen 1:26, 27), Thomas noted,

> it is an affirmation that man is a spiritual person called to fulfill himself by establishing mastery over nature . . . Man is finite spiritual freedom. *He is no doubt evolved from nature* and is subject to its mechanical and organic necessities, but in his sense of selfhood and personhood, unlike the subhuman beings,

---

21. Ibid., 362 (emphasis added).

> he knows that . . . he can transform nature and subject it to his purposes.[22]

According to Thomas, the clue to interpretation of creation lies in emphasizing that God created the world in Jesus Christ and he interprets the doctrine of creation in the light of redemptive history. For him, creation cannot be given priority over the redemption of human beings, as the creation of all things is through Christ, by Christ and for Christ.[23] For him, creation is not something that has happened in the past but continues to happen as "God creates" rather than, "God created." Thomas said,

> Creation is the world in motion towards its fulfillment in the coming *eschaton*. The *eschaton* is the creative power, the inner dynamic of the world in process, of the history of mankind towards integration in the lordship of Christ.[24]

Sumithra notes, "Rejecting the doctrine of creation, Thomas rejects also the doctrine of human depravity. Man 'falls' in his destructive and selfish ambitions and is created in his nobler works."[25] For Sumithra, "This figurative interpretation of biblical passages also shows that [Thomas] does not take the inspiration of the Bible seriously."[26] Sumithra concludes that, for Thomas, God is not unchangeable and absolute but, like human beings and other creations, is a part of the evolving process.[27]

Thomas interprets the doctrines of fall and redemption in the light of this understanding of evolving human history of which even God is a part. For him, the fundamental sin of human beings, the one original sin, is the refusal of the human spirit to acknowledge the sovereignty of the creator (one who continues to create) and to recognize their dependence on him.[28] For Thomas, the fall is the denial of the fulfillment of human destiny, as the creation/the redemption reveals human history as destiny. Redemption, he believes, is not the restoration of the human state that existed prior to the fall, but the freedom of God's children to grow into adulthood as human

---

22. M. M. Thomas, "The Secular Ideologies of India and the Secular Meaning of Christ," in *Readings in Indian Christian Theology*, vol. 1, eds. R. S. Sugirtharajah and Cecil Hargreaves (Delhi, India: ISPCK, 1993), 94–95 (emphasis added).
23. T. M. Philip, *The Encounter between Theology and Ideology: An Exploration into the Cummunicative Theology of M. M. Thomas* (Madras, India: CLS, 1986), 36.
24. Thomas as quoted in Sumithra, *Christian Theologies*, 178.
25. Sumithra, *Christian Theologies*, 177.
26. Ibid.
27. Ibid., 178.
28. Philip, *Encounter between Theology and Ideology*, 47.

beings. It is not the recovery of the lost paradise but a claiming together with God of the New Heaven and New Earth, a new place for the existence of the community of God's adult children.²⁹ Thomas sees the redemptive act of God as the New Creation of the world and humanity in Jesus Christ, and Jesus Christ as the new man through whom this new humanity is created in the image of God. Here, Sumithra's comments on Thomas' view of "the image of God" are insightful:

> [Thomas] says that the traditional understanding of man as being created in the image of God needs to be re-cast, so he defines the image of God in man as "the obligation to respond to the call in freedom is the core of his personality, the basis of his eternal status as a person." This means that freedom and responsibility are the key elements of God's image in man . . . Here Thomas is consciously following the process theology since he says that not only man, but God also, is in process of evolution. So, he finds the evolution of man an inevitable necessity.³⁰

Again, in Thomas, we see no clear concern about the inevitability of physical death in his understanding of human history or how the human "State-after-Death" of eternal life or final judgment at the hand of God fits into this process of evolution. It would seem that Thomas is strongly influenced by the Secular Marxist ideology which accepts that this life is all there is and there is no need to consider seriously what happens after death.

According to Thomas, the church is called to be the witness and symbol of *koinonia* in Christ where all the human beings realize their true personhood reconciled to God and the world.³¹ The church is called to be the sign of forthcoming unity of humanity, and this unity must become the goal for Christians, that is, the church. The true nature of the church is a body immersed in society. According to Thomas, the church must endeavor to discern how Christ is at work in the revolution of contemporary society and must share in this work with him. Thus, the mission of the church, says Thomas, is to participate in the contemporary revolutions of the world.³² The mission of the church is *primarily* the task of humanization, and redemption

---

29. Jacob Thomas, *Ethics of World Community: Contribution of Dr. M. M. Thomas based on Indian Reality* (Calcutta, India: Punthi Pustak, 1993), 63.
30. Sumithra, *Christian Theologies*, 176.
31. Thomas, *Ethics of World Community*, 194.
32. Sumithra, *Christian Theologies*, 179.

is only one aspect of this task of humanization, serving the spiritual aspect of humanity. The church should participate in the life of the society and should be involved in the struggle to build a New Community for the benefit of humanity.[33] Explaining Thomas' view, Sumithra comments,

> The recipients of Christian mission are not individuals anymore but structures such as cultures, religions and ideologies. The method is no more proclamation, but now it is participation or as he calls it the confession of participation. The bearers are no more the called and sent missionaries, but rather organizations or the churches who do the work. He has enough to say why the verbal communication of the gospel is utterly inadequate for our time. So he comes to the conclusion that evangelism in our time equals service. Unless the church exercises its prophetic ministry of constructive criticism, the priestly ministry of the suffering servant, it has lost its salt. Following from here he goes on to give details of the task the church has in several areas of national and international life – the political, the economic, the cultural, the social, the religious, etc.[34]

Boyd also noted, "Thomas rejects the conservative evangelical tendency to limit the work of the Christian mission to preaching and church-growth; the gospel of salvation must work itself out also in the realm of history and politics, and in the campaign to provide conditions where men can live as real men."[35]

Thomas developed his theology of dialogue as a method of interaction between various modern forces with the hope of preparing them to participate in their common search for a humanized world and to transform their vision in their encounter with each other for a more just world community. His main concern is to build a new secular human community and dialogue is a theological necessity in the light of Christian mission.[36] As to Thomas' attitude towards other faiths, Sumithra notes,

> the church must have *koinonia*, or open fellowship, without any barrier. For this reason he discusses baptism whether it should be an entrance ticket into the church or privilege of the member

---

33. Boyd, *Introduction to Indian Christian Theology*, 319.
34. Sumithra, *Christian Theologies*, 179–180.
35. Boyd, *Introduction to Indian Christian Theology*, 319.
36. Thomas, *Ethics of World Community*, 80.

of the church . . . These insights lead him also to the formation of the church in Hindu and other religious systems . . . And so he comes up with what he calls "the Christ-centred Hindu church." All this is in line with his understanding of the pluralistic response of man to Christ.[37]

Thomas did not consider the spiritual aspect of human beings solely in isolation but in its integral relation with other aspects of society. Hence he had little concern for what happens beyond this world of society and had no serious thoughts about the "State-after-Death." He attempted to combine his Christian faith with Marxist thought and Hindu religiosity for the service of humanity, becoming syncretistic in his approach. Consequently, in my opinion, he failed to communicate the uniqueness of the gospel of Christ. Thomas did not treat the Bible as the primary source and the final authority for his theologizing; instead, he borrowed heavily from philosophy, sociology, political science and other religions, using them as his authority for reforming society. His evolutionary views of both humanity as well as God draw heavily on naturalism and modern science rather than from the Bible, the main source of Christian theology.

John Hick

John Harwood Hick was born on 20 January 1922 in Scarborough, England. Raised in a nominal Christian home (with exposure to other faiths),[38] he was converted to an evangelical faith at the age of eighteen while he was studying law at University College, Hull. He then went on to study philosophy at Edinburgh University.[39] During World War II, as a conscientious objector,

---

37. Sumithra, *Christian Theologies*, 180.
38. Hick (*An Autobiography* [Oxford, England: Oneworld Publications, 2002], 27–31) notes that as a child he attended a local parish church (C of E) and that his maternal grandma "was into all sorts of religious explorations and I was interested in all of them with her" and that his mother Aileen believed in spirits and mediums and along with her friends had also used ouija boards and that Aileen was very 'psychic' and used to see apparitions and did two healings. One of his mother's friends lent him some theosophical literature and he found Theosophy (19th century western philosophy formed with elements from Hinduism and Buddhism) to be the "first coherent religious philosophy," "much more so than the Christianity." Although he rejected it initially, from this grew an interest in eastern religions which became dormant during his evangelical Christian years until he later decided to reject the evangelical faith and beliefs like the divinity of Christ (Ibid., 31–35).
39. Chester Gillis, "John Harwood Hick," in *A New Handbook of Christian Theologians*, eds. Donald W. Musser and Joseph L. Price (Nashville, TN: Abingdon, 1996), 221; Hick, *An Autobiography*, 33.

Hick joined the alternative service of the Friends' (or Quakers') Ambulance unit and then, after the war, completed his MA at Edinburgh in 1948 and PhD at Oxford in 1950. He then studied theology at a Presbyterian seminary, Westminster College, Cambridge, from 1950 to 1953 to train as a minister.[40] Hick became the minister of Belford Presbyterian Church in Northumberland in early August of 1953.

Hick married Hazel Bowers at Belford Presbyterian Church at the end of August, 1953 and continued to serve there until he went on to teach philosophy in January, 1956 at Cornell University in Ithaca, NY.[41] Hick taught at Princeton Seminary in 1959 and then returned to the UK in 1964 to teach first at Cambridge University, and then, in 1967, he became the H. G. Wood Professor of Theology at Birmingham University. He remained there until 1980 when he returned to USA, teaching at Claremont Graduate School, CA until 1992. Hick returned to Birmingham at the age of 70 as Fellow of the Institute for Advanced Research in the Humanities.[42] In 2002, aged 80, he published, *John Hick: An Autobiography*, through Oneworld Publications, Oxford, England.

Theology of Religious Pluralism

Analyzing Hick's works on philosophy and theology, Chester Gillis notes, "His philosophical and theological work reveals a radical reinterpretation of the entire corpus of Christian doctrine."[43] Hick himself cites some who commented that, "with regard to Christology, 'Hick was especially problematic . . . because he was himself an apostate evangelical.'"[44] In the last quarter of the twentieth century, Hick became well-known as a Pluralist as noted in the following:

> John Hick towers over all other pluralists in influence and renown. Beginning with his 1972 call for a Copernican Revolution in dealing with the world religions, John Hick has raised the questions, pushed the boundaries, coined the paradigmatic

---

40. Gillis, "John Harwood Hick," 221; Hick, *An Autobiography*, 36, 71, 78.
41. Hick, *An Autobiography*, 88, 102.
42. Gillis, "John Harwood Hick," 221.
43. Ibid.
44. Hick, *An Autobiography*, 35. Hick notes evangelicals opposed his joining the PC (USA) Presbytery of San Gabriel, CA, in 1983–84 and "The very conservative Fuller Seminary in Pasadena was also a strong anti influence" (Ibid., 267).

phrases and thereby prepared the fertile ground for normative pluralism. Recognizing his pivotal role in contemporary theology, Hick's *An Interpretation of Religion* (Yale) received the 1991 Grawemeyer Award for the most significant new thinking in religion.[45]

As I have footnoted above, Hick earlier found Theosophy to be his "first coherent religious philosophy . . . much more so than the Christianity." Hick's theory of *Pluralism* in his later life is basically a restatement of Theosophical Hindu-Buddhist religious ideas of ultimate reality and how humans should respond to those ideas of reality. Obviously, *Pluralism*, when understood in this way, is in direct conflict with Judeo-Christian, even Muslim, views.

Hick has correctly discerned the strong influence of modern naturalistic[46] (western) worldview in the prevailing "assumption that the idea of an afterlife began in fear of extinction and a desire for a better life beyond the grave" and he also has correctly assessed that the belief in an afterlife "did not arise as wish-fulfillments" but "as part of a moral conception of the universe in which there is a judgment of the soul and the rewards of heaven are balanced by the punishment of hell."[47] Yet, he seems to imply that this belief of after-life is a human after-thought in that the "belief in a desirable afterlife . . . came later."[48] Hick recognizes the presence of the concept of an all-powerful Personal God

---

45. Dennis L. Okholm and Timothy R. Phillips, eds., *Four Views on Salvation in a Pluralistic World* (Grand Rapids, MI: Zondervan, 1996), 13.

46. Hick insightfully notes, "In our western world, beginning around the seventeenth century, the earlier pervasive religious outlook has increasingly been replaced by an equally pervasive naturalistic outlook, and during the twentieth century this replacement has become almost complete. Naturalism has created the 'consensus reality' of our culture. It has become so ingrained that we no longer see it, but see everything else through it. The main reason for this is clearly the continuing and most welcome success of the sciences in discovering how the physical world works, and in using this knowledge for our benefit in many fields, not least medicine . . . But in the case of events that can be experienced either naturalistically or religiously, the latter is precluded by the dominant faith of our culture. And when philosophizing about the history of religions a naturalistic interpretation is likewise routinely accepted as self-evidently more plausible than a religious one. Thus for example, when we hear someone speak of a moment when they had a strong sense, or feeling, of God as an unseen, all-enveloping, benign presence, the naturalistic assumption automatically rejects this as illusory and points to psychological mechanisms that might have produced it. It is firmly assumed that there is no reality beyond the physical (including, once again, the functioning of human brains), so that the religious person's sense of a divine presence can only be some kind of self-delusion. That the presence of a transcendent reality might be mediated to us by means of our own innate psychological structure is not even considered as a serious possibility" (John Hick, *The Fifth Dimension: An Exploration of the Spiritual Realm* [Oxford, England: Oneworld Publications, 1999], 14–15).

47. Hick, *Fifth Dimension*, 4.

48. Ibid.

continually intervening in human history in the traditional faiths of Judaism, Christianity and Islam, yet he thinks that this personal aspect of God is a human apprehension of Reality rather than an absolute fact of reality. Hick notes,

> This is the insurmountable problem for the concept of God as a limitless powerful supernatural Person who is continually intervening, sometimes openly and sometimes secretly, in the course of human affairs. Such an anthropomorphic image pervades Judaism, Christianity and Islam in their traditional forms, and almost all western atheists have naturally enough pursued them into the same trap. They have accepted an anthropomorphic God as that which, quite reasonably, they reject. But many religious people are also atheists in relation to that particular concept of God. "Atheism" is thus much too general a term to be useful, unless accompanied by a clear statement of the kind of God that one does not believe in. However . . . we are exploring the non-anthropomorphic conception of the ultimately Real that has always been present within the mystical strands of the great traditions. This does not clash in any way with the sciences – unless one illicitly incorporates the naturalistic assumption into them – but it does go far beyond them.[49]

One might ask, how does Hick distinguish between what is an anthropomorphic and what is a non-anthropomorphic notion of the ultimately Real and how does he discern which is true? Okholm and Philips point out the contradiction within this view of *Pluralism*:

> *Pluralism*, which argues that many religions are salvific, on first glance appears to be an accurate and appropriate label. However, does the pluralists' definition of salvation reflect every specific religion's understanding of this condition? At times Troeltsch appears to verge on this sort of relativism, but most contemporary pluralists do not. In order to escape relativism, John Hick defines saving religions as those involving a "transformation of human existence from self-centeredness to God-or Reality-centeredness." Yet this definition contradicts a more traditional Christian or Muslim understanding of salvation. As a result,

---

49. Ibid., 18.

the term *pluralism* conceals its own normative truth-claims regarding religion.[50]

Here Vinoth Ramachandra's response to Stanley Samartha's Pluralism (and hence to Hick prior to Hick's above comment) is worth noting:

> Samartha, like Professor John Hick . . . seeks to avoid a choice between personalist and nonpersonalist understandings of deity by using instead the language of "Transcendence," "Mystery," "Sat," "Ultimate Reality" and other highly abstract concepts. But . . . a choice has already been made in adopting the *advaita Vedanta* worldview as a framework for pluralism: for personal theism, whether in the form of the Semitic faiths or the *bhakti* tradition in India, has been demoted to a lower level of reality. Those believers who speak of God as personal being imply, at the very least, that God communicates with us, enters into personal relationships with us and has a purpose for the world. In asserting that Ultimate Reality/Mystery is unknowable, or that what can be known is so seriously distorted by our conceptual and cultural limitations that we cannot make any true statements about that Reality/Mystery, Samartha is imposing limits not only on our human ability but on that Reality/Mystery . . . The nonpersonal "God behind God" is clearly one who does not speak. This is a dogmatic assertion, an assumption that is necessary for Samartha's entire programme . . . There is an in-built bias towards the nontheistic Indian faiths. But this makes his strictures on "exclusivist Christian arrogance" sound extremely hollow, if not downright hypocritical.[51]

Ramachandra is correct in pointing out that Hick and Samartha have already made a choice by adopting the nonpersonalist views of God from the *Advaita Vedanta* (monistic) worldview as a framework for their Pluralism and that they have already assigned the personalist view of God to a lower level of reality. By making this choice, Hick and others are, themselves, exclusivist and are inconsistent when accusing particularists of being exclusivists. Ramachandra continues to show the fallacy of this view of Pluralism,

---

50. Philips, *Funeral Rites in Islam*, 15.
51. Ramachandra, *Recovery of Mission*, 13–14.

> Given the widely differing connotations of the terms in the world's religions, surely the onus of proof that their ultimate referents are identical lies with Samartha. How does he know that one Mystery underlies all the diverse "symbols," or even that "The Truth is greater than the sum of all its apprehensions?" Is he laying claim to a non-symbolic, privileged access to the Transcendent: a vantage point from which he can now survey the whole world of religion and identify them as but historically and culturally conditioned responses to the same Transcendent? And how, one wonders, would such a vantage point itself escape the historical and cultural conditioning that Samartha argues is endemic to all human beliefs?[52]

Hick's conservative position changed gradually, as Hick himself notes, in connection with his Princeton experience in 1959: "The Seminary regarded me as soundly conservative in my theology, as indeed I thought I was – otherwise I would have opted without hesitation for Union or McGill . . . However, it turned out before long that I was not conservative enough."[53] This shift may have begun in 1961 while at Princeton when he attempted to join the local Presbytery of New Brunswick and was asked if he could affirm the *Westminster Confession* (1647). He responded negatively about a number of things but, more specifically, he did not affirm the virgin birth of Jesus and did not consider it essential for the doctrine of incarnation.[54] At the second of the two presbytery meetings then, Hick said this:

> Now a word specifically about the virgin birth of our Lord. Left to myself I do not have anything to say about this at all – and in this, as the ministers here will certainly know, I am following the example of the majority of the New Testament writers: Paul, John, Mark, Peter, James, and Jude all believe in Christ as the Word Incarnate, but none of them mentions the idea of virgin birth; and I am content to follow them in this. However if I am specifically challenged to say something about it, I have to say simply that I do not affirm it; it plays no part in my personal faith. I do not assert that it is impossible, or that it may not be

---

52. Ibid., 15.
53. Hick, *John Hick*, 119.
54. Ibid., 125.

true; and I have no quarrel with those who do affirm it; but I am not myself able to affirm it.[55]

Hick assumes that since certain of the writers of the New Testament do not mention the virgin birth of Jesus, they did not affirm it. Arguing that the absence of a statement of truth negates truth is an untenable position. For example, that Jesus did not categorically state that he is God does not negate his divinity. Hick's negative position on the virgin birth of Jesus is contradicted by both Matthew and Luke who affirm it. Consistency is a problem for Hick. In one case, Hick affirms that of which the Bible is silent and, in another, he negates that to which the Bible gives specific testimony. Hick rightly shows how Jesus Christ as the Word incarnate is a prominent topic in John and other writings, but fails to note that this topic is not mentioned explicitly in any of the Synoptics.

D. A. Carson summarizes Hick's gradual shift from an evangelical Christian position to a radical pluralistic one:

> Hick's views have gradually evolved from those of a conservative ... In the seventies he came to the conclusion that if Christianity as popularly believed is true, other religions are correspondingly false, and that much of the human race is therefore damned to eternal perdition. He saw no recourse but to shift from *Christo*centrism to *theo*centrism, arguing that we should all come "to the realization that it is *God* who is at centre, and that all religions ... serve and revolve around him." ... this means Hick must "de-center" Christ and the incarnation. The latter must be taken as mythological and metaphorical, not as literal or definitive. In time Hick came to see that even these proposals were not radical enough. He saw that he was still thinking and writing of God as personal, though some of the world's religions espouse an impersonal view of God. He was still a "covert theist" ... Hick now prefers to speak of *Reality*-centeredness.[56]

The result is that Hick has put Christianity on the same level with all other religions, where the focus is on the manifestations of God, all of which he considers equally valid.

---

55. Ibid.
56. D. A. Carson, *The Gagging of God: Christianity Confronts Pluralism* (Grand Rapids, MI: Zondervan, 1996), 146.

State-after-Death

Having traced the broader shift of Hick's perspectives, I will now consider Hick's thoughts on the "State-after-Death" which he discusses in his *Death and Eternal Life*, first published in 1976. In the preface of *Death and Eternal Life*, Hick notes that:

> *The notion of a global as distinguished from a one-tradition theology of death requires an inter-cultural as well as an inter-disciplinary approach*; and this inevitably involves dealing with a vast amount of material second hand, using work done by experts in the diverse disciplines involved. I have accordingly not hesitated to seek the help of colleagues in other fields. None of these must be held in any way responsible for what I have said in discussing their subjects, but they have nevertheless saved me from numerous errors as well as often pointing me in profitable directions; and I am deeply grateful to them.[57]

Though I may not agree with Hick's conclusions, I do appreciate his serious attempt to construct a global theology of death, as I too am attempting to do. I find his comment helpful as he acknowledges his dependence on secondary sources due to the enormity of the task involved. However, in the preface of the 1994 edition of *Death and Eternal Life*, Hick expresses the above comment in a slightly different way:

> But perhaps the main feature of the book that has encouraged me to make it available again is that it treats *the subject of death on a global basis, seeking insights from both east and west*, and from psychology, parapsychology, sociology, and philosophy, as well as from religion. For truth-seeking requires not only accurate reasoning but also *an openness to ideas and information from any and every relevant source*.[58]

By this note, Hick makes his intentions very clear. He is *not* merely using *an inter-cultural as well as an inter-disciplinary approach*, as noted in the 1976 edition, *but* is going a lot further in dealing with *the subject of death on a global basis, seeking insights from both east and west* and borrowing *ideas and information from any and every relevant source*. With these sources he

---

57. Hick, *Death and Eternal Life*, 15 (emphasis added).
58. John Hick, *Death and Eternal Life* (Louisville, KY: Westminster/John Knox Press, 1994), 17 (emphasis added).

is synthesizing a *New* global philosophy of death which is the *Old* Hindu-Buddhist understanding of death. Hick's exposure to Theosophy quite early on in his life and also his active involvement with the people of other faiths, when he moved to the chair of theology at Birmingham University, UK in 1967, was a critical factor in this new perspective of his theology.[59] It is important to note here Hick's following comment, in which he refers to Paul Tillich and the personal interaction he had with Tillich:

> I asked him a series of critical questions, which he answered fully in his usual manner of enveloping the questioner's point of view in his own system . . . Although I never adopted his complex theological system, I saw him as a major force in opening up a new range of possibilities and thus as a wholly positive influence, today alas largely neglected. In his later years he visited Japan, held extensive dialogues with Zen philosophers in Kyoto, and opened his mind to an even more radical range of possibilities. *Indeed he said in one of his last public lectures that if he had his time over again he would re-think his entire system on a multi-faith basis. At that time he was far ahead of me in this, though I have since caught up, at least on that issue.*[60]

Later on, Hick also notes about himself that, "It was after these visits to India and Sri Lanka, and partly as a result of them, that I wrote my longest book, *Death and Eternal Life* (1976)."[61] Hick was not only learning about what takes place after death according to other faiths during his trips to India and Sri Lanka, but was also letting these perspectives influence and objectively change his Christian theological understanding, and hence produced a new radical philosophy of the "State-after-Death."

Let us now consider Hick's concept of *Death and Eternal Life* (1976). Hick himself summarizes its contents in this way in his autobiography:

> Amongst a wide range of topics I treated the mainly Hindu and Buddhist belief in reincarnation more seriously than any but a very few . . . western philosophers . . . I criticized the standard Christian doctrine of an eternal heaven or hell on the ground that, in almost all cases, at death we are not yet ready for either an eternal heaven (or heaven via purgatory) nor have we

---

59. Cf. Hick, *John Hick*, 159ff.
60. Ibid., 111 (emphasis added).
61. Ibid., 225.

> deserved an eternal hell, or obliteration. We need further moral and spiritual growth or development – for which the traditional purgatory doctrine does not allow. And such development happens in this life, to the extent to which it does happen . . . bounded as it is by birth and death. It is the pressure of these boundaries, as distinguished from an endless vista of the same life, that gives urgent meaning to our time here. We have to get on with whatever we are . . . to do . . . so continued progress may well be in further finite lives.[62]

Here Hick is questioning the authority of God's word in the letter to the Hebrews which notes, "it is appointed for men to die once, after that comes judgment" (9:27), referring to our *one* finite life on earth before we face the judgment of God for either eternal heaven or hell. Although Hick's background is in the Reformed tradition, rather than believing in "justification by faith" in Jesus Christ, Hick has converted to a religion of works (Hindu, Buddhist and other religions). His theology of "salvation by works" requires an extended period of time and more finite lives. Thus Hick imposes his own authority and human standard over God's authoritative word. The implication of Hick's perspective is that the "good news" of the gospel is not good enough to enable people of pluralistic religious contexts to participate by faith in Christ in the promise of an eternal heaven as their "State-after-Death."

Having criticized the Christian doctrine of eternal heaven or hell, Hick supports something akin to the Buddhist ideas of rebirth and proposes a "Buddhistic gospel" of gradual development and spiritual perfection by passing through several finite lives:

> My eventual conclusion is that something like the Buddhist conception of rebirth is quite likely to be true. This depends upon a distinction between the present conscious self, which is not immortal but is a temporary and changing expression of a deeper reality, an underlying psychic structure, a dispositional or karmic continuant, which affects and is affected by the activities of the present self, and which will be expressed again many times in new conscious personalities, reflecting a gradual development towards unity with the eternal ultimate reality . . . To repeat the way that I have put it in *The Fifth Dimension*, so long as we

---

62. Ibid.

cling to our fragmentary and very imperfect ego its approaching demise is the worst possible news and we will go to great lengths to shut it out of our minds. But if we can each come to see oneself as the present moment within a long creative process and can trust in the value of that process, we can accept our mortality without fear or resentment and can try to live to the full within our present life span.[63]

Thus, Hick has rejected the unique gospel of eternal life in Jesus Christ, and wants to convince the world (mainly western world) that his evolutionary view is more plausible than the Christian gospel. Hick refers to certain surveys done in western society to prove his point:

A simpler and more popular version of reincarnation belief seems to be surprisingly widespread in contemporary western society, surveys reporting that about seventy per cent of people, including church members, profess some kind of reincarnation belief. In most cases they probably have in mind the popular conception of the present self living again, rather than the more complex Buddhist/Hindu idea. I imagine that they have seen the implausibility of the traditional Christian belief, but share the basic cosmic optimism of all the great world religions and find some kind of reincarnation to be the most plausible possibility.[64]

This, then, is Hick's global theology of "State-after-Death": all the belief systems of the world religions are absorbed into one Hindu-Buddhistic universalism, where all becomes well for everyone after several events of rebirth, through a progressive reformation of one's self or works, without condemnation of anyone to hell. The ultimate question is to ask John Hick, "Why did Jesus Christ come into the world and what is the meaning of Jesus' death if not to make salvation possible in one life? Why does the Christian church exist and why did Jesus leave the church with the mandate to preach the Christian gospel to people of other faiths in this time of religious pluralism?"

---

63. Ibid. Hick continues to elaborate further to show the plausibility of his new theory of "State-after-Death": "We are like the runners in a relay race: the torch has been handed to us and for a short time the whole project depends upon us. Our life thus has an urgent meaning. We are contributing something unique, not only to the world that will continue after our death but also to our own future selves who will, one after another, embody the basic dispositional character-structure – the soul, or jiva, or karmic nexus – which we have inherited and are now all the time modifying in small ways for good or ill" (Ibid., 226).

64. Ibid., 226.

Hans Küng

Hans Küng was born on 19 March 1928 in the strongly Catholic town of Sursee in Switzerland. He was the eldest of seven children with one brother and five sisters.[65] He grew up in a loving and devout middle class Catholic family. His father, Hans Küng senior, ran a thriving shoe business that he had inherited from his father, Johann Küng. His mother, Emma Gut, a self-confident farmer's daughter also helped run the shoe business.[66] In 1948, at the age of twenty, Hans Küng went to study philosophy and theology for seven years at the Pontificia Universitas Gregoriana in Rome to become a priest in the Catholic Church.[67] During his study in Rome, Küng came into "intellectual contact with important philosophers and theologians" and into "personal contact with some of the leading theological and ecclesiastical figures of the time, such as Joseph Lortz, Hans Urs von Balthasar, Yves Congar, and Augustinus Bea."[68]

While in Rome, Küng wanted to grapple with the fundamental barrier between Catholics and Protestants from the time of Luther and began studying the doctrine of justification. He studied Protestant theologian Karl Barth's views on justification in light of Catholic theology in his *Licentiate* thesis at the Gregorian University. Küng notes,

> Something that I couldn't have expected to begin with now happens after all: at the end of laborious research and intellectual grappling which finally leads to a thick and detailed manuscript of around 220 pages with much small print, as early as the summer semester of 1955 in Rome I can formulate as the result of my theological licentiate work: "Generally speaking, in the doctrine of justification there is a fundamental agreement between the teaching of Barth and the teaching of the Catholic Church." So in the light of this there would be no basis for a schism. Its theological core and basic motive collapse. From both the Catholic and the Protestant side it can be asserted that the justification of man takes place through the grace of God

---

65. Hans Küng, *My Struggle for Freedom: Memoirs*, trans. John Bowden (Grand Rapids, MI: Eerdmans, 2003), 17, 24.
66. Ibid., 21–28.
67. Ibid., 40–42.
68. Werner G. Jeanrond, "Hans Küng," in *The Modern Theologians: An Introduction to Christian Theology in the Twentieth Century*, ed. David F. Ford (Oxford, UK: Blackwell, 1997), 162.

solely on the basis of trusting faith, which is to be active through works of love. I begin to understand what a momentous result for ecumenism I have here in my hands in 1955.[69]

After his ordination in Rome in 1954 and his *Licentiate in Theology* in 1955, Hans Küng went on to study in Paris at the Sorbonne and the Institut Catholique, for his doctorate in theology. Even though his supervisor, Louis Bouyer, thought his licentiate thesis was quite sufficient for a doctoral dissertation, he continued to work on it for another year or so to provide additional supporting evidence from the Bible and the history of theology. His dissertation was accepted on Thursday 21 February 1957 and was granted the *doctor theologiae*.[70] I will briefly survey Küng's theology to determine his views on "State-after-Death," especially in light of the variety of beliefs held in pluralistic contexts.

Theological Development

Küng's dissertation with its focus on the fundamental barrier between Catholics and Protestants brought him wide recognition within the academic community and played a key role in his theological career. In 1960, at the young age of 32 and just prior to the Second Vatican Council, Küng was installed in the chair of fundamental theology at the University of Tübingen's Roman Catholic Faculty of Theology. Küng was appointed as a consultative theologian for the Second Vatican Council (1962–65) and was duly immersed in the conflict between the reformists and the traditionalists within the Roman Catholic Church.[71]

Soon after this he dealt with important ecclesiological questions in his published books, such as *Structures of the Church* (1962), *The Church* (1967), and *Infallible?* (1970). He questioned the hierarchical authority of the Roman Catholic Church and, more specifically, the infallibility of the pope. After nine years of controversy, Pope John Paul II withdrew the Roman Catholic Church's permission for Küng to teach Roman Catholic theology. So Küng

---

69. Küng, *My Struggle for Freedom*, 123.
70. Ibid., 125–136. From July 1955 Küng came to a personal contact with Karl Barth and Barth wrote in his letter of introduction for Küng's dissertation that he has accurately presented Barth's views and Barth gave his assent to the consensus Küng found in Catholic theology with Barth's view (Ibid., 123, 124, 130–134). Jesuit theologian Karl Rahner also highly approved of Hans Küng's dissertation (Ibid., 143).
71. Jeanrond, "Hans Küng," 163.

left the faculty of Roman Catholic Theology and began to teach ecumenical theology in the new Institute for Ecumenical Research within the University of Tübingen, and remained there until his retirement in 1996. Werner G. Jeanrond summarizes Hans Küng's overall theological development this way:

> Küng's theological development to date may be roughly divided into four periods: (1) his concentration on ecclesiological questions until 1970; (2) his treatment of major articles of Christian faith (God, Jesus Christ, and Eternal Life) during the 1970s; (3) his reflection on theological method and the dialogue between Christianity and other world religions and between religion and culture since 1983; and (4) from 1990 onward his two related projects on global responsibility and on the religious situation of our time, which are connected with all his previous concerns.
>
> All these periods are inspired by a strong commitment both to dialogue with all current religious, political, and cultural forces in the world in general and to Christian ecumenism in particular. Küng's commitment to Christian and even global ecumenism must not be confused with a new kind of essentialism, according to which all Christian traditions or even all religious traditions are essentially the same. Rather, Küng wishes to bring Christians of all backgrounds and the different religious traditions of humankind into a mutually critical conversation.[72]

We are particularly concerned about Küng's theology of "State-after-Death" in relation to this topic within the context of world religions in global pluralism and the implications of Küng's thinking for communicating the Christian gospel in pluralistic contexts.

State-after-Death

In his book *Eternal Life?* (1984), Hans Küng deals mainly with his theology of "State-after-Death." In this book Küng tackles a number of complex questions related to the belief in life after death. He covers issues such as: the meaning of death and eternal life (whether eternal life is a wish or a reality); the belief of reincarnation or rebirth in the religions of Indian origin;

---

72. Ibid.

and the hope of resurrection from the dead in Christianity. Küng discusses the symbolic character of heaven and hell (and whether hell is eternal) in Christianity. Finally, Küng deals with the consequent medical, philosophical, and theological problems that this study engenders. Küng notes in the preface of *Eternal Life?* – about the nature of the book he produced:

> I did not want to produce a long-winded theological treatise on eschatology, but – as in the books *On Being a Christian* and *Does God Exist?* – to answer the pressing questions of our contemporaries on the basis of present-day theological studies without digressing too much . . . So these three books now appear to be dovetailed into one another, and after a dozen years I am glad to be able to say that the theological path then taken with *On Being a Christian* has proved itself . . . and can be followed consistently, untroubled by theological fashions.[73]

This comment reflects the kind of method Küng uses to theologize in his contemporary context. Küng's theological perspectives are based on two horizons, "a theology from the perspective of Christian origins and the Christian center, against the horizon of today's world" and an interaction between "God's revelatory speaking in the history of Israel and the history of Jesus" with "our own human world of experience."[74] For Küng, however, the Christian message has primacy over the horizon of human experience, as he notes,

> All this means that a drastic, paradigmatic upheaval can take place in Christian theology – if it is to be and remain Christian – always and only on the *basis* of the Gospel, and ultimately *on account* of the Gospel, but never *against* the Gospel. The Gospel of Jesus Christ himself – much as the testimonies to him must be deeply probed by means of historic-criticism – is no more at the theologian's disposal, to rule on its truth, than history is for the historian or the Constitution for the constitutional lawyer.[75]

Thus, on the surface, it seems Küng is quite orthodox in his Christocentric theologizing and, unlike Hick, is not replacing it with a "Theocentric" theology

---

73. Hans Küng, *Eternal Life?*, trans. Edward Quinn (New York, NY: Doubleday, 1984), xiv-xv.
74. Küng cited in Grenz and Olson, *20th-Century Theology*, 262.
75. Ibid. Here and in the previous reference Grenz and Olson cites from Küng's *Theology for the Third Millennium*, trans. Peter Heinegg (New York, NY, and London: Doubleday, 1988).

for the sake of inter-religious interactions and relationships. It would seem, therefore, that Küng is committed to communicating the unique gospel of Jesus Christ without compromise to universalistic thinking. But is it really so? There is reason to look deeply at his above comment that, "The Gospel of Jesus Christ himself – *much as the testimonies to him must be deeply probed by means of historic-criticism.*" It would appear that his understanding is that *this* gospel of Jesus Christ is "hidden" in the Bible and needs to be discovered by "historic-critical" exegesis if it is to become the norm of theology. Grenz and Olson rightly point out the ambiguity of Küng's theological method:

> Nowhere is this ambiguity more evident than in his position concerning the theological norm. According to Küng, Scripture is supposed to stand over all ecclesiastical traditions, whether ancient or modern, as the *norma normans non normata* (supreme norm judging all norms) of Christian theology. Yet in his estimation Scripture is itself thoroughly historical and fallible; consequently it must be judged by rigorous historical-critical exegesis. Once the historical-critical method of interpretation is introduced, Küng shifts his supreme norm of theology to the gospel within Scripture – Jesus Christ. But this norm must be drawn from Scripture and applied to Scripture and tradition by the historical-critical method. What is Küng's actual final criterion? Is it Scripture, the "gospel" within Scripture or the historical-critical method?[76]

If the Bible, the source of the gospel of Jesus Christ, is fallible, then what confidence can we have in the Word of the gospel and then what confidence can the people of other faiths have in that gospel, even if it is communicated correctly in pluralistic contexts? Let us now look at some of the instances of his method in his book *Eternal Life?* (1984).

Referring to belief in an eternal life and the decision-making it involves in general, that is in all the religions of the world, Küng notes the following:

> This trusting self-commitment to an ultimate meaning of reality as a whole and of our life, to the eternal God, to an eternal life, is rightly described in general usage as *"faith"* in God, *in an eternal life*. At the same time it is of course a question of belief in a wide sense, which would be better described as trust or hope. That is

---

76. Grenz and Olson, *20th-Century Theology*, 269.

to say, a belief of this kind need not be provoked by the biblical proclamation; it is possible in principle also for non-Christians and non-Jews, for Hindus, Confucians and Buddhists . . . and of course especially for Muslims, who appeal to the Koran (inspired by the Bible).[77]

When Küng says that, "a belief of this kind need not be provoked by the biblical proclamation," he is undoubtedly referring to the *"faith"* that Apostle Paul speaks about in Romans 10:17 (NASV 1995), "So *faith* comes from hearing, and hearing by the word of Christ." Yet it appears that Küng is not distinguishing the uniqueness of this *faith* from any other religious faith. Likewise, in essence, Küng does not distinguish between the Bible as the Word of God, as opposed to other sacred writings through which religious words generate the same kind of belief. Küng is not interested in dealing with that which is truly *God's revealed word*, rather, with what is the general human response to an ultimate meaning of reality in all the religions. This is the position of John Hick, as we have seen before. Consequently, when Küng studies the theme of resurrection in the Bible, he is not tracing that theme within *God's progressive revelation* in the Scriptures, but rather, he is dealing "with the question of the *stages in the development of faith in the resurrection in the Judeo-Christian Scriptures*, which Islam also adopted."[78] Perhaps for Küng this is doing theology *from below*, from human experiences recorded by fallible human witnesses in the fallible human book, the Bible, rather than from a Bible that is the infallible Word of God.

As a result, Küng concludes that the human belief in the resurrection from the dead was a late phenomenon in the Old Testament and comments:

> Anyone who is accustomed as a Christian, without reflection, to assume a continuity in the history of salvation between the Old Testament and the New should be quite clear about what this means: *All the patriarchs of Israel*, Abraham, Isaac and Jacob, Moses and the Judges, the kings and the prophets, Isaiah, Jeremiah and Ezekiel, for their own part passed from such an end into darkness; and yet they had lived and acted in an unswerving belief in God. For more than a thousand years, *none* of these Jews *believed in a resurrection of the dead* or in an eternal life in the positive sense of the term, in a "Christian" heaven. With

---

77. Küng, *Eternal Life?*, 78.
78. Ibid.

remarkable consistency they concentrated on the present world, without bothering about what was in any case a dismal, dark, hopeless hereafter.[79]

In response to Küng, I will show in the material that follows that in Genesis 22, Deuteronomy 32 and 1 Samuel 2, Hosea 6, Ezekiel 37, Isaiah 26 and Daniel 12, there are signposts for the theme of resurrection from the dead within the progressive revelation of the Old Testament. We will find these insights become clearer and brighter (from implicit to explicit) as we travel along the paths of revelation of Old Testament Scripture. Küng notes, however that,

> Certainly in the history of Christian interpretation we find a constant appeal to Old Testament texts in order even at this point to secure the Christian idea of the resurrection. But the various Old Testament statements, which speak of a "resurrection," are meant to be *figurative, metaphorical*, and cannot without more ado be taken as real in their imagery.[80]

In response to this, I would refer to the Synoptic Gospels (cf. Mark 12:26–27; Matt 22:31–32; Luke 20:37–38) where Jesus' incisive response (God is not the God of the dead, but of the living) refers to Moses at Horeb in the Old Testament (Exod 3:6). Jesus says this to refute the Sadducees' position that there is no resurrection from the dead. This shows the presence of belief in life after death in the Old Testament.

Küng speaks of non-Jewish influences on the Old Testament when he comments: "the question of the resurrection, we find in the last chapter of this (originally apocalyptic) book of Daniel a passage which is presumably influenced by Persian ideas."[81] In response to this I will point to Colin Brown's statement,

> Whereas the biblical passages speak of awakening from death, as from sleep, the Persians thought of it as a reconstitution of the body through the reunion of its elements. In conclusion it may be said that the Jews had a conception of resurrection before they came into contact with the Persian Empire. The thought of an after-life has its deepest root in the awareness of the living God himself; because Yahweh lives and is the covenant God

---

79. Ibid., 83.
80. Ibid.
81. Ibid., 85.

of Israel, his people, there is an on-going relationship and life. This awareness developed in the course of history in Israel's many vicissitudes and partly also *in contrast* with surrounding religious beliefs.[82]

It is quite interesting to note, as does Old Testament scholar Daniel Block,[83] that until about 1985 biblical scholars maintained that there was no belief in life after death in ancient Israel (especially in the Old Testament itself). Most argued that belief in life after death was really a late development among the Jewish people during or after the Babylonian exile as is reflected in the intertestamental literature. Block continues to show that,

> Many believe that the Pharisaic acceptance of the doctrine . . . derives from a limited number of late texts that reflect Persian influence, and that the Sadducees, who rejected the notion, were the true heirs of OT belief. That some scholars have recently reversed the roles of these two parties is welcome: many now insist that the Saducean position represented a conscious departure from both Hebrew and common Semitic beliefs.[84]

Again, Küng failed to accept Jesus' incisive refutation of the Saducee's position of no resurrection from the dead by referring to Moses at Horeb (Exod 3:6) and Jesus' own resurrection as the validation of *literal* and not *figurative* resurrection.

Of course, according to Küng,[85] Jesus himself was fallible and was conditioned by his contemporary culture, for example, in his imminent expectation of the kingdom of God and that some later writings in the New Testament tried to cover it up:

> It is certain that Jesus lived, preached and worked – as his first community and Paul did later – in the *horizon of apocalyptic ideas*. How otherwise could the awareness of living at a turning point of time have been indicated? His consciousness of living at the end of an earlier age and the beginning of a new? No, like many of his contemporaries, Jesus lived in a state of apocalyptically depicted

---

82. Colin Brown, "Resurrection," in *The New International Dictionary of New Testament Theology*, vol. 3, ed. Colin Brown (Grand Rapids, MI: Zondervan, 1986), 275 (emphasis added).
83. Daniel Block, *The Book of Ezekiel: Chapters 25–48*, The New International Commentary on the Old Testament, No. 26 (Grand Rapids, MI: Eerdmans, 1998), 392.
84. Ibid.
85. Küng, *Eternal Life?*, 91–92.

> *imminent expectation*: the kingdom was to come. With him an entire apocalyptic generation was expecting in the immediate future the kingdom of God... and was mistaken. This is too well documented in the earliest strata of the synoptic tradition to be disputed and – because of the scandal of this fact – it was softened down in the later writings and strata of the New Testament.[86]

Thus, as noted before, Küng, on the surface, seem quite orthodox in his theology, by continuing to keep Jesus Christ at the center and, unlike Hick, Küng is clear that the gospel of Jesus Christ must be communicated in pluralistic religious situations. But, we have to ask, what kind of Jesus is this and why would the people of other faiths consider this Jesus unique compared to any other human being? Küng himself does what he says later writers of the New Testament seemed to have done, that is, he is raising ambiguity about the absolute nature of the kingdom Jesus talked about:

> Unlike the apocalyptic writers, Jesus in particular was not interested in satisfying human curiosity. He neither dated nor located the kingdom of God, nor did he describe in detail the course of the apocalyptic drama...
>
> ... With the imminent expectation it is a question less of a mistake on the part of Jesus than of a *time-conditioned, time-bound world vision* which Jesus shared – like a number of other things – with many of his contemporaries. Jesus and his contemporaries were "mistaken" then in the sense and only in the sense that generations of human beings were "mistaken" in their belief in the Ptolemaic world picture before Copernicus... Today the really important question is whether the admittedly extremely urgent *matter*, with which Jesus was concerned in his preaching of the advent of God's kingdom, still has a meaning: in the completely changed horizon of understanding of humanity today.[87]

If Jesus himself was "mistaken" like rest of his contemporaries, what guarantee is there that he was also not mistaken in his overall ministry? This kind of thinking reveals Küng's view of a fallible Jesus which would carry detrimental implications when communicating the gospel in religiously pluralistic

---

86. Ibid.
87. Ibid., 92.

contexts. The gospel would be received as an unreliable human perception of truth. Küng goes on to question the accounts of Jesus' death in the later writings of the New Testament and in this way he challenges the authority of the biblical record:

> The question therefore cannot be suppressed: Did he *not die in vain*? Even if we can assume that Jesus expected his violent death, we still do not know exactly what he thought and felt as this death came upon him. According to Mark, the earliest of the evangelists, there were none of Jesus' followers at the foot of the cross who might have passed on his last words; only some Galilean women, without Jesus' mother, watched from a distance. The disciples had fled. It would have been natural to fill in these gaps in our information with impressive or touching details in the style of Jewish and Christian legends of the martyrs. In fact this did happen later in a way that was incidentally very appropriate: in Luke a prayer for his enemies – who did not know what they were doing – and the conversion of one of the criminals crucified with him, who would that very day be with him in paradise; in John the parting with loving care from his mother and the beloved disciple.
>
> There is nothing of all this in the earliest Passion account. There are no edifying embellishments, no impressive words or gestures, no reference to an unshakable inward resignation (like that of Socrates). His death is described here with staggering simplicity: "Jesus gave a loud cry and breathed his last." This loud inarticulate cry accords with the fear and trembling before death mentioned by all three Synoptists and toned down only in Luke, with a reference to an angelic manifestation, as a sign of God's closeness.[88]

Küng continues to speak about the implausibility of the gospel accounts in connection with the resurrection of Jesus. Drawing solely upon historical-critical analysis Küng writes:

> A close analysis of the Easter accounts actually reveals unsurmountable *discrepancies and inconsistencies* in the tradition. It is true that attempts have constantly been made to

---

88. Ibid., 94–95.

combine the material harmoniously into a uniform tradition. But in vain. Agreement is lacking, to put it briefly, (1) in regard to the persons involved . . . ; (2) in regard to the locality of the events . . . ; (3) in regard to the whole sequence of appearances: . . . Everywhere harmonization turns out to be impossible.[89]

Küng continues to question the historicity of the resurrection accounts,

> The various extensions, displacements and developments of the Easter message – quantitatively expressed, eight verses in Mark and fifty-four in John – cannot however lay claim *a priori* to historicity merely on the basis of the description of the sources, but might have a largely legendary character.[90]

But then Küng also understands that the clear implication of his conclusion will cause some to question the reliability of the resurrection message which, at least, seems not what he wants to do. So he comments:

> In view of the complexity of these findings, . . . There are those who may possibly find themselves faced with the question as to whether perhaps all the Easter stories amount to no more than legend. The answer is that this is not so in the sense that everything here might be pious invention. But it is true in the sense that the Easter stories with their time-conditioned restraints in form and content are meant to illustrate, make concrete and defend the reality of the new life of the risen Christ. What at first may seem alarming to a person with a traditional education, on closer examination may turn out to have a truly liberating effect. The Easter message is not identical with the details of the Easter stories here described. It is no more identical with these than the biblical message of creation is identical with the details of the biblical narrative of the six days' work of God the Creator. I can believe in the truth of Easter without having to accept as literally true each and every one of the Easter stories.[91]

Later on, Küng, again diminishes the importance of the empty tomb by noting that, "It was not by the empty tomb but by the 'appearances' or 'revelations' – probably objective or subjective visions or hearings . . . that

---

89. Ibid., 100–101.
90. Ibid., 102.
91. Ibid., 102–103.

Jesus' disciples came to believe in his resurrection to eternal life" and also by that "whatever is thought about the historicity of the empty tomb, neither Jesus' resurrection nor ours is dependent on an empty tomb. The reanimation of a corpse is not a precondition for rising to eternal life."[92] Though the empty tomb may not have been enough to convince even the disciples about Jesus' resurrection, it was an important piece of historical evidence for Jesus' resurrection that God in his sovereignty allowed to be recorded in the Holy Scriptures and it is there as history to give confidence and proof that is needed by the skeptical human mind. New Testament scholar N. T. Wright, convincingly argues, "the best *historical* explanation is the one which inevitably raises all kinds of *theological* questions: the tomb was indeed empty, and Jesus was indeed seen alive, because he was truly raised from the dead" and how, if the two "historical conclusions" are taken away, "the belief of the early church becomes itself inexplicable."[93] In contrast to N. T. Wright, Küng writes,

> Historically ascertainable are the death of Jesus and after that the Easter faith and the Easter message of the disciples; the historian goes into these two public events, the death of Jesus and the faith of the disciples. But the resurrection itself is not a public event and cannot be pinned down or objectified.[94]

In an interview in *The Christian Century*, 18–21 December 2002, pp. 28–31, N. T. Wright argues about the historicity of the resurrection and what part both the empty tomb and the post-resurrection sightings play in the authenticity of the event. I agree with Wright that the plausibility and historicity of the resurrection of Jesus is stronger than all seeming contradictions. The real problem lies in the fact that Küng does not consider the Bible as the infallible Word of God, so he cannot accept what is recorded therein as historic truth. We also see this deference in Küng's comment about what is "body" in the term *bodily resurrection*. To him this "body" is not actual physical body but an "identical personal reality,"[95] having no continuity with the present physical body, whereas the disciples understood this as the physical body raised and significantly transformed.[96]

---

92. Ibid., 104.
93. N. T. Wright, *The Resurrection of the Son of God*, Christian Origins and the Question of God, No. 3 (Minneapolis, MN: Fortress Press, 2003), 10.
94. Küng, *Eternal Life?*, 105
95. Ibid., 111.
96. Wright (*Resurrection of the Son of God*, 478) notes concerning the resurrection

However, no matter how much we question Küng's pretense of orthodoxy with respect to the resurrection of Jesus, we cannot ignore his serious engagement with the perspectives on the "State-after-Death" in engagement with other religions, especially with the idea of reincarnation. Küng notes about reincarnation:

> despite the numerous accounts of events in this field, there are no scientifically undisputed, universally recognized facts, as John Hick too has to admit when he tries to establish a reconciliation between the Indian belief in reincarnation and the Christian belief in resurrection. None of the accounts – mostly coming from children or from the countries where there is a belief in reincarnation – of a recollection of a previous life could be verified, any more than the obviously legendary story, written many centuries after Buddha's death, about his recollection of the one hundred thousand lives he had lived.[97]

Thus, Küng,[98] contrary to John Hick, does well in looking into arguments for and against reincarnation and in conclusion shows that it is not proved to be true and that even the Chinese traditions reject it:

> To sum up then – considering all the arguments for and against – it cannot in any case be said that the doctrine of reincarnation has been proved. In fact, despite all its attractiveness, there are quite weighty arguments against the idea of rebirth which are not to be ignored; it is also notable that educated Indians, Chinese and Japanese often show considerable skepticism in regard to the idea of reincarnation. Not only does it not solve many problems that it claims to solve, but it also created a number of new ones. In any case, with a view to a responsible decision, it may be worthwhile to turn to the alternative solution as presented in this case by the Jewish-Christian-Islamic tradition, which in this present respect is confirmed by another and often neglected tradition of the East:

---

language used by the disciples, "We should not project on to others the limitations of our imaginations" and refers to Küng (*On Being a Christian*, trans. Edward Quinn [Garden City, NY: Doubleday 1976], 350f) that he "stresses the unimaginability of the resurrection as part of his argument that 'the resurrection of Jesus was not an event in space and time.'" To Wright, scholars like Küng want to hang on to resurrection language "to keep up a pretence of orthodox respectability" but in reality use that language to mean something quite different.

97. Küng, *Eternal Life?*, 64.
98. Ibid., 61–65.

that is, the Chinese tradition which exercises its influence also in Korea, Japan and Vietnam. Before the introduction of Buddhism people in China did not believe in a reincarnation and even afterward the scholars of the Confucian tradition continued to reject the idea, since they found it to be beneath man's dignity to give equal respect to all sentient beings and to imagine their deeply revered ancestors as beasts of burden or even as insects.[99]

Also, though Küng does not consider the Bible infallible, unlike Hick, he seems to have a more orthodox view of hell as we see in the following quote:

> What then is to be said about hell and the punishment of hell? We can now recapitulate what has been said:
>
> • Hell in any case is not to be understood mythologically as a place in the upper or underworld, but theologically as an exclusion from the fellowship of the living God, described in a variety of images but nevertheless unimaginable, as the absolutely final possibility of distance from God, which man cannot of himself *a priori* exclude. Man can miss the meaning of his life, he can shut himself out of God's fellowship.
>
> • The New Testament statements about hell are not meant to supply information about a hereafter to satisfy curiosity and fantasy. They are meant to bring vividly before us here and now the absolute seriousness of God's claim and the urgency of conversion in the present life. This life is the emergency we have to face.
>
> • Anyone who fails to perceive the seriousness of the biblical warnings of the possibility of eternal failure judges himself. Anyone who is inclined to despair in face of the possibility of such a failure can gain hope from the New Testament statements about God's universal mercy.
>
> • The eternity of the "punishment of hell" (of the "fire"), asserted in some New Testament metaphorical expressions, remains subject to God and to his will. Individual New Testament texts,

---

99. Ibid., 64.

which are not balanced by others, suggest the consummation of a salvation of all, an all-embracing mercy.[100]

It seems that Küng is also concluding that the "punishment of hell" is only a possibility and is meant as a warning from God, but not as an absolute reality. Thus, Küng allows for "salvation for all" based on God's all-embracing mercy. It appears, therefore, that Küng is in tension between orthodoxy and a more Universalist-pluralistic position. What, then, is expected of Christians in their attitude toward other faiths? According to Küng:

- Instead of indifferentism, for which everything is all the same, somewhat more *indifference* toward supposed orthodoxy, which makes itself the measure of the salvation or perdition of mankind, and wants to enforce its claim to truth with the tools of power and compulsion;

- instead of relativism, for which there is no absolute, more sense of *relativity* toward all human establishing of absolutes, which hinder productive co-existence between the different religions, and more sense of *relationship*, which lets every religion appear in the fabric of its interconnections;

- instead of syncretism, where everything possible and impossible is mixed and fused together, more will to achieve a *synthesis* in the face of all denominational and religious antagonisms, which are still exacting a daily price in blood and tears, so that *peace* may reign between religions, instead of war, hatred and strife.

Given all the religiously motivated intolerance, one cannot stop demanding tolerance and religious freedom. But at the same time too there must be no betrayal of freedom for the sake of truth. The *question of truth* must not be trivialized and sacrificed to the utopia of future world unity and the religion of world unity.[101]

It seems that, unlike Hick, Küng does not want to openly deny the ultimate uniqueness of Christian truth, however vague that becomes in his case. For Küng, there is an essential Christianity that must be retained in the quest

---

100. Ibid., 141–142.
101. Hans Küng, "Is There One True Religion?," in *Christianity and Other Religions*, eds. John Hick and Brian Hebblethwaite (Oxford, UK: Oneworld Publications, 2001), 127.

for unity among the religions. One has to ask, however, if this non-critical idea of openness and tolerance does not carry the very risk of indifference, relativity and compromise which he speaks against. In the end, Christians must learn to speak in love the message that there is no other way to God except through Jesus Christ. We are reminded of Jesus' saying, "He who is not with me is against me, and he who does not gather with me scatters" (Matt 12:30; Luke 11:23).

Summary and Implications

M. M. Thomas, to a much greater degree than Devanandan, brings a liberal theological style that leads to an open compromise with other faiths. Thomas, while favoring formal dialogue with people of other faiths, went too far in looking for elements of truth in non-Christian ideologies and religions. Thomas begins his theology with people rather than with solid biblical foundations. This led to Thomas giving up the uniqueness of the Christian gospel in favor of integration and syncretization with other socio-philosophical perspectives. More human-centered than God-centered, Thomas' theology sought to deal first with the corporate issues of power structures, dehumanization, injustices and historic social development, rather than with personal salvation through the gospel of the one and only Lord and Savior Jesus Christ.

The pluralist theologian John Hick and the reformist Catholic theologian Hans Küng do stand out among Christian theologians of the Twentieth Century as having courage and insight to discuss "State-after-Death" in dialogue with world religions. In our engagement with religious pluralism, we cannot ignore the works of John Hick and Hans Kung. Even though there have been countless missionary practitioners to people of other faiths in the last two hundred years, I am disappointed that no evangelical scholar of repute has engaged seriously with the special issue of "State-after-Death" in relation to the people or the perspectives of other world religions. For this reason, I appreciate the contributions that both John Hick and Hans Küng have made by interacting with the perspectives of world religions, especially in the area of what happens after death.

However, in the process of engaging the perspectives of other faiths, both have strayed from a Scriptural basis for understanding the "State-after-Death." Perhaps Hans Küng wandered off less in this matter than did John Hick, who has moved from being *Christocentric* to *Theocentric*, and finally to *ultimate-Reality-centric*. Even so, their contributions have important implications for the communication of Christian thought to the people of other faiths. It would be fair to say, however, that both are more concerned about the noble goal of peaceful co-existence with people of other faiths, than with lovingly pointing them to the One who has taken upon himself the sins of the world.

4

Hermeneutics for Biblical Perspective

In this chapter, I will consider the methodology to use to understand the biblical perspective of "State-after-Death." I have noted in the Introduction that the purpose of this study is to examine selected views in pluralistic contexts and their relationship to the Bible and the early church's views to seek a more effective model of theology of "State-after-Death" in pluralistic contexts. "What does it mean to be 'biblical'?," as asked by the evangelical theologian and scholar Kevin Vanhoozer. Vanhoozer notes, "how easy it is to use Scripture to prove this or that doctrine, or to justify this or that practice, only to be accused of distorting the text."[1] It is obvious that, in the history of the Christian church, all theologies or theological traditions are based upon distinct interpretations of biblical texts. Yet, as Vanhoozer says, "If theology is largely biblical interpretation, then it is important to work with sound hermeneutic principles."[2] Thus, it is crucial to determine sound methodological principles that must be followed to "correctly handle the Word of Truth" (2 Tim 2:15).

There are many publications on the subject of hermeneutics in general, and "Biblical Hermeneutics" in particular. Since it is impossible to assess all of them in this study, I will choose to deal with Anthony C. Thiselton, a well-known scholar and a leading exponent of the *multidisciplinary* approach to biblical hermeneutics. I shall also consider the work of the New Testament scholar, Grant R. Osborne in his, *The Hermeneutical Spiral*, and the recent work of Kevin J. Vanhoozer, *Is There a Meaning in This Text?*

---

1. Kevin J. Vanhoozer, *Is There a Meaning in This Text?: The Bible, the Reader, and the Morality of Literary Knowledge* (Grand Rapids, MI: Zondervan, 1998), 9.
2. Ibid.

Definition and Scope

The term, "hermeneutics," is derived from a Greek verb 'ερμηνευω which means "to interpret." Thiselton defines 'hermeneutics' briefly as, "the theory of interpretation."[3] While traditionally, hermeneutics meant quite narrowly "the study of rules or principles for the interpretation of particular texts," Thiselton points out that hermeneutics is concerned with "the interpretation and understanding of any act of communication," be it written, verbal or symbolic.[4] Osborne notes that traditionally, hermeneutics meant, the "science . . . for interpreting an individual author's meaning" but many tend to define it as an "elucidation of a text's present meaning rather than of its original intent."[5] Osborne argues for the importance of original meaning without neglecting also the applied component. For him "hermeneutics encompasses both what it meant and what it means," that is, "hermeneutics is the overall term while exegesis and 'contextualization' (the crosscultural communication of a text's significance for today) are the two aspects of that larger task." Osborne continues,

> Three perspectives are critical to a proper understanding of the interpretive task. First, hermeneutics is a science, since it provides a logical, orderly classification of the laws of interpretation . . . Second, hermeneutics is an art, for it is an acquired skill demanding both imagination and an ability to apply the "laws" to selected passages or books . . . Third and most important, hermeneutics when utilized to interpret Scripture is a spiritual act, depending upon the leading of the Holy Spirit.[6]

However, according to Thiselton, many theorists see hermeneutics raising "prior and more fundamental questions about the very nature of language, meaning, communication and understanding."[7] Thus, for Thiselton, "hermeneutics,"

> involves an examination of the whole interpretative process. This raises issues in the philosophy of language, theories of meaning,

---

3. Anthony C. Thiselton, "Hermeneutics," in *New Dictionary of Theology*, eds. Sinclair B. Ferguson, David F. Wright and J. I. Packer (Downers Grove, IL: InterVarsity, 1988), 293.
4. Ibid.
5. Grant R. Osborne, *The Hermeneutical Spiral: A Comprehensive Introduction to Biblical Interpretation* (Downers Grove, IL: InterVarsity, 1991), 5.
6. Ibid.
7. Thiselton, "Hermeneutics," 293.

literary theory, and semiotics (theory of signs), as well as, in biblical hermeneutics, those which also arise in biblical studies and in Christian theology.[8]

Thiselton points out, further, that hermeneutics is no longer considered merely "a supplementary tool" for "correct" interpretation, but rather "a profound reflection on the very basis and purpose of interpretation and of how we decide what would count in the first place as a 'correct' interpretation."[9] For him, whether we can claim an interpretation is "correct," "productive," "valid" or "responsible" still remains a hermeneutical question. His advice is that we should first, "enquire into the conditions under which any kind of interpretation is possible or appropriate to certain given purposes of reading, writing or understanding."[10]

Finally, Vanhoozer sees "meaning as a *theological* phenomenon, involving a kind of transcendence, and the theory of interpretation as a *theological* task."[11] In spite of the complexity of current debate regarding the theories of interpretation, Vanhoozer says that, "meaning and interpretation are too important to be left to the specialists."[12] Thus, he urges every Christian to tackle the subject of biblical interpretation, personally, for themselves, taking authority from the Protestant emphasis on priesthood of all believers. Vanhoozer challenges the emerging view among some scholars, who hold "meaning as relative to the encounter of text and reader," by a strong defence that "meaning is independent of our attempts to interpret it."[13]

At this point, we must at least recognize the obstacles that block the way through this hermeneutical morass before we overcome them. These are: the distance of time between the text and the reader, the distance of time between the events and their recordings in the text, the interpretive purposes of those who wrote the text, and the differences of culture, language and geographical conditions between the text and the reader.[14] However, this is where the help of the Holy Spirit is crucial for the task of hermeneutics in interpreting Scriptures, as we have seen in Osborne and noted above.

---

8. Ibid.
9. Ibid.
10. Ibid.
11. Vanhoozer, *Is There a Meaning in This Text?*, 9, (emphasis added).
12. Ibid., 10.
13. Ibid.
14. Klein, Blomberg and Hubbard (*Introduction to Biblical Interpretation* [Dallas, TX: Word, 1993]) characterize these obstacles as kinds of distance. These are not dealt with here at length due to the limited scope of this chapter.

The Hermeneutical Spiral

Osborne points to three interdependent levels in a wholistic hermeneutical methodology: "'what *it* meant' (exegesis)," "'what it means to *me*' (devotional)" and "'how to share with *you* what it means to me' (sermonic)."[15] For him, "biblical interpretation entails a 'spiral' from text to context, from its original meaning to its contextualization or significance for the church today."[16] He prefers the image of "spiral" rather than "circle" (proposed by scholars of the New Hermeneutic), as he senses that in "a closed circle" the priority of the text might be lost. For Osborne, it is

> an open-ended movement from the horizon of the text to the horizon of the reader . . . spiralling nearer and nearer to the text's intended meaning as I refine . . . and allow the text to continue to challenge and correct those alternative interpretations, then to guide . . . its significance for . . . today.[17]

Earlier, Thiselton envisaged this interaction of *The Two Horizons* and noted, "The goal of biblical hermeneutics is to bring about an active and meaningful engagement between the interpreter and text, in such a way that the interpreter's own horizon is reshaped and enlarged."[18] Thiselton continued,

> In one sense it is possible to speak, with Gadamer, of the goal . . . as a "fusion" of horizons. In practice, because the interpreter cannot leap out of the historical tradition to which he belongs, the two horizons can never become totally identical; at best they remain separate but close . . . The problem of historical distance . . . should not give undue pessimism . . . If the problems . . . are not trivial, neither are they insoluble, and there is always progress *towards* a fusion of horizons. The Bible . . . does speak today . . . to correct, reshape, and enlarge the interpreter's own horizons.[19]

Furthermore, Thiselton argued for the priority of the horizon of the text, especially for those who believe that God speaks through the Bible today.

> To hear the Bible speak . . . with its due authority, the distinctive horizon of the text must be respected and differentiated in the

---

15. Osborne, *Hermeneutical Spiral*, 6.
16. Ibid.
17. Ibid.
18. Anthony C. Thiselton, *The Two Horizons* (Exeter, UK: The Paternoster Press, 1980), xix.
19. Ibid.

first place from the horizon of the interpreter. This is not only a theological point. As . . . from the writings of Gadamer, it also arises from general hermeneutical theory.[20]

One important point to note is that Thiselton conceived the imagery of "spiral" before Osborne.[21] Thiselton wrote that,

> Although it has now become a fixed . . . term . . . "hermeneutical circle" is in one respect an unfortunate one. For although the center of gravity moves back and forth between the two poles . . . , there is also . . . progressive understanding . . . better conveyed by . . . such image as that of the spiral.[22]

The Process of Interpretation

For Osborne, the interpretation process has ten stages[23] and two main parts: exegetical (textual) research and theological (contextual) research.[24] *Exegetical research* is subdivided into "inductive study," (interaction with the text directly) and "deductive study" (interaction with exegetical tools and scholars' comments and reworking of findings). Inductive study gives us "a preliminary idea regarding the meaning and thought development of the text" and deductive study helps us "to unlock the in-depth message under the surface of the text."[25] These two studies correct one another in the search for the original intended meaning of the text. "One major purpose of deductive study is to take us away from the contemporary meaning of the word-symbols in the text, which, because of our pre-understanding and personal

---

20. Ibid., xx.
21. Ibid., 104; Osborne, *Hermeneutical Spiral*.
22. Thiselton, *Two Horizons*, 104.
23. See Osborne, *Hermeneutical Spiral*, 13. Osborne (Ibid., 14–15) adapted this figure from Eugene A. Nida and Charles R. Taber's study of the process of translation in *The Theory and Practice of Translation* (Leiden: E. J. Brill, 1974) and notes, "The theory is based on the belief that the crosscultural communication of ideas is never a straight-line continuum, for no two languages or cultures are linked that closely. A 'literal' or unitary approach always lead (sic) to miscommunication. Instead, each communication unit must be broken up into 'kernel ideas,' or basic statements, and then reformulated along the lines of the corresponding idioms and thought patterns of the receptor culture. This is necessary not only at the basic level of translation but also at the broader level of interpretation as a whole. It is the exegetical aspect . . . which uncovers the kernel ideas, and the process of contextualization which reformulates them so that they speak with same voice to our culture today."
24. Osborne, *Hermeneutical Spiral*, 12–14.
25. Ibid., 14.

experiences, we cannot help but read back into the text."[26] For Osborne, "genre analysis," is crucial for discovering the originally intended meaning of the text and so he puts it as a major section in his book in between "general" and "applied" hermeneutics.

Finally, *theological research* helps complete the interpretation process by moving from the textual meaning (what it meant) to the contextual meaning (what it means for us today). For Osborne, the "hermeneutical spiral" takes place both at the level of finding original meaning in the exegetical research and also at the level of theological research. In the theological (contextual) research, the spiral moves from biblical theology to systematic theology to homiletical theology, spiraling upwards for a better understanding of the text's significance for our context today.[27] Osborne discusses the ten stages of interpretation in his whole book. Referring to the problem of meaning, he notes, "These . . . are indeed very real and complex . . . difficult philosophical issues involved . . . The appendices discuss the theoretical answer, while the book as a whole attempts to provide the practical solution to this dilemma."[28] Next, we consider the philosophical and theoretical issues of the problem of meaning of the text.

The Problem of Meaning of the Text

The problem of meaning of a text has to do with the inter-relationship between the author, the text itself and its reader. Osborne asks an important question: "The author 'produces' a text while a reader 'studies' a text. Yet which of the three is the primary force in determining its meaning?"[29] He notes that in various proposed theories of meaning, the *focus* has moved from one to the other of the three. He asks, "Since an author is no longer present to explain the meaning . . . is the text 'autonomous' from the author? And since the reader provides the grid by which the text is interpreted, what place does the text itself have in the process of understanding?"[30]

Though some are skeptical about 'Reader-oriented criticism,' Osborne argues that, "the difficulties of objective interpretation are far too great" to

---

26. Ibid.
27. Ibid.
28. Ibid., 7–8.
29. Ibid., 366.
30. Ibid.

ignore its positive points.³¹ This is because all readers look at texts on the basis of their own background and inclinations. He notes that, "It is not only impossible but dangerous to put our knowledge and theoretical tradition aside as we study a biblical text. That very knowledge provides categories for understanding the text itself."³² However, our traditions have the potential to control the text and influence its meaning, and so, the meaning tends to be produced more by us, the readers, than by the text itself. Osborne argues that this should not be and seeks to establish that "the priority of determining the author's intended meaning is the true core of biblical interpretation."³³

Earlier, Thiselton identified the underlying problem in hermeneutics as two-sided (its *Two Horizons*): the 'historical conditioning' of the present reader/interpreter and that of the ancient text.³⁴ Thiselton sees this problem raising four issues.³⁵ First, there is the current interpreter's pre-understanding and its influence in the task of hermeneutics. Second, as we accept this pre-understanding, we should not shift our focus entirely from the past text to the present.³⁶ Third, as the New Testament authors' pre-understanding was theologically informed (e.g. by Christology), so, following their tradition, present interpreters need to "approach the text from a particular theological angle." Fourth, we need to find out what part philosophical description can play to solve these and other problems in our task of hermeneutics.

At the end of his detailed study in *The Two Horizons*, Thiselton concludes that "the use of philosophical description" does assist the interpreters, first of all, "to define the nature of the hermeneutical task."³⁷ Second, it provides "conceptual tools for the interpretation of parts of texts," and third, it assists an interpreter "to detect his own presuppositions and enlarge his own critical capacities." As a result, for Thiselton, the use of philosophical description instead of "leading to a one-sided or distorted interpretation" provides "the interpreter with a broader pre-understanding in relation to which the text may

---

31. Ibid., 367.
32. Ibid.
33. Ibid.
34. Thiselton, *Two Horizons*, 10–17.
35. Ibid., 17–22, 22–23.
36. Thiselton critiques Bultmann's hermeneutics here: "in neglecting to give adequate place to the Old Testament as a history of publicly accessible tradition, Bultmann has made the hermeneutical problem more difficult. For if the hermeneutical question is reduced to a wholly present question about meaning 'for me,' it becomes almost impossible to heed Wittgenstein's warnings about private language" (Thiselton, *Two Horizons*, 23).
37. Thiselton, *Two Horizons*, 445.

speak more clearly in its own right."[38] It would be appropriate for us, at this point, to briefly survey the major historical theories of biblical hermeneutics and what part philosophy may have played in their formulations.

Historical Theories of Hermeneutics

Thiselton[39] reminds us that, though J. C. Dannhauer was probably the first one to have used the term "hermeneutics" in *Hermeneutica Sacra* (Strasburg, 1654), yet "reflection about interpretation and interpretative processes began long before . . . within the Bible itself, whenever earlier traditions or writings are reviewed from the standpoint of later ones." Thiselton points to how Jesus interpreted his death according to the Old Testament and interpreted Old Testament according to his own deeds (e.g. Luke 24:25–27; Greek διερμηνευσεν, "interpreted"). Thiselton also shows that "the theory and practice of allegorical interpretation" (a search for a meaning below the surface of the text) began in the pre-Christian times among some Stoic philosophers, was passed on from Greek thought to Jewish circles and then grew within the Christian church.[40] He notes that Origen argued that Paul used allegorical interpretation whereas some others still argue that Paul used typology, that is, instead of correspondence of *ideas*, typology depends on correspondence of *events*. Thiselton adds,

> Clement of Rome (c. AD 96) provides a very early example of Christian allegorical interpretation . . . Clement of Alexandria, a century later, argued that the interpreter should expect hidden meanings in the biblical writings . . . Origen argued that the interpreter should begin with the plain or grammatical meaning, but should then 'rise from the letter to the spirit.' . . . His own use of allegorical interpretation moved too far in the direction of . . . Gnostic[s] . . . By way of response and reaction, the fathers of Antioch . . . Theodore of Mopsuestia (350–428) and John Chrysostom (344/354–407), opposed the allegorical excesses of Alexandria.[41]

---

38. Ibid.
39. Thiselton, "Hermeneutics," 293ff.
40. Ibid., 294.
41. Ibid.

In the medieval period, Origen's threefold sense of interpretation developed into fourfold (multiple) sense: the literal or letter-sense (the basic meaning), the allegorical or typological sense, the moral sense (significance for practical conduct) and the anagogical sense (the relationship of basic meaning to the fulfillment of God's purposes in eternity).[42] The Reformers then argued that the Bible itself is the final judge of whether the church traditions are valid. Luther stressed that the primary meaning of the Bible is not obscure but clear and Calvin argued that a passage has only one meaning. This does not mean that the Reformers downplayed the importance of hermeneutics; instead, they upheld the necessity of its rigorous task.[43]

In the 17th century, Baruch (Benedict) Spinoza (1632–1677) contended for the importance of querying about a particular biblical text's authorship, date, occasion and purpose. In the 18th century, J. S. Semler (1725–1788) argued that historical-critical enquiry should be made "without reference to doctrine or theology," but Thiselton remarks that, "historical-critical enquiry need not, and indeed should not, exclude theological considerations."[44] Following this, a new era of hermeneutics began with the works of Friedrich Schleiermacher and others followed him in that tradition.

Romanticist Hermeneutical Tradition

The Romanticist Tradition includes Schleiermacher, Wilhelm Dilthey and Emilio Betti. Schleiermacher (1768–1834) felt that the weakness of previous works is that these seem to use hermeneutics only when difficulties arose. Whereas previous scholars used hermeneutics as "an instrumental service-discipline" to validate their *a priori* understanding or assumptions about a text, Schleiermacher tried to disentangle the subject "from what he called 'regional' concerns."[45] Therefore post-Schleiermacher hermeneutics has become "an *interdisciplinary* or *multidisciplinary* subject" dealing with "philosophical issues about the nature of human understanding, linguistic questions about texts, theological enquiries about biblical texts, and social concerns about

---

42. Ibid., 294–295. According to Thiselton, though this four-fold sense may have produced edifying results, yet "often the primary meaning of the text became buried and lost under layers of pious tradition" (Ibid., 295).
43. Thiselton, "Hermeneutics," 295.
44. Ibid.
45. Anthony C. Thiselton, "Biblical Theology and Hermeneutics," in *The Modern Theologians*, ed. David F. Ford (Malden, MA: Blackwell, 1997), 520–521.

interpersonal communicative action."[46] Schleiermacher's hermeneutics involve expertise both in the field of "linguistics (or grammatical)" and in "understanding people (or psychological)," and that an interpreter must "step out of one's own frame of mind into that of the author."[47] Schleiermacher responded to Immanuel Kant's *Critique of Pure Reason* with a theory of understanding in which there were two poles of knowledge: the interpersonal, *relational* (divinatory) part with the critical, *rational* (comparative) part. Divinatory knowledge brings creative understanding and comparative knowledge gives critical understanding. Without rejecting the rational critical testing of comparative method, in keeping with his links with pietism and Romanticism, Schleiermacher does a balancing act and uses the interpersonal, relational divinatory method to capture that which escapes abstract reason.[48]

Wilhelm Dilthey (1833–1911) succeeds Schleiermacher in the Romanticist model and focuses more on the historical reconstruction of the author's life-experience (*Erlebnis*). Thus, Dilthey stresses more the social, interpersonal or "psychological" dimension of Schleiermacher's hermeneutics instead of its grammatical or "linguistic" features.[49] Osborne notes, "Interpretation for him involves the union of subject and object in a historical act of understanding."[50] This is Dilthey's "rediscovery of the I in the Thou," which means one's self is re-discovered in the act of one's reading. Dilthey borrows "the idea of readers identifying with authors" from Schleiermacher but goes further to claim that perhaps the readers can understand the meanings of texts better than the authors themselves.[51] Thus, for both Schleiermacher and Dilthey after him, the hermeneutical key is the "flow of life" ("stream of life" in Wittgenstein's

---

46. Ibid., 521.
47. Anthony C. Thiselton, *New Horizons in Hermeneutics* (Grand Rapids, MI: Zondervan, 1992), 206–207; Thiselton, "Biblical Theology and Hermeneutics," 521; Thiselton, *Interpreting God and the Postmodern Self* (Grand Rapids, MI: Eerdmans, 1995), 54; Osborne, *Hermeneutical Spiral*, 368. Thiselton identifies following major themes in Schleiermacher's system of hermeneutics: "(a) understanding consists in re-experiencing the mental processes of the author of a text; (b) it is grasping the meaning of the parts through divining the whole, and understanding the whole through grasping the parts; (c) it involves perceiving the individuality of the author as a human user of shared language; (d) it seeks to understand more than a text may have explicitly expressed, and hence to achieve a fuller grasp of the author's thoughts or purpose than the author articulated or perhaps understood" (Thiselton, *New Horizons in Hermeneutics*, 216).
48. Thiselton, *Interpreting God*, 41–42.
49. Thiselton, "Biblical Theology and Hermeneutics," 512; Osborne, *Hermeneutical Spiral*, 368.
50. Osborne, *Hermeneutical Spiral*, 368.
51. Ibid., 369.

terms) and to "re-live" the authors' life-experiences is to reconstruct their life-worlds and attempt to enter these life-worlds by sharing in their forms ("form of life" in Wittgenstein's terms).[52]

The next important personality of the Romanticist tradition is Emilio Betti (1890–1968) who believes that hermeneutics as an intellectual discipline and educational training is essential for the life of a society.[53] This is because when people recognize that an interpretation is open to correction and revision it promotes greater tolerance among them. Following Schleiermacher, Betti sees interpretation, mainly as the reverse process to that of composition, in which interpreters need to reach behind the words of the text to the life-experience that produced them and the main train of thought behind them.[54] Thus, for Betti, "imaginative *reconstruction* . . . is required for understanding."[55]

Existentialist Model of Hermeneutics

Instead of the Romanticist historical reconstruction of author's life-world, the Existentialist model focused on the text's present effect on readers. This paradigm shift is noticed in Karl Barth's early writings and in Rudolf Bultmann.[56] Instead of a "purely historical enquiry," Thiselton notes that Barth and Bultmann wanted "to let the New Testament texts speak as proclamation, as address, as promise or as warning" to the present reader.[57] Thiselton contends that Bultmann (1884–1976) was influenced by many ideas including that of Kierkegaard and early Heidegger:

> Behind both the dialectical theology of the early Barth and the hermeneutical theory of Bultmann stood the existentialist thought of Kierkegaard, although in the case of Bultmann a multiplicity of influences were at work ranging from Neo-Kantianism and the early Heidegger to Lutheran pietism and form criticism.[58]

Thiselton argues that the Existentialist model failed to be a new beginning for "reader-related interpretation" because "existentialism is profoundly

---

52. Thiselton, *New Horizons in Hermeneutics*, 559.
53. Thiselton, "Hermeneutics," 296; *New Horizons in Hermeneutics*, 252.
54. Thiselton, "Hermeneutics," 296; *New Horizons in Hermeneutics*, 252.
55. Thiselton, *New Horizons in Hermeneutics*, 252.
56. Ibid., 272.
57. Ibid.
58. Ibid.

individualistic," which is opposite of the "post-Gadamerian emphases on the positive role of traditions and reading-communities."[59] Also, a needless polarization is set up between the two presumed *alternatives* of language: "factual, descriptive functions" against "value-laden, proclamatory, and transforming functions." This is done to show that the proclamatory functions only could or should act independently of the factual, descriptive functions of language. Discussing early Heidegger's influence on Bultmann, Thiselton continues,

> In theology, Rudolf Bultmann shared some . . . of Heidegger's perspectives. Bultmann believed that the biblical writings only apparently or secondarily presented generalizing and descriptive statements about God and man. Their primary purpose, he urged, was the existential or practical function of calling persons to appropriate attitudes and responses of will. For example, the utterance, "God will judge the world" is to be interpreted less as a statement about a future event than as a call to responsibility before God in the present moment. The affirmation "Jesus is Lord" represents not so much a statement about Christ's cosmic status as a confession that Christ directs and controls my own life.[60]

However, Thiselton also thinks that Existentialist hermeneutics contributed constructively in that it highlighted the importance of 'reader-situations' in biblical studies.[61] He adds that, "within a frame in which the role of the community in interpretation" is recognized, "a Kierkegaardian stress on the *disruption* of social and religious convention in transforming and creative understanding has a valuable place as a *supplementary* hermeneutical model."[62] The biblical authors, and more specifically Jesus and Paul, in their mode of communication were concerned about the nature of their audience and readers.[63] For Thiselton, 1 Corinthians 9:20–23 and Acts 14:15–18, 17:22–31 show Paul entered into the "world" of his readers and hearers. Thus, the Existentialist model of hermeneutics discovered the dimension of "self-

---

59. Ibid.
60. Thiselton, "Hermeneutics," 296.
61. Thiselton, *New Horizons in Hermeneutics*, 272–273.
62. Ibid., 273.
63. Thiselton (*New Horizons in Hermeneutics*, 273) refers to J. Arthur Baird's note on T. W. Manson's study on the language of Jesus in which Manson claimed that Jesus' teachings were conditioned by the nature of his audience.

involvement" and "audience-related address" in these texts which the texts presume.[64]

For Thiselton,[65] the heart of the problem of Bultmann's hermeneutics is the relation between the self-involving (or existential) functions of language and the language that asserts that certain statements are facts. Thiselton notes, "the more heavily they emphasize the language of self-involvement, human experience, and divine address, the further they move away from *description, narrative, report, and statement.*"[66] Thus, for Bultmann, it became more a matter of "either-or" rather than a "both-and" issue. Thiselton shows, from the conclusion of Bultmann's *Theology of the New Testament*, that for Bultmann, the interpreter can *either* view the New Testament as a source for the reconstruction of history *or* view it as writings that have something to say to the present, but it cannot be *both.*[67] Thiselton shows that, for Bultmann, "myth" is not merely imagery used to describe the transcendent, even though this is one of his three definitions.[68] Rather, "myth" *appears* to portray events such as atonement and resurrection as "objective" events, as historically true, but in reality *the form* of the language disguises *the function* of the language and so these are not objective events. This leads Thiselton to conclude that Bultmann's hermeneutical program of demythologizing is one-sided and "would be disastrous for theology and do violence to our understanding of the New Testament if it is regarded as a comprehensive hermeneutic."[69] However, Thiselton sees the way forward in the work of Donald Evans, J.L. Austin and others (scholars of "speech-act" theory) who "show that self-involving language *pre-supposes,* rather than offers an *alternative* to, the language which makes truth-claims about states of affairs or events."[70]

Gadamer's Model of Hermeneutics

Though related to the Existentialist model, following his later works, Heidegger's student, Hans-Georg Gadamer (b.1900) presents an ontological

---

64. Thiselton, *New Horizons in Hermeneutics*, 273.
65. Ibid., 275.
66. Ibid.
67. Ibid. Thiselton discusses in detail in (*Two Horizons*, 205–292) what influenced Bultmann to "polarize the either/or of history and faith, or description and address, with such uncompromising sharpness" (*New Horizons in Hermeneutics*, 275).
68. Thiselton, *New Horizons in Hermeneutics*, 281–282.
69. Ibid., 282.
70. Ibid.

model of hermeneutics.[71] In Gadamer's model "language and meaning" relate to "the disclosure of truth" in such a way that it "transcends and calls attention to the reality of the 'world' projected and mediated by a work of art."[72] Thiselton explains it in this way:

> A game, or a work of art, projects a "world" which shapes the judgments of the player or the interpreter who enters it. The reality of a game clearly transcends the content of the consciousness of a player; its structure, its goals, and its variable shape as a series of particular temporal events, determine what counts as appropriate knowledge and action for the player. No one game is simply a replica of another. Similarly interpretation or understanding is not static. As a paradigm of hermeneutics, Gadamer's work offers a distinctive third approach, in contrast to the so-called Romanticist models of Schleiermacher and Dilthey, and to the existentialist models of Bultmann and others.[73]

Gadamer felt that post-Enlightenment rationalism was wrong when insisting on "'method' as the means of grasping truth."[74] For Gadamer, "method" is "a hindrance to truth," as it follows too closely "the generalizing techniques of science" and tries to "determine in advance the terms on which truth should be understood. Deceived by method in science, an interpreter tries to 'master' texts, life, or art, rather than letting them confront him or her on their own terms."[75] For Gadamer, Descartes' Enlightenment "method" of "the total reconstruction of all truths by reason" is misconceived. Instead, Gadamer calls us to get back to the elements present in the classical concept of wisdom. For "wisdom goes deeper than knowledge and draws on tradition for transmitting reinterpretations and actualizations of truth in events" and does not just "subsume the individual under a universal category."[76]

Osborne notes that Gadamer is not interested in ascertaining the author's intent because, for Gadamer, the text has gone through an alienation from the

---

71. Thiselton (*New Horizons in Hermeneutics*, 10) notes, for Gadamer, "understanding and conscious judgments are founded on broader realities accessible through language as, in principle, a universal phenomenon. In this sense, Gadamer sees his hermeneutics as taking an *ontological* turn towards language." However, for Gadamer, "the *actualizations* of this broad linguistic tradition occur only in *changing, historically-finite, events*."
72. Thiselton, "Hermeneutics," 296.
73. Thiselton, *New Horizons in Hermeneutics*, 10.
74. Ibid., 6.
75. Thiselton, "Biblical Theology and Hermeneutics," 530.
76. Ibid.

author in the act of writing.⁷⁷ Osborne explains Gadamer's view in this way: "when I study those passages where Paul reflects on his past life . . . I do not study Paul but the texts he wrote, and the texts speak to me in my present situation rather than re-create the original author's past situation."⁷⁸ Gadamer uses interpreter's "pre-understanding" in a positive way compared to the Enlightenment's view of it as a barrier to understanding. As the interpreter with "pre-understanding" questions the text, the thought-world of the text in dialogue with the interpreter reshape the asked questions. Thus, in Gadamer's "hermeneutical circle" (originally from Fuchs and Ebeling, the founders of New Hermeneutic), there is a "fusion of horizons," the horizons of past text and present interpreter merge.⁷⁹ Osborne concludes,

> In sum, Gadamer's aesthetic hermeneutic moves from the author and the text to a union of text and reader, with roots in the present rather than in the past. Yet there are several weaknesses inherent to this theory. As is true also of the New Hermeneutic, *it is not clear how Gadamer avoids the danger of subjective interpretation.* For him there are two controls against subjectivity – the past horizon of the text and the present community of the interpreters . . . However, *there are no clear criteria for avoiding subjectivism.* In fact, each moment of reading can produce a new and innovative understanding.
>
> Also, *Gadamer does not develop a methodology for distinguishing true from false interpretation . . . develops no criteria for noting inadequate understandings . . . has an uncritical view of the role of the reader in interpretation* . . . Finally, *Gadamer gives tradition an uncritical role in the act of coming-to-understanding* . . . However, *there is no stability in this approach, for tradition is ever developing and changing depending on the community and the data.*⁸⁰

Thiselton notes that Gadamer sees tradition and its effects in a more positive way than Heidegger.⁸¹ For Gadamer, tradition, with its prejudices, does transmit wisdom and "allows for a 'formation' (*Bildung*) which 'builds.'

---

77. Osborne, *Hermeneutical Spiral*, 369–370.
78. Ibid., 370.
79. Ibid.
80. Ibid., 371 (emphasis added).
81. Thiselton, "Biblical Theology and Hermeneutics," 531.

In particular, this process is achieved through a mutual respect between those within different horizons, through a genuine 'listening,' each to the other, in dialogue."[82] Thiselton feels this brings to theology a new sense of understanding of what it means to "listen" to "the other," the text or God or another person, without imposing our own terms which we have chosen as the "grid" or "method." Thiselton comments,

> This has profound consequences for reappraisals of reason. Reason alone is not enough; but credulity alone would not be "wisdom." Like Hegel and Wittgenstein, Gadamer's creative genius treads a razor edge from which it can fall into either of two opposite difficulties. Some see Gadamer as upholding tradition; others see him as legitimizing a move toward contextual relativism and postmodernism. Both responses are partly true and partly false, and demand that we read Gadamer with care.[83]

More than others, Gadamer is not only credited for formulating a general hermeneutical theory, but also his model of hermeneutics is considered a turning point in the history of hermeneutical theories. Though, there are some literary theories (Structuralism, Reader-Response Criticism and Deconstruction)[84] that have impacted hermeneutics, Thiselton shows post-Gadamerian hermeneutics have mainly been responses to Gadamer's model.

---

82. Ibid.
83. Ibid.
84. Osborne (*Hermeneutical Spiral*, 371–385) discusses these in detail. He notes, Structuralism is "unconcerned with the author's intended meaning and seek only to uncover the structure behind the writer's expressed thought, the 'common world' of the underlying codes that address us directly" (Ibid., 373) and "with structuralism and post-structuralism we have moved even further from the object/text to the subject/reader" (Ibid., 376); he notes, Reader-Response Critics like Stanley Fish, "have a skeptical attitude toward the author and the text, they have an uncritical . . . attitude toward interpretive communities and reading strategies" (Ibid., 380); and that in Deconstruction theories "readers deconstruct not only the original author-text referent but also all 'understandings' of the text throughout history" (Ibid., 383). Thiselton includes Reader-Response Criticism in Socio-Pragmatic model of post-Gadamerian hermeneutics, and argues that, though Deconstruction theories may have some value, "they remain primarily negative and context-dependent" and that "'undoing' in Paul de Man, and 'play' in Derrida, involves something more radical than correcting traditions" (Thiselton, *New Horizons in Hermeneutics*, 590).

Post-Gadamerian Hermeneutics

Thiselton insightfully points out that since Gadamer there have been four distinct directions of response to his hermeneutics.[85] Thiselton sums it up,

> If Gadamer's work is perceived as a crossroads or as an intersection, some theorists move forward with a firmer emphasis on *metacritical evaluations* of theoretical criteria and pragmatic operations. Others move in the direction of exploring the socio-ethical aspects of historical tradition and language, and expound a hermeneutics which embodies a *socially relevant critical theory*. A third . . . leads towards the very opposite conclusion. The finite, context-relative actualizations of an otherwise inaccessible reality and truth are perceived to inhibit any metacritical exploration, and hermeneutics comes to represent a descriptive account, even a narrative account, of *the pragmatic effects of texts within given social communities*. Finally, some attempt to turn back from Gadamer's position, and offer defenses of more *traditional* approaches in hermeneutics.[86]

First, the *Metacritical* direction follows Gadamer's stress on "practical wisdom" rather than "theoretical reason." As the practical judgments of each community are continually being passed on through the historical flow of tradition, "established patterns and practices become embedded in language" which "gives contingent, historically finite, conscious, acts of judgment their currency."[87] Gadamer did not trust the scientific "method" of Enlightenment rationalism, as it reflected theory separated from the "contextual contingencies," the contingent events of historical contexts. For him, "practical wisdom" is based on truth realized from contextual events. For Gadamer, "method" is only "a derivative and over-generalized tool" but "rationality rests on a broader base."[88] These insights led to the formation of a metacritical perspective. Thiselton noted earlier that the key question of *metacriticism* is:

> can we critically rank the different criteria by which we judge what counts as meaningful or productive effects of texts within

---

85. Thiselton, *New Horizons in Hermeneutics*, 11–16.
86. Ibid., 11.
87. Ibid.
88. Ibid.

this or that context in life? . . . Some trans-contextual basis is sought for the comparative evaluation of contextual criteria of interpretation and indeed for the purposes in relation to which each set of criteria gains its currency.[89]

Thus we see, in metacriticism, there is a search for a trans-contextual or transcendental basis by which a comparative evaluation can be made of a critic's own personal and contextual agenda. The metacritical perspective was followed and further modified by Wolfhart Pannenberg, Jürgen Habermas, and Karl-Otto Apel, and also Paul Ricoeur.[90] In my judgment, the metacritical perspective is most essential today due to the unusual rise of conflicting claims of truth in our post-modern pluralistic era.

Second, the *Socio-Pragmatic* model follows Gadamer's model in the opposite direction to that of the *metacritical* one and argues that, "Since each 'actualization' of texts or of historical language differs from previous or subsequent actualizations, it is possible to argue that all particularizations of truth remain radically context-relative."[91] As two performances of a game are not exact replicas, according to socio-pragmatic model, "we cannot predict, through some overview or metacritical formula, how one . . . will differ from another in a new context."[92] Richard Rorty and Stanley Fish are the best-known representatives of this context-relative socio-pragmatic model of hermeneutics. Stanley Fish is also well known as a proponent of "Reader-Response Criticism" of literary theories. Thiselton refers to Christopher Norris (who sees this approach as an *American "pragmatist cultural politics"*) and Cornel West (a black American theologian) as he critiques Rorty and Fish:

> Norris sees . . . social powerlessness and philosophical vulnerability of Rorty's approach. Rorty, he urges, provides an example of how social pragmatism professes open-minded tolerance while in practice tending to privilege its own liberal cultural values. Its status quo philosophy . . . can only allow the oppressed to remain oppressed, for it offers no basis . . . to challenge the status quo . . . Cornel West . . . attacks the bland and inept incapacity

---

89. Ibid., 6.
90. Thiselton (*New Horizons in Hermeneutics*, 358–359) shows that, for Ricoeur, hermeneutics is a metacritical discipline, and quotes him, "hermeneutics ultimately claims to set itself up as a critique of critique, or *meta-critique*." I will cover Habermas, Pannenberg and Apel under socio-critical model and deal with Ricoeur separately.
91. Thiselton, *New Horizons in Hermeneutics*, 11.
92. Ibid., 12.

of socio-pragmatic philosophy to offer socio-critical theory or norms for action. West asks: "Does Rorty's neo-pragmatism only kick the philosophical props from under bourgeois capitalist societies, and require no change in our cultural and political practices?" West notes that Dewey himself, to whom Rorty . . . appeals, acknowledges that wholesale relativist historicism has only four possible consequences: either a paralyzing scepticism, or the view that "might is right", or sheer intuitionism, or a self-situating contextualism. None of these four alternatives provides a critical theory for social action, as Rorty and Fish concede.[93]

Thiselton[94] continues to show the difficulty and ineffectiveness of such pluralism in Rorty's socio-pragmatic model of hermeneutics, which will be useful for us as we deal with pluralistic perspectives of "State-after-Death." Thiselton notes,

> Rorty seeks painfully and unsuccessfully to address this moral dilemma . . . The liberal pluralist within him sees moral progress in the acknowledgement that even the most diverse people are somehow "like us". But the ironist within him can define a universal only in negative terms: neither we nor our institutions can really know what it is like for someone else to suffer loss or pain. Like . . . the ancient sceptics, the only universal is one of renunciation. But this seemingly humble and tolerant pluralism while . . . appearing to affirm minorities and the weak, in practice can offer no argument for constraints upon those who oppress them. Indeed Rorty acknowledges . . . he simply has no answer of principle to the question "why not be cruel?" *The mistake is to confuse the role of historical contingency and contextualism in challenging the status of some absolutized foundationalism outside time, place, and history, with a positive dialectical relation between contextual contingency and ongoing metacritical exploration and testing in the form of an open system . . . in which neither contingent life-world nor explanatory system has the last word, but contribute to some interactive whole.*[95]

---

93. Ibid., 400–401.
94. Ibid., 401.
95. Ibid. (emphasis added).

Third, the *Socio-Critical* direction of post-Gadamerian hermeneutics is seen in the works of Jürgen Habermas, Wolfhart Pannenberg and Karl-Otto Apel, with the concern for the socio-ethical implications of biblical hermeneutics. By using some metacritical socio-ethical values, they aim to uncover unconscious social and ideological distortions in the interpretation of texts. Thiselton summarizes Habermas, Pannenberg and Apel's model of socio-critical hermeneutics unlike Rorty and Fish's model in this way:

> They argue that *given social interests* and not merely bare, finite contextual contingencies, lie behind different actualizations of texts or of truth. The task of *socio-critical* hermeneutics is to unmask these social interests through an emancipatory technique, which serves freedom, justice, and truth. In his earlier work Habermas examines the relation between knowledge and human "interests". In his later work, he argues convincingly that the questions raised by hermeneutics at a metacritical and social level necessitate exploration of *both* the historically finite contingencies of the hermeneutical *life-world* and a broader trans-contextual critique involving, in some sense, *system*. Pannenberg's volume *Theology and the Philosophy of Science* reflects a similar dual concern, but with perhaps a more controlling interest in system.
>
> Karl-Otto Apel also attempts to move beyond the given of social and linguistic practices in particular contexts to some kind of provisional or anticipatory notion of the universal as a basis for metacriticism. But like Gadamer, he appreciates the contextual boundaries of historical finitude. Following Wittgenstein, he accepts the particularity of given language-games in the public world. But unlike Rorty and Fish, Apel does not believe that this locks the interpreter or the philosopher into some localized ethnocentric world. Apel also seeks a broader understanding of human rationality, and refuses to restrict enquiry to the socio-pragmatic level. Human inter-subjectivity, he argues, reaches beyond particular communities.[96]

The fourth direction of post-Gadamerian hermeneutics, for Thiselton, is a return to more traditional models of hermeneutics. E.D. Hirsch brings this

---

96. Thiselton, *New Horizons in Hermeneutics*, 12.

traditional model of the priority of author's intention and meaning of the text back into the task of hermeneutics. Osborne comments,

> *Meaning* for Hirsch is grounded in the author's choice of language and so is *unchanging*, while *significance* applies that *meaning . . . so does change*. While relativists (he calls them "cognitive atheists") deny such a distinction, Hirsch finds support in Husserl's concept of "brackets." The mind "brackets" alien information until it can work back to it. In this way, Hirsch argues, *one can move behind preunderstanding to the text and discover the author's intended meaning.*[97]

While some defend Hirsch's model, Thiselton notes, others consider it to be "'a hermeneutics of innocence' which cannot be sustained in a post-Gadamerian era."[98] Thiselton affirms Hirsch's warnings against a radical surrender of "humanist paradigms without remainder in exchange for postmodernist assumptions" and contends that many of Hirsch's arguments are true for certain kinds of text, but "his largely pre-Wittgensteinian conceptual and methodological tools do not match the complexity of the issues formulated in post-Gadamerian theory."[99] For Thiselton, this is because,

> First, Hirsch's language about the importance of author's intention needs to be transposed into the kind of post-Wittgensteinian theoretical terms adopted by Searle and others in claims about the "directedness" of texts. (This is distinct from Hirsch's use of Wittgenstein's "language Game" for genre) . . . Issues . . . about human agency and linguistic communicative interaction need to be introduced . . . also. Second, it only postpones rather than solves the problem if we follow Hirsch in restricting "meaning" to a largely *semantic* notion of meaning or only to more straightforward models of inter-personal communication. It does not help to use the term "significance" as a catch-all for more complex and more context-relative examples as if these functioned only as subjective connotations, all of the same kind. What meaning *is*, as Wittgenstein observes, depends on

---
97. Osborne, *Hermeneutical Spiral*, 393 (emphasis added).
98. Thiselton, *New Horizons in Hermeneutics*, 13.
99. Ibid.

the language-game from within which meaning-currency is drawn.[100]

However, while critiquing Hirsch's traditional model, Thiselton is not trying "to reduce all kinds of textual meaning to socio-pragmatic meaning-*effects*" because, he argues, "as Wittgenstein urges, we presuppose some kind of criteria which will allow us to determine when some 'mistake' or misunderstanding has occurred" and that "If meaning were only meaning-effects, texts could never be misunderstood."[101] Thiselton contends,

> Intersubjective regularities in the public world prevent the collapse of communicative meaning into what Wittgenstein termed . . . "private" language, i.e. that for which no criteria of *what might count as a mistake* could be sustained. This provides a more constructive ground on which to examine the various claims of post-Gadamerian hermeneutics than to turn back to Hirsch's own over-simplified arguments.[102]

Ricoeur's Hermeneutics of Suspicion

Finally, a further response of post-Gadamerian hermeneutics in the *metacritical* direction is that of Paul Ricoeur, emerging from "psycho-analytic" models, and called a "hermeneutic of suspicion."[103] Although the views of Freud, Marx and Nietzsche (three masters of suspicion) seem to be contrary to that of Christian theology, for Thiselton, "their insistence that the human mind can deceive itself . . . in the interests of individual or of social power, resonates with biblical . . . assertions about the deceitfulness . . . and duplicity of the human heart."[104] Thiselton continues,

> On this basis Ricoeur presses into the service of hermeneutics the critical tools of Freudian theory. Freud's interpretation of dreams, and his notions of dream-text and dream work, offer parallels for Ricoeur with interpretations of myths, symbols, metaphors, and other multi-layered or double-layered texts. Freud's concept of overdetermination underlines the complexity

---

100. Ibid.
101. Ibid.
102. Ibid.
103. Ibid., 13–14.
104. Ibid., 14.

of interpreting complex processes for which different levels of explanation can be suggested, or in which different levels of understanding may operate.

... Critical tools serve to destroy the idols which we project into the sacred Word...[105]

For Thiselton, Paul Ricoeur (b. 1913) is probably of same stature as Gadamer "in the extent of his influence on, and importance for, late twentieth-century hermeneutical theory."[106] Thiselton thinks this is because Ricoeur's theory has

> *constructively interdisciplinary* character. [Ricoeur] began with interests in phenomenology and existentialism and moved into questions of interpretation in linguistic theory, psychoanalysis, structuralism, theories of texts, metaphor, and narrative and Christian theology and religions.[107]

This is Ricoeur's main contribution and is similar to Habermas, Apel and Pannenberg. Contrary to Gadamer and Rorty, Ricoeur insisted on "explanation" (method) and "understanding" (truth) be kept together in a dialectical relationship.[108] Having rejected "method," Ricoeur felt, Gadamer has "left no metacritical or even critical procedure for testing the validity of traditions in effective-historical consciousness."[109] For Ricoeur, "hermeneutics properly remains a metacritical discipline" which means both the unmasking task of "explanation" and the creative task of "understanding."[110] Thiselton explains,

> Where explanation is critical, socio-critical, or metacritical, understanding may nevertheless operate at a "post-critical" level. Explanation entails the *willingness to expose and to abolish idols* which are merely projections of the human will; understanding requires *a willingness to listen with openness to symbols* and to "indirect" language. The two major areas of hermeneutics, explanation and understanding, thus invite respectively metacritical or socio-critical *suspicion* which in turn bring about re-valuations, and also post-critical *retrieval* embodying

---

105. Ibid., 14.
106. Ibid., 344.
107. Ibid., 344–345.
108. Ibid., 344, 348.
109. Ibid., 344.
110. Ibid.

openness towards a new "possibility" which may entail renewal or change. For humankind is fundamentally finite and deeply fallible, and yet is also able to reach "beyond" to what Heidegger termed "possibility."[111]

Thus, Thiselton also notes that, "Side by side with a critical use of tools of suspicion, Ricoeur also aims to recover the power of symbols, metaphor, and narrative . . . A hermeneutic of retrieval aims at restoring the power of language for creative and productive purposes."[112] Ricoeur thinks that, "cerebral concepts and factual reports *reflect already-perceived actualities*, metaphors and narratives *create possible ways of seeing or understanding* the world and human life."[113] Thus, for Ricoeur, "Metaphor produces *new possibilities* of imagination and vision; narrative creates *new configurations* which structure individual or corporate experience."[114] Following Heidegger, Ricoeur says that, metaphors do not create *actuality* but *possibility* and calls this the "potentiality-for-being."[115] Thiselton comments,

> If metaphor, therefore, presents *possibility* rather than *actuality* it is arguable that metaphoric discourse can open up new understanding more readily than purely descriptive or scientific statement. Ricoeur's hermeneutics of metaphor also reflects the "turn" of the later Heidegger increasingly towards poetry and art, and his relative disparagement of scientific or conceptual thinking as merely "calculative."[116]

Thiselton quotes the heart of Ricoeur's view of metaphor, "Metaphor presents itself as a strategy of discourse that, while preserving and developing the creative powers of language, preserves and develops the *heuristic* power wielded by *Fiction*."[117] Yet, for Ricoeur, metaphor does say "something about reality." Ricoeur argues that metaphor is a "dual linking of 'fiction' and 're-description'" and is not a substitute "for an ordinary word which one could have found in the same place."[118] Thiselton notes, "Ricoeur rejects, then, the tradition that views metaphor as mere ornament, together with the positivistic

---

111. Ibid., 344.
112. Ibid., 14.
113. Ibid., 351.
114. Ibid.
115. Ibid.
116. Ibid., 352.
117. Ibid.
118. Ibid., 352–353.

view . . . that metaphor constitutes a generally misleading abuse of language, which encourages illusion."[119]

However, Ricoeur's more innovative and influential contribution in hermeneutics is to knit this view of metaphor with his approach to narrative. Ricoeur thinks that, "With narrative, the semantic innovation lies in the inventing of another work of synthesis – a plot. By [which] . . . goals, causes, and chance *are brought together within the temporal unity of a whole and complete account.*"[120] For Ricoeur, this synthesis of the heterogeneous connects narrative with metaphor. "But while a metaphor or a conceptual theme may transpose scattered aspects of thought into some coherent working structure, Ricoeur stresses that the narrative orders scattered sequential *experiences and events* into a *coherent structure of time.*"[121] Thiselton notes that, following established narrative theory, Ricoeur makes a "distinction between '*plot*' as a *construct of human time* and '*story*' as a sequence of events, situations, and settings in *natural time.*"[122]

For Ricoeur, narrative components both contribute to the plot to build a "whole," and derive their significance from their place within the whole. The "whole" is the narrative-world of the reader and Ricoeur contends that, when this "re-figured" world grabs the reader, the narrative-effects are "revelatory and transformative." For Ricoeur, "The effects of fiction, revelation, and transformation are essentially the effects of reading."[123] It is important for us to understand Ricoeur's position on "historical" narrative in relation to "fictional" narrative. Thiselton notes,

> Ricoeur believes that "the way has been paved for a full recognition of the fictional character of history by the general critique of the positivistic epistemology of history." Whereas . . . for positivists, the historian's work is "to unearth facts," in contemporary epistemology history becomes "imaginative reconstruction." The decisive new factor, Ricoeur believes, is the view of history as "a literary artifact" which has emerged from literary theory and from semiotics . . . The historian *makes* the story into a completed whole, and writes from a given vantage-point, perhaps adding a conceptual argument about "what it adds up to." Yet Ricoeur is

---

119. Ibid., 353.
120. Ibid., 354.
121. Ibid.
122. Ibid.
123. Ibid., 355.

unwilling to *identify* historical narrative with fiction . . . "History is both a literary artifact *and* a representation of reality." On the other hand, "fiction" and "representation of reality," Ricoeur insists, "are not antithetical terms."

Ricoeur concludes: "Both history and fiction refer to human actions, although they do so on the basis of two different referential claims. Only history may articulate its referential claim in compliance with rules of evidence common to the whole body of science . . . Fictional narratives may assert a referential claim of another kind, appropriate to the split reference of poetic discourse." . . . Although, therefore, both fiction and history are "true," they are true in different senses.[124]

Thiselton notes that Vanhoozer has reservations about Ricoeur's ambivalence regarding the relation between history and fiction. Thiselton quotes Vanhoozer, "Ricoeur fears that descriptive language stifles the passion for the possible by confining us within the limits of the present, and closes our imagination to the future."[125]

Thiselton asks whether Ricoeur has restricted the "reference" in historical narrative from reaching "beyond intra-literary and intra-linguistic world of 'refiguration'" by assigning "such a decisive role to the transforming and revelatory power of plot-configuration and plot-movement" in fiction.[126] This is Vanhoozer's argument too as he thinks Ricoeur is approaching biblical narrative in the same way as the scholars of the New Hermeneutic. Vanhoozer sees Ricoeur as having merely switched "subjectivity" to a new key so that only the human self is left as the "object of reference."[127] Though Thiselton, along with Vanhoozer, recognizes "an ambiguity in Ricoeur's account of the status of historical narrative and its relation to the power of fiction," yet he thinks this ambiguity is not a contradiction.[128] This is because, Thiselton feels, it has not been made clear whether discussion is at the interpretative, critical or metacritical level. To that end, Thiselton highlights Ricoeur's affirmation that "hermeneutics ultimately claims to set itself up as a critique of critique, or

---

124. Ibid., 356–357.
125. Ibid., 357.
126. Ibid., 358.
127. Ibid.
128. Ibid.

meta-critique" as Ricoeur discusses the need for critical engagement between Gadamer's model and Habermas' critique of ideology.[129]

Ricoeur repeatedly rejects the individualism of a "narrow and narcissistic 'I' of immediate consciousness" and insists that texts expand the horizon of readers.[130] Referring to Speech-act theory and Ricoeur, Thiselton notes, "The creative emphasis in Searle and in Recanati of shaping the world to fit the eventful word of promise finds expression in Ricoeur's connection between 'possibility' and eschatological hope." For Thiselton, "The language of promise, of hope, and of eschatology has an important place in Ricoeur's biblical hermeneutics."[131]

Due to the limited scope of this study, I will now need to move on from this brief survey of the history of hermeneutical theories to the most crucial issue in hermeneutics, the issue of the authorial intent and its priority in meaning and understanding.

The Priority of Authorial Intent in Meaning

Until now I have been mainly referring to the works of one of the chief scholars of hermeneutics, Anthony C. Thiselton and, to some extent, Grant R. Osborne. Now I want to look into Kevin J. Vanhoozer's major work, *Is There a Meaning in This Text?*, in which he makes a strong case for the priority of authorial intent in the meaning of the text. His book represents a theologically informed effort to restore the priority of authorial intent as a central factor for epistemological conviction. He takes post-modern hermeneutics seriously and treats Reader-Response critics, Deconstructionists, and others with respect. Vanhoozer gives a sensitive and thorough response to the pessimism and epistemological nihilism of post-modernity. Vanhoozer seems to be fully aware of the multi-disciplinary hermeneutical task at hand:

> Such is the task I here undertake – to respond, from an explicitly Christian theological point of view, to the modern and postmodern challenges to biblical interpretation by marshaling a host of interdisciplinary resources and bringing them all to bear on the problems of textual meaning: Is there a meaning? Can we know it? What should we do about it? . . .

---

129. Ibid., 358–359.
130. Ibid., 371.
131. Ibid.

> The present work challenges what amounts to an emerging consensus that sees meaning as relative to the encounter of text and reader. The interpretation of Scripture, on this view, owes as much to community tradition as to the canonical text itself. The view here defended – that meaning is independent of our attempts to interpret it – is a minority opposition view in the parliament of contemporary literary theory.[132]

Apart from the Introduction and Conclusion, Vanhoozer's book has two main parts, each of them dealing with the three loci of meaning: author, text and reader. In the Introduction, Vanhoozer outlines "The Three Ages of Criticism," the three periods of preoccupation with the author, text, and reader respectively.[133] In a sense, his threefold division parallels the division of philosophy into metaphysics, epistemology and ethics. He treats these three areas of metaphysics, methodology, and morals of meaning and relates them to the three periods of emphasis on the author, text and reader. In part 1, he "sets out the major challenges to contemporary hermeneutics," and deals with postmodern skeptical hermeneutics in chapters 2–4. In part 2, he presents at great length his "alternative constructive proposals for interpretation"[134] and proposes a Trinitarian hermeneutic in chapters 5–7 and then gives his conclusion in chapter 8.

In chapter 2, he describes how the author was important in hermeneutical considerations before and what led to the demise of its authority and intention in modern hermeneutical discussion. He gives the case against author and the hermeneutic realism and, of those, especially dealing with the influence of Derrida's post-structuralism and Fish's neo-pragmatism against author's intention.[135] In chapter 3, he analyzes the undoing of the text and discusses the loss of respect for meaning, the rise of allegorical interpretation and loss of determinacy in the text. He examines the arguments for hermeneutical relativism, which he calls "hermetic" instead, like the hermetic writings derived from the confusion of Hermes with Thoth (Egyptian god of wisdom), "writings that are characterized by occultism and obscurity."[136] In chapter 4, he tackles the undoing of the reader and the cosmic shift in epistemology, which accompany a radical reader-response opinion that sees the text as inactive

---

132. Vanhoozer, *Is There a Meaning in This Text?*, 10.
133. Ibid., 25.
134. Ibid.
135. Ibid., 26.
136. Ibid., 27.

Hermeneutics for Biblical Perspective 159

and the reader as the real producer of meaning. Some "reader-response" critics do see the text as active, providing signs and indeterminacies (which invite interpretive participation of readers), and see meaning as the product of the *joint-interaction* of the text and the reader. But the radical critics give readers the full freedom to do whatever they want to do with the text.[137]

In part 2, Vanhoozer begins with his response to the challenges of chapter 2 in chapter 5 and "makes the case for a realism of meaning by rethinking the role of the author."[138] Vanhoozer sees the author as intrinsic to the existence of text and argues for the validity of the text being interpreted in harmony with the author's truth-intention. He uses philosophical resources, like the common-sense realism of Thomas Reid and the speech-act theory of J. L. Austin and John Searle, to present his case for authorial intention based on the concept of "author as a communicative agent."[139] He argues, meaning is a form of *doing*, and if the author is the subject or *doer* of that *doing*, then we must respect the *doer* and the *doing* and interpret what has been *done* (the text) with the *doing* and the author or *doer* in mind. In this, Vanhoozer relates human *doing* to God's creation, and bases human authorship to God as a communicative agent, in God's ability to communicate himself through revelation and incarnation.[140]

In chapter 6, Vanhoozer responds to the challenges of chapter 3 and presents the understanding of interpretation and literary knowledge based on the concept of "communicative rationality and the text as a communicative act," in harmony with the Socio-critical theory of Jurgen Habermas, and the new Reformed epistemology of Alvin Plantinga and Nicholas Wolterstorff.[141] Borrowing the term "thick description" from anthropologist Clifford Geertz,[142] he claims, "meaning can be adequately known through a process of 'thick description' that views the text as a complex literary act and respects its various levels, including the canonical."[143] In chapter 7, Vanhoozer responds to the undoing of the reader in chapter 4 and presents a theory of hermeneutical responsibility. He considers the morality or ethics of interpretation and the

---

137. Vanhoozer notes, "Chapter 4 relates the ethics of interpretations to questions concerning human freedom and responsibility and to issues of politics and ideology" (*Is There a Meaning in This Text?*, 28).
138. Vanhoozer, *Is There a Meaning in This Text?*, 26.
139. Ibid.
140. Ibid.
141. Ibid., 27.
142. Ibid., 250.
143. Ibid., 27.

responsibilities of the interpreter.[144] He sketches what it means to be an understanding person and moves on from philosophy to theology proper.[145]

Finally, in chapter 8, the Conclusion, Vanhoozer pulls everything together and summarizes his perspective using three sets of concepts: (a) "Trinitarian Hermeneutics," which is more than a philosophical framework, but a declaration that God, as a communicative agent, somehow underwrites language;[146] (b) "The Verbal Icon and the Authorial Face," in which he refers to the idolatry, whereby the reader projects himself/herself upon the text which he/she seeks to understand,[147] instead of genuinely seeking to hear and to be led beyond oneself;[148] (c) "Hermeneutic Humility and Literary Knowledge," in which he discusses the two deadly sins of pride and sloth. Pride prematurely claims absolute knowledge without appropriate effort, while sloth "prematurely claims the impossibility of literary knowledge."[149]

In his special treatment on Ricoeur, Vanhoozer shows that even though Ricoeur defends textual meaning, Ricoeur is not a defender of the priority of author's intended meaning, because to him text is independent of the author. Vanhoozer explains,

> Ricoeur represents a mediating position between the traditional position that focuses on the author's intent and Derrida's undoing of it. There is a meaning in the text, but it is dissociated from the author. Because it is fixed in writing, discourse is both decontextualized from its original situation and depsychologized from its original author. Ricoeur develops the concept of discourse by means . . . of concepts: *work* and *world* . . .
> . . . Whereas the text as work must be analyzed and explained, the world of the text must be understood or appropriated.[150]

Then Vanhoozer goes on to critique Ricoeur's method of hermeneutics in this way:

---

144. For Vanhoozer, ethical interpretation is a spiritual act in which the spirit of understanding is not a spirit of power or play but the Holy Spirit (Vanhoozer, *Is There a Meaning in This Text?*, 29).
145. Vanhoozer, *Is There a Meaning in This Text?*, 29.
146. Ibid., 456.
147. Ibid., 459.
148. Ibid., 460.
149. Ibid., 462–463.
150. Ibid., 215.

> What exactly does an interpreter appropriate? Not the intention of the author, not even the historical situation of the author and his or her original readers, but the meaning of the text itself . . . Interpretation uncovers not the mind of an author, but a perspective, a "way of looking at things," a proposed world. In short, . . . a possible way of being that is not merely a self-expression of the author. In this regard, Ricoeur speaks of the "narrative voice," the voice that commends the world of the text to the reader. Though cut off from its author, the text still has an "intention": the projected world that it proposes for our consideration and response. The question remains whether we can discover this world without recourse to the notion of the author.[151]

Thus, for Vanhoozer, Ricoeur is trying to uproot the text from its ground of the authorial intention and assigning the text itself an "intention". However, he shows that Ricoeur is still tacitly appealing to the author in his analysis of written discourse. Vanhoozer notes,

> What Ricoeur rejects as the object of interpretation is the author's intention construed as a psychological event. Yet he admits that written discourse implies an author: "It is impossible to cancel out this main characteristic of discourse without reducing texts to natural objects, i.e., to things which are not man-made, but which, like pebbles, are found in the sand." To consider the text as an authorless entity is to commit what Ricoeur himself calls the "fallacy of the absolute text." Ricoeur goes to some pains, however, to explain in just what way the author is of continuing relevance for interpretation. What he wants to say, I believe, is that authorial intention becomes a dimension of the text, just as an artisan carves, paints, or otherwise projects oneself into one's handiwork. What Ricoeur actually does instead is to refer to the "intention" *of the text*. Strictly speaking, however, texts do not have intentions, nor do they act. We do not ascribe agency to texts, nor do we praise or blame books, we rather direct our praise or blame to their authors. For only persons say something to someone about something.[152]

---

151. Ibid.
152. Ibid., 216.

Vanhoozer critiques how people use the text when they don't intend to discern authorial intent as he argues for the priority of authorial intent in meaning. He asks, "If one is not reading for the author's intended message, what exactly is one doing?"

> (1) "I am trying to reconstruct the original historical situation." . . . is more interested in the context than in the text itself . . . however, interpreters are not trying to recreate the background so much as to determine *what happened*.
>
> (2) "I am trying to reconstruct the history of the text's composition." Again . . . is only marginal to the task of interpretation and understanding. It is an instance of looking *at* the mirror instead of in it.
>
> (3) "I am trying to uncover the ideological interests that motivated the author and to criticize them in light of what we now believe about human liberation, morality, and human rights." . . . Does one not first have to recover "what is said/done" (by the author) in order to go on to criticize it? And is not the task of determining "what is said" precisely what I have acknowledged to be the goal of interpretation? If so, then this position articulates not an alternative definition of meaning so much as a step beyond it, towards evaluating the author's enacted intention.
>
> (4) "I am reading to see what I can get out of the text." But is interpretation purely a private matter? Is there no sense in which what one gets out of a text is to be shared . . . ? This position, if taken to its extreme, is better classified as invention or creation, even 'authoring.' . . . this option treats the text as though it had been written by the reader . . . the meaning is the sense the words have borne had the *reader* written them.
>
> (5) "I am exploring the sense potential of the text. I am reading for the text's intention, not the author's" . . . But is it cogent? What does it mean to speak of the text's "sense potential?" If it means the sense I think these words *now* bear (to me here and now), then this position dissolves into the preceding one. On the other hand, if it refers to the sense potential the words had in their original context, then we are determining what the author

might, or *could have*, intended. But this is to make the author's intended meaning the goal of interpretive process.[153]

All of these ways of looking at the text are very well represented in our present world. Vanhoozer in his brief list has helpfully characterized where modern hermeneutics has brought us at the beginning of the Twenty-First Century and shows their futility in favor of the priority of authorial intention for understanding the meaning of the text. He is not dogmatic but sensitive to the possible strengths of opposing arguments of modern Reader or even Text-oriented hermeneutics, yet he reasons well to strengthen the confidence on the authorial intent. However, it is not clear what to make of his grounding of hermeneutics in the doctrine of the social Trinity with the emphasis on the "threeness" of Godhead rather than the "oneness." Not all are comfortable thinking along this line. Some prefer to stress more strongly the Unity of the Godhead rather than the Trinity of the Godhead, both of which they may affirm. One concern is how effective Vanhoozer's model of hermeneutics will be for the interpretation of Scripture in pluralistic contexts.

A Proposed Model of Hermeneutics

Following the Purpose Statement of this study, in this chapter I have attempted to determine methodological principles to be followed in order to understand the biblical perspective of "State-after-Death" correctly in pluralistic contexts. There is a general tendency in pluralistic contexts to assign multiple meanings to biblical texts. Hence, it is important for us to have sound hermeneutical principles to deduce reliable and responsible meaning of biblical texts. Based on my study here, I propose a tentative model of hermeneutics. Before I discuss the characteristics of this model, I must qualify the model to be tentative only because I am open to see my understanding corrected, reshaped and enlarged. Vanhoozer[154] considered "pride" and "sloth" as the two deadly sins of interpretation and so my intention is to remain humble (cf. 1 Cor 13:12) and not to be slothful, in order that I may grow in my understanding and make some modifications to this model of hermeneutics in the future.

This model would take the horizon of pluralistic contexts seriously and would sensitively "listen" to the issues which arise from out of that horizon in order to understand its pre-understandings. Yet, the priority of the horizon

---

153. Ibid., 253–254.
154. Ibid., 462–463.

of the Bible will be maintained, for even though the issues and the questions arise from the context, it is the horizon of the Word of God that must correct, reshape and enlarge the horizon of the context. It is God who must have the last word through his Word. In this tentative model, I propose three methodological principles or three main characteristics: (1) The priority of authorial intention, (2) The metacritical perspective, and (3) The constructive use of narratives.

1. The priority of authorial intention. This principle is crucial for the interpretation of the Scripture, for that matter, of any text. Vanhoozer has reasoned well for its defence and I will not prove again its validity. However, this particular quote from Osborne, where he refers to himself and his text *The Hermeneutical Spiral,* is instructive:

> We are again at the heart of the problem. You, the reader, do not know me, the author. The text of this book does not truly reflect my personality. That is, of course, obvious; the question, however, is whether it adequately reflects my thoughts on the possibility of meaning. Can you as reader understand my opposition to polyvalence, or is this text autonomous from my views? . . . I am writing in the library . . . Certainly many of the professors here, schooled in the existential or historical-critical approaches and . . . in the German culture, will read these arguments from a quite different perspective. The question is not whether they will agree but whether they can understand my arguments. I will not be around to clarify my points, so certainly this written communication lacks the dynamics of oral speech. Moreover, those readers without the necessary philosophical background will definitely struggle with the concepts herein.
>
> . . . does this mean that no amount of clarification can impart the meaning that I seek to communicate in these . . . ? I think not. This issue has two aspects: can we know what another person meant in a written account, and is it important to know that original intended meaning?[155]

My answer to both of these questions is a resounding, "Yes." Though, it may be *difficult* to understand absolutely what the author meant, it is *possible* to get to the author's intended meaning adequately, at least the gist of the meaning.

---

155. Osborne, *Hermeneutical Spiral,* 376.

As a response to the questions, let us look at this chapter. The whole purpose of writing this chapter is to present a model of hermeneutics in order to construct a basis for understanding the biblical perspective on the topic of death and after-death. It is extremely important that a study of this kind expresses clearly the author's intention as we study this difficult topic from the Scriptures. The biblical narrative is normative for our study and must be dealt with carefully. Thus, we have to keep looking for the authorial intention. When speaking of the Bible, we are not only referring to the human authors or scribes who penned the Scriptures, however important they may be. Indeed, the human authors of the Bible are very important and their intended meaning is a first consideration. Yet the evangelical conviction is that God is the ultimate author of the Bible and while God used the human authors and their understanding to communicate the message, God's truth recorded in the Bible is more than what the authors, themselves, may have understood. In other words, the human authors may not have understood *absolutely* what God was trying to communicate through *their* writings, though they definitely understood it *adequately* in order to communicate it.

Thus, God's intended meaning will not contradict with what the human authors of the Bible meant by what they recorded, but it may mean something greater than what the human authors wanted to convey. Perhaps this is parallel to what we saw earlier in one of the directions of post-Gadamerian response in hermeneutics, in the *metacritical* direction, in which *Rationality* is understood to have been resting on a *broader base* than the *critical "method"* of post-Enlightenment Rationalism. In order to understand God's meaning in the Bible, we not only need to use the critical faculties of our mind, we need to humbly depend on the Holy Spirit to teach us the deeper aspects of what God means by His Word. Both Osborne and Vanhoozer concur with this when they say that the act of interpretation is a *spiritual* act or exercise which is dependent on the Holy Spirit.[156]

2. The metacritical perspective. I noted from Thiselton earlier that the key question that *metacriticism* asks is whether we can "critically rank the different criteria by which we judge what counts as meaningful or productive effects of texts within this or that context in life."[157] Thus there is a search for a trans-contextual or transcendental basis by which a comparative evaluation can be made of a critic's own contextual agenda. This metacritical perspective

---

156. Ibid., 5; Vanhoozer, *Is There a Meaning in This Text?*, 29.
157. Thiselton, *New Horizons in Hermeneutics*, 6.

is even more essential today due to the plethora of conflicting claims of truth in this post-modern pluralistic era of religions and ideologies. Everyone seems to have their own claim to the Truth. Nowadays, truth is what one subjectively makes it to be and thus what is true to one may not be the Truth for another. In such situations of relativity, even contradiction, complicated further by pluralism, there is a need for a transcendental basis for mutual critique, even as Ricoeur affirms, "hermeneutics ultimately claims to set itself up as a critique of critique, or *meta-critique*."[158]

The transcendental basis for Thiselton's metacritical perspective is "the love of God" to his creation (Rom 5:5) as expressed in the biblical narratives of the cross and resurrection of Christ.[159] Similarly, David Bosch in his task of "critical hermeneutic" approach, sees this "Jesus event" as the always-relevant trans-contextual basis. Bosch describes missiology, "as relating the always-relevant Jesus event of twenty centuries ago to the future of God's promised reign by means of meaningful initiatives for the here and now."[160] For the biblical perspective on "State-after-Death" in pluralistic contexts, "the cross and the resurrection of Christ" is the transcendental basis for our *metacritical* hermeneutics. In the Bible, we see how the early disciples and the New Testament writers used the Christ-event as that transcendental basis to interpret the Old Testament (e.g. Peter's sermon in Acts 2, Stephen's message in Acts 7 etc.). In spite of the highly developed interpretive traditions of Jewish, Qumranic and Rabbinic communities, Jesus and the early disciples argued that the Jewish religious authorities were misreading the Old Testament when failing to see the obvious references to Jesus in the Old Testament. Even the Apostle Paul himself did not see this in the Old Testament before his conversion, but afterwards he writes:

> We are not like Moses, who would put a veil over his face to keep the Israelites from gazing at it while the radiance was fading away. But their minds were made dull, for to this day the same veil remains when the old covenant is read. It has not been removed, because only in Christ is it taken away. Even to this day when Moses is read, a veil covers their hearts. But whenever anyone turns to the Lord, the veil is taken away. (2 Cor. 3:13–16 NIV US)

Relating *metacriticism* with *hermeneutical pluralism*, Thiselton comments,

---

158. Ibid., 359.
159. Ibid., 609–610.
160. Bosch, *Transforming Mission*, 24.

I shall argue that *in one sense hermeneutical pluralism is inevitable* because, on the basis of the historical situatedness of the interpreter and his or her reading-community *within a prior life-world, . . . we cannot assess one reading-model in terms of another*. To seek to *impose* some universal model, or even to impose a model . . . as "primary" would be to operate in the same authoritarian terms that social pragmatists use but disguise as liberal pluralism. On the other hand, *Christian theology would move into self-contradiction if it ceased to evaluate the prohibition of idolatry, the message of the cross, and the universality of eschatological promise as merely context-relative;* as the *product or construction* of a particular social culture with no claim to offer a *universal critique* of life and thought, and even a *metacritique* of other criteria of thought, understanding, and action.[161]

Thiselton stresses the need to understand the axes of "life-world and trans-contextual critique" as a priority in order to be fully aware of "the degree of complexity" in their interactions "in a theory of hermeneutics which is compatible with Christian theology."[162] Thiselton insightfully explains the relationship between *pluralism* and *metacritique* by the following example of a young couple in love:

The example of the young couple whose criteria of relevance and interest become transformed when they fall in love, and when they interact with each other's "group", brings into focus one way of understanding the relation between metacritique and pluralism. In one sense their experience affirms the reality and inevitability of pluralism: what, up to that moment, they had taken for granted as the *only* obvious way of understanding and evaluating the world has become relativized as no more than one option among others. But in another sense, their love-relationship has now *enlarged* their understanding, with the result that their former interests and stereotypifications appear from their new and transformed vantage-point to be relatively *narrow, ill-informed*, and *self-centered*. Whether or not they have ever encountered the term "metacritical", their new attitudes will at very least imply fresh *judgments*, including *re-assessments*

---

161. Thiselton, *New Horizons in Hermeneutics*, 612.
162. Ibid.

of earlier *criteria* of relevance, i.e. a *critical re-ranking* of their earlier *critical norms*.[163]

Thus we see how appropriate and helpful the *metacritical* perspective will be as an important characteristic for the model of hermeneutics in pluralistic religious contexts.

3. The constructive use of narratives. Earlier, Thiselton noted how innovative and influential Ricoeur is in his contribution when highlighting the importance of narrative in biblical hermeneutics. For Ricoeur, "Narratives present *possibilities of human action*, as understood in terms of *a schema of time*."[164] For Ricoeur, narrative components both contribute to the plot to build a "whole," and derive their significance from their place within the whole. The "whole" is the narrative-world of the reader and Ricoeur contends that, when this "re-figured" world grabs the reader, the narrative-effects are "revelatory and transformative."[165] Thus, Ricoeur encourages us to see the importance of the power of narrative in the hermeneutical task, especially when we are thinking of pluralistic contexts.

However, as soon as we delve into Ricoeur's view on "historical" narrative in relation to "fictional" narrative we find ourselves in murky waters. Vanhoozer has some reservations about Ricoeur's ambivalence regarding the relation between history and fiction and rightly so. Vanhoozer contends Ricoeur is approaching biblical narrative like the scholars of the New Hermeneutic and that he, Ricoeur, has merely switched "subjectivity" to a new key, and as a result only the human self is left as the "object of reference."[166] Though Thiselton, along with Vanhoozer, recognizes "an ambiguity in Ricoeur's account of the status of historical narrative and its relation to the power of fiction," yet he thinks this ambiguity is not a contradiction.[167] For Thiselton, this is because it is not specific whether the discussion is going at interpretative level, critical level or metacritical level. However, even when we may disagree with Ricoeur's view on history and fiction, we need not throw out the baby with the bath water and disregard the power of narrative in hermeneutics.

With regard to biblical narratives, Charles E. Van Engen's comments are helpful. Showing "The Importance of Narrative Theology," he notes, "Narrative theology is an attempt to build bridges both between the various

---

163. Ibid.
164. Ibid., 354.
165. Ibid., 355.
166. Ibid., 358.
167. Ibid.

horizons in Scripture and from Scripture to our day."[168] He believes that, the "Movement of Narrative theology" can be helpful to Mission theology, and uses themes and sub-themes of biblical narratives to build on Bosch's "critical hermeneutics." Van Engen contends that narrative theology is more than story and dogmatics. In his Evangelical assessments, he points to five positive elements of narrative theology that evangelicals can make use of:

1) Narrative theology deals with the text as a whole.

2) Its interest is in the interaction of the text with the community.

3) It helps in the relationship between the two horizons of text and the reader.

4) It helps to read the Scripture from a wholistic perspective which affirms God's salvation as reaching and transforming every aspect of the human experience.

5) It is useful for its methodological contribution for biblical theology and in inductive Bible study, evangelism, preaching, contextualization and conversion.

He also highlights five deep concerns that evangelicals have about narrative theology:

1) It may deny the authorial intent of the text, which is a non-negotiable.

2) It tends to deny or limit the referential function in literature that God himself is talking to us in the Scripture. "The referential quality of Scripture is not negotiable."[169]

3) It tends to downplay the contextual grounding of the text.

4) It focuses on literary structure and as a result ignores the historicity of the text.

5) It tends to downplay the concept of truth, the metaphysical implications of the faith.

Finally, Van Engen suggests the areas in which narrative theology may contribute: in Trinitarian mission, wholistic mission, universal

---

168. Van Engen, *Mission on the Way*, 45.
169. Ibid., 61.

mission, corporate mission and contextual mission. Of course, as a model of hermeneutics for pluralistic religious contexts, I want to see how "it may provide images, pictures, metaphors, and stories that are necessary for rounding out the propositional, textual, and historical aspects of today's global theological conversations in missiology."[170]

I would like to conclude by highlighting that God, as a communicative agent, loves to communicate through imagery and narrative. I am greatly fascinated by God's use of imagery in communicating propositional truth. Acts 10 and 11 show us God's use of imagery in Peter's vision about all kinds of four-footed animals, reptiles and birds and God saying, "Get up, Peter, kill and eat." Soon we find out that the divine message has much deeper meaning than removing Jewish taboos. Vinoth Ramachandra comments:

> The narrative records a process of "double conversion." On the one side, we see Peter repenting of his racial prejudice under the deepening impact of the gospel on his thinking and as a result of witnessing the same gospel at work in another's life. On the other side, Cornelius, upright and God-fearing though he was, still needed to hear the gospel from Peter's lips (not even from those of an angel!) in order to receive forgiveness of sin and the gift of the Holy Spirit. The result is the stupendous sight, unimaginable in their contemporary world, of a Jewish peasant and a Roman centurion living together under one roof.[171]

Only God can bring about that change. Yet, one cannot downplay the communicative power of the imagery of Peter's vision. In that pluralistic context of a Jewish Christian and a gentile God-fearer, what a breakthrough God brings through the use of imagery, in that communicative act of Peter's vision.

In conclusion, I will use this model of hermeneutics with the three pronged characteristics (the priority of authorial intention, metacritical perspective and constructive use of narratives) to investigate the Old Testament and the New Testament perspective of "State-after-Death" for pluralistic contexts in the next four chapters.

---

170. Ibid., 67.
171. Ramachandra, *Recovery of Mission*, 268.

5

State-after-Death in the Old Testament

In this chapter and the next, I will look into the Old Testament teachings on "State-after-Death" in order to understand the biblical perspective on the theme for pluralistic contexts. My inquiry will show that what takes place at death and afterward is a major component of God's mission in the Old Testament and that God desires to rescue humankind from one after-death situation to another. Our special interest is with the history of Israel within the context of Near-East pluralism. I will use the hermeneutical model discussed in the previous chapter, with its three dimensional approach (priority of authorial intention, metacritical perspective and constructive use of biblical narratives), to investigate Old testament perspectives on "State-after-Death." In our metacritical perspective of hermeneutics, the death and the resurrection of Jesus Christ is the transcendental or trans-contextual basis for interpreting Scriptures and for doing Christian theology in pluralistic religious contexts.

Over a hundred years ago in the summer of 1906 in his lectures at Durham, UK, C. F. Burney cautioned about two important issues that are pertinent for our study.[1] As he traced the growth of religious beliefs about life after death in the Old Testament history of Israel, Burney pointed out first that,

> We must remember . . . the growth of . . . religious beliefs . . . the evolution of the idea is, strictly speaking, logical rather than historical . . . In the history of all intellectual processes it constantly happens that there arise minds which are above and

---

1. C. F. Burney, *Israel's Hope of Immortality* (Oxford, UK: Clarendon Press, 1909), 5–7.

in advance of the age which gives them birth; which overleap certain stages in the unfolding of truth, and rise at once to conceptions which may not become the common property of their race until perhaps generations have passed by and the intermediate stages of thought have been slowly and laboriously worked out. Thus we are likely to go astray if we attempt to draw up a strictly chronological outline of the development of . . . religious beliefs.[2]

Second, Burney showed that some statements of the Old Testament have "a deeper significance when read in the fuller light of New Testament revelation."[3] For example, Jesus taught that when God spoke to Moses at Horeb, "I am the God of your father, the God of Abraham, the God of Isaac and the God of Jacob" (Exod 3:6, NIV) God implied that there is life beyond death since, "God is not the God of the dead, but the God of the living." Thus, we see in the Old Testament the beginnings of belief in a "State-after-Death" that are more fully revealed in the New Testament.

Some Introductory Questions

The possibility of death in the human race is mentioned almost immediately as the Old Testament begins in the creation account. In Genesis 2:17, God commanded Adam not to eat from the tree of the knowledge of good and evil, "for in the day that you eat of it you shall surely die" (ILB). Thus, death is The Punishment (or the consequence that will follow) if Adam disobeys God's command regarding the tree. Eve knew this as well, as she repeated the warning to the serpent in Genesis 3:3, "but God said, 'You shall not eat of the fruit of the tree which is in the midst of the garden, neither shall you touch it, lest you die'" (RSV). What did God communicate about death to Adam and Eve and to all of humanity by that statement? In this early account of creation we do not find a great deal of elaboration about the subject of death and what happens at and after death. Yet we see that, from the very beginning in the early passages of Genesis, "State-after-Death" is a vital component of God's salvific mission.

Commenting on the Old Testament perspective on death, Robert Martin-Achard notes, "At the outset, the Old Testament informs us that man

---

2. Ibid., 5–6.
3. Ibid., 6.

is not immortal; there is nothing eternal in him. No part of him is immune from death."[4] He contends that the Old Testament rejects the doctrine of immortality of human soul and argues that, though often considered basic to Christian faith, it is a belief that actually came into prominence through Plato's philosophy.[5] However, he concedes that though the dead are no longer alive, yet they continue in existence "under such conditions as do not deserve the name of life."[6] Later on, referring to the earlier passages of Genesis, Martin-Achard goes on to comment that,

> Before the Fall, between Adam and death . . . there stands the Living God; His presence is sufficient to ward death off, to conceal it; Adam, standing before God, is able to ignore it . . . But when God withdraws, nothing is left to Adam but the presence of death . . . Man, then, is born mortal, but by his sin he renders death effective; it enters as a reality into his existence; henceforth he lives as one who has heard the capital sentence pronounced against him . . . By his disobedience, Adam has transformed the human situation into a curse; in this sense, death, through the threatening shadow it constantly throws on his life, is truly the wages of sin. Thus, accidentally, man becomes that "being-for-death" that is at the core of Heidegger's thought.[7]

Along with Martin-Achard's comment, Murray J. Harris' remark is to the point, "Man and woman were not created unable to die but were created able not to die, although after the fall death became a universal biological necessity."[8] Adam and Eve were not created immortal but with the ability to choose "to die" or "not to die" and they chose death through their disobedience. As a result, after the fall the whole of humanity has on them the curse of death. From the very beginning of the Old Testament, "State-after-Death" becomes

---

4. Robert Martin-Achard, *From Death to Life: A Study of the Development of the Doctrine of the Resurrection in the Old Testament*, trans. John Penney Smith (Edinburgh and London: Oliver & Boyd Ltd, 1960), 17.

5. Martin-Achard notes that, "for the Israelites, the soul is not, in essence, superior to the body, and cannot develop without it; . . . not . . . an uncreated and thus imperishable reality; its destiny depends, not on its nature, but on the Living God . . . death . . . concerns the whole being of man" (*From Death to Life*, 17).

6. Martin-Achard, *From Death to Life*, 17.

7. Ibid., 19–20.

8. Murray J. Harris, "Death," in *New Dictionary of Theology*, eds. S. B. Ferguson, D. F. Wright, and J. I. Packer (Downers Grove, IL: InterVarsity, 1988), 188; and *Raised Immortal: The Relation between Resurrection and Immortality in New Testament Teaching* (London: Marshall, Morgan & Scott, 1983), 194.

a crucial component of God's mission. Humankind now must suffer the absolute and inevitable fact of death. To meet this catastrophe God now will provide a way to overcome the "State-of-Death." God, the creator of life will be revealed as the Redeemer and Renewer of life.

As we observe the onset of death in the early passages of Genesis, we also see in the rest of the Old Testament a continuation of the reality of death as the history of Israel unfolds over a period of a thousand years in a variety of life settings. The Old Testament focuses mainly on Israel's earthly life in which God revealed himself to his people, who often failed even as they struggled to obey, serve and worship him. Thus, an attempt to trace the growth of the idea of "State-after-Death" in the religion of Israel is fraught with difficulty.[9] The Israelites showed little interest in what happens at death. King Hezekiah, recovering from his sickness and impending death, says,

> Lo, it was for my welfare that I had great bitterness; but thou hast held back my life from the *pit of destruction*, for thou cast all my sins behind thy back. For *Sheol* cannot thank thee, *death* cannot praise thee; *those who go down to the pit* cannot hope for thy faithfulness. The living . . . he thanks thee, as I do this day (Isa. 38:17–19 [RSV], italics added).

Some scholars even argue that the Old Testament, in general, does not teach anything about "State-after-Death" that is religiously significant and that the texts that may allude to some sort of afterlife are negligible in the context of broader biblical worldviews.[10] In my judgment, if there is little said about death, it is because in most of the Old Testament God is establishing Israel as a special nation among the nations as the first priority before giving a fuller revelation of what actually happens at death and beyond. The Old Testament refers frequently to the dead being "gathered unto their fathers" or "sleeping with their fathers" (e.g. Gen 25:8, Gen 35:29, etc.) which may either simply mean that they joined their ancestors in the death state and the grave,

---

9. Burney, *Israel's Hope of Immortality*, 5.
10. Segal ("Judaism," in *Life after Death in World Religions*, ed. Harold Coward [Maryknoll, NY: Orbis Books, 1997], 13–14) points this out quite vividly when he argues how the Israelite's destiny in the afterlife is not "cited as a reason for sacrificial atonement" or how in the list of curses for disobedience, there are "plagues and fevers, defeat and conquest, famine, desolation, and exile" yet no mention of the fate that awaits sinners upon their physical death. He argues that in the Torah "God's grace or wrath" continues beyond one's life span "by extending it to one's progeny" and in the "continuity of future generations" rather than some "supernatural afterlife." However, he acknowledges that "there are texts in the Hebrew Bible that . . . seem to refer to at least a limited kind of afterlife."

or such references may give a picture of joining faithful ancestors in some supernatural "State-after-Death."

It is important to note, as Martin-Achard shows, that in the recent past some scholars have strongly stressed the *similarities* of the Israelites' view of life and death with that of Babylonians, Egyptians and other ancient peoples. He notes,

> Hebrew conceptions in this sphere have often been likened to Mesopotamian, Egyptian or even Greek ideas. The comparison is legitimate, the resemblances observed by the specialists being numerous. A perusal of the works of L. Durr, A. Bertholet, A. Lods, and E. Dhorme, to cite only these, is enough to carry conviction. Writers such as J. Pedersen and H. Wheeler Robinson and others have made a point of stressing the parallels that may be traced between the psychology of the Israelites and that of primitive peoples . . . In short, in face of life or death, the Hebrew reacted in very much the same way as once the Babylonian and the Egyptian did.[11]

Nicholas J. Tromp argues the same point, showing the similarities of vocabulary and style of Ugaritic texts with that of the Old Testament texts, as he notes:

> As the documents found at Ras Shamra belong to an environment where culture was geographically widespread but not subject to frequent changes, an affinity with Old Testament times and culture is obvious. In spite of skeptical voices it can hardly be denied that students of Ugaritic have contributed not a little to a better understanding of the text of the Old Testament . . . Ugaritic texts . . . shows remarkable similarity with biblical Hebrew, both in vocabulary and style.[12]

So Tromp "tries to obtain a better perspective of Israelite views on Death and the Beyond with the help of conceptions found" in the Ugaritic texts.[13]

However, recent scholar Philip S. Johnston argues for the *dissimilarities* between the views of the "State-after-Death" from the epics of ancient Near Eastern literature of Mesopotamia, Ugarit and Egypt with the Old Testament

---
11. Martin-Achard, *From Death to Life*, 1–2.
12. Nicholas J. Tromp, *Primitive Conceptions of Death and the Nether World in the Old Testament* (Rome: Pontifical Biblical Institute, 1969), 1.
13. Ibid., 2.

because of the inherent differences between polytheism and Yahwism. Johnston notes,

> In marked contrast, Israel's canonical literature contains no such epics about descent to the underworld or return from it, guided by various deities. By its very definition it could not, since it specifically refused the necessary polytheism. Nor does it have any detailed description of the deceased's journey through the underworld to a place of judgment. Such speculation clearly lay outside the parameters of orthodox Yahwism and was avoided by its authoritative writers. Instead . . . life itself was the starting-point and the focus for Israel's faith, while death and its aftermath were of little concern. Israelite faith concerned a living relationship with Yahweh in the present, not speculation about the future. This in itself distinguishes Israel's literature significantly from that of her neighbors.[14]

Yet, Johnston accepts that the Israelites did have some concept of what followed death even though "State-after-Death" is not a major or recurrent theme of the Old Testament and their response to it can be discerned from the numerous passages that refer to death.[15] Perhaps Tromp too, however minutely, acknowledges the differences in the descriptions of human death in the Old Testament and in the Ugaritic texts, when he notes,

> For two reasons, parallel lines in the strict sense of the word cannot be established for our subject. In the OT the myth is a broken one; it is reduced to scattered motifs and allusions.
>
> On the other hand, the Ras Shamra evidence hardly contains any direct information as to human death and afterlife; relevant material is mainly found in the Baal-cycle, where the death of that vegetational god is described. It is clear, however, that these passages reflect conceptions of human death.[16]

Thus, I conclude, on one hand, that the Old Testament, because of its inherent monotheism, does offer a picture of "State-after-Death" *dissimilar* to other religious texts of ancient Near Eastern peoples.

---

14. Philip S. Johnston, *Shades of Sheol: Death and Afterlife in the Old Testament* (Downers Grove, IL: InterVarsity, 2002), 69–70.
15. Ibid., 70.
16. Tromp, *Primitive Conceptions of Death*, 2–3.

On the other hand, while Johnston rightly shows that there is no "detailed description of the deceased's journey through the underworld to *a place of judgment,*"[17] it is clear that there is *judgment* at or after death. From the outset, the Old Testament depicts God's judgment over humanity in the judgment of Adam and Eve. Later, we find that one's "State-after-Death" would depend on God's judgment at or after death if God is going to judge every deed done in one's lifetime. For example, Ecclesiastes 12:1, 5b, 7, 13, and 14 says,

> Remember also your Creator in the days of your youth, before the evil days come, and years draw nigh; . . . because man goes to his eternal home . . . , and the dust returns to the earth as it was, and the spirit returns to God who gave it . . . The end of the matter; all has been heard. Fear God, and keep his commandments . . . For God will bring every deed into judgment, with every secret thing, whether good or evil (RSV).

Thus, the writer of the letter to the Hebrews in the New Testament notes, "it is appointed for men to die once, after that comes judgment" (9:27) to confirm to the scattered Jewish believers in Christ in the first century the above Old Testament assumption of judgment after death.

In spite of the difficulty of the task, due to lack of overwhelming Old Testament references, Burney however felt that it was still possible to broadly trace the growth of the belief in a life after death in the religious life of Israel. For Burney, in the history of Israel, "There were . . . great national crises which involved . . . the reconstruction of belief upon wider and sounder bases. A large part of Israel's literature groups itself about these periods of crisis and has to do with the vexed questions and phases of transition in religious thought which they involved."[18] This is because in the Old Testament, God was initially establishing Israel as a nation to set the stage in this world, especially in the midst of diverse religious contexts of the Near-East, for his ultimate mission to rescue humans from the penalty of death and its "State-after-Death." From the beginning, God gave subtle but clear hints before he gave a fuller revelation of the state beyond death.

Next, we will study the meaning of the most important Old Testament term for "State-after-Death," that is, *Sheol* and similar terms meaning "the pit" or "destruction."

---

17. Johnston, *Shades of Sheol*, 69 (emphasis added).
18. Burney, *Israel's Hope of Immortality*, 7.

Sheol and Similar Terms

In the Old Testament the Hebrew term *Sheol* is found sixty-five (or sixty-six)[19] times. As it has no definite article, it is considered a proper name by scholars[20] and is a feminine noun (BDB:982). *Sheol* generally means the underworld, the realm where the deceased go deep down under the earth. Three other Hebrew terms *bor*, *be'er* and *shahat* for "pit" clearly mean the underworld in about thirty-six of their occurrences.[21] Also the Hebrew term *'abaddon* (or destruction), occurring six times, clearly means the underworld. Thus *Sheol* and these other terms occur about one hundred times in the Old Testament and paint a similar picture of the underworld. However, the underworld is a minor theme in the Old Testament compared to death itself as the stem 'die/death' (*m-w-t*) occurs exactly one thousand times.[22]

The Origin of Sheol

As we noted above, Martin-Achard stresses the *similarities* of the underworld view of the Israelites with that of other Near-Eastern peoples and argues that if the Israelites did borrow this idea from their neighbors they did it quite early on. He notes,

> The Israelites, like most of the primitive peoples, believe that the dead are gathered together in the vast and usually sub-terranean region that is set apart for them. The world of the dead, the Sheol of the Hebrews, corresponds in every particular to the Hades of the Greeks and the Arallu of the Assyro-Babylonians. Certain scholars consider that the Israelites borrowed this idea of a kingdom of shadows from their neighbours; but if this theory be established, the borrowing is certainly very early and perhaps dates to before the entrance of the Hebrews into Palestine.[23]

---

19. It occurs 65 times in the MT and in Isa 7:11 (following early versions LXX, Aquila, Symmachus, Theodotion and Peshitta) the word for 'ask' is emended to 'to Sheol' (Johnston, *Shades of Sheol*, 71fn6).
20. Martin-Achard (*From Death to Life*, 37); Johnston (*Shades of Sheol*, 71).
21. ACUTE (*The Nature of Hell* [Carlisle, UK: Paternoster/ACUTE, 2000], 38fn4); Johnston (*Shades of Sheol*, 83–84) notes that *bor* means the underworld 19 times in 10 passages (possibly in 3 others), *be'er* means it twice, and *shahat* means it 15 times in 11 passages.
22. Johnston, *Shades of Sheol*, 72–73.
23. Martin-Achard, *From Death to Life*, 36–37. Martin-Achard (Ibid., 37fn1) cites this as the opinion of A. Jeremias (1887, 1903), G. Beer (1902:7ff.), A. Lods (1906:209ff.), and E. Dhorme (1907:5ff.).

Whether the Israelites truly borrowed the idea of underworld from their neighbors, even if it was earlier than their entry into Palestine, is not certain. Yet, following Johnston,[24] it seems certain that Israelites rejected their neighbors' inherent polytheistic meanings of the idea of the underworld as it was incompatible with the belief in One True God. The etymology of *Sheol* is unknown and so is no help towards its meaning.[25] Johnston argues further about the uniqueness of the term *Sheol*,

> The distinctiveness of the term 'Sheol' to Hebrew is frequently noted in discussion of its etymology, but seldom in consideration of its meaning. Since the underworld was a widespread concept in the Near East, it is remarkable that Hebrew has a name for it which is virtually unique. Whether intentional or accidental, this allowed the Israelites and their writers to invest the term with their own religious outlook, without the conceptual baggage that other shared terms might carry. The linguistic distinctiveness permitted a clearer expression of theological distinctiveness.[26]

Johnston (in his footnote 55) points out how the uniqueness of the term *Sheol* "elicits scant scholarly comment" and notes how one scholar recognizes the uniqueness of the term, yet suggests the Israelites borrowed the underworld idea from their Near-Eastern neighbors, "without seeing the anomaly of this."[27] It seems clear that the Israelites responded to the naturalistic views about "State-after-Death" of their polytheistic neighbors by resolutely choosing a unique term *Sheol* with its distinct monotheistic theological meaning.

The Description of the Underworld

As mentioned above, *Sheol* is the underworld, the place where the dead go, a place deep down, under the earth. Johnston describes it this way,

> It is clearly below ground: to go there one "descends" (*y-r-d*), and to escape one 'ascends' (*'-l-h*); it is often qualified by adjectives of depth; it is cosmologically opposite to 'heaven' (Job 11:8; Ps

---

24. Johnston, *Shades of Sheol*, 69.
25. While Martin-Achard (*From Death to Life*, 37) says the etymology is still in dispute, both Johnston (*Shades of Sheol*, 78) and Burney (*Israel's Hope of Immortality*, 8) about hundred years apart consider the origin of the word unknown.
26. Johnston, *Shades of Sheol*, 79.
27. Ibid.

139:8; Isa 7:11; Amos 9:2; cf. Deut 32:22); one digs towards Sheol (Amos 9:2); the earth opens its mouth and rebels descend there (Num 16:30, 33); it is a cavernous communal tomb (Ezek 32:18–32); and is associated with worms, maggots and dust (Job 17:16; Isa 14:11).[28]

In the King James Version, the term *Sheol* is translated "hell" thirty-one times, "grave" thirty-one times and "pit" three times, whereas the NIV usually translates *Sheol* as "grave," but occasionally as "realm of death" (Deut 32:22) or "depths of the grave" (Amos 9:2). Johnston argues that even though *Sheol* may have different nuances in different contexts of the Old Testament, the meaning carries the single basic idea of the "underworld" and contrary views are not sustainable.[29]

Burney refers to the underworld in Job 10:21–22 as a "land of darkness and deep shade . . . of gloom, like black darkness . . . deep shade without any order . . . where the light is like black darkness."[30] He points out that the residents of *Sheol* are *Repha'im* (or "shades") which means "'relaxed' or 'flaccid' ones, mere semblances of their former selves."[31] Referring to the taunt-song against the King of Babylon (Isa 14:3 ff), Burney argues that *Sheol* has to be different from the grave. While the body may rest in the grave or be cast out dishonorably, the shade (though disembodied) "has a semblance of its former self by which it is recognizable" and is doomed to existence in *Sheol*.[32] Burney corroborates this possibility from the narrative where the witch of Endor brings up the shade of Samuel as "an old man . . . covered with a garment" for King Saul in 1 Samuel 28:14 while acknowledging that the Hebrews' understanding of the relationship between the dead body and the shade is a probable one.[33]

Referring to Genesis 1:1–2:4, Lloyd R. Bailey points out that since the creation narrative of the second day does not carry the words, "it was good," the rabbis surmised that *Sheol* must have been created on that day.[34] According to Bailey, this shows that the rabbis understood *Sheol* to be an

---

28. Ibid., 73.
29. Ibid., 73–75.
30. Burney, *Israel's Hope of Immortality*, 8.
31. Ibid.
32. Ibid., 10.
33. Ibid., 10–11.
34. Lloyd R. Bailey, *Biblical Perspective on Death* (Philadelphia, PA: Fortress Press, 1979), 52, endnote 122.

opposite of "good" yet felt that it was "a divinely ordained part of the structure of things."[35] For Johnston, "Sheol is at the opposite theological extreme to Yahweh, and the dominant feature for its inhabitants is their separation from him" because there "they are cut off from him and forgotten" (Ps 88:5), there "they cannot remember, praise or thank" him (Ps 6:6; Isa 38:18; Jonah 2:5). Accordingly, Johnston concludes that "Sheol is a fitting place for the wicked who forget God (Pss 9:17; 31:17; 55:15), but one which the righteous dread (Pss 16:10; 30:3; 49:15; 86:13)."[36] Yet *Sheol* does not provide an escape from God (Amos 9:2; Ps 139:8), because it is thoroughly accessible to God (Job 26:5; Prov 15:11) and cannot limit or restrain God's power (Deut 32:22; Isa 7:11; Job 11:8).

Tromp argues that the Old Testament does not have a "formal doctrine" on the destiny of the dead and that the realities of death and beyond have to be only "understood and expressed in a mythical-symbolical way."[37] Yet Tromp states that "Sheol is not beyond Yahweh's power . . . Yahweh has full control over Sheol."[38] Johnston argues that for *Sheol* to be within God's power it has to be literal, just as the derogatory remark, "Go to hell," has its root in the belief that there is a real hell, so also, *Sheol,* to be open before God (Job 26:6, 14), has to be real.[39] Tromp argues that Job 26:6, 14, means that God does not know *Sheol* in an "intellectualistic sense of knowing" but when he knows it, it is "in his hands" (Ps 95:4), meaning, he controls it.[40] This explanation is unconvincing since he cannot control what he does not literally know. Tromp further argues his point by referring to God and chaos, that God is not in chaos but he controls it. In the same way, one could argue that God does not need to be in *Sheol* in order to know (and see) it in detail to control it.

Johnston further contends that, "Yahweh has access to Sheol does not imply that its inhabitants have access to him."[41] For its inhabitants, Johnston notes,

> Sheol is a place of no return (Job 16:22), a place of captivity with gates (Isa 38:10) and bars (Jonah 2:6). The 'cords of Sheol' may also suggest captivity (Pss 18:5; 116:3), . . . Job's wish to be

---
35. Ibid., 132.
36. Johnston, *Shades of Sheol*, 75.
37. Tromp, *Primitive Conceptions of Death*, 196.
38. Ibid., 197.
39. Johnston, *Shades of Sheol*, 75.
40. Tromp, *Primitive Conceptions of Death*, 200–201.
41. Johnston, *Shades of Sheol*, 76.

hidden temporarily in Sheol (14:13; cf. 18–22) initially seems to question this finality, but the wish is hypothetical, an attempt to move beyond his perceived impasse with God, and does not qualify the general picture.[42]

Johnston further describes *Sheol*,

It is a place of darkness (Job 10:21; Ps 88:6, 12; cf.143:3; Lam 3:6; Sirach 22:11), of inactivity and silence (Pss 94:17; 115:17). Only two prophetic oracles portray any form of activity. In one the denizens of Sheol must be roused to greet a newcomer, and they then describe themselves as weak (Isa 14:9f.). In the other, the long dead declaim that others 'have come down, they lie still' (Ezek 32:21). These texts simply confirm that inactivity is the norm.[43]

Johnston contends, "Death, and implicitly Sheol, is the great leveler of all, small or great, slave or free (Job 3:13–19)."[44] He argues against any social distinctions among the residents of *Sheol*, as their enfeebled existence does not permit that (Isa 14; Ezek 32) and he does not accept the two compartments theory.[45]

The Underworld as the Destiny of the Dead

For Burney, *Sheol* is the abode of all the dead (pictured in Job 30:23) both morally good and bad without distinction.[46] Atkinson concurs and contends that there is no biblical foundation for two divisions there. He translates *Sheol* simply as "grave," as does the NIV, and for him the difference between the godly and the ungodly is manifest in resurrection.[47] Though some may see the possibility of two compartments in *Sheol* in Isaiah 14:15 and Ezekiel

---

42. Ibid.
43. Ibid.
44. Ibid.
45. Ibid., 76–77.
46. Burney, *Israel's Hope of Immortality*, 9. Truett E. Bobo ("The Intermediate State," PhD dissertation, Fuller Theological Seminary, 1978, 7–12) argues against W. G. Shedd & L. Berkhof's position of *Sheol* as the abode of the wicked only, and following W. Eichrodt, G. Von Rad & others, he sees it as the abode of all dead.
47. Basil Atkinson, *Life and Immortality: An Examination of the Nature and Meaning of Life and Death as They are Revealed in the Scriptures* (Taunton, UK; E. Goodman, n.d.), 46–47.

32:23, (also in later Inter-Testamental literature) Johnston argues that the Old Testament does not assert that view.[48]

Table 1: Nuances of Sheol in the Old Testament
(after Johnston, *Shades of Sheol*, 80)

Main Emphasis		Number of Texts	Texts[49]
1. Cosmological extremity		5	Deut 32:22; Job 11:8; Ps 139:8; Isa 7:11 (57:9); Amos 9:2
2. Underworld	general term	6	1 Sam 2:6; Job 17:13, 16; 26:6; Prov 15:11; Isa 57:9
	place of confinement	4	2 Sam 22:6; Ps 18:6; Job 7:9 (14:13; 17:16); Ps 116:3
	existence	3	Ps 6:6; Isa 14:11; 38:18
3. Underworld	personified	7	Prov 1:12; 27:20; 30:16; Song 8:6; Hos 13:14 (x2); Hab 2:5
4. Escape	deliverance	5	Pss 16:10; 30:3; 49:15; 86:13; Jonah 2:2
	avoidance	2	Prov 15:24; 23:14
5. Destiny	everyone	2	Ps 89:48; Eccl 9:10
	righteous	7	Gen 37:35; 42:38; 44:29, 31; Job 14:13; Ps 88:3; Isa 38:10
	ungodly	25	Num 16:30, 33; 1 Kgs 2:6, 9; Job 21:13; 24:19; Pss 9:17; 31:17; 49:14 (x2); 55:15; 141:7; Prov 5:5; 7:27; 9:18; Isa 5:14; 14:11, 15; 28:15, 18; Ezek 31:15–17; 32:21, 27

Here, as we have noted before, especially following Johnston's table above, *Sheol* has different nuances in different contexts of the Old Testament. Johnston's survey of the different nuances of meaning of *Sheol* in different contexts by classifying the related Old Testament texts which I have shown above is very helpful. Johnston's survey shows that *Sheol* is used to mean "the

---

48. Johnston, *Shades of Sheol*, 77.
49. The texts in parentheses are not counted in the number of occurrences as these have "a significant further connotation" (Johnston, *Shades of Sheol*, 80).

human destiny" most frequently in the Old Testament and when it means "the human destiny" the predominant reference is to the destiny of the ungodly. As Johnston argues,

> This use accounts for half of all occurrences, and is attested across the whole range of the Old Testament literature: psalmodic, reflective, prophetic and narrative. For the Hebrew writers this was clearly the most notable aspect of the underworld. By contrast, Sheol occurs relatively infrequently in cosmology, underworld description or personification, and these were not important biblical themes. However, modern scholarship has tended to focus attention on these latter aspects.[50]

Thus, we see that although many scholars tend to consider *Sheol* as the *abode of all dead,* both the godly and the ungodly, from Johnston's above clasification of *Sheol*'s nuances of meaning, it seems clear that the writers of the Old Testament see it predominantly as the *destiny of the ungodly,* often referred to as "the wicked" (Isa 5:14; Pss 9:17; 31:17; 141:7; Job 21:13), "sinners" (Job 24:19), "the foolish rich" (Ps 49:14), "scoffers" (Isa 28:15, 18) and "the immoral" (Prov 5:5; 7:27; 9:18). Of course, Johnston also points out that sometimes *Sheol* is "feared by the righteous in extreme circumstances (though more often they seek deliverance) and very occasionally it is envisaged for everyone."[51] He notes,

> certain individuals, who are otherwise presumed to be righteous, envisage descent to Sheol, specifically Jacob, Hezekiah, Job and a psalmist (Gen 37:35 etc.; Isa 38:10; Job 17:13–16; Ps 88:4). However, they all speak in the context of extreme trial, whether loss, illness, affliction or abandonment; and Hezekiah, Job and the psalmist interpret their circumstances explicitly as divine judgment . . . So arguably the righteous only envisage Sheol when they face unhappy and untimely death, which they interpret as divine punishment. By contrast, when they face a contented death at the end of a full and happy life, or where this is narrated, there is no mention of Sheol.[52]

---

50. Johnston, *Shades of Sheol*, 80.
51. Ibid., 81.
52. Ibid., 81–82.

We have seen in Johnston's table that only twice is *Sheol* used in the Old Testament as the *destiny of all dead*: Psalm 89:48–49 and Ecclesiastes 9:7–10. Johnston shows that "in Psalm 89 it is humanity as created for falsehood, i.e. sinful and under judgment, which is destined for Sheol."[53] He also shows that, in Ecclesiastes, God's *judgment* ("though less prominent than other themes") of all deeds (12:14) is the final theme and *all of the dead* going to *Sheol* (9:7–10) is simply a "part of Qohelet's reflection on the absurdity of observable life," and is *not* its final word.[54] In conclusion, agreeing with Johnston, *Sheol* is mainly the final destiny of all who are under God's judgment, that is, the wicked, and perhaps the afflicted righteous, or *all* sinners but not the general destiny of all human dead.

Alternative to Sheol

If, according to the Old Testament, *Sheol* is not the general destiny of all the dead but only of those who are under the judgment of God – the ungodly and the wicked – then what happens to those who are godly in God's sight and not sent to *Sheol*? What does God do with them after their death in the Old Testament? What is their "State-after-Death"? Is there an alternative to *Sheol* in the Old Testament? It seems that there is no specific place mentioned in the Old Testament as an alternative to *Sheol* (and similar terms); that is, there is no reference to a specific place, like *Sheol*, that indicates the destiny of the righteous, godly dead. Yet, in the Old Testament, some texts seem to point to a kind of hope for the godly of a continuing fellowship with God beyond death. Now I will consider those Old Testament texts about "State-after-Death."

Enoch and Elijah

We find some clues for an alternative to *Sheol* in the Old Testament in the final destiny of two notable men of God, Enoch and Elijah, both of whom did not experience death but continued fellowship with God beyond physical life. Genesis 5:23, 24 (NIV) has, "Altogether, Enoch lived 365 years. Enoch walked with God; then he was no more, because God took him away." Within the overall context of Genesis, chapter 5 gives a human genealogy from the

---

53. Ibid., 82.
54. Ibid., 83.

first man, Adam, until Noah and then speaks of the great flood during Noah's lifetime in chapter 6. In the rest of chapter 5, starting from Adam until Noah, every person died after a full life except for Enoch. However there is little explanation of what happened to him. Johnston points out that,

> Scholarly interest tends to focus on ancient parallels, and the date of composition or redaction. But what often escapes notice is that Enoch's fate does not occasion later theological comment or devotional fervour in Israel's religious literature. Nowhere in the Hebrew Bible is there an explanation of its significance, or a prayer for a similar destiny. Enoch's mysterious experience remained singular in Israel's story and unassimilated in her theology.[55]

Outside the Old Testament canon, we do see some elaboration of the Enoch tradition from the second century before the Christian era onwards in at least three Books of Enoch which are part of the Apocalyptic Pseudepigrapha. According to Martin-Achard, these Pseudepigraphal writings make Enoch "not only the custodian of the mysteries of the things to come, but also the heavenly High Priest, and even the New Testament."[56] He comments,

> The lot of Enoch remains exceptional . . . it marks the break in the order imposed upon the descendants of Adam . . . It is important to emphasise that the believers in Israel . . . primarily exalted the Patriarch's piety and the uncommon lot it procured him; the personal destiny of Enoch perhaps had the effect of inspiring some of the faithful to hope that the life of a man absolutely dedicated to God would not necessarily end in Sheol, but would find its reward and fulfillment in Yahweh.[57]

All the same, there is little detail in the Old Testament canon about Enoch's departure from the earth and what it meant to the common faithful of Israel.

Next, in 2 Kings 2:1–12 we find the Lord (*YHWH*) took Elijah to heaven without his physically dying on earth. "When the LORD was about to take Elijah to heaven in a whirlwind, Elijah and Elisha were on their way from Gilgal" (2 Kgs 2:1, NIV). Elijah wanted to persuade Elisha to remain there so that Elijah could depart but Elisha would not leave Elijah alone as long he was

---

55. Johnston, *Shades of Sheol*, 199–200.
56. Martin-Achard, *From Death to Life*, 66–67.
57. Ibid., 69.

alive on earth. When they went to Bethel, the company of prophets reminded Elisha that the Lord (*YHWH*) was going to take Elijah away, yet Elisha would not separate from him. The same thing happened in Jericho and then they both went to the Jordan, where Elijah parted the water and they crossed over on dry ground. After that Elisha asked Elijah for the double portion of his spirit and while the two of them were walking together, "suddenly a chariot of fire and horses of fire appeared and separated the two of them, and Elijah went up to heaven in a whirlwind . . . and Elisha saw him no more." (2 Kgs 2:11–12, NIV).

In 2 Kings 2:15–18, the company of prophets recognized, "the spirit of Elijah is resting on Elisha" yet they did not believe Elisha and wanted to search for Elijah's body. They "searched for three days but did not find" Elijah's body and Elisha rebuked them for not believing him (2:17–18). Johnston perceptively comments,

> But here again Elijah's fate remains a singular event, which does not become a model for Elisha or other prophets, and which receives no theological reflection. The only later acknowledgement of it in the Old Testament occurs in the penultimate verse of the prophetic corpus, with its concluding prediction that God will send "the prophet Elijah before the great and terrible day of Yahweh comes." (Mal 4:5)[58]

Thus, the State beyond the physical existence on earth, of both Enoch and Elijah stands out compared to the rest of the notable people of God in the Old Testament as they did not experience death but went on to be with God forever. We see no theological reflection on their final destiny in the Old Testament canon of Scripture, and Elijah is only mentioned once in Malachi 4:5. Perhaps this reflects ignorance or lack of interest in Enoch and Elijah's State beyond death among the ancient faithful of Israel and that Elijah was only considered a potential heavenly messenger much later in the post-exilic period. Johnston notes that Enoch and Elijah's final destiny was not explicitly considered a model "for the righteous: not in narrative of impending death, not in prophetic aspiration, not in wisdom musing, nor – most strikingly – in the numerous psalms which grapple with the inequity and reality of death."[59]

However, though Enoch and Elijah's final fate was somehow put on the sidelines of the Old Testament perspectives of "State-after-Death," it must be

---

58. Johnston, *Shades of Sheol*, 200.
59. Ibid.

recognized that their final destiny was never explicitly or implicitly denied or rejected. Neither is the possibility of continued fellowship with God beyond death for the *righteous* and the faithful entirely ignored or rejected. Next we will look at a few of the Psalms that seem to allow this possible continued communion with God beyond death like Enoch and Elijah.

The Psalms

As we have noted, the final destiny of Enoch and Elijah seems *not* to be a model in most of the Psalms that struggle with impending death and it seems these Psalms considered physical death as the final end of a living relationship with God. Consequently, there was a sincere plea throughout the Psalms that the people will be saved from their enemies and impending physical death. For example, "No one remembers you when he is dead" and "It is not the dead who praise the LORD, those who go down in silence" (Pss 6:5; 115:17). King David prayed, "The cords of death entangled me; the torrents of destruction overwhelmed me" (Ps 18:4) and God saved him from death and his enemies; and he said, "He reached down from on high and took hold of me; he drew me out of deep waters. He rescued me from my powerful enemy, from my foes" (Ps 18:16–17). However, a few Psalms seem to give an alternative view of ultimate destiny and hence a different "State-after-Death" from *Sheol* which we now consider.

Psalm 16

According to Gunkel,[60] this is an Individual Lament because it begins with a plea for protection. Craigie claims that, even though 16:1 may imply a prayer for protection in the midst of a crisis, or for continued protection from crisis, in general terms it is a Psalm of Confidence especially because of 16:5–11.[61] Martin-Achard too considers this to be a Psalm of Confidence and notes, "The writer is voicing his happiness at being in communion with the Living God; thanks to this he has tasted a serene joy, he has discovered the well-spring of a veritable and inexhaustible felicity."[62] In 16:10–11, the Psalmist shows that his total confidence is on God, "For you do not give me up to Sheol, or let your

---

60. Cited in Johnston, *Shades of Sheol*, 201(fn 5) from Hermann Gunkel's commentary on Psalms in German (*Die Psalmen* [Göttingen: Vandenhoeck & Ruprecht, 1926], 51).
61. Peter C. Craigie, *Psalms 1–50*, Word Biblical Commentary, No. 19 (Dallas, TX: Word Books, 1983), 155.
62. Martin-Achard, *From Death to Life*, 148.

faithful one see the Pit. You show me the path of life. In your presence there is fullness of joy; in your right hand are pleasures forevermore" (NRSV).

According to Craigie[63] and others, the Psalmist was facing the immediate threat of death and was confident that he would be restored to a full life in God's presence here and now. For these scholars, this passage should not be interpreted either messianically or in terms of individual eschatology. They see the Psalmist in an immediate crisis and confident of an immediate deliverance. Craigie comments, "the psalmist acknowledges that God makes him know, or experience, the 'path of life,' not the afterlife, but the fullness of life here and now which is enriched by the rejoicing."[64] Thus, for these scholars, the Psalmist will finally go to *Sheol* like all others after a long fruitful life on earth. It is important to note that though Derek Kidner admits that some see in this Psalm nothing more than a recovery from an illness, yet he contends that "the contrast in Psalms 49 and 73 between the end of wicked and that of righteous supports a bolder view."[65] But Martin-Achard refers to the opinion of H. Gunkel and C. Barth (a son of Karl Barth) that, "There is absolutely no question of resurrection or immortality here" and he too seems to agree with them that there is no hint of resurrection or immortality here.[66]

However, based on the authorial intent, Johnston is right in contending that this passage invites a different interpretation. Johnston notes concerning the Psalmist,

> But if he felt instinctively that Sheol was not a fitting fate for Yahweh's 'faithful one', then he could be affirming an equally instinctive confidence in deliverance from it, and a personal if undefined hope for some form of continued communion with Yahweh beyond death. After all, as he says in v. 11, he is on the path of life, not death, sated with divine joy and endless pleasure. The form of this continued communion . . . remains vague: no

---

63. Craigie, *Psalms 1–50*, 155ff.
64. Ibid., 158.
65. Derek Kidner, *Psalms 1–72: An Introduction and Commentary on Books I and II of the Psalms*, Tyndale Old Testament Commentaries, No. 14a. (Leicester, UK: InterVarsity, 1973), 86. Klaas Spronk (*Beatific Afterlife in Ancient Israel and in the Ancient Near East* [Kevelaer, Germany: Butzon and Bercker; Neukirchen-Vluyn: Neukirchener Verlag, 1986], 74ff) gives a summary of different scholars' views relating the hope for a continuation of the communion with YHWH and the belief in the final resurrection of the dead in the Old Testament. Some thought the former was a preparation for the latter, whereas others saw in them twofold developments, and some even saw in the former view the influence of Greek concept of immortal soul.
66. Martin-Achard, *From Death to Life*, 151–152.

spatial location is indicated, no name (contrasting with the name Sheol) is mentioned, no fellow beneficiaries are acknowledged – in fact no details are given at all. Only Yahweh's presence and blessing are clear. Caught in the tension between an underworld associated predominantly with the ungodly . . . and the lack of a clear alternative for the faithful, the psalmist affirms that some alternative is eminently appropriate.[67]

Though Martin-Achard contends that the Psalmist is not thinking about dying and being resurrected by God from the grave, yet in some sense he sees death has been overcome.[68] He comments about the Psalmist and his communion with God, "he does not understand how its persistence will be possible, but that does not trouble his mind, because it depends on God . . . after Easter, the faith of the psalmist became the great certainty."[69] I find Johnston's response helpful, as he points out that the tension that the psalmist goes through (with *Sheol* mainly for the ungodly and a lack of clear alternative for the faithful) gives a "forward-looking, prophetic perspective" to the Psalm. This tension is duly resolved as "sketched at the margins of the Old Testament, in resurrection and post-mortem distinction between righteous and wicked" in Isaiah 26:19 and Daniel 12:2, and that resolution is fully realized in Christ's resurrection.[70]

Psalm 49

Scholars conclude this is a Wisdom Psalm, giving special instruction to all peoples on earth irrespective of their national, social or economic status as spelled out in 49:1–2.[71] In 49:3–4 we see the clear signs of a Wisdom Psalm

---

67. Johnston, *Shades of Sheol*, 201–202.
68. Martin-Achard, *From Death to Life*, 152.
69. Ibid., 153.
70. Johnston, *Shades of Sheol*, 202.
71. Martin-Achard (*From Death to Life*, 153), Kidner (*Psalms 1–72*, 182), Broyles (*Psalms, New International Biblical Commentary*, No. 11 [Peabody, MA: Hendrickson Publishers, 1999], 221), Anderson (*Out of the Depths: The Psalms Speak for Us Today* [Philadelphia, PA: The Westminster Press, 1983], 218), Johnston (*Shades of Sheol*, 202). Craigie (*Psalms 1–50*, 358) though puts it in the general category of the wisdom psalms yet sees it differ from some other types of wisdom psalms, which deal with general themes of morality basic to the wisdom tradition (e.g. Psalm 1). For Craigie, this psalm is concerned with a single issue (a "proverb" or "enigma," v 5) the issue of death, specifically in the context of wealth and power. He notes, "There is first a basic category, in which the moral essence of the wisdom tradition is expressed in a didactic form; the Book of Proverbs is an example . . . The second category contains works of a more theoretical nature, exploring the difficult intellectual and theological issues raised in moral wisdom . . . Psalm 49 falls into the second category and has some similarity to the themes of the Book of Job, particularly . . . in which Job raises the empirical problem of the apparent success and prosperity of the wicked and rich (Job 21:7–15)."

as the Psalmist uses terms like wisdom, understanding, proverb and riddle. In 49:5–6 the Psalmist presents the problem of the righteous suffering persecution at the hands of the wicked, those who put their trust in wealth. He then uses wisdom truth to provide the solution for the problem raised in 49:7–9 that "human wealth is powerless to prolong life and to ransom people from the pit, i.e. the underworld."[72] The Psalmist shows in 49:10–14 that all people will die, be they wise or foolish, leaving their wealth behind and no matter how wealthy or important a person is on earth their ultimate destiny is death and *Sheol*. We carefully note here that in 49:14 the Psalmist is emphasizing the final fate of the ungodly in contrast to the Psalmist's fate in 49:15.[73] Thus in 49:14 *Sheol* is shown to be the final home of the unrighteous and the wicked rich.

However in 49:15 the Psalmist pointedly shows the other half of the solution of the riddle (49:5–6), that God is going to ransom him (or the righteous) from the power of *Sheol* and receive him. "What humans are powerless to do, God will do for his faithful follower: God will provide for him an alternative destiny to the underworld."[74] The following comment by C. Ryder Smith is illuminating,

> Unlike some other Psalmists this one does not say "God will slay the wicked *before their time*," for he knows that often wicked men do, in fact, live long and prosperous lives. His answer is, in effect: "The righteous do not pass permanently to Sheol when they die. This is the fate of the wicked, and of the wicked only, as it ought to be." What then happens to the righteous? This Psalmist's answer is "God will ransom (*padah*) my soul from the hand of Sheol, for he will take me" (verse 15). The context requires the "take" here means "take me to himself" (cf. Gen 5:24). The "emotional reaction of the *chasid* to the new concept of Sheol passes clearly at last . . . , into the *conviction* that Sheol is not the final destiny of righteous men. Its basis is 'When the man who is faithful to God dies, God will still be faithful to him. God can [do] no other.'"

---

72. Johnston, *Shades of Sheol*, 203.
73. Martin-Achard (*From Death to Life*, 155) refers to W. Staerk, A Bentzen and H. Gunkel's opinion that v. 15 was not part of the original psalm but added in and that to them the central idea of the psalm is that death is the final leveler of all people and their inequalities on earth. However, Martin-Achard correctly argues that without v. 15 "there is no progression in its thought" and that most scholars consider it authentic as it is found in the earliest versions and as it is "marking the culminating point of this Wisdom poem."
74. Johnston, *Shades of Sheol*, 203.

Whatever may be true of other Psalmists, this one had "solved the riddle."[75]

Of course, some scholars do not see in 49:15 the *alternative* final destiny for the righteous but an immediate rescue from the imminent danger of death. C. Barth cited by Johnston argued that this Psalmist, like all the other Psalmists, while rejoicing in immediate rescue from the power of *Sheol*, still does not deny his eventual destiny in *Sheol*.[76] However, the context of this Psalm nowhere implies a temporary problem of imminent death for all people as the main riddle of the Psalm but, rather, the injustices of the wicked rich as opposed to the godly and the poor. The Psalmist's solution is that the wicked will be punished and sent to *Sheol* and the righteous will escape *Sheol* and have their final destiny with God. This Psalm cannot be simply about the Psalmist's temporary rescue from immediate death here and now and continuation of life on earth under the tyranny of the wicked. Even if the former oppressors are punished in *Sheol*, a new generation of wicked may arise on earth to oppress the rescued Psalmist again.

Craigie argues that 49:15 (in Hebrew) is not the Psalmist's words of hope but rather he is quoting the wealthy, "their (imaginary) words of self-confidence: 'Surely God will redeem me . . . ' (v. 16). They think their position of privilege in this life will give them also a position of privilege when it comes to death."[77] I respectfully disagree because the Psalmist could have added, "They say," prior to the quote in verse 15 or even used the third person pronoun. Johnston argues that "there is no textual hint that this is a false statement, and it would give little comfort to the righteous that they would share the same fate as their foes."[78] Johnston also argues that 49:19 shows the difference in the final destiny of the wicked and the righteous, in that, if it is taken out of context, it may mean that all people, godly or ungodly, go to *Sheol* after death. However, in this context the Psalm probably speaks about the Psalmist's persecutor whose ancestors were presumably equally ungodly and so he will end up with them.[79]

Martin-Achard does not see an obvious explicit reference to resurrection in this Psalm, yet he feels that the Psalmist here possibly thinks that "he will

---

75. C. Ryder Smith, *The Bible Doctrine of the Hereafter* (London: The Epworth Press, 1958), 64–65.
76. Johnston, *Shades of Sheol*, 203.
77. Craigie, *Psalms 1–50*, 360.
78. Johnston, *Shades of Sheol*, 204.
79. Ibid.

escape not only premature death or the judgment that is going to smite all the ungodly, but by some dispensation, death itself as well" and he will dwell with God forever.[80] He believes the study of Psalm 73 will help us reach a more conclusive solution to the issue of what is the *alternative* final destiny of the righteous.

Psalm 73

As in Psalm 49, Psalm 73 is also a Wisdom Psalm dealing with the prosperity of the wicked and the Psalmist's personal reaction to that enigma. Then he enters the sanctuary of God and comprehends the real, ultimate destiny of these wicked persons, whom he envied (73:17). Verse 17, generally seen as a temple experience, is widely considered the turning point of the Psalm and verse 24 the high point of the Psalmist's affirmation.[81] According to Martin-Achard, the Psalmist provides the same solution as in Psalm 49, except that he "lays even more stress upon the privilege of the man who lives close to God."[82] As in 49:15, here the Psalmist begins to unfold the other half of the solution, the final destiny of the righteous, in verse 23. Let us consider verses 23–24: "Yet I am always with you; you hold me by my right hand. You guide me with your counsel, and afterward you will take me into glory" (NIV).

Here the Psalmist begins to proclaim that, in spite of his foolish reaction to the prosperity of the wicked and the suffering of the righteous, he is *always with* God, meaning, he continues to have fellowship with God in the midst of suffering. Not only that, God holds his right hand, guides him with wise advice and this fellowship with God will continue *afterward* as God *takes* (or *receives*) him *into glory*. Johnston notes that scholars are divided whether this "*into glory*" refers to this life or to some life after death and he shows how it is possible to argue both views from the immediate context of the Psalm.[83] So he cites the alternative approach of Martin-Achard,[84] which for Johnston, "refocuses the issue from the time-frame of the psalmist's hope to its nature," to the daily presence of God in Psalmist's life.[85] However, Kidner explains more convincingly why this *glory* perhaps has more to do with a "State-after-Death" into God's presence than *glory* in this present life:

---

80. Martin-Achard, *From Death to Life*, 157–158.
81. Johnston, *Shades of Sheol*, 204.
82. Martin-Achard, *From Death to Life*, 158.
83. Johnston, *Shades of Sheol*, 205.
84. Martin-Achard, *From Death to Life*, 165.
85. Johnston, *Shades of Sheol*, 205.

The word *afterward*, or 'in the end', makes it clear that the last line looks beyond the steady progress of the middle sentence, to the climax of the whole. Whether that climax . . . is the comparatively modest one of promotion to earthly honour . . . or the crowning joy of passing into God's presence, is something of an open question. To the present writer, the second is altogether the more likely. Verbally, the word *receive* suggests it, and doubly so, by its use in the story of Enoch (Gen. 5:24, "for God took him"; the verb is the same) and in Psalm 49:15. In the latter, the line "for he will receive me" completes a couplet which begins "But God will ransom my soul from the power of Sheol." Further, the thrust of the present paragraph is towards God alone, from its opening theme, "continually with thee," to its supreme confession in 25f., "Whom have I in heaven but thee?" This mounting experience of salvation, "grasped, guided, glorified," is a humble counterpart to the great theological sequence of Romans 8:29f., which spans the work of God from its hidden beginning, "whom he foreknew," to the same consummation as here, "he also glorified." We may well conclude that if eternal life was visible to a discerning eye even in the saying "I am the God of Abraham, . . . Isaac, and . . . Jacob," as our Lord pointed out, here it lies open for all to see.[86]

Perhaps Johnston is also persuaded that this Psalm points to hope beyond death as he concludes, "Nevertheless, the stronger the Israelite writer's sense of divine presence in this life, the more likely the development of a concept of hope that transcending [sic] death."[87] He also notes that the redactional study may show that later redactors placed this Psalm in the middle of the Book of Psalms, since they may have understood this Psalm as pointing to a supreme example of hope beyond death. I will not cover here other verses in Psalms (17:15; 27:13; 139:18b), which may also point to this hope, yet I recognize traces of that hope in them within the progressive nature of revelation.

---

86. Derek Kidner, *Psalms 73–150: An Introduction and Commentary on Books III-IV of the Psalms*, Tyndale Old Testament Commentaries, No. 14b (Leicester, UK: InterVarsity, 1975), 25.

87. Johnston, *Shades of Sheol*, 205–206.

Proverbs

There are a few proverbs that may project an alternative hope of life beyond death in God's presence for the righteous instead of *Sheol*. These are Proverbs 12:28; 15:24; 23:14. We will look first at Proverbs 12:28, "In the path of righteousness there is life, in walking its path there is no death" (NRSV). The first half of this verse is clear but the second half causes a lot of difficulties in translation due to some variations in earlier and later manuscripts. Kidner cites two suggestions with no change in the consonantal text: "And the journey of her pathway is no-death!" and "But [there is] a way [which is] a path to (*'el*) death" and notes, "The second of these is the smoother construction; it also fits the prevailing pattern of antitheses. But the first is closer to the existing text, and has had fresh support claimed for it from Ugaritic."[88] However, Johnston notes that "many scholars reasonably propose 'but the way of abomination/folly leads to death,'[89] and some suggest that the extant text reflects a later, more developed eschatology."[90]

Yet for Johnston, even if this erases "the immediate reference to immortality" from the second half of the verse, "the general reference to life" in the first half of the verse remains. In my opinion, as long as we are not absolutely sure that the second half of the existing text's verse is a later emendation to the original text, there is definitely a good chance that this is a reference to an alternative to *Sheol*, in keeping with the first half's "general reference to life" as Johnston suggests. Why would the later copyists change the meaning of the second half so drastically if it were not true?

Next in Proverbs 15:24 has, "For the wise the path of life leads upward, in order to avoid Sheol below. If you beat them with the rod, you will save their lives from Sheol" (NRSV). In 15:24, the comparison of "upward" and "below" could mean "life with God beyond death" as opposed to "punishment in Sheol below" but as Johnston points out, some scholars only see in it life on earth here and now or "a later (Hebrew) reinterpretation of an originally this-

---

88. Derek Kidner, *Proverbs: An Introduction and Commentary*, Tyndale Old Testament Commentaries, No. 15 (Downers Grove, IL: InterVarsity, 1964), 100.

89. For example, in Murphy and Huwiler (*Proverbs, Ecclesiastes, Song of Songs*, New International Biblical Commentary, No. 12 [Peabody, MA: Hendrickson Publishers, 1999], 62–63) and also in Murphy (*Proverbs*, Word Biblical Commentary, No. 22 [Dallas, TX: Word Books, 1998], 88, 92) and Murphy also notes "In any case, immortality cannot be understood here as life with God beyond death. Sheol is the consistent perspective in this book" Murphy and Huwiler (*Proverbs, Ecclesiastes, Song of Songs*, 62).

90. Johnston, *Shades of Sheol*, 208.

worldly proverb (preserved in the LXX)."[91] However, Johnston also points out that LXX may have used a different Hebrew text or LXX may have adapted in translation and that the existing canonical Hebrew text is not necessarily a later text than the LXX.[92]

In Proverbs 23:14, we see the "life and death" antithesis as in 15:24 and it seems there is an alternative for the undisciplined child that will save him/her from going to *Sheol* at death if disciplined in this life. But, again, as it does not elaborate on what the alternative to *Sheol* is, most scholars would consider it to be just prosperous life on earth as opposed to pre-mature death and *Sheol*. However, we cannot ignore the traces of an alternative to *Sheol* in these verses of Proverbs as a part of the progressive revelation that is more fully revealed later on in Scripture.

Job 19:25–27

> For I know that my Redeemer lives, and that at the last he will stand upon the earth; and after my skin has been thus destroyed, then in my flesh I shall see God, whom I shall see on my side, and my eyes shall behold, and not another. My heart faints within me! (NRSV)

This passage has given a lot of difficulties[93] to translators and interpreters over the years due its "unusual theme, poetic form and awkward Hebrew" and scholars are divided as to whether Job expects vindication in this life or after death.[94] Johnston thinks a literal translation would be like this,

> 25 And I, I know my *go'el* living, and last upon dust he will stand.
>
> 26 And after my skin [masc.] this [fem.] is flayed, and from my flesh I will see God.
>
> 27 Which I, I will see to/for me, and my eyes will see and not a stranger, my kidneys are consumed in my bosom.[95]

---

91. Ibid., 207–208.
92. Ibid., 208.
93. See Martin-Achard (*From Death to Life*, 166). He cites C. Kuhl: "Versiculus brevis, septem constans vocculis, at undequaque *difficultatibus* septus" (emphasis added). Also Johnston (*Shades of Sheol*, 211); Andersen (*Job: An Introduction and Commentary*, Tyndale Old Testament Commentaries, No. 13 [London: InterVarsity, 1976], 193).
94. Johnston, *Shades of Sheol*, 209.
95. Ibid., 211.

In spite of the textual difficulties and possible range of translations, Andersen cautions against two extreme interpretations of this passage, "There is no need for the loud note of Job's certainty of ultimate vindication to be drowned by the static of textual difficulties. But too much of later resurrection theology should not be read back into the passage, as in AV."[96] Though Christians generally use the fuller revelation of New Testament perspective of "State-after-Death" to interpret this Old Testament passage, Johnston wonders if Job, himself, understood clearly whether it was going to be an after-death vindication or vindication in this life.[97] After a thorough examination of the passage, Johnston concludes,

> So in beleaguered yet defiant faith, Job asserts that he will have a defender who will stand on earth and support him, and that after all his suffering he will get the one thing that matters most, an opportunity to present his case to God. This interpretation makes most sense . . . , even if it removes both the resurrectional and the messianic elements. It is just possible that he envisages some form of vindication after death, though without any indication of physical change or continued communion with God.[98]

It seems that Johnston leaves room for the possibility that Job may have envisaged some form of vindication beyond death.

However, even though Martin-Achard sees Job's confident expectation of God's intervention at the eleventh hour, he argues for Job's vindication here on earth and sees "no reference to the Hereafter" in verse 25.[99] He argues that verse 26 also shows that, "he is neither referring to his resurrection, nor . . . to a judgment of which he would be a far-off and posthumous witness."[100] and that verse 27 confirms the exegesis of verses 25–26 that, "Job will see God, in person, with his own eyes . . . while he is still alive, and not in the Beyond."[101]

By contrast, Andersen points out that, by referring to the end of Job's account (especially 42:5) and by "*relying* also on a general belief that the hope of personal resurrection is not present in the book," some scholars "maintain that Job still expects vindication in this life, *in spite of all that he has said*

---

96. Andersen, *Job*, 193.
97. Johnston, *Shades of Sheol*, 209, 214.
98. Ibid., 213.
99. Martin-Achard, *From Death to Life*, 168.
100. Ibid., 172.
101. Ibid., 173.

about the imminence of his death."¹⁰² However, Andersen sees in this passage Job's hope of a positive encounter with God after death "as a genuine human being," even though he admits that this "passage falls short of a full statement of faith in personal bodily resurrection." He argues quite convincingly why it is so:

> We think that there are several good reasons for accepting the second position. First, there would be no need for Job to deposit a written testimony, if he expects to be vindicated before he dies. Secondly, the word translated *earth*, as used in Job, is constantly connected with Sheol, and the statement that the Redeemer *lives* is a direct answer to the fact that a man dies (14:10). The repetition of the word *after* (-wards) in the prominent position at the beginning of verses 25b and 26a suggests an interval, or even, with the meaning *at last*, something eschatological. Finally, the argument that Job does not expect personal reconstitution as a man, because this idea entered Judaism only towards the very end of the biblical period, can be dismissed in light of much recent research that shows interest in the after-life as an ancient concern for Israelite faith. In particular, the outcome of our study of such passages as Job 14:13ff, if valid, shows that the hope of resurrection lies at the very heart of Job's faith.¹⁰³

In spite of the difficulties of translating the passage, as well as other scholars' views of what exactly happened at the end of the Book of Job, I find Andersen's position is more convincing than Martin-Achard's. As Andersen says, even though the Book of Job may not have a full-fledged, explicit and detailed description of the hope of personal bodily resurrection, yet there are clear indications of an alternative to *Sheol* for the righteous man like Job in the presence of God, after or beyond death, instead of mere vindication for him in his earthly life only. Soon we will consider the passages from the Old Testament which deal more explicitly with the resurrection from the dead within the progressive revelation of the Scriptures.

---

102. Andersen, *Job*, 194 (emphasis added).
103. Ibid.

Summary and Implications

I began this chapter by looking at Genesis 2:17ff. where God pronounced the first sentence of death on Adam and Eve as punishment for their disobedience. Adam and Eve were created with the ability to choose "to die" or "not to die." They chose death through their disobedience, resulting in the fall, after which the whole of humanity suffered the curse of death. My intention was to show from the Old Testament that "State-after-Death" is a critical component of God's universal mission whereby human beings can be rescued from one form of final destiny for another. We found that the Old Testament focuses mainly on Israel's earthly life in which God revealed himself to his people as they were called to obey, serve and worship God only, though they often failed. Yet in spite of the difficulty of tracing the growth of the understanding of life after death in ancient Israel, we were able to observe a progressive revelation of the concept of "State-after-Death" in the Old Testament as part of God's universal mission.

Sheol and similar terms generally mean "the underworld," or the realm where the deceased go deep down, under the earth. Israelites responded negatively to neighboring Near-Eastern pluralistic views of "State-after-Death" by choosing the unique term *Sheol* with its distinct monotheistic theological meaning for the underworld. They did not absorb the polytheistic assumptions of surrounding non-Yahwist peoples. In the Old Testament the underworld is a real and literal place away from God, a place of no return, of darkness and gloom, yet not totally outside of God's control. Finally, with the help of Johnston's survey of underworld references in the Old Testament, we conclude that it is mainly the destiny of those under God's judgment, the ungodly and sinners, and *not* the general destiny of all human dead, whether righteous or unrighteous.

That led us to study where the righteous would go or be after their death, an alternative to *Sheol* in the Old Testament. Several texts in the Old Testament seem to point to a hope for the godly or the righteous through a continuity of fellowship and communion with God, even beyond physical death. Our study of Enoch and Elijah, different Psalms, Proverbs and the classic passage of Job 19:25–27 all indicate a hope for the righteous and the faithful beyond death. In the next chapter, I will look into the references from the Old Testament that seem to more explicitly deal with resurrection from the dead within the progressive revelation of the Scriptures.

6

Resurrection from Death in the Old Testament

Having looked at Sheol and a possible alternative to *Sheol*, we will now seek indications in the Old Testament of a more specific "State-after-Death," namely, the possibility of resurrection from the dead. We ask whether this is a significant component of God's ultimate plan to rescue humankind in the religiously plural context of the Old Testament, to bring them from one form of the after-death state to another. N. T. Wright notes,

> Nobody doubts that the Old Testament speaks of the resurrection of the dead, but nobody can agree on what it means, where the idea came from, or how it relates to the other things the scriptures say about the dead. But since the Jewish world of Jesus' and Paul's day looked back to these texts as the principal sources for their widespread belief in resurrection, we must take care at least to examine the relevant texts.[1]

With this in mind, I will examine the Old Testament texts which seem to touch on resurrection from the dead within the progressive revelation of the Scriptures.

Resurrection from the Dead

In the introductory questions of the last chapter, we saw that in Genesis 2:17ff God pronounced the sentence of death on Adam and Eve and through them to all of humanity as a punishment for their disobedience. We noted Martin-

---

1. Wright, *Resurrection of the Son of God*, 108.

Achard's statement that God's "presence is sufficient to ward death off,"[2] as witnessed in the Old Testament. Is this God of the Old Testament able *only* to ward off death with his presence or is he *also* able to raise people from the dead? We will now consider this question.

Genesis 22

Enoch's state beyond death was an alternative to *Sheol* and the Lord (*YHWH*) took Elijah to heaven without his physically dying on earth. This shows that the God of the Old Testament is *able* to ward off the experience of death and take us to himself eternally. In the narrative of Genesis 22, we observe Abraham's faith and understanding of God, who is able to do more than simply ward off death. Abraham's conversation with both his servants and his son is a very important window into his underlying understanding of "State-after-Death." Kidner comments:

> From Abraham the harrowing demand evokes only love and faith, certain as he is that the 'foolishness of God' is unexplored wisdom. So, he is enabled, in the surrender of his son, to mirror God's still greater love, while his faith gives him a first glimpse of resurrection.[3]

In 22:5b, Abraham says to his servants, in the presence of his son Isaac, "We will worship and then we will come back to you." Kidner notes about verse 5 that Abraham believed God could raise Isaac from the dead immediately:

> The assurance that Isaac as well as Abraham would *come again* from the sacrifice was no empty phrase: it was Abraham's full conviction, on the ground that 'in Isaac shall thy seed be called' (21:12). Hebrews 11:17–19 reveals that he was expecting Isaac to be resurrected; henceforth he would regard him as given back from the dead.[4]

Again, in verse 8, Abraham responds to Isaac's query about the lamb for the burnt offering that *God will provide*. Here again, Abraham shows his full faith in God and the way God will intervene. What was in Abraham's mind? John E. Hartley comments,

---

2. Martin-Achard, *From Death to Life*, 19–20.
3. Derek Kidner, *Genesis: An Introduction and Commentary.* Tyndale Old Testament Commentaries (Leicester, UK: InterVarsity, 1967), 142.
4. Ibid., 143.

> The verb "provide" is literally "see." With this assertion, was Abraham refusing to face what was about to take place, or was he venturing a statement of great faith? This assertion, along with the one made to his servants about returning, suggests Abraham had a hope deep within himself that God would not let him kill the child of promise. The writer of Hebrews read the text in this way. (11:17–19)[5]

Hartley is right in seeing in both verse 5 and verse 8 that, "Abraham had a hope deep within himself that God would not let him kill the child of promise."[6] Yet, in verse 10 Abraham, resolved to obey God, prepares to sacrifice his son. If Abraham believed only that God would not let him kill his son of promise, then he would have waited until God provided him the lamb for the sacrifice. However, his continued preparation (verses 9–11), shows his underlying faith that his God was able to raise his son back to life, even if his son is killed. This is just as the writer of Hebrews (11:19) sees it. We noted in our chapter on hermeneutics that "the cross and the resurrection of Christ" is the transcendental basis for our *metacritical* hermeneutics on "State-after-Death" in pluralistic contexts. Based on that perspective, Genesis 22 would seem to be a prophetic picture of the future death and, especially, *resurrection* of Christ.

Thus, at the outset of the formation of the people of God, Israel, we already see in the Old Testament the seeds of belief in resurrection from the dead. We have shown that this is not because Israel had borrowed this idea from some neighboring peoples. Rather, it was because the God of the Old Testament is the one true and living God, who revealed himself to Abraham and had promised to give him descendants through his son Isaac. And Abraham believed God.

Next, we will explore the theme of resurrection from the dead in Deuteronomy 32 and 1 Samuel 2.

Deuteronomy 32 and 1 Samuel 2

Deuteronomy 32 gives the Song that Moses recited to the whole assembly of Israel prior to his death and their entry into Canaan. In verse 39, God

---

5. John E. Hartley, *Genesis,* New International Biblical Commentary, No. 1 (Peabody, MA: Hendrickson Publishers, 2000), 208.
6. Ibid.

proclaims his own uniqueness above all else and invincible power, not only to kill people but to bring them back to life. Similarly, at the birth of Samuel, Hannah states, "The LORD kills and brings to life; he brings down to Sheol and *raises up*" (1 Sam 2:6, ESV). These references affirm God's absolute power to give life and point to the possibility (and the faith) that God will bring the dead back to life again, especially in the second half of 1 Samuel 2:6 "he brings down to Sheol and *raises up*."

Johnston notes, "Both statements are categorical. They flow from an absolute confidence in Israel's god as all-powerful, and are the straightforward theological development of this faith."[7] Later on Johnston concludes that,

> All this suggests that Yahweh's power to "raise up from Sheol" is a potentiality which is affirmed rather than an actuality which has been witnessed. As supreme god, Yahweh obviously can "make alive," even though there is no recorded occurrence of this happening in the Mosaic or early monarchic tradition. This is who Yahweh is, not what he has done.[8]

It is true that apart from Enoch and Elijah, physically disappearing from the earth and ascending to heaven, "there is no recorded occurrence of [resurrection] in the Mosaic or early monarchic tradition." But did Moses (actually God is speaking in Deut 32:39) and Hannah merely proclaim what God *can* do rather than what he *would* ever do? Would they have remembered what happened to Enoch and Elijah as they spoke those words? Would they have remembered that Abraham believed God before he received the promised son? Or what did Abraham consider God would do as he went on to slay his son Isaac in obedience to God? I contend that these verses are sign-posts for the belief in resurrection in the Old Testament and imply that God was going to accomplish this truth in ultimate human destiny. These verses seem to be God's prophetic truth fulfilling the promises to Abraham in Genesis 12:1–3.

Though not dealing with resurrection, as such, but referring rather to Deuteronomy's use of the history of the Old Testament, Christopher Wright remarks on Deuteronomy 32:21 and 27:

> God has no illusions (v. 21). Neither has Moses (v. 27). But then, neither God nor Moses nor the Bible as a whole deals

---

7. Johnston, *Shades of Sheol*, 219.
8. Ibid.

in illusions. The future prophetically described in the Song of Moses, whether predictive or retrospective, was no illusion, but a matter of historical fact as the centuries of Israel's OT history unfolded and ultimately became the basis for an equally non-illusory eschatological theology of history and mission in the hands of Paul.[9]

Perhaps this remark ought to be applied to resurrection from the dead in the Old Testament. Following the above remark, Deuteronomy 32:39 and 1 Samuel 2:6 (as also Gen 22) are predictive parts providing the basis for a *non-illusory eschatological theology* of "State-after-Death." These verses affirm not merely that God *can* raise the dead, but also implicitly point to the possibility that he *will* raise the dead in the last day. One must not ignore the predictive/prophetic value of these verses for a theology of "State-after-Death" within the progressive revelatory process of the Scriptures.

Other Old Testament passages provide more of a basis that God *will* raise people from the dead. Martin-Achard says, "These important texts are so many signposts on the way followed by the Chosen people until they reached the revelation of a truth which became a fundamental dogma of Judaism and was subsequently adopted by the disciples of Christ, as it was by those of Muhammad."[10] We will continue to show that, in the process of progressive revelation of the Scriptures, the implicit concept (signposts, according to Martin-Achard) of the resurrection from the dead in the Old Testament becomes clearer in the passages discussed below.

Hosea 6

Hosea is an eighth century (BCE) prophet calling on Judah and Israel to repent because of the impending judgment from God. He reminds them that the king of Assyria cannot cure or heal them (5:13) because it is God who will tear and carry them off like a lion (5:14) until they repent and seek God's mercy (5:15). Israel seems to have heard Hosea's call for repentance and responds with 6:1–3 (NRSV):

> 1) "Come, let us return to the LORD; for it is he who has torn, and he will heal us; he has struck down, and he will bind us up.

---

9. Christopher J. H. Wright, *Deuteronomy*, New International Biblical Commentary, No. 4 (Peabody, MA: Hendrickson Publishers, 1996), 297.
10. Martin-Achard, *From Death to Life*, 74.

2) After two days he will revive us; on the third day he will raise us up, that we may live before him.

3) Let us know, let us press on to know the LORD; his appearing is as sure as the dawn; he will come to us like the showers, like the spring rains that water the earth."

According to Martin-Achard, "The consensus of opinion is that vs. 1–3 contain a penitential psalm voiced by the Israelites in manifestation of their repentance . . . [It] expresses their desire to return to God; it implies their acknowledgement of their misdeeds, and, above all their certainty that they will be heard by Yahweh."[11] Of course, the scholars are divided as to whether this passage refers to resurrection from the dead or recovery to normal health in this life only. Martin-Achard notes the two groups, "According to W. von Baudissin, E. Sellin, W. Baumgartner, and T. H. Robinson . . . here the Israelites are referring to resurrection; for J. Wellhausen, W. Nowack, and K. Budde, on the other hand, Israel is an invalid, relying on the help of God for relief. This is also the opinion of J. J. Stamm."[12] Martin-Achard considers this passage refers to a national restoration rather than the resurrection of individual Israelites.[13] I believe, instead of an "either-or," this passage along with many other Old Testament passages has a "both-and" meaning.

While the Israelites were certainly looking for national restoration, it seems there is also a brighter (though implicit) indication here that points to the resurrection from the dead. Kidner explains it well:

> Notice . . . how radical a cure is looked for. Bandaging and healing (1) provide one way of expressing it, but bringing back to life (2) does better justice to man's plight and to God's power. Admittedly the words "revive" and "live" need mean no more than "heal" and "recover"; but they can also and more properly express the meeting of a need as desperate as that which faced Ezekiel in the vision of his people as a heap of dry bones . . . Nothing short of resurrection is fit to describe such need and such salvation; and while the mention of *the third day* would

---

11. Ibid., 78.
12. Ibid., 80.
13. Ibid., 81. Later on Martin-Achard refers to Hosea 13:14b "O Death, where are your plagues . . . ?" and considers whether the Apostle Paul's exegesis of that verse in 1 Corinthians 15:55 is a correct one and concludes that it is not if considered in its immediate context (Ibid., 86–93).

sound to Hosea's hearers as the mere equivalent of "very soon," *the prophet may have spoken more significantly than he knew*; for it is only in Christ's resurrection that His people are effectively raised up, as both Paul and Peter teach us. And when Paul finds, apparently, not only the resurrection but even "the third day" to be "in accordance with the scriptures" (1 Cor 15:4), it is at least possible – though one should put it no higher – that this passage as well as "the sign of Jonah" was in mind.[14]

Similarly, David A. Hubbard saw this prayer as seeking resurrection from the dead because, the "wounding is unto death,"[15] as a three-day duration fits the time for decomposition of the body, and the verbs "revive us" (1 Sam 2:6) and "raise us up" (Isa 26:19) are frequently used for resuscitation and resurrection. Hubbard noted, "If recovery from sickness not revival from death . . . is the meaning, the time frame seems trivial. A three-day illness, especially in antiquity, would have been no big thing."[16] Johnston thinks this passage is using the metaphor of "renewal of life" for national restoration of Israel and the images that Hosea uses are perhaps fused together "so that healing from grievous (or fatal) wounds and resurrection from the dead are alternate images for the renewal of a moribund nation."[17]

For Johnston, those who see "the third-day" as a clue for resurrection and the passage referring to Christ are going beyond the evidence and, while it is possible that Hosea and his hearers were aware of the idea of resurrection from the dead, that is not clearly seen here.[18] If this passage is ultimately God's word, then perhaps, as Kidner noted above, "the prophet may have spoken more significantly than he knew."[19] The trans-contextual and transcendent basis of Christ's death and resurrection in our *metacriticism* is significant here for interpretation. N. T. Wright comments,

> From a later perspective, this appears as it stands as a prayer of faith in the life-giving, restorative power of YHWH. However,

---

14. Derek Kidner, *Love to the Loveless: The Message of Hosea*, The Bible Speaks Today (Downers Grove, IL: InterVarsity, 1981), 66 (emphasis added).
15. David A. Hubbard, *Hosea: An Introduction and Commentary*, Tyndale Old Testament Commentaries, No. 22a (Downers Grove, IL: InterVarsity, 1989), 125.
16. Ibid.
17. Johnston, *Shades of Sheol*, 222. Both Johnston (Ibid) and N. T. Wright (*Resurrection of the Son of God*, 118) cite John Day (1996:246f; 1997:126f) referring to death (and resurrection) in this passage and Johnston does accept death as *a* theme in Hosea.
18. Johnston, *Shades of Sheol*, 222.
19. Kidner, *Love to the Loveless*, 66.

in its original context it almost certainly was intended as a description of a prayer that the prophet regarded as inadequate. It indicated a failure to repent at a deep level, a simplistic hope that maybe YHWH could be bought off. Once again, it is entirely possible that later readers, including later biblical writers, would have taken it in a more positive sense. When read in this sense, the passage has a claim to be the earliest explicit statement that YHWH will give his people a new bodily life the other side of death. It appears to have influenced Daniel 12, perhaps via Isaiah.[20]

Thus, from this later perspective, resurrection from the dead (in Hos 6) has become an explicit component of God's ultimate plan whereby his people will be rescued, within the progressive revelation of the Scriptures.

Ezekiel 37

Ezekiel 37:1–14 is the most familiar section in the entire Book of Ezekiel among the faithful Jews and Christians. Many a sermon has been preached on Ezekiel's awe-inspiring vision in which God takes him by his spirit to a valley of dry bones and makes these dry bones come back to life again. Blenkinsopp informs us, "Much . . . early Christian interpretation of this famous passage found in it proof of the bodily resurrection, a belief well established in Judaism by the beginning of the common era."[21] Martin-Achard notes, "The Jews, and afterwards the Christians, read an announcement of the resurrection of the dead in the last days into this passage from the prophet of Exile; at that time according to Ezekiel, the dead will come forth from their graves, and their bodies and souls will be reunited."[22] Martin-Achard refers to the Targum, which declares this is the resurrection of the ten tribes of Israel and their reunion with the tribes of Judah. He also refers to church fathers like Justin Martyr, Irenaeus and Tertullian who saw in this passage evidence for the resurrection of the body.[23] He points out that Jews use this chapter liturgically

---

20. Wright, *Resurrection of the Son of God*, 118–119.
21. Joseph Blenkinsopp, *Ezekiel*, Interpretation: A Bible Commentary for Teaching and Preaching (Louisville, KY: John Knox Press, 1990), 171.
22. Martin-Achard, *From Death to Life*, 93–94.
23. Martin-Achard notes that Tertullian refuted the Gnostic view that Ezekiel 37 is about restoration of Israel and not resurrection of individuals (Martin-Achard, *From Death to Life*, 94). However, Martin-Achard himself agreed with his contemporary exegetes who question Tertullian's position against the Gnostics and concluded that Ezekiel really used symbolic

at the Passover, as did the Christians as early as Jerome on the Holy Saturday before Easter.

Blenkinsopp makes an interesting comment,

> In spite of the possibility of contamination by contact with the dead (Num 19:16–18; 2 Kgs 23:14, 16; Ezek 39:15–16), Ezekiel is led in trance through the field, wondering at the great number of bones of those long dead. The question that he hears addressed to him – "Mortal, can these bones live?" – seems to call for only one answer. Ezekiel, however, does not answer, since he knows that the power of God extends even into the realm of death. He is then commanded to proclaim a message not to the obtuse, as in his inaugural vision, but to the dead, summoning them back to life. He does so, and it comes to pass before his eyes.[24]

In light of Blenkinsopp's comment above, Ezekiel's astounding response to God brings to mind Peter's vision of unclean animals in Acts10:9ff, and how he reacted to God in verse 14 ("Surely not, Lord"), whereas Ezekiel follows God's leading with no sense of distaste or abhorrence. Ezekiel's response, "O Lord GOD, you know," is simply an acknowledgement of ignorance and humility before God, yet with a full confidence that all things are possible with God, even raising bones back to life. Referring to Ezekiel 37:3 (in connection with Deut 32:39, 1 Sam 2:6 and Ps 104:29–30), and Ezekiel's knowledge of YHWH as the Lord of both spheres of the living and dead, Christopher Wright notes,

> The same double affirmation is made by Hannah, and by the psalmist in relation to all life on earth. As well as these liturgical declarations, Ezekiel would have known the stories of those rare occasions in the Old Testament of the resuscitation of the dead through the powerful prayer of Elijah and Elisha, and of the startling revival of a corpse upon contact with the bones of Elisha. So, yes, Ezekiel would have willingly . . . [accepted] the power of Yahweh to revive the dead . . . recently dead people . . . whose bodies were fully intact and scarcely cold. But *bones*? Dry bones of the long dead? . . . It was more than could be imagined,

---

terms of resurrection for Israel's national restoration and was not interested in the resurrection of the dead even though Ezekiel's use of this symbolism raised hope among the Jews and Christians for renewal of life after death (Ibid., 102). Johnston too notes that "it says nothing about personal resurrection, even if it was later interpreted in that way" (*Shades of Sheol*, 223).

24. Blenkinsopp, *Ezekiel*, 171.

let alone believed. Ezekiel's answer is understandably cautious. "He had the knowledge not to deny God's ability, but he lacked the faith to believe in it." So he bounces the question back to God himself.[25]

I fail to see any evidence in Ezekiel's response (v. 3) to suggest that he lacked the faith to believe God could raise the bones back to life. Moreover, he shows no hesitation to obey God and prophesy to the dead bones (v. 7). Elsewhere in the Scriptures (e.g. Sarah in Gen 18:10–15) God detected lack of faith, just as Jesus detected it among his disciples and others. These instances of doubt were dealt with immediately. Also, my understanding of faith is, faith IN God, that is, God is able to do whatever he chooses to do. So, instead of arrogantly throwing the question back to God, I think in verse 3, Ezekiel is making a gentle but confident statement of faith.

Blenkinsopp contends that it would be a mistake to write off any hint of personal resurrection here,

> While the modern, critical reader will inevitably raise questions about the historicity of narratives such as these, they at least testify to the belief that the power of God could triumph over death, which of course is quite different from the contemporary Christian and Jewish belief in the survival of death in a postmortem existence. While, therefore, Ezekiel's vision certainly deals with the restoration of Israel – as the explanation in vs. 11–14 makes absolutely clear – it would probably be mistaken to exclude systematically any hint of the postmortem destiny of the individual.[26]

Christopher Wright argues that, the main point of Ezekiel's message in its context:

> was to bring hope *to Israel as a people*. His vision and its interpretation were not intended to teach a doctrine of bodily resurrection, but to compare the restoration of Israel to the imaginary bringing back to life of the bones of a massive army of slain soldiers. The language is symbolic and metaphorical, and its application was for the still living, not the already dead.

---

25. Christopher J. H. Wright, *The Message of Ezekiel: A New Heart and a New Spirit. The Bible Speaks Today* (Downers Grove, IL: InterVarsity, 2001), 305.

26. Blenkinsopp, *Ezekiel*, 173.

That is, Ezekiel's vision promised the exiles that there would be a living future for Israel in the return from exile; it did not promise that those who had died in 587 or those who would die during the exile itself would literally come back to life to share in that return. That kind of resurrection hope seems to have developed later.[27]

However, Christopher Wright sees Ezekiel's message as an important link in a theological chain to which the biblical theme of resurrection is connected:

> Nevertheless, there is no doubt that Ezekiel's vision of dry bones and their revival functions as a very important link in a theological chain to which the full biblical hope of resurrection is anchored. At one end is the connection . . . between Ezekiel's vision of God breathing life into the lifeless bodies of Israel's defunct army and the Genesis tradition of God breathing the breath of life into the human-shaped pile of dust that then became a living human being. God's renewal of Israel was like a rerun of creation. Or, to put it the other way round, what God was about to do for Israel would be like the first act in the renewal of humanity as a whole. Here again, as in so many ways, the links between Israel and humanity are apparent. Israel has been called in the first place, through Abraham, to be a blessing to all the nations of the earth. Their election and redemption were for the sake of the rest of humanity. Likewise, therefore, just as their sin and punishment mirrored the fallenness of the whole race, so too their restoration would prefigure God's gracious purpose of redemption for humanity. Resurrection for Israel anticipated resurrection for all.[28]

Christopher Wright concludes that the resurrection of Jesus fulfills Ezekiel's vision:

> So the resurrection of Jesus *did* fulfil the vision of Ezekiel through his personal embodiment of the restoration of Israel. But, in line with the thrust of our earlier point, the restoration of Israel through Jesus was also the first stage of God's wider project of the redemption of the human race. The breath that breathed life into

---

27. Wright, *Message of Ezekiel*, 309.
28. Ibid., 310.

the dead came from the four winds – that is, the Spirit of God is at work everywhere in the world, in all directions. That which was focused with tremendous resurrection power on Ezekiel's dead bodies, and then on the dead Messiah, is the same power that is available to the ends of the earth to bring life, salvation and the hope of bodily resurrection to all who trust in the one who sends it.[29]

Of course, as we mentioned before, even if the prophets, like Ezekiel, may not have known about personal resurrection from the dead, yet speaking the Word of God "the prophet may have spoken more significantly than he knew."[30] However, as Block notes, it is interesting to see that the biblical scholars until about 1985 maintained that there was no belief in life after death in ancient Israel,

> Many believe that the Pharisaic acceptance of the doctrine (see Acts 23:6–9) derives from a limited number of late texts that reflect Persian influence, and that the Sadducees, who rejected the notion, were the true heirs of OT belief. That some scholars have recently reversed the roles of these two parties is welcome: many now insist that the Sadducean position represented a conscious departure from both Hebrew and common Semitic beliefs.[31]

This note from Block, once again, strengthens the possible presence of the theme of resurrection from the dead in this passage of Ezekiel. The possible hint of personal resurrection in Ezekiel's vision at least highlights that "State-after-Death" is a central element of God's plan to rescue his people from death as the punishment of sins.

Isaiah 26

Isaiah chapters 24–27 are generally called the Apocalypse[32] of Isaiah because their literary and theological elements set them apart from the previous and subsequent chapters. In chapter 24, we see the Lord's judgment and the total

---

29. Ibid., 310–311.
30. Kidner, *Love to the Loveless*, 66.
31. Block, *Book of Ezekiel*, 392.
32. Martin-Achard (*From Death to Life*, 123); "apocalyptic or at least proto-apocalyptic" Johnston (*Shades of Sheol*, 224).

destruction of the earth but then from chapter 25 to 27 we see how the Lord will protect his people Israel. Those who trust in him will be delivered from Assyria and Egypt and will be brought back to worship him on the holy mountain of Jerusalem. Referring to chapters 24–27, Johnston notes, "In this bewilderingly bright kaleidoscope of vivid images and momentous themes, there are also glimpses of triumph over death, most notably in 25:6–10: 'he will swallow up death forever' (v. 8)."[33] In my opinion, this is one of God's clear biblical signposts to resurrection from death, because he is the God of the living and not the dead.

Now consider the next, even more explicit, assertion of Isaiah 26:19, "But your dead will live; their bodies will rise. You who dwell in the dust, wake up and shout for joy. Your dew is like the dew of the morning; the earth will give birth to her dead" (NRSV). In the Old Testament, this clearly affirms hope of the resurrection from the dead. Webb observes,

> What about those who die in the time of waiting, who have put their trust in the LORD but experienced no fulfillment? Will they suffer the same fate as the wicked, described in verse 14, and miss out on the triumph to come? Verse 19 issues a resounding "No!" Their waiting will not be in vain. They will be raised from death to share in the final victory. Here again is that victory over death already glimpsed in 25:8.[34]

Johnston notes, "The imagery clearly envisages the personal resurrection from the death of at least some Israelites . . . The application may be national, but the imagery presupposes a concept of individual resurrection."[35] Martin-Achard admits that, "In the form of a prayer, Isa XXVI. 19 proclaims the resurrection of the dead . . . reserved for certain members of the Chosen People, perhaps only for martyrs . . . denied . . . to the heathen . . . impious Jews . . . (XXVI. 14)" but he also says, "The concept of resurrection does not appear to be absolutely novel to the writer of the prayer; here he is probably

---

33. Johnston, *Shades of Sheol*, 224. Martin-Achard agreeing with many other scholars dates chapters 24–27 quite late, from the fourth century BCE and considers this part of v. 8 was not "part of the original text, but are a sort of interpretation of vss. 7–8" and was added in the third century BCE (*From Death to Life*, 129). Motyer (*The Prophecy of Isaiah* [Leicester, UK: InterVarsity, 1993], 219–220) specially argues against the late dating of Isaiah 26:19 and exclaims "How insubstantial this is!"

34. Barry Webb, *The Message of Isaiah: On Eagle's Wings*, The Bible Speaks Today (Leicester, UK: InterVarsity, 1996), 111.

35. Johnston, *Shades of Sheol*, 225.

voicing the thought of the pious Jews."³⁶ Of course, some who question its validity as the Word of God, may consider it to be merely the writer's own human conjecture. Motyer's remarks on Isaiah 26:19 concludes well,

> In sum, therefore, the verse is a promise of life for the world, the fulfillment of 25:6–10a . . . In this regard, the terms of the present verse go beyond the figurative to the literal and declare a full resurrection, including the resurrection of the body. Within the progressive revelation of the Old Testament only Daniel 12:2 is comparable.³⁷

Next, we consider Daniel 12 and see that resurrection from the dead is an important component of God's ultimate plan to rescue his people.

Daniel 12

1) "At that time Michael, the great prince, the protector of your people, shall arise. There shall be a time of anguish, such as has never occurred since nations first came into existence. But at that time your people shall be delivered, everyone who is found written in the book.

2) Many of those who sleep in the dust of the earth shall awake, some to everlasting life, and some to shame and everlasting contempt.

3) Those who are wise shall shine like the brightness of the sky, and those who lead many to righteousness, like the stars forever and ever.

4) But you, Daniel, keep the words secret and the book sealed until the time of the end. Many shall be running back and forth, and evil shall increase" (NRSV).

This is the final reference for the concept of resurrection from the dead within the canon of Old Testament Scripture and this is the clearest signal for that concept, proclaiming bodily resurrection of both righteous and the

---

36. Martin-Achard, *From Death to Life*, 137.
37. Motyer, *Prophecy of Isaiah*, 219. ACUTE (*Nature of Hell*, 39) notes, "Two Old Testament passages refer clearly to resurrection: Isaiah 26:19 (cf. v. 14) and Daniel 12:2. Of these only the latter mentions a resurrection of both the righteous and unrighteous to separate fates."

unrighteous individuals, one to everlasting life and the other to everlasting contempt at the end of human history.[38] Johnston notes, "Finally, one text speaks unmistakably and unambiguously of personal resurrection."[39] Yet Johnston finds the description here quite limited because to him the verses seem to focus on Daniel's people and also the phrase "many of . . . " probably means "many and not all" people and so not a general resurrection for all humans.[40] But Baldwin notes,

> But the use of the word "many" in Hebrew is not quite parallel with its use in English. Hebrew *rabbim*, "many," tends to mean "all," as in Deuteronomy 7:1; Isaiah 2:2, where "all nations" becomes "many peoples" in the parallel verse 3; and in Isaiah 52:14, 15; 53:11, 12, where this key-word occurs no less than five times, with an inclusive significance. As Jeremias points out, the Hebrew word *kol*, "all," means either "totality" or "sum"; there is not word for "all" as a plural. For this *rabbim* does duty, and so comes to mean "the great multitude," "all"; cf. "Multitudes who sleep in the dust of the earth . . . " (NIV). The emphasis is not upon many as opposed to all, but rather on the numbers involved.
>
> *In the light of this usage our author can be seen to be thinking of a general resurrection prior to judgment.* Jesus almost certainly has this verse in mind in Matthew 25:46 and John 5:28, 29. As in chapters 2 and 7, the world as we know it has come to an end and an entirely new order has come, because the everlasting God has broken into time. He is the source of everlasting righteousness (9:24) and of *everlasting life*, wording first coined here in the Old Testament, though other writers express the conviction that the warmth of fellowship with the Lord that they enjoyed on earth could not be ended merely by death (16:11; 17:15; 73:23,24; Isa 26:19). Mention of the tree of life and the possibility of living for ever (Gen 3:22) must have kept the thought before the Israelite believer from early times.[41]

---

38. Martin-Achard (*From Death to Life,* 141) notes Daniel 12:1 "calls the final scene in human history to mind".
39. Johnston, *Shades of Sheol,* 225.
40. Ibid., 226. Similarly, Martin-Achard (*From Death to Life,* 145) notes, "According to this passage, the resurrection is not universal; it primarily concerns the Chosen People, and only some of its perished members."
41. Joyce G. Baldwin, *Daniel: An Introduction and Commentary,* Tyndale Old Testament Commentaries, No. 21 (Leicester, UK: InterVarsity, 1978), 204–205 (emphasis added).

I agree with Baldwin *contra* Johnston and Martin-Achard that this passage refers to the general resurrection for all before the final judgment. This is because general resurrection would also reflect God's plan concerning all peoples on earth as he promised to Abraham, the Father of the Chosen People Israel in Genesis 12:3b, that "in you (or by you) *all the families of the earth* shall be blessed (or bless themselves)" (NRSV, emphasis added). Again, "all peoples shall be blessed," and not just Israel, as Johnston, Martin-Achard and many others affirm. We can see again that resurrection from the dead is a critical component of God's universal mission as an alternative to a hopeless destiny, within the progressive revelation of the Old Testament.

Summary and Implications

We have studied further passages that implicitly or explicitly deal with the concept of the resurrection from the dead by considering Genesis 22, Deuteronomy 32 and 1 Samuel 2, Hosea 6, Ezekiel 37, Isaiah 26 and finally Daniel 12. In all of these we found "signposts" (a term borrowed from Martin-Achard) of the promise of resurrection from the dead within the progressive revelation of the Old Testament. These "signposts" became clearer (from implicit to explicit) as we moved through the Old Testament narratives. These indications of resurrection hope, in the midst of neighboring pluralistic views during the Old Testament times, show that "State-after-Death" is a critical component of God's mission to provide an alternative to a hopeless final destiny of humankind. Consequently "State-after-Death" would be an important and a fruitful area for conversation today when the global church, as agents of God's mission, (a) engages with the Hindu, Muslim and Secular Humanist peoples in pluralistic contexts *within* and *outside* the Christian church, and (b) effectively communicates the gospel of Jesus Christ in global pluralistic contexts.

As we now study the New Testament in the next two chapters, the truth of resurrection from the dead will be more fully revealed through the death and resurrection of Christ.

7

State-after-Death in the Synoptics and John

As we begin to look at "State-after-Death" in the New Testament, we recognize at the outset the strong Jewish background of the early church as well as the pluralistic Greco-Roman religious contexts in which it was written. Jewish understanding regarding "State-after-Death" had developed further during the interval between the Old and New Testament under Persian, Greek and Roman rule. Though I am not going to look at this development in-depth due to the limited scope of this study, yet we note, for heuristic purposes, that there was some continuity of thought on death and after-death from the intertestamental literature to the New Testament.[1] However, New Testament thought was also distinct from that of the intertestamental period.

The Greek term *Hades* is a key term in the New Testament understanding of "State-after-Death". This is more so because linguistically *Hades* connects the Old Testament and the New Testament in this area. Douglas K. Stuart notes of the Old Testament term *Sheol*: "The LXX renders it by Gk. *hades* (Hades), as apparently does the NT, at least in direct quotations of the OT."[2] Stuart notes further, "The NT view of HADES as a place of confinement for

---

1. For example, the books of Enoch which are dated from about third century BCE onwards give some of the views of State-after-Death of that period and show some similarities with New Testament perspective. Craig A. Evans (*Noncanonical Writings and New Testament Interpretation* [Peabody, MA: Hendrickson Publishers, 1992], 23) notes, "*1 Enoch* contributes much to intertestamental views of . . . heaven, judgment, resurrection . . . This book has left its stamp upon many of the NT writers, especially the author of Revelation." Evans notes that *2 Enoch* refers to "abodes of heaven and hell are already prepared for righteous and sinners" and "ethical teachings, which at times parallel those of the NT and Proverbs" (Ibid., 23). I am not convinced that these books truly influenced many of the New Testament authors, as much as the unique teachings and work of Jesus Christ regarding State-after-Death.
2. Douglas K. Stuart, "Sheol," in *The International Standard Bible Encyclopedia*, vol. 4, ed. Geoffrey W. Bromiley (Grand Rapids, MI: Eerdmans, 1988), 472.

the wicked (Rev 20:13) until their destruction in GEHENNA (Matt 10:28; Rev 20:14–15) goes beyond the far more neutral OT usage of Hebrew *šŏl*, and it corrects the often bizarre intertestamental uses of Gk. *hades*".[3] However, we have seen earlier, following Johnston, that *Sheol* is used mainly in the Old Testament as the final destiny of all who are under God's judgment, that is, the wicked, and perhaps the *afflicted* righteous, or *all* sinners and *not* as the general destiny of all human dead. Thus, to understand *Hades* in the New Testament we must bear in mind this Old Testament understanding of *Sheol*.

In order to understand "State-after-Death" in the New Testament, we will study this topic in the Synoptic Gospels and in the gospel and letters of John in this chapter, and the letters of Paul and the Book of Revelation in the next. Because both Old and New Testaments are God's Word progressively revealed through many centuries and through different authors, what God began revealing (perhaps dimly to some) in the Old Testament about "State-after-Death" is more fully (and brightly) revealed in the New Testament. For this study, both the Testaments are the *primary* source for doing Christian theology in pluralistic contexts. I will continue to use the three-dimensional model of hermeneutics (the priority of authorial intention, metacritical perspective, and constructive use of biblical narratives) to investigate the "State-after-Death" in the New Testament. In this metacritical perspective, we re-emphasize the death and resurrection of Jesus Christ as our trans-contextual foundation for doing theology.

The Synoptic Gospels

New Testament insights into what happens at and after death go significantly further than the Old Testament. Jesus' teaching and ministry explicitly promise eternal life beyond death to those who believe, transforming the concept of "State-after-Death" for believers. Jesus pronounces an opposite "State-after-Death" for unbelievers. The report *The Nature of Hell*, produced by a special working group of the Alliance Commission on Unity and Truth among Evangelicals in the United Kingdom (ACUTE), states, "Christ's teaching and work also brought new revelation on the destiny of unbelievers and on the cosmos as a whole."[4]

---

3. Ibid.
4. ACUTE, *Nature of Hell*, 42.

We will look at the important terms: *Hades* and *Gehenna* in the Synoptic Gospels after examining the theme of resurrection from the dead. As C. F. Evans poignantly comments, "Of the synoptic gospels it would not be sufficient to say simply that they conclude with resurrection narratives, *for it is only in the light of faith in the risen Lord that they were written at all.*"[5]

Resurrection from the Dead

Murray J. Harris describes the general New Testament understanding of resurrection thus, "In its fullest sense, resurrection is God's raising of persons from the realm of the dead to new and unending life in his presence. It is an event leading to a state."[6] As noted earlier in Block, most biblical scholars until around 1985 maintained that there was no belief in life after death in ancient Israel, that the Pharisees' belief in resurrection reflects Persian influence and that the Sadducees were the true heirs of Old Testament belief. However, some have recently reversed their position on this and "many now insist that the Sadducean position represented a conscious departure from both Hebrew and common Semitic beliefs."[7] Most of these scholars argued that belief in life after death was actually a late development among the Jewish people after or during the Babylonian exile (as reflected in intertestamental literature). On neighboring non-Israelite religious influence, especially Persian Zoroastrianism, Colin Brown concludes,

> W. W. von Baudissin has pointed out that the terminology employed by the Jews in discussing the resurrection is typically Semitic and does not recall Iranian expressions . . . Whereas the biblical passages speak of awakening from death, as from sleep, the Persians thought of it as a reconstitution of the body through the reunion of its elements. In conclusion it may be said

---

5. C. F. Evans, *Resurrection and the New Testament* (London: SCM Press Ltd, 1970), 4 (emphasis added). C. Brown comments regarding C. F. Evans: "His form-critical analysis leads him to see a great fragmentation within the NT. Hence, what matters is not to believe in the historical accuracy of the stories but the central proclamation that they enshrine" and that "for Evans the cause of the resurrection faith of the early church remains obscure" (Brown, "Resurrection," 299); also M. J. Harris notes, "Both the staunchest defenders of the Resurrection and its remorseless critics recognise the centrality of the resurrection of Christ in apostolic Christianity . . . Where the two groups differ is in their evaluation of the historical evidence on which belief in the Resurrection was based" (Harris, *Raised Immortal*, 5).

6. Murray J. Harris, "Resurrection, General," in *New Dictionary of Theology*, eds. S. B. Ferguson, D. F. Wright, and J. I. Packer (Downers Grove, IL: InterVarsity, 1988b), 581.

7. Block, *Book of Ezekiel*, 392.

that the Jews had a conception of resurrection before they came into contact with the Persian Empire. The thought of an after-life has its deepest root in the awareness of the living God himself; because Yahweh lives and is the covenant God of Israel, his people, there is an on-going relationship and life. This awareness developed in the course of history in Israel's many vicissitudes and partly also in contrast with surrounding religious beliefs.[8]

In the Synoptic Gospels (cf. Mark 12:26–27; Matt 22:31–32; Luke 20:37–38), Jesus' incisive response ("God is not God of the dead, but of the living") as a refutation of the Sadducees and its reference to Moses at Horeb (Exod 3:6) strongly affirms the presence of belief in life-after-death in the Old Testament. Brown refers to R. N. Longenecker, who "sees Jesus as confounding the Sadducees for whom every word of the Torah possessed validity, by employing their own methods of exegesis against them."[9] Brown also helpfully cites W. L. Lane's comments[10] regarding Jesus' above response to the Sadducees,

> The concept "God of the dead" implies a blatant contradiction, especially in the context of the Sadducean understanding of death as extinction, without the hope of resurrection. If God has assumed the task of protecting the patriarchs from misfortune during the course of their life, but fails to deliver them from that supreme misfortune which marks the definitive and absolute check upon their hopes, his protection is of little value . . . In citing Exodus 3:6 Jesus showed how resurrection faith is attached in a profound way to the central concept of biblical revelation, the covenant, and how the salvation promised by God to the patriarchs and their descendants in virtue of the covenant contains implicitly the assurance of the resurrection. It was the failure to appreciate the essential link between God's covenant faithfulness and the resurrection which had led the Sadducees into their grievous error.[11]

---

8. Brown, "Resurrection," 275.
9. Ibid., 264.
10. W. L. Lane, *The Gospel According to Mark*, NLC (Grand Rapids: Eerdmans, 1974), 430.
11. Brown, "Resurrection," 263–264.

Donald Hagner refers to Jesus' rebuke to the Sadducees in Mark's and Matthew's accounts (but not so in Luke's) and argues that,

> The implication that Jesus sees . . . is that the patriarchs were still alive, since God spoke of his relationship with them in the present tense ("I am") and would take no pleasure in being the God of the dead . . . And if they are alive, there can be no problem in their eventual resurrection. It is to this last point, the possibility of resurrection, that the remark about the Sadducees not knowing the power of God is directed. For God, who has the power initially to create, has also the power to give new, resurrection life.[12]

Hagner further points out that the Sadducees assumed wrongly in presenting the case of a woman who had seven successive husbands in that they thought the resurrection life would be exactly like the present earthly life. He comments, "There will be, to be sure, continuity with this life. But also . . . there will be features of discontinuity . . . That is, in regard to marriage there will be discontinuity between this life and the life to come."[13] Referring to Luke's account, Hagner notes,

> The age of the resurrection, in short, will involve a new order, an eschatological order, which corresponds to the hope of the prophets (cf. Isa 25:7; 26:19; see also Rev 21:4). Luke's version of Jesus' words also highlights a significant feature of that new eschatological order ("that age"): it will be inhabited by "those who are considered worthy of a place in that age" (20:35). The criterion whereby the worthiness of those inhabitants is established is not specified. What is clear, however, is that to be a "child of God" is to be, by definition, also a "child of the resurrection" (20:36).[14]

Lloyd R. Bailey sees this discussion of Jesus with the Sadducees regarding resurrection as one of the occasional exceptions to the low level of speculation on the nature of life after death in the Synoptic Gospels and, therefore, he

---

12. Donald Hagner, "Gospel, Kingdom, and Resurrection in the Synoptic Gospels," in *Life in the Face of Death: The Resurrection Message of the New Testament,* ed. Richard N. Longenecker (Grand Rapids, MI: Eerdmans, 1998), 106.
13. Ibid., 107.
14. Ibid.

seems to ignore it, mentioning it only in an endnote.[15] However, he does accept that "a resurrection of the dead is assumed" in the Synoptic Gospels.[16]

Joanne E. McWilliam Dewart also contends that the resurrection of the dead "is conspicuously infrequent, either as a theme or a problem, in the Synoptic Gospels, and Jesus appears to have had little to say about it". She considers the above reference, "The only synoptic text discussing (rather than merely alluding to) the resurrection of the body."[17] She comments that instead of convincing the Sadducees of the resurrection of the dead, Jesus focuses here "on the power of God and the nature of the resurrection life." She notes that Jesus' reproofs imply that "the Sadducees are so bound, even in their imaginations, to the material world that they cannot envisage an afterlife in which the body will be spiritual."[18] Dewart is interpreting the nature of resurrection life in the above text as total discontinuity from the present material earthly life to non-material spiritual life, which is different from Hagner's view which sees in the resurrected life both continuity and discontinuity with the present earthly life.[19]

At this point, I must note that just as Jesus reasoned with the Sadducees to prove the truth of the resurrection from the dead, he also confirmed this truth by his deeds by miraculously raising dead persons while here on earth. In the Synoptic Gospels, we see the raising of Jairus' daughter (cf. Mark 5:21–43; Matt 9:18–26; Luke 8:40–56), the raising of the widow's son at Nain (only in Luke 7:11–17), Jesus commissioning the twelve disciples with the instruction to raise the dead (especially Matt 10:8), and in Jesus sending a message to John the Baptist in prison that "the dead are being raised up" (Matt 11:4; Luke 7:22). Hagner notes that though "there is no breaking in of the new [eschatological] age in these" resurrections, yet "in the radical movement from death to life, these events are in their own way signs and

---

15. Bailey, *Biblical Perspective on Death*, 140.
16. Ibid., 92.
17. Joanne E. McWilliam Dewart, *Death and Resurrection*, Message of the Fathers of the Church Series, No. 22 (Wilmington, DE: Michael Glazier, 1986), 26.
18. Ibid., 26–27.
19. There has been much debate recently about Murray J. Harris' view (with Norman Geisler and others), which stresses more the discontinuity aspect (that after resurrection Jesus sometimes materialized into a physical body but was essentially nonmaterial spiritual body) even though Harris still does affirm literal physical resurrection of Jesus (Harris, *Raised Immortal*, 53–57; cf. Wayne Grudem, *Systematic Theology* [Grand Rapids, MI: Zondervan, 1994], 610–613). Grudem (*Systematic Theology*, 832–835) argues that the New Testament indicates strongly that there will be considerable continuity with the earthly body along with some definite discontinuity in the transformed resurrected body.

anticipations of the eschatological resurrection of the dead, for they display the authority of Jesus over death."[20] Finally, Osborne draws our attention to, "the enigmatic raising of the saints in Matthew 27:51–53," which he thinks "provides a theological bridge from the cross to the empty tomb" as the death and resurrection of Jesus "are inextricably linked as a single event in salvation-history" that guaranteed the eventual "raising and uniting of the true 'saints' of God, both past and future."[21]

Next we examine Jesus' own predictions of his death and resurrection in the Synoptic Gospels.

Jesus' Death-Resurrection Predictions

In the second half of each of the Synoptic Gospels, Jesus' prediction of his death and resurrection are recorded in three main parallel segments: (1) Mark 8:31–33; Matthew 16:21–23; Luke 9:22; (2) Mark 9:30–32; Matthew 17:22–23; Luke 9:43b–45; (3) Mark 10:32–34; Matthew 20:17–19; Luke 18:31–34. Hans F. Bayer notes that, these "three major . . . predictions serve as significant landmarks in the unfolding narratives. Like birth pangs signalling a delivery, they point to Jesus' inescapable mission awaiting him in Jerusalem," that is, his passion and resurrection.[22] Comparing the three passages from Mark, Harris points out that some scholars contend "that the original saying was basically this: 'The Son of Man will suffer many things and be killed and after three days he will rise'" and that "the evangelists have each expanded the original form to correspond to events as they knew them."[23] But I think Harris is correct in noting that "there seems little reason to discount the possibility that Jesus uttered the prophecy on more than one occasion and in slightly different words each time."[24]

For some scholars, the real contention is that these are not genuine predictions but prophecies compiled after the events (*vaticinium ex eventu*), after the death and resurrection of Jesus by the gospel writers. However, the theological formulations typical of early creeds (such as, "according

---

20. Hagner, "Gospel, Kingdom, and Resurrection," 101.
21. Grant R. Osborne, "Resurrection," in *Dictionary of Jesus and the Gospels*, eds. Joel B. Green, Scot McKnight and I. Howard Marshall (Downers Grove, IL: InterVarsity, 1992), 678.
22. Hans F. Bayer, "Predictions of Jesus' Passion and Resurrection," in *Dictionary of Jesus and the Gospels*, eds. Joel B. Green, Scot McKnight and I. Howard Marshall (Downers Grove, IL: InterVarsity, 1992), 630.
23. Harris, *Raised Immortal*, 6.
24. Ibid.

to scriptures," "for our sins," "raised from the dead as the first fruits" and "exalted by his right hand") are lacking in these predictions, which make it "more likely that these are indeed historical reminiscences."[25] Referring to Mark's "after three days" (but Matthew and Luke's "on the third day") in these predictions, Hagner comments that it "is essentially synonymous with 'on the third day,' because of the common manner of reckoning time inclusively (i.e. any part of three days may also be referred to as 'after three days')" and so there is no contradiction here between these two phrases.[26] This also confirms why Matthew, himself, uses "after three days" (27:63) in referring to the chief priests and the Pharisees' version of Jesus' prediction. Perhaps this also explains why, in the next verse, the chief priests and the Pharisees wanted the tomb made secure "until the third day" (Matt 27:64).

Apart from these three major predictions, there are many more explicit or implicit references to the death and resurrection of Jesus in the Synoptic Gospels. An example is, Jesus' indirect prediction of his resurrection from the dead after his transfiguration on the mountain when he commanded that Peter, James and John not tell anyone what they had seen until he was raised from the dead (Mark 9:9 and Matt 17:9). Jesus' enigmatic statements reported by his opponents (Mark 14:58 par. Matt 26:61; Mark 15:29 par. Matt 27:40), that he would destroy the temple and build another in three days, and his reference to the sign of Jonah (Matt 12:38–42 par. Luke 11:29–32), also predict his death and resurrection. In addition the allusions to Jesus' exaltation (Mark 12:10–11; Matt 21:42; Luke 20:17; and Mark 12:36; Matt 22:44; Luke 20:42–43) and second coming (Mark 8:38; Matt 16:27; Luke 9:26; and Mark 13:26; Matt 24:30; Luke 21:27), as well as his ascension and future return (Mark 14:62; Matt 26:64; Luke 22:69) all presuppose that he would rise again after his death.[27]

These predictions of Jesus' death and resurrection in the Synoptic Gospels, confirm the truth of the resurrection from the dead for which Jesus argued with the Sadducees. Some scholars note the strangeness of the disciples not understanding when Jesus predicted his resurrection (Mark 9:10, 32; Luke 9:45) and conclude that belief in resurrection from the dead was not common among the Jews of Jesus' earthly days in Israel. But Bayer points out, "from the perspective of the disciples, resurrection was to occur at the end of the age

---

25. Osborne, "Resurrection," 675; also cf. Harris, *Raised Immortal*, 6–7.
26. Hagner, "Gospel, Kingdom, and Resurrection," 104.
27. Cf. Ibid., 104–105.

to all people (Dan 12:2)"²⁸ and this is also seen in Martha's response to Jesus when her brother Lazarus died (John 11:24). Hagner comments that,

> It was not . . . the concept of a future resurrection from the dead that was incomprehensible to them. Rather, it was the idea of the imminent [death and] resurrection of the one they had just confessed to be the Messiah, and whose glory they had seen on the Mount of Transfiguration.²⁹

Next we consider the most crucial aspect of our study, the three resurrection narratives of Jesus in the Synoptics.

The Narratives of Jesus' Resurrection

Jesus' resurrection narratives in the three Synoptic Gospels (Mark 16:1–8; Matt 28:1–20; Luke 24:1–53) give a more comprehensive understanding of the phenomenon of resurrection from the dead because, ultimately, it is his resurrection that paves the way for believers' resurrection. Ulrich Wilckens notes,

> Just as belief in the Resurrected One would be robbed of its decisive criterion if it were not expressly the Crucified One, whose resurrection was being spoken of, so too, conversely, any belief which . . . restricted itself to the Cross, would be robbed of its power; for only one who believes in the Resurrected One can see the salvation of the world as founded in Christ's death on the Cross. True salvation in the Christian sense is to be obtained through no other power than the power of love. But there can only be true salvation since through Jesus' resurrection divine proof has been given that love is all-powerful. Power without love brings destruction; but love without power is ineffectual.³⁰

---

28. Bayer, "Predictions of Jesus' Passion and Resurrection," 633 (5).
29. Hagner, "Gospel, Kingdom, and Resurrection," 106.
30. Ulrich Wilckens, *Resurrection*, trans. A. M. Stewart (Atlanta, GA: John Knox Press, 1978), 27. However, Brown's survey notes, "Wilckens stresses the oneness of Christian traditions with pre-Christian literature . . . There is thus an apocalyptic stamp about certain descriptions of the risen and ascended Christ, and this raises the question of how valid such descriptions can be for us today" (Brown, "Resurrection," 287). For example, for Wilckens (*Resurrection*, 70) forty (days) in Acts 1:3 is not "a historically correct specific chronological measurement" but "a biblical number" (Ps 95:10 forty years in wilderness; 1 Kings 19:8 forty days fast) and Luke was using it to show "limited length of time" (cf. Harris [*Raised Immortal*, 52, 90] argues for forty days). Brown also notes that Willi Marxsen while questioning the

There is no detailed record of Jesus' actual resurrection in the Synoptic Gospels (nor in John's gospel)[31] as it was not seen by any of the New Testament witnesses. According to Matthew 28:4, however little they did see during the actual event, the guards were so afraid that they shook and became like dead men. However, Hagner highlights the three significant themes common to the Synoptic narratives of what took place immediately after the resurrection event itself: the empty tomb, the female witnesses and the appearances of the risen Jesus.[32]

Referring to the empty tomb of Jesus and the sightings of the risen Jesus, New Testament scholar N. T. Wright argues convincingly in his recent, *The Resurrection of the Son of God*, that if these two "historical conclusions" are taken away, "the belief of the early church becomes itself inexplicable". And further "the best *historical* explanation is the one which inevitably raises all kinds of *theological* questions: the tomb was indeed empty, and Jesus was indeed seen alive, because he was truly raised from the dead."[33] A few years ago in an interview in *The Christian Century*, N. T. Wright commented on the historicity of Jesus' resurrection and what part the sightings of the risen Jesus played. He pointed out that many leaders of first-century Jewish movements had died, yet a claim for resurrection would have been very unusual. Wright imagines Josephus, the first-century Jewish historian, contemplating this claim of Jesus' resurrection:

> [Josephus] hears about the demise of a messianic . . . or prophetic leader, and is told that this leader has been raised from the dead. He is going to ask: What do you mean he's been raised from the dead? And he will not be satisfied if the answer is: Well, I had this vision, or I felt my heart warmed, or I felt that God had forgiven me for letting the leader down. He would say, "Well, fine, I'm glad you had that experience. But why did you say he's been raised from the dead?" My point is that resurrection is something that had a quite clear meaning at that time. It was something that every pagan knew doesn't happen. And a lot of

---

resurrection of Jesus followed Wilckens in noting that "the witnesses who had experience of this happening were obliged to make it known 'with the resources of the tradition'" (Brown, "Resurrection," 285).

31. cf. Harris, *Raised Immortal*, 62–64. Hagner ("Resurrection," 108) notes "a purely fictional description of the event in the *Gospel of Peter* 35–42 . . . indirectly demonstrates the historical sobriety of the canonical Gospels."

32. Hagner, "Gospel, Kingdom, and Resurrection," 107–111.

33. Wright, *Resurrection of the Son of God*, 10.

Jews (the Sadducees and some others) believed it doesn't happen. Those who did affirm the resurrection did not think it was just a way of saying, "He is Lord."[34]

N. T. Wright thus shows that at that time people clearly understood that resurrection does not happen, and if someone claimed it happened, they would see it as an exceptional actual event. N. T. Wright presented a plausible explanation for the historicity of Jesus' resurrection, and the part which the empty tomb and the sightings of the risen Jesus play, when he continued,

> The historian has to offer a plausible hypothesis of why the disciples used the language of resurrection. My hypothesis is that there were two things: an empty tomb and sightings of Jesus. An empty tomb by itself doesn't mean that much, nor do visions – many people have had visions, particularly after somebody they love has just died . . . I think the historian is faced with two parts of an arch with the piece in the middle – the resurrection – missing . . . Are these just two isolated phenomena?
>
> The historian cannot prove the resurrection in the same way that one can prove that Jerusalem was destroyed in 70 AD. But I think the historian can say: Here are the plausible explanations. And there is an extreme implausibility of virtually all the rival suggestions, such as the one that James, the brother of the Lord, was walking around in the garden at the same time, and because he looked rather like Jesus, the women saw him in the half light. That story is not going to last more than an hour or two.[35]

The women who witnessed the resurrection in the Synoptic narratives were the first witnesses of the resurrection and, Hagner notes, that this "underlines *the historical truth of the story*, for no one in that culture would have invented a story that gave such a key role to women. Even the disciples, at first, disregarded the report of the women, crediting it to be 'an idle tale' not worthy of belief (Luke 24:11)."[36] Having noted the historical plausibility of Jesus' resurrection, we too can confidently proclaim with Paul, "But Christ has indeed been raised from the dead, the firstfruits of those who have fallen asleep" (1 Cor 15:20) and that because of Jesus' resurrection all the believers now have the hope that they too will be raised from the dead some day.

---

34. N. T. Wright, interview in *The Christian Century* (18 December 2002): 28–31.
35. Ibid.
36. Hagner, "Gospel, Kingdom, and Resurrection," 109 (emphasis added).

Thus, having conquered death as he had predicted, the risen Jesus (Matt 28:16–20) went to the Galilee of the Gentiles (Matt 4:15) and on a mountain (like the mount of transfiguration) commanded his disciples with authority to make disciples of *all the nations* (*panta ta ethne*), instead of his earlier commission to go only to "the lost sheep of Israel" (Matt 10:5–6). He promised to be with them always, until the very end of the age.[37]

We now consider the topic of hell in the Synoptics and, in particular, the two terms, *Hades* and *Gehenna*, in order to understand "State-after-Death" of the unbelievers.

Hades and Gehenna

The report *The Nature of Hell* of the UK Evangelical Alliance is very helpful here, highlighting how, throughout the Synoptic Gospels, the concept of hell is referred to most in Matthew's gospel and that only one passage in Mark's gospel (9:43, 45, 47, 48) refers to hell.[38] The passage from Mark and all the references from Luke's gospel about hell, except for the parable of the rich man and Lazarus (Luke 16), are included in Matthew's gospel. Below is a table adapted from ACUTE[39] that sharpens the picture of the references to hell:

Table 2: Words and Images of Hell in the Synoptics

(after ACUTE, *The Nature of Hell*, 44–45)

Matthew	Mark & Luke	Concepts and Images	Context
Matt 3:7, 12	Luke 3:7, 17	Wrath Unquenchable fire	John the Baptist's teaching
Matt 5:22		Fire, Gehenna	Jesus' teaching
Matt 5:29, 30 Matt 18:8, 9	Mark 9:43, 45, 47 Mark 9:48	Fire, Gehenna, eternal fire .. .. .. Undying worm, unquenched fire	Jesus' teaching
Matt 7:13		Destruction	Jesus' teaching

---

37. Cf. Hagner, "Gospel, Kingdom, and Resurrection," 114; Evans, *Resurrection and the New Testament*, 83–84.

38. ACUTE, *Nature of Hell*, 42–47.

39. Ibid., 44–45.

Matthew	Mark & Luke	Concepts and Images	Context
Matt 8:12	Luke 13:28	Darkness, weeping, gnashing of teeth	Parable: great feast
Matt 22:13		Darkness, weeping, gnashing of teeth	Parable: wedding banquet
Matt 25:30		Darkness, weeping, gnashing of teeth	Parable: lazy servant
Matt 24:51		Weeping, gnashing of teeth	Parable: wicked servant
Matt 10:15	Luke 10:12	Judgment	Jesus' teaching
Matt 11:23	Luke 10:14	.. .. ..	
Matt 11:24	Luke 10:15	Hades	
Matt 10:28		Destruction, Gehenna	Satan
	Luke 12:5	Gehenna	
Matt 12:41	Luke 11:32	Judgment	Jesus' teaching
Matt 12:42	Luke 11:31	Judgment	
Matt 13:42		Fire, weeping, gnashing of teeth	Parable: wheat / tares
Matt 13:50		Fire, weeping, gnashing of teeth	Parable: net
Matt 16:18		Hades	Peter's faith
Matt 23:15		Gehenna	Pharisees
Matt 23:33		Condemned, Gehenna	
Matt 25:41		Eternal fire	Parable: sheep & goats
Matt 25:46		Eternal punishment	
	Luke 16:23, 24, 25, 26, 28	Hades, torment, agony, fire, great chasm	Story: rich man & Lazarus

As mentioned earlier, linguistically *Hades* connects to and provides some continuity with the Old Testament understanding of "State-after-Death," and *Sheol* is translated *Hades* in the LXX.[40] From the above table we find that *Hades* is used in the Synoptic Gospels in three different contexts. In two of these, *Hades* is indirectly depicted as a place of punishment:

---

40. Stuart, "Sheol," 472. Also, where the New Testament quotes directly from the Old Testament (e.g. Acts 2:27, 31 and in some manuscripts 1 Cor 15:55) it has *Hades*.

1) In Matthew 11:24, par. Luke 10:15, Jesus pronounces judgment upon Capernaum that it will be brought down to *Hades* because of unbelief.

2) In Matthew 16:18, Jesus responds to Peter's confession by saying that "the gates of *Hades* shall not prevail against" Christ's church.

3) In Luke 16:19–31, the rich man is "in *Hades* being in torment" and sees "Abraham far away and Lazarus in his bosom" (16:23). He describes his State[41] in *Hades* as "in agony in this fire" (16:24) and separated "by a great chasm" (16:26) from Abraham and Lazarus and cannot cross to where they are.[42]

In the Book of Revelation 1:18, 6:8 and 20:13b, 14, *Hades* is used together with death where we see that the risen Jesus has the keys of *death* and *Hades*; *death* and *Hades* were given power to kill; *death* and *Hades* give up their dead for the final judgment and finally *death* and *Hades* are thrown into the lake of fire.

However, unlike *Hades*, the New Testament term *Gehenna* is not used in the LXX for any of the Hebrew underworld terms. However, according to Hans Bietenhard, "It is the Gk. form[43] of the Aram. *gehinnam*, which in turn goes back to the Heb. *gehinnom*. This originally denoted a valley lying to

---

41. In the debate about whether the story of the rich man and Lazarus literally happened or is a parable, the real problem is the assumption that if the story is a parable then it does not give any factual information about State-after-Death (cf. Robert A. Morey, *Death and the Afterlife* [Minneapolis, MN: Bethany House Publishers, 1984], 84–85). Apart from teaching the possible reversal of destiny after death for the rich and the poor (cf. Craig A. Evans, *Luke*, New International Biblical Commentary, No. 3 [Peabody, MA: Hendrickson Publishers, 1990], 249), I think Jesus uses the story to teach that a terrible torment is awaiting for the ungodly after death in *Hades* but a heavenly bliss for the believer along with Abraham in the presence of God (cf. Jesus' response to the Sadducees with "I am the God of Abraham . . ." meaning Abraham is alive in the presence of God). Jesus is also teaching that a great chasm separates *Hades* and where Abraham is (in the presence of God) and that there is no second chance after death, and so to escape *Hades* one must believe the Scriptures while on earth before death.

42. In view of some intertestamental literature's use of *Hades*, some scholars suggest different compartments in *Hades* for the righteous and the unrighteous. However, this story strongly infers, along with other New Testament uses of *Hades* and the Old Testament perspective of *Sheol* (see previous chapter) that *Hades* is a place for unbelievers. Thus Jesus promises that "the gates of *Hades* shall not prevail against" Christ's believers, the church (Matt 16:18). Also Paul says, for him "away from the body" means "at home with the Lord" (2 Co 5:8b) and in Rev 20:14 we see that death and *Hades* are thrown into the lake of fire (*Gehenna*), the second death.

43. ACUTE (43): *geenna* (Greek), Gehenna (Latin); Bietenhard transliterated γεεννα to *Gehenna*.

the south of Jerusalem . . . , the valley of the son (or sons) of Hinnom (Josh 15:8; 18:16; Isa 31:9; 66:24; Jer 32:35; 2 Chr 33:6)."[44] This "Valley of Hinnom" was infamous for idolatry and child sacrifice and was where Kings Ahaz and Manasseh (2 Kgs 16:3; 2 Chr 28:3; 33:6; Jer 7:31; 32:35) burned sacrifices to Molech and even sacrificed their own sons by fire to this god. King Josiah destroyed this paganized valley (2 Kgs 23:10; though his reform did not last long) and the Prophet Jeremiah called it the "Valley of Slaughter," since many would be killed there because of God's judgment on Jerusalem and Judah (Jer 7:31–32). Later on this valley may have become Jerusalem's rubbish heap[45] and in all probability a fire continually burned there to consume the rubbish, perhaps even unclaimed dead bodies. Ajith Fernando remarks that "its history made it an appropriate place from which to derive a name for the place of eternal punishment which is often described as a place with fires of torment."[46]

Yet, however subtle, there seems to be some distinction between *Hades* and *Gehenna* in the New Testament as Gary A. Lee notes,

> The NT seems to distinguish Gehenna from Hades: Gehenna is the place of final judgment, and Hades is the intermediate place where the ungodly await their final judgment (cf. Rev 20:14, where Death and Hades are cast into the lake of fire at the last judgment). As the place of final punishment, Gehenna receives both body and soul (Matt 10:28 par. Luke 12:5), whereas Hades receives only the soul (Acts 2:27, 31; . . .). Thus Jesus urged His listeners to avoid Gehenna at all costs (Matt 5:29f.; 18:9; Mark 9:43, 45, 47), for it is the place where "the fire is not quenched" (Mark 9:48). Those who call their brothers "fools" (Matt 5:22) and the "scribes and Pharisees, hypocrites" (Matt 23:29, 33) are liable to Gehenna (the rabbis consigned various groups to Gehenna . . .). Like the rabbis, Jesus used the term "child of hell" (Gk. *huios geennes*, Matt 23:15) as an epithet for the ungodly.[47]

---

44. Hans Bietenhard, "Hell, Gehenna," in *The New International Dictionary of New Testament Theology*, vol. 2, ed. Colin Brown (Grand Rapids, MI: Zondervan, 1986), 208–209.
45. According to ACUTE (*Nature of Hell*, 43), we do not have any biblical or other early reference for this as a rubbish heap, though reference to ashes may suggest that (Jer 31:40).
46. Ajith Fernando, *Crucial Questions about Hell* (Eastbourne, UK: Kingsway, 1991), 26.
47. Gary A. Lee, "Gehenna," in *The International Standard Bible Encyclopedia*, vol. 2, ed. Geoffrey W. Bromiley (Grand Rapids, MI: Eerdmans, 1982), 423. Cf. Bietenhard, "Hell, Gehenna," 208–209.

Whether or not one accepts this distinction between *Hades* and *Gehenna*, both terms are used in the New Testament to name a place of punishment and torment for unbelievers, either immediately after death or after the final judgment.

The term *Gehenna* occurs eleven times in the Synoptic Gospels and once in James 3:6, where the tongue is, itself, set on fire by *Gehenna*. Thus, it appears twelve times in the New Testament and then in various Jewish and Christian writings.[48] Following the table above, we summarise that, in all of its occurrences in the Synoptic Gospels, it is used by Jesus himself as he speaks in four different contexts:

1) In Matthew 5:22 in Jesus' teaching on the mount he says, "anyone who says, 'You fool!' will be in danger of the fire of *Gehenna*."

2) In Matthew 5:29, 30; 18:8, 9 and Mark 9:43, 45, 47 he says it is better to enter life (or the kingdom of God) maimed than with the whole body go to *Gehenna*.

3) In Matthew 10:28, par. Luke 12:5, he commands us to fear God who can destroy or send both body and soul to *Gehenna*.

4) In Matthew 23:15 he tells his listeners that some of the teachers of the law and the Pharisees, make their converts twice as much "sons of *Gehenna*" as they are already. In Matthew 23:33 Jesus calls them snakes and brood of vipers and asks how they will escape *Gehenna*.

Importantly, in the second context Jesus compares *Gehenna*, "the eternal fire" in Matthew 18:8 with the "*Gehenna* of fire" in the next verse 18:9. In Mark 9:43, *Gehenna* is "the unquenchable fire" and, finally, in Mark 9:48 he quotes Isaiah 66:24 to describe *Gehenna*, "where their worm does not die, and the fire is not quenched." In all of these the punishment in *Gehenna is unceasing*. Some argue from Matthew 10:28, which speaks of the destruction of body and soul, that these will be annihilated in *Gehenna*. (Although annihilation is a related topic, I will not pursue it further as it is beyond the scope of this study, but note here that the parallel to Matthew 10:28, Luke 12:5, refers only to *Gehenna* without the accompanying destruction of body and soul.)

In addition to *Hades* and *Gehenna*, further concepts and images in the Synoptic Gospels in Table 2 describe the unbelievers' "State-after-Death".

---

48. ACUTE, *Nature of Hell*, 43.

For example, God's "coming wrath" and its "unquenchable fire" in John the Baptist's teaching in Matthew 3:12. In Matthew 25:31–46, in the parable of the sheep and the goats, Jesus mentions "eternal fire" in verse 41 and "eternal punishment" in verse 46, confirming the eternalness of the punishment to the unrighteous. Finally, Jesus speaks in harsh metaphors (given in the table above) of the state of unbelievers after death with language such as, darkness, weeping, gnashing of teeth and the "fiery furnace" (Matt 13:42, 50).

The Gospel and Letters of John

We turn now to John's gospel and letters for further perspectives on "State-after-Death". With regards to unbelievers, ACUTE states that, "John's gospel and letters differ noticeably from the synoptic gospels in that they contain no reference to Gehenna, Hades, torment, fire, etc.," but "portray unbelief in terms of 'perishing', 'death' and 'condemnation/judgment.'"[49] However, George Eldon Ladd notes that, "it is clear that the four Gospels[50] were written from the perspective of Jesus' resurrection." Then Ladd shows the importance of resurrection in John's gospel,

> The Gospel of John bears witness to Jesus' conviction that he must die and rise again, but in very different terms from the Synoptics . . . "Unless a grain of wheat . . . but if it dies, it bears much fruit" (John 12:24). Here, in a metaphor, Jesus is made to predict his own death, but beyond death is a new emergence into life to bear much fruit . . . In the parable of the Good Shepherd . . . (John 10:11, 18) . . . "I lay down my life, *in order that* I may take it again." This indicates that the resurrection is not a mere event following Jesus' death, but the essential completion of his death. Resurrection is the purpose of his death.[51]

To understand what happens after death in John's gospel and letters, we look first at the general theme of resurrection from the dead as we did in the Synoptic Gospels.

---

49. Ibid., 47. Except when Jesus says that some branches are thrown into the fire and burned (John 15:6).

50. As Ladd (*I Believe in the Resurrection of Jesus* [Grand Rapids, MI: Eerdmans, 1975], 29) quotes C. F. Evans "Christianity of the New Testament – is a religion of resurrection" so I say the whole of New Testament was written from the perspective of Jesus' resurrection.

51. Ladd, *I Believe in the Resurrection of Jesus*, 33–34; cf. also Bailey, *Biblical Perspective on Death*, 95.

Resurrection from the Dead

Though Bailey contends that the topic of resurrection from the dead "is pushed to the margins of discussion"[52] and C. F. Evans states that the concluding narratives of resurrection appearances in John's gospel "are not strictly necessary to his thought,"[53] Andrew T. Lincoln's assertions are quite convincing:

> The dominance of the resurrection message in the Fourth Gospel is beyond dispute. While all the Gospel accounts are written from a post-resurrection perspective, the perspective in the Fourth Gospel is not only explicit in the narrator's asides (cf. 2:22; 7:39; 20:9) but also much more determinative for the shaping of the narrative than in the Synoptic Gospels. The preresurrection setting of Jesus and the postresurrection setting of the fourth evangelist and his readers have been telescoped together, so that much of the narrative is to be read on these two levels at the same time. Of the four Gospels, it is John's Gospel, in chapters 20 and 21, that allots the most space to the resurrection accounts and that provides the greatest number and variety of resurrection appearances.
>
> Furthermore, the Fourth Gospel has eternal life – with its clear associations with resurrection – as a pervasive theme. The term "life" occurs thirty-six times in John's Gospel. On seventeen of those occasions it is accompanied by the adjective "eternal." And in a number of key sayings of Jesus, eternal life is linked explicitly to resurrection, with the most striking of these sayings being the "I am" formulation in 11:25: "I am the resurrection and the life."[54]

N. T. Wright too sees the theme of resurrection in John's gospel and notes that while John is "very different from others, resembles them (and also Paul) in this respect: it too bears witness to the centrality and rich variety of 'resurrection' ideas . . . John has allowed 'resurrection' themes to be heard at several points in . . . his gospel . . . The new life which will be consummated

---

52. Bailey, *Biblical Perspective on Death*, 94.
53. Evans, *Resurrection and the New Testament*, 4.
54. Andrew T. Lincoln, "'I Am the Resurrection and the Life': The Resurrection Message of the Fourth Gospel," in *Life in the Face of Death: The Resurrection Message of the New Testament*, ed. Richard N. Longenecker (Grand Rapids, MI: Eerdmans, 1998), 122.

in the resurrection . . . works backwards into the present."⁵⁵ Of course, one cannot ignore the emphasis on "realized eschatology" in John.⁵⁶ However, Marianne Meye Thompson points out, the apparent "contradiction in terms to speak of having 'eternal life,' the life of age to come, in the present, for eternal life is that life which does not end – and yet John clearly expects the death and resurrection of believers . . . Thus eternal life is also the appropriation by faith of unseen yet present realities . . . and become more fully realized in the next."⁵⁷ Thus the theme of the resurrection from the dead is implied very early on in the prologue of John's gospel (1:4) and also in 1 John both in the beginning (1:2) as well as in the end (5:20) through the reference to Jesus being the "life" or "eternal life."⁵⁸ After the prologue refers to "life" (1:4), John carries forward the theme of resurrection in the second half of the temple incident (2:19–22) where Jesus speaks of himself and the destruction of the temple and rebuilding it in three days. To that we now turn.

When we consider the enigmatic remark in Mark 14:58, par. Matthew 26:61 (also Mark 15:29, par. Matt 27:40), we find John alone interprets it in light of Jesus' resurrection. John states that, "he had spoken about the temple of his body" and that "after he was raised from the dead his disciples remembered he said this before" (2:21–22). Hagner notes, "It is the Fourth Gospel that solves the puzzle by explicitly applying this saying to Jesus' resurrection . . . Thus John gives his readers the key to the right interpretation of this resurrection saying, which is expressed somewhat enigmatically in the Synoptic Gospels."⁵⁹ One wonders how some scholars can conclude that the subject of resurrection has no place in John's gospel, because there is no other plausible explanation why John would interpret Jesus' temple remark that way.⁶⁰

The truth about resurrection from the dead, in general, comes out most clearly in John's account of Jesus' response to the charge of his detractors that he was making himself equal with God: "For just as the Father raises the dead and gives them life, even so the Son gives life to whom he is pleased to give

---

55. Wright, *Resurrection of the Son of God*, 440.
56. Cf. Bailey, *Biblical Perspective on Death*, 94.
57. Marianne Meye Thomson, "John, Gospel of," in *Dictionary of Jesus and the Gospels*, eds. Joel B. Green, Scot McKnight and I. Howard Marshall (Downers Grove, IL: InterVarsity, 1992), 381.
58. The implication of Jesus' response to the Sadducees with regard to resurrection in the Synoptics that "God is not God of the dead, but of the living" (Mark 12:27, Matt 22:32 and Luke 20:38) confirms that.
59. Hagner, "Gospel, Kingdom, and Resurrection," 105.
60. Cf. also Wright, *Resurrection of the Son of God*, 440–441.

it . . . for a time is coming when all who are in their graves will hear his voice and come out – those who have done good will rise to live, and those who have done evil will rise to be condemned" (5:21, 28, 29 NIV). Reflecting on John 5:19–30,

Murray J. Harris concludes,

> This whole passage, therefore, like John 6:54, reflects a combination of 'realized eschatology' with its stress on the present fulfillment of divine promise (vv. 24–5) and 'futurist eschatology' with its emphasis on the future consummation of divine promise (vv. 28–9). There are some scholars who dismiss all future elements in John's eschatology as either concessions to traditional Jewish beliefs or later editorial insertions. But the data prove intractable. The distinctive element in the eschatology of the Fourth Gospel is not the eradication of the Jewish doctrines of future judgment (see 5: 22, 27, 29), future resurrection (see 5:29; 6:39–40, 44, 54; 11:23), or future eternal life (see 4:14, 36; 5:39; 6:27; 12:25), but (i) the addition of the present dimension to the doctrines of judgment (3:18; 5:22, 27), resurrection (5:21, 24–5; 11:25), and eternal life (3:15–16, 36; 5:24; 6:33, 40, 47, 54; 17:3); and (ii) the role of Jesus in judging (5:22, 27), raising the dead (5:21, 28; 6:39–40) and granting eternal life (4:14; 5:24; 6:27), both now and in the future.[61]

John shows us in 5:19–30 that Jesus has the authority to raise the *spiritually* dead (5:24) and that he is raising them now (5:25) and, moreover, in the future it will be Jesus' voice that will raise all the *physically* dead in the end for the final judgment to either eternal life or condemnation (5:28, 29). John continues to highlight Jesus' power to raise the dead and, thus, the teaching about future resurrection from the dead in the end ("at the last day") in 6:39, 40, 44 and 54. The limited scope of this section restricts us from looking at all the references to resurrection that permeate John's gospel, yet we cannot overlook the crucial symbolic event of Jesus raising Lazarus from the dead in John 11.

Lazarus, the brother of Martha and Mary, from Bethany (less than two miles from Jerusalem) died after an illness and was buried in a tomb for four days when Jesus came and raised him from the dead, returning life to him as

---

61. Harris, *Raised Immortal*, 152.

he had before (John 11:1–12:11).⁶² Lincoln argues that this is a momentous event within the narrative of John's gospel,

> Whereas in the Synoptic Gospels it is the temple incident . . . , in John's Gospel it is the raising of Lazarus that is the catalyst for the decision of the Sanhedrin to put Jesus to death. This seventh and climactic sign of Jesus' public ministry is recounted creatively and dramatically by overlaying it with the theme of Jesus' own destiny and with the concerns of later followers about the death of believers.⁶³

Lazarus' resurrection is not only a critical sign for the death and resurrection of Jesus Christ but, more importantly, it opens the way for clear teaching from Jesus about the believers' final destiny after death, especially in his dialogue with Martha. Even while Martha expresses her disappointment that Lazarus would not have died if Jesus has been there earlier (11:21), yet, with great confidence in Jesus, she continues, "But even now I know that whatever you ask from God, God will give you" (11:22, ESV). As Jesus assures her that Lazarus will rise again, Martha misunderstands and thinks Jesus is referring to the future general resurrection (11:24). Then Jesus makes his historic claim, "I am the resurrection and the life" (11:25) and draws her attention from a mere hope of future resurrection in the end to himself as the One who "will effect resurrection and impart life" to the believer.⁶⁴ Harris paraphrases John 11:25–26:

> Jesus said to her, "I myself am the pledge and agent of resurrection; I myself am the giver of immortality to the resurrected dead. Accordingly, with regard to resurrection, the person who believes in me, even if death overtakes him, will nevertheless be raised up in resurrection life; and, with regard to immortality, every person who will gain resurrection life as a believer in me will never die but will live for ever."⁶⁵

It seems that initially Martha was focusing her attention on Christ, as she knows Jesus has a special relationship with God, by stating that God always

---

62. Harris (*Raised Immortal*, 214) and Wright (*Resurrection of the Son of God*, 443) point to the conditional nature of his resurrection, that Lazarus remained mortal after his resurrection and would die again.
63. Lincoln, "I Am the Resurrection and the Life," 139.
64. Harris, *Raised Immortal*, 212.
65. Ibid.

gives him what he asks (John 11:22). But then Jesus through his claim in 11:25–26 wants to take her (and all of us) a step further to know that not only does he have a special relationship with God but also that he, himself, is the giver of life. In essence, he (Jesus) who is speaking is God himself. Perhaps, even after that remark of Jesus, Martha shows her lack of faith about who Jesus is when she does not want the stone removed because of a possible bad odor from Lazarus' decaying body (11:39). Yet Jesus continues to draw the attention of all who are standing there to himself, that they might believe in him and that God has sent him (11:42). It is through believing in him that they will have resurrection life (21:31). Harris concludes, "The central theme of John 11:1–44 is the lordship of Jesus over death . . . Those who are united to him in faith . . . are not guaranteed immunity from physical death but they are guaranteed triumph over death through resurrection (v. 25b) and then a ceaseless supply of resurrection life (v. 25a)."[66]

As far as the letters of John are concerned, there seem to be no references to resurrection in the Second and the Third letter. But the First letter does refer to resurrection life. It is implied from beginning to end, 1 John 1:2 to 5:20, through references to Jesus as "life" or "eternal life." Whereas the world is passing away, as this age is ending and God's rule is coming, so those who do the will of God *abide forever* (2:17). God has promised *eternal life* to those who remain in the Father and in the Son (2:25). We (the believers) have passed from *death to life*, anyone not loving *remains in death* (3:14). God sent his one and only Son that we *might live* through him (4:9). We, (the believers) will have *confidence on the day of judgment* (4:17). God gave us *eternal life*, he who has the Son *has life* he who does not have the Son of God *does not have life* (5:11, 12).

Narratives of Jesus' Resurrection

Finally, as we have seen in the narratives of Jesus' resurrection in the Synoptic Gospels, John 20 and 21 also give us a more comprehensive understanding of the reality of resurrection from the dead, because, ultimately, it is Jesus' resurrection that paves the way for the possibility of the believers' resurrection from the dead and eternal life with him. If Jesus himself was not raised, then his words in John 11 that believers will be raised from the dead and have endless resurrected life would not have any meaning. We have seen how

---

66. Harris, *Raised Immortal*, 214.

Hagner highlights the three significant themes common to the Synoptic Gospels about Jesus' resurrection: the empty tomb, the female witnesses and the appearances of the risen Jesus.[67] In John 20 and 21, we see the same themes except that only one female witness, Mary Magdalene, is mentioned and more detailed interactions are given between the risen Jesus and individual disciples like Mary Magdalene, Thomas and Peter.[68] Thus, the themes of the empty tomb, the witness of a woman and the appearances of the risen Jesus present in John's narratives confirm in the same way the historical truth of Jesus' resurrection as we have seen in the Synoptics.

Referring to John 21, Grant R. Osborne points out that most scholars consider this chapter to be an appendix or epilogue added after the completion of the gospel.[69] If that is true, the question is whether John himself wrote it later or someone else. Osborne notes, "The latter is suggested by 21:24–25, which seems to be the imprimatur of a church official attesting to the validity of the Beloved Disciple's witness. Yet the chapter's language, style and emphases parallel the rest of the Gospel . . . and one can tentatively equate the authors of chapters 20 and 21."[70] Yet, whoever the author of John 21 may be, "it clearly stands thematically within the mainstream of Johannine ideology"[71] and so for the purpose of this chapter does not nullify the historical truth of Jesus' resurrection.

However, there is one other problem that scholars wrestle with in all four gospels: the location of the resurrection appearances, as Osborne notes,

> Scholars have discussed at length the significance of the Galilee versus Jerusalem appearance traditions, especially since they do not occur together in any single Gospel account (John 21 is an appendix added later . . .). Many believe that the Galilee tradition is prior, since it is found in the oldest tradition (Mark 14:28; 16:7). However, this is not a necessary conclusion, for even in Matthew – where the Galilee appearance takes center stage – there is a "Jerusalem" appearance to the women (Matt 28:8–10). The Redactional interests of the Evangelists may have

---

67. Hagner, "Gospel, Kingdom, and Resurrection," 107–111.
68. Of course, only Luke (24:13–35) gives the detailed interaction on the road to Emmaus between the risen Jesus and the two of his followers Cleopas and his friend who later report this to the Eleven.
69. Grant R. Osborne, *The Resurrection Narratives: A Redactional Study* (Grand Rapids, MI: Baker, 1984), 176.
70. Osborne, "Resurrection," 686; cf. also Osborne, *Resurrection Narratives*, 189–191.
71. Osborne, *Resurrection Narratives*, 176.

been reason enough for them to center on one tradition. C. F. D. Moule (1957–58) presents a quite plausible thesis that as festival pilgrims . . . the disciples would have remained in Jerusalem for the feast of unleavened bread (thus the appearances of Matt 28:9–10; Luke 24:13–49; John 20:11–29), gone back to Galilee for the interim between the feasts (Matt 28:16–20; John 21) and finally returned to Jerusalem for Pentecost (the ascension in Luke 24:50–53; Acts 1:6–11).[72]

Following Osborne and Harris, we find C. F. D. Moule's explanation convincing, and it also explains the reference to the forty days of Jesus' post-resurrection appearances to his disciples in Acts 1:3 as literally forty days rather than some symbolic biblical number as others suggest. Thus, the narratives of Jesus' resurrection in all four gospels confirm the historicity of the event and also confirm that the ultimate destiny of believers in Christ is that they will be resurrected bodily in the future and will continue in resurrected life forever.

Unbelievers' State-after-Death

At the beginning of this section we noted that in John's gospel and letters the terminologies used to describe the unbelievers' destiny after physical death "differ noticeably from the Synoptic Gospels in that they contain no reference to Gehenna, Hades, torment, fire,"[73] instead their final destiny is referred to in terms of "'perishing', 'death' and 'condemnation/judgment'."[74] We see this in the classic verses of John 3:16, 18: "whoever believes in him shall not *perish* but have everlasting life . . . Whoever believes in him is not *condemned* [or judged], but whoever does not believe stands *condemned* [or judged] already" (NIV). The letters of John, refer only once to the destiny of unbelievers, 1 John 5:16, concerning sin that leads to *death* as a final destiny and not just leading to physical death.

The purpose of John's gospel is that its readers may believe (or continue to believe) in Jesus and by believing have *life* in his name (John 20:31). D. A. Carson comments helpfully:

---

72. Osborne, "Resurrection," 683; cf. Harris, *Raised Immortal*, 50–53.
73. However, one exception is that "fire" is mentioned once in John 15:6.
74. ACUTE, *Nature of Hell*, 47.

> In short, John's Gospel is not only evangelistic in its purpose (which was a dominant view until this century . . .), but aims in particular to evangelize Jews and Jewish proselytes. This view has not been popular, but is gradually gaining influence . . . It may even receive indirect support from some recent studies that try to interpret the Fourth Gospel as a piece of mission literature. The best of these display generally excellent exegesis, but give little attention to the fact that with very little adaptation the same exegesis could justify the thesis that the Gospel of John was not written *to* believers *about* mission but *to* outsiders to *perform* mission.[75]

If Carson's assertion is true that John's gospel was written "in particular to evangelize Jews and Jewish proselytes" then it can be assumed that its Jewish hearers were fully aware of unbelievers' "State-after-Death." Therefore, no further elaboration from John is needed except to see it compared to condemnation, judgment, death and "to perish," the opposite of eternal life. However, if it were written to the believers either to strengthen their faith or to persuade them to do mission, then there was no need to elaborate at this point on the final destiny of unbelievers. John's message is that Jesus came to save and so those who reject him are, in effect, condemning themselves. Even if John were writing to the non-Jews of the pluralistic religious contexts of the Greco-Roman world, his message is clear about "State-after-Death."

Summary and Implications

In the Synoptic Gospels, we saw that the New Testament perspective goes significantly beyond the Old Testament. Jesus promises eternal life for believers and the opposite for unbelievers. Jesus reasons convincingly with the Sadducees about the truth of resurrection, miraculously raises dead people, and predicts his own death and resurrection. The resurrection narratives of Jesus offer three predominant themes: the empty tomb, the witness of women, and the appearances of the risen Jesus. These convincingly prove his bodily resurrection. Thus, believers have new hope because of Jesus' own resurrection, and there would be continuity as well as discontinuity with the physical body. Unbelievers, however, will be consigned to *Hades* (like *Sheol* in OT) immediately after death, as an intermediate state of temporary

---

75. D. A. Carson, *The Gospel According To John* (Grand Rapids, MI: Eerdmans, 1991), 91.

punishment, before experiencing the fires of *Gehenna* after the final judgment, to suffer there eternally.

In the gospel of John, resurrection of the dead and eternal life are dominant themes. There will be a general resurrection of all people, the righteous and the unrighteous, the former for eternal life and the latter for condemnation. Jesus predicted his death and resurrection in his saying concerning the destruction of the temple and its rebuilding in three days. Resurrection from the dead shows most clearly in John's account of Jesus' response to the charge that he was making himself equal with God because he claimed to raise the dead and give life just like God the Father does. Lazarus' resurrection is not only a sign for the immediate death and resurrection of Jesus but, most importantly, it gives Jesus' clear teaching in his dialogue with Martha on what happens after the death of a believer. Jesus takes authority over death and through Jesus believers will triumph over death. In John's first letter, the theme of resurrection is implied throughout.

As with the Synoptic Gospels, the narratives of Jesus' resurrection in John's gospel carry the themes of the empty tomb, female witness (only Mary Magdalene) and the appearances of the risen Jesus. These confirm the historical truth of Jesus' bodily resurrection. Thus the narratives of Jesus' resurrection in all four gospels confirm the historicity of the event and affirm the ultimate destiny of believers in Christ. They will be bodily resurrected in the end and will continue in resurrected life forever. As for the unbelievers' "State-after-Death" and final destiny, there is no mention of *Hades* and *Gehenna* in John's gospel, as a place of punishment, but it does mention *perishing, death* and *condemnation/judgment,* while the letters mention *death* (not just physical death) as a final destiny only once (1 John 5:16).

We have seen in our study of the New Testament so far that "State-after-Death" is a critical component of the Divine mission whereby God opens the way for humans to be spared a hopeless final state and receive life-after-death through the resurrection of the Lord Jesus Christ. We found that, in spite of the pluralistic contexts of the Greco-Roman world of the New Testament, God revealed his unique message of hope after death to his people, available because of Jesus' death and the resurrection. This message was radically different from the existing pluralistic views. This study of "State-after-Death" in the New Testament shows us further that, as for the early disciples of Jesus Christ amid their mixed religious environment, the issue of "State-after-Death" would be an important and fruitful area for conversation. The same is true for the present-day global Christian church, as the Agents of God's mission: (a) engages with the Hindu, Muslim and Secular Humanist peoples *inside* and *outside* the Christian church and (b) effectively communicates the gospel of Jesus Christ in those pluralistic contexts of the world.

In the coming chapter, we will explore Paul's letters and the Book of Revelation.

8

State-after-Death in Paul's Epistles and in Revelation

For this investigation of the letters of Paul and the Book of Revelation I will continue to use the three dimensional approach (the priority of authorial intention, metacritical perspective and constructive use of biblical narratives) for working with the biblical texts concerning death and after-death. In this metacritical method, as noted before, we assume the death and the resurrection of Jesus Christ is the transcendental or trans-contextual basis for doing Christian theology in pluralistic religious contexts.

The Letters of Paul

Paul's letters are the earliest written documents of the New Testament[1] and therefore the earliest window into understanding the New Testament church's views on "State-after-Death". Due to the massive body of scholarship that examine this issue in Paul's letters, we must be highly selective in this study. Even N. T. Wright notes this in his writing:

> This investigation of Paul must itself be seriously curtailed. Most aspects of Paul's thought link up with most other aspects in a wonderfully complex web of ideas, biblical echoes, implicit narratives and practical instructions. The resurrection (of Christians, and of Jesus) is central in much of this, and to follow through all the ramifications of what Paul says would entail writing detailed commentaries on many sections of many letters,

---

1. E.g. Bailey, *Biblical Perspective on Death*, 87; Wright, *Resurrection of the Son of God*, 211. We will not delve into the arguments of authorship but only look into what are commonly considered Paul's letters within the traditional biblical scholarship.

and engaging in discussion with a whole world of monographs and articles. Here to keep length under control, I must refer to detailed discussions elsewhere [Yet he took 190 pages to write it!].[2]

Wright deals mainly with resurrection from the dead, but I look also into the final destiny of unbelievers'. Because of this broader intention I must be even more restrained in selecting textual and scholarly references seeking to understand Paul's perspective on "State-after-Death". Like John, Paul does not explicitly deal with *Gehenna* and *Hades*[3] but does refer to other terms closely related to unbelievers' final destiny. We begin with Paul's view on resurrection from the dead.

Resurrection from the Dead

Referring to Paul's viewpoint on resurrection, C. F. Evans notes,

> Paul, for all the emphasis he is led . . . to put on the cross, attests the centrality of the resurrection both in statements which arise from and express his own theology, and in formulae which he has adopted as already traditional by his time. He connects it with the deepest things, and at one point can affirm categorically that denial of the resurrection amounts to a denial not of one element in the Christian faith, nor of one truth among others, but of the Christian faith itself. (1 Cor 15:12ff.)[4]

Of course, Paul being a Pharisee (Acts 23:6; 26:5; Phil 3:5) believed in the resurrection of the dead (Acts 23:6–8; 24:21) even prior to encountering the risen Jesus on the Damascus Road. Larry J. Kreitzer notes that Paul "understood his encounter of the risen Lord Jesus Christ in light of [resurrection]" and also cites R. J. Sider that, "as a good first-century Pharisee, Paul could not conceive of the resurrection of the dead in purely immaterial terms."[5] Harris, however,

---

2. Wright, *Resurrection of the Son of God*, 212. Also Pheme Perkins (*Resurrection: New Testament Witness and Contemporary Reflection* [Garden City, NY: Doubleday & Co, 1984], 264) notes that "The Pauline tradition makes the most exhaustive use of resurrection symbolism in the New Testament . . . Paul finds a variety of ways to present the death and resurrection of Christ as the pattern that determines the shape of Christian life in the Spirit."

3. In some manuscripts a direct quote from Hosea 13:14 in 1 Cor 15:55 has *Hades*. If an author belonging to the Pauline circle wrote the letter to the Hebrews, Heb 10:27 refers to judgment and raging fire.

4. Evans, *Resurrection and the New Testament*, 4.

5. Larry J. Kreitzer, "Resurrection," in *Dictionary of Paul and his Letters*, eds. Gerald F.

amplifies Paul's definition of resurrection. Harris says that it "implies not only restoration to life but also transformation and exaltation" and that it "applies first of all to the resurrection of Christ, but it also applies to both the present spiritual resurrection and the future bodily resurrection of believers."[6] We shall review some of the resurrection references in Paul's letters.

I will begin with 1 Thessalonians, commonly dated sometime during CE 49–52, written by Paul in Corinth after his visit to Thessalonica (Acts 17:1-8).[7] In 1:9-10, Paul commends the Thessalonians for their faith and for leaving the idols of paganism to serve the true and living God and "to wait for his Son from heaven, whom God raised from the dead." Then, in 4:13–5:11, Paul deals with the final state of the believers who have died and of those who remain when Jesus returns. In it Paul urges the Thessalonians to continue to encourage each other on that premise. Wright notes,

> In this passage he [Paul] clearly indicates that those who have already died will, at some future date be raised from the dead 'in the same way' (*houtos*, 4:14). Jesus' resurrection will be the model for that of his people. Those currently dead will rise up (*anastesontai*, 4:16), and so possess "salvation" rather than being the objects of "wrath" (5:9). The words Paul uses, the nature of his argument, and the underlying story-line, all make it crystal clear that he belongs . . . right in the middle of second-Temple Jewish beliefs about resurrection. Take Jesus out of this picture, and what is being asserted – the future resurrection to salvation from wrath, for those presently dead who belong to the people of the one god – is familiar from our study of Judaism: it is the position of the Pharisees. Whatever other beliefs Paul revised following his conversion, resurrection remained constant. This means that we are bound to see resurrection as *bodily*, not only because of the terminology (there is no evidence that the *anastasis* root meant anything other than bodily resurrection, either in the paganism

---

Hawthorne, Ralph P. Martin and Daniel G. Reid (Downers Grove, IL: InterVarsity, 1993), 807.

6. Harris, "Resurrection and Immortality in the Pauline Corpus," in *Life in the Face of Death: The Resurrection Message of the New Testament*, ed. Richard N. Longenecker (Grand Rapids, MI: Eerdmans, 1998), 149. See footnote #3, Chapter 7 for Harris's view along with Grudem's view regarding the resurrected body.

7. Cf. Wright, *Resurrection of the Son of God*, 213; D. J. Williams, *1 and 2 Thessalonians*, New International Biblical Commentary, No. 12 (Peabody, MA: Hendrickson Publishers, 1992), 10; William Hendriksen, *I & II Thessalonians* (Edinburgh, UK: Banner of Truth Trust, 1955), 16.

that denied it or the Pharisaic Judaism that affirmed it), not only because of the obviously Jewish context, but also because of the narrative logic. Resurrection is something new, something the dead do *not* presently enjoy; it will be life *after* 'life after death'.[8]

Dealing with the intermediate state of the believers who had already died, until the return of Jesus, N. T. Wright rejects the idea of "soul sleep."[9] Though "soul sleep" (generally defined as a period of unconscious "State-after-Death" for the soul until the final resurrection) is an important topic, it is beyond the limited scope of this study. The study of "State-after-Death" here is a broad philosophical concept, directly related to the communication of the gospel of Jesus Christ with its promise of eternal life beyond death and it is not about the specific details of Intermediate State. This study is dealing with the larger issue of eternal destiny after death and so it will not consider the controversial issues of "soul sleep" in the intermediate state or "annihilation in hell." Referring to Paul's writing in 2 Corinthians 5:8 and Philippians 1:23, and here in 1 Thessalonians 4:13–5:11, with words such as, "the dead in the Messiah" (4:16), and those who have fallen asleep "continue (and will continue)" to "live with him" (5:10), to be "with Jesus" (4:14), or "with the Lord" (4:17), Wright points to "the paradox and tension inherent" in this intermediate state for the believers with the Lord.[10] For Wright, this inherent tension highlights the importance of bodily resurrection in the future, as he contends Paul is affirming here.

Next, we turn to the two most important references in Paul's letters to resurrection from the dead: 1 Corinthians 15 and 2 Corinthians 4:7–5:10. George E. Ladd noted that, "Paul preserves for us the earliest tradition of the resurrection appearances of Jesus."[11] As we consider the theme of resurrection from the dead in 1 Corinthians 15 and 2 Corinthians 4:7–5:10 we must recognize that, "Whole books have been written on 1 Corinthians 15 alone, and massive monographs and commentaries . . . clamour for attention."[12] Therefore, we are compelled to be extremely selective as to sources and our reflections on them.

---

8. Wright, *Resurrection of the Son of God*, 215.
9. Ibid., 216. Wright contends that Paul does not refer to the 'soul' (*psyche*) to depict the intermediate state and "it is the *body* that 'sleeps' between death and resurrection" but not in an unconscious state (Ibid).
10. Wright, *Resurrection of the Son of God*, 216.
11. Ladd, *I Believe in the Resurrection of Jesus*, 104. According to Ladd, Paul wrote to the Corinthians around CE 55 or 56 (Ibid).
12. Wright, *Resurrection of the Son of God*, 277.

Wright points out that the previous theory of A. C. Thiselton, that 1 Corinthians 15 was written by Paul to sort out the Corinthians' view of *over-realized* eschatology by pointing to a *future* resurrection, is now being abandoned by scholars for a new theory of Richard Hays.[13] This new view suggests Paul is responding to Corinthians' need for a *more adequate* eschatology, as they were syncretizing their Christian beliefs with ideas from pagan philosophy and popular-level Stoicism instead of Jewish-style eschatology. On one hand, the new theory seems more plausible, as Paul also deals with other issues that relate to paganism such as, the Greeks looking for human wisdom (1 Cor 1 & 2), the Corinthians' pagan background (1 Cor 6:9-11), food sacrificed to idols (1 Cor 8) and idolatry in Israel's history (1 Cor 10). On the other hand, both theories may be equally true, as Longenecker notes,

> Evidently some Christians at Corinth were claiming that a future, personal, corporeal resurrection of believers in Jesus was (1) *irrelevant*, since the eschatological hope of the gospel was already fulfilled in a believer's present, spiritual experience; (2) *impossible*, since the corporeal body in Greek religious thought was excluded from divine redemption – perhaps, also, in reaction to crude Jewish ideas about resurrection as being simply revivification, reanimation, or resuscitation; and (3) even *unnecessary*, since believers were thought to possess already an immortal soul, which, now being redeemed by Christ, made any further action by God superfluous. Such a scenario seems evident from a "mirror reading" of Paul's statements in the passage. For in 1 Cor 15:12–58 the apostle sets out (1) the *fact* of a Christian's future, personal, corporeal resurrection in vv. 12–34 (as signaled by the use of *hoti*, "that", which appears twice in v. 12), (2) the *manner* of a Christian's resurrection in vv. 35–49 (as signaled by the use of *pos*, "how", which appears in v. 35), and (3) the *necessity* for a Christian's resurrection in vv. 50–58 (as signaled by the use of *dei*, "necessary", which appears in v. 53).[14]

Thus, in 1 Corinthians 15, Paul is giving the authentic response of a relevant theology of "State-after-Death" for Corinthian believers to meet the pluralistic

---

13. Ibid., 279–280.
14. Longenecker, *Life in the Face of Death*, 186.

challenges of their own philosophical Greek (pagan), as well as Jewish, contexts in Corinth (cf. 1 Cor 1:22–24).

Influenced by the pluralistic views of their context, some Corinthian Christians denied future bodily resurrection of believers (1 Cor 15:12). Paul faces that challenge squarely and argues at length in 1 Corinthians 15 that, "what the creator god did for Jesus is both the *model* and the *means* of what he will do for all Jesus' people."[15] However, some New Testament scholars doubt whether Jesus' resurrection was an actual event, even though Paul witnesses to it in verses 1–11. Wright notes,

> Bultmann, famously, criticized Paul for citing witnesses to Jesus' resurrection, as though he considered it an actual event, instead of being merely a graphic, "mythological" way of referring to the conviction of the early Christians that Jesus' death had been a good thing, not a bad thing. The inauthenticity of an entire stream of twentieth-century New Testament scholarship is thus laid here; if Paul really allowed himself, in so serious and sober an introduction to a carefully crafted chapter expressing the central point that underlay an entire letter, to say something as drastically misleading as Bultmann imagined, he is hardly a thinker worth wrestling with in the first place. But in fact Bultmann was simply wrong: the resurrection of Jesus was a real event as far as Paul was concerned, and it underlay the future real event of the resurrection of all God's people.[16]

N. T. Wright is correct because Paul himself argues in verses 12–19 that if Jesus' resurrection was not a real event then the gospel preached is useless, their faith is futile and there would be no salvation for believers. Furthermore, those who have died believing in Christ for salvation are all lost, because their sins are still intact. Wright had noted earlier, "The gospel is anchored in the resurrection of Jesus . . . if this did not happen then the gospel, with all its benefits, is null and void."[17]

As to the question of what kind of body the resurrected body of believers will be, Ladd shows from 1 Corinthians 15:44 that it will be a corporeal body animated and empowered by the Spirit of God,

---

15. Wright, *Resurrection of the Son of God*, 316.
16. Ibid., 317–318.
17. Ibid., 317.

Paul sums up his argument by saying, "It is sown a physical body, it is raised a spiritual body" (v. 44). These words are subject to misinterpretation and taken to mean that the resurrection will be in "spiritual", i.e. non-corporeal bodies. This cannot be Paul's meaning. The translation "physical body" is not accurate; as a matter of fact, the Greek word has no equivalent term in English. The Greek word is *psychikon*, from *psyche* which means life or soul. The physical – i.e., mortal – body is not made of *psyche*; it is a body animated by *psyche*. In the same way the resurrection body will not be made of *pneuma* – spirit. It is true that some Greek philosophers did not consider *pneuma* to be non-material as we do; they thought of *pneuma* as a very fine, invisible, celestial substance capable of interpenetrating all other forms of being. However, this idea is not found in Paul. *Pneuma* to him is God's pneuma – the Holy Spirit. The resurrection body will be one which is completely animated and empowered by the Spirit of God.[18]

Paul continues to amplify this truth by his comparison of Adam and Jesus in verses 45–49. Adam and Jesus had the same kind of material body while they were on earth. If not, Jesus was not fully human. In verse 49b, Paul is speaking about believers bearing the image of the risen Jesus as opposed to the image of Jesus before his death, as it would seem that there was *some* discontinuity in the materiality or corporeality of the two bodies of Jesus, though not *total* material discontinuity as the body that was buried was the same body that was literally raised and transformed.

According to Paul, the believers too, whether dead or alive, will go through that same transformation (v. 51) and this, for Paul, is a new "mystery" or enigma. Referring to this "mystery," Longenecker notes that a discernible shift seems to have occurred in Paul's statement from what he wrote in 1 Thessalonians 4, in that, "resurrection has to do with transformation, not merely with the revivification, reanimation, or resuscitation of a dead corpse."[19] Thus, following the model of Jesus' resurrection, it is not a question

---

18. Ladd, *I Believe in the Resurrection of Jesus*, 116. Wright (*Resurrection of the Son of God*, 348–352) makes the same point as he discusses this verse in more detail and concludes with the old Jerusalem Bible translation, "when it is sown it embodies the soul, when it is raised it embodies the spirit. If the soul has its own embodment, so does the spirit have its own embodiment."
19. Longenecker, *Life in the Face of Death*, 190.

of "*either or*" but rather "*both and*" and the believers' transformation will include the revivification of the material body at the resurrection.[20] I have quoted Ladd, above, in confronting the enigma between physical body and spiritual body (1 Cor 15:44), and it is also important to note his conclusion:

> We conclude, then, that the witness of the Gospels and the witness of Paul are in *substantial* agreement. Neither of them represent the resurrection of a dead corpse to physical, earthly life. Both Paul and the Gospels, though admittedly in different ways, describe the resurrection in terms of continuity of person and personality but discontinuity in the relationship of the resurrection body to the physical body. Such is the witness of the New Testament. What is the historian to make of this witness?[21]

Harris, discussing *complete material* continuity, suggests that Ladd here asserts "that there will be a personal, but not a material, continuity between" the physical body and the resurrection body for a believer.[22] Ladd does not say *complete material* discontinuity when discussing the relationship between the resurrection body and the physical body. Nevertheless, I do agree with Ladd that there is *some* discontinuity between the two bodies of a believer and I think N. T. Wright is correct when he refers to Paul's theology as

> a theology in which the present physical body is not to be abandoned, nor yet to be affirmed as it stands, but is to be transformed, changed from present humiliation to new glory (Philippians 3:21), from present corruption and mortality to new incorruption and immortality. This is indeed the defeat of death, not a compromise in which death is allowed to have the body while some other aspect of the human being (the soul? the spirit?) goes marching on.[23]

Next, I will briefly consider the passage of 2 Corinthians 4:7–5:10 to see if there is any noticeable change in Paul's theology regarding resurrection

---

20. Grudem (*Systematic Theology*, 833–834) notes that the details of how it will occur is not clear as the Bible does not specifically mention it. He responds, however, to the objection that "some bodies completely decay, are absorbed into plants, and then eventually into other bodies, so that nothing of the first body can be found" by simply noting "God can keep track of enough elements from each body to form a 'seed' from which to form a new body (see Gen 50:25; Job 19:26; Ezek 37:1–14; Heb 11:22)."
21. Ladd, *I Believe in the Resurrection of Jesus*, 129.
22. Harris, "Resurrection and Immortality," 155.
23. Wright, *Resurrection of the Son of God*, 358.

for believers. Many scholars suggest that 2 Corinthians is a composition of different "Pauline letters (or, portions of letters), which have been brought together to form our present canonical letter" mainly because of certain internal changes of style between chapters 1–7 (or 1–9) with chapters 10–13.[24] However, as far as Paul's theme of resurrection is concerned in 2 Corinthians 4:7–5:10, that would not be of any significance because this passage is contained within chapters 1–7, the so called "Conciliatory Letter" within 2 Corinthians. I also notice that some have proposed for many years that there is a significant change from 1 Corinthians to 2 Corinthians in "a move away from a Jewish-style eschatology, involving the resurrection of the body, towards a more hellenistic model."[25] But Wright responds,

> The main thrust of [2 Cor 4:7–5:10] is to insist on seeing the present in the light of the future. The present is full of suffering, especially for the apostle; but he sees it as organically connected to the future in which there is resurrection (4:14), glory (4:17), a new body (5:1), and judgment (5:10). This path of suffering is thus the embodiment of the covenant-renewing death of the Messiah, and itself carries, remarkably, something of the same significance; and it is also the beginning of, and the signpost to, the renewal of creation which follows from covenant renewal (5:17). This line of thought is necessarily different to that in 1 Corinthians, but I shall argue that Paul is drawing on exactly the same underlying ideas. He has changed his perspective, in that he now speaks openly of his own death as likely to occur before the final resurrection (5:1–10); he draws on different aspects of his controlling narrative about present and future, since he is making different points; but he has not changed the narrative, or the theology, itself.[26]

I agree with Wright that there may have been some development in Paul's thought regarding the resurrection of believers within the progressive nature of God's revelation from 1 Thessalonians to 1 Corinthians and then to 2 Corinthians. But Paul's underlying theology of the resurrection of the body for the believers of Christ remains the same. There are other passages such as, Romans 8:19–25 and Philippians 1:21–26; 3:10–11 and 20–21; 4:5, where

---

24. Longenecker, *Life in the Face of Death*, 191–192.
25. Wright, *Resurrection of the Son of God*, 361.
26. Ibid., 361–362.

Paul deals with the resurrection of the believers at Christ's return. We will not look at these, however, due to the limitations of this chapter, but I will note a conclusion from Longenecker, who has looked at these passages,

> Nonetheless, whatever shifts of thought, mood, or personal expectation might be postulated, it needs to be emphasized and enunciated clearly that the focus of Paul's teaching regarding the resurrection of believers was always on Christ's Parousia and the resurrection of believers that would then take place. *And it is this resurrection message that remains constant in his teaching.*[27]

We note here that, though the believers' final destiny is secure, their works will be tested by fire (1 Cor 3:10–15). Next, I will consider the "State-after-Death" of unbelievers.

The State-after-Death of Unbelievers

We have already noted that, like John, Paul does not explicitly deal with *Gehenna* and *Hades*[28] but he does use other terms that are closely related to the final destiny of unbelievers. The classic reference is Romans 6:23, where *death* (*thanatos*) is considered "the wages of sin," the final punishment or consequence of sin, and is the total opposite of "the gift of God," which is *eternal life* through our Lord Jesus Christ. In Romans 5:12, Paul has already alluded to the Genesis 3 account of the fall and shows how *death* entered all of humanity through one man's disobedience as a consequence or punishment of sin. James R. Edwards makes this helpful comment on Romans 5:12,

> Paul's starting point is thus the empirical reality of death. The grim stalker of life is, to be sure, the result of an equally horrid disobedience to God by the rebellious human will, but Paul does not explore this connection or the way in which human sin and death result from Adam's disobedience . . . He is content to say typologically what he said in 3:23, "All have sinned and fall short of the glory of God." The curse of Adam's sin is death, and death,

---

27. Longenecker, *Life in the Face of Death*, 201 (emphasis added).
28. In some manuscripts a direct quote from Hos 13:14 in 1 Cor 15:55 has *Hades*. If an author belonging to the Pauline circle wrote the letter to the Hebrews, Heb 10:27 refers to judgment and raging fire.

as Paul taught elsewhere, is "the last enemy to be destroyed" (1 Cor 15:26).[29]

Paul sees death as not merely physical or bodily death but also as a complete death of the relationship between God and his human creation. Through one man, Adam, death *reigned* (Rom 5:17) and so no one can escape that destiny. But God himself has made a provision of grace through another man, Jesus, who has *conquered* death and can reestablish that relationship. Edwards commenting on Romans 5:17 says:

> From a human perspective one or the other will rule: disobedience or obedience, sin or righteousness, death or life. It is not a question of *whether* we will submit to such masters, only to *which* ones we will submit. Either death reigns or life reigns, but not both. To be human is to stand at a crossroads of choice: there is the way of the past, the way of death, or the way of the future, the way of life in Christ. There is the first Adam, and there is the last Adam. But that is only the human perspective. Paul writes from the divine perspective, assuring us that the influence and effect of Christ's work defeat the tragic effects of Adam's trespass. The sin of one is cancelled by the righteousness of the other; the curse of one is overcome by the grace of the other. The one causes death, the other swallows up death in life. In every way Christ surpasses Adam.[30]

Thus, like John, instead of dwelling on *death* and the unbelievers' "State-after-Death," Paul is emphasizing God's offer of righteousness and *life* through Jesus Christ for all who *believe,* just as "Abraham believed God, and it was credited to him as righteousness" (Rom 4:3, 11).

Paul speaks openly about God's *wrath* and righteous *judgment*. We see this in many places. In Romans 1:18 Paul says, "God's wrath [is] against all ungodliness and unrighteousness of humans;" in Romans 2:5, he refers to "the *day* of God's wrath" and the revelation of his righteous judgment and in Romans 2:16, "God will judge on that *day* through Jesus Christ." Similarly, the disobedient and the unrepentant are the objects of God's wrath (Rom 2:5, 9:22; Eph 2:3, 5:6). God's wrath comes upon unbelievers and there is trouble and distress for the disobedient, evil doers and unbelievers (Rom 2:8, 9; cf. Rom

---

29. James R. Edwards, *Romans,* New International Biblical Commentary, No. 6 (Peabody, MA: Hendrickson Publishers, 1992), 148–149.

30. Ibid., 151.

3:5; 4:15, 16, 5:9; 12:19; Col 3:6; 1 Thess 2:16). The unbelievers will perish or are perishing (Rom 2:12; 1 Cor 1:18; 2 Cor 2:15; 4:3; 2 Thess 2:10–12).

In 2 Thessalonians 1:6–10, Paul speaks explicitly about the coming judgment and wrath of God that awaits unbelievers and that their final destiny is the exact opposite of what will happen to the believers in Jesus Christ when he returns (vv. 8–9).

> 6. God is just: He will pay back trouble to those who trouble you 7. and give relief to you who are troubled, and to us as well. This will happen when the Lord Jesus is revealed from heaven in blazing fire with his powerful angels. 8. *He will punish those who do not know God and do not obey the gospel of our Lord Jesus. 9. They will be punished with everlasting destruction and shut out from the presence of the Lord and from the majesty of his power* 10. on the day he comes to be glorified in his holy people and to be marveled at among all those who have believed. This includes you, because you believed our testimony to you. (NIV, emphasis added)

Thus, for Paul, if the believers will be resurrected from the dead, be transformed and have *eternal life* when Christ returns, then the unbelievers will face *everlasting destruction* (and separation) from the presence of the Lord and from the glory of his power.

The Book of Revelation

Finally, I will look into the "State-after-Death" of both the believers and the unbelievers in the last book of the New Testament canon, the Book of Revelation. Though much of this book is mysterious or enigmatic in character because of its innumerable unusual symbols, yet the apocalyptic style presents objective truths about the final judgment of God and the eventual destiny of both the believers and the unbelievers. The Book of Revelation claims to be the authoritative word of God (1:2) and closes with this warning (22:18–20 NIV),

> 18. I warn everyone who hears the words of the prophecy of this book: If anyone adds anything to them, God will add to him the plagues described in this book. 19. And if anyone takes words away from this book of prophecy, God will take away from him his share in the tree of life and in the holy city, which are

described in this book. 20. He who testifies to these things says, "Yes, I am coming soon." Amen. Come, Lord Jesus.

Revelation has a profound message about future punishment for some, blessings for others and proclaims that the Lord Jesus is coming back soon for the believers.

Traditionally, early church fathers and scholars accepted that the author of the Book was the beloved disciple of Jesus, the apostle John, also considered the author of the gospel and the three letters of John.[31] However, Robert W. Wall notes,

> more recent arguments against attributing Revelation's authorship to the Apostle John constitute a considerable challenge to the ancient consensus. Most scholars now agree that the John of Revelation is neither the author of the Fourth Gospel nor the Apostle John. We agree with this conclusion (although the evidence on both sides of the issue remains inconclusive). The internal reasons seem clear and persuasive . . .[32]

Who, then, is this John of Revelation? Although I still remain unconvinced that it is not the Apostle John, I am comfortable with Wall's assertion,

> The most one can suggest . . . is that John belongs to a school of Christian prophets which sought to preserve and transmit to others the Apostle John's unique witness to the risen Lord Jesus. Even if one concludes that the evidence does not support this particular conclusion, the ongoing authority of Revelation is not ultimately determined by the ideology which equates an apostolic writer with an apostolic writing. The church's recognition that John's Revelation belongs to the Christian biblical canon and continues to serve the "one holy catholic and *apostolic* church" stems from its confidence that this composition constitutes a normative witness to the "word of God and the testimony of Jesus Christ." (cf. Rev 1:2)[33]

---

31. Richard C. Lenski, *The Interpretation of St. John's Revelation* (Minneapolis, MN: Augsburg Publishing House, 1943), 5–12; Robert W. Wall, *Revelation*, New International Biblical Commentary, No. 18 (Peabody, MA: Hendrickson Publishers, 1991), 7.
32. Wall, *Revelation*, 7–8.
33. Ibid., 9–10.

In Revelation 1:9–10, John was exiled to the island of Patmos[34] because of his proclamation of "the word of God and the testimony of Jesus" and there on the Lord's Day[35] he received the vision and revelation from God. As to when and why it was written, the general consensus of scholars is late in the first century, and as a response to the spiritual crisis that occurred due to the persecution that believers were facing along the coastline of southwest Asia.[36] Furthermore, Wall suspects that the writer John also had "an evangelistic purpose" in that "his desire is that even the non-believer respond to his message of God's triumph over the anti-Christian kingdom and be converted."[37] For the limited purpose of this chapter and accepting the apocalyptic nature of the text, I will follow through the Book of Revelation, looking into important references that deal with "State-after-Death" or the ultimate destiny of both believers and unbelievers in the Lord Jesus Christ.

One of the overall biblical teachings, that God is going to judge the kingdoms of this world one day, is overwhelmingly highlighted in this last book of the Bible because it is God's judgment that brings about two different destinies, one for the righteous and the other for the unrighteous. As Allison A. Trites notes, "It is the person of God in the Apocalypse who must be reckoned with as the divine judge (note the use of the noun *krima*, 'judgment,' in 17:1 and 18:20, and the verb *krinein*, 'to judge,' in 16:5; 18:8, 20; and 19:2)."[38] However, God's initial judgment of *death* on Adam and through him to all humanity (Gen 3) has been conquered by Jesus. At the very outset of his revelation to John, Jesus confirms in 1:18, "I am the Living One; I was dead, and behold I am alive forever and ever! And I hold the keys of death and Hades" (NIV). Like the Gospels and Paul's letters, the message is clear from the beginning in the Book of Revelation that believers need no longer fear God's judgment and the punishment of *death* and *Hades*. Because of his resurrection, Jesus holds the keys of *death* and *Hades*.

---

34. Allison A. Trites notes that Patmos was "an island in the south Aegean Sea just off the coast of Asia Minor and west of Miletus and Ephesus" (Trites, "Witness and the Resurrection in the Apocalypse of John," in *Life in the Face of Death: The Resurrection Message of the New Testament*, ed. Richard N. Longenecker [Grand Rapids, MI: Eerdmans, 1998], 271).

35. Wall (*Revelation*, 65) notes Boring (*Revelation* [Louisville: John Knox Press, 1989], 82) suggesting it was an idiom for "Easter" at that time.

36. Bailey, *Biblical Perspective on Death*, 95; Wall, *Revelation*, 5, 10. Some historians date it in the late 60s CE during the Neronic time but for Wall (*Revelation*, 5) it reflects "the *Sitz im Leben* ("life setting") of the Asian church during the Domition period (AD 81–96)." (Assuming it was Apostle John, he would have been quite elderly at that time.)

37. Wall, *Revelation*, 14.

38. Trites, "Witness and the Resurrection," 272.

Next, in the seven letters to the seven churches in Asia Minor, the same message is given to the believers about their final destiny, as Christ's exhortations calls them to *overcome*:

1) 2:7 "To him who *overcomes*, I will give the right to eat from the tree of life, which is in the paradise of God."

2) 2:10 "Do not be afraid of what you are about to suffer. I tell you, the devil will put some of you in prison to test you, and you will suffer persecution for ten days. Be faithful, even to the point of death, and I will give you the crown of life. 2:11 . . . He who *overcomes* will not be hurt at all by the second death."

3) 2:17 "To him who *overcomes*, I will give some of the hidden manna. I will also give him a white stone with a new name written on it, known only to him who receives it."

4) 2:26 "To him who *overcomes* and does my will to the end, I will give authority over the nations – 2:27 . . . – just as I have received authority from my Father." 2:28 "I will also give him the morning star."

5) 3:5 "He who *overcomes* will, like them, be dressed in white. I will never blot out his name from the book of life, but will acknowledge his name before my Father and his angels."

6) 3:12 "Him who *overcomes* I will make a pillar in the temple of my God. Never again will he leave it. I will write on him the name of my God and the name of the city of my God, the new Jerusalem, which is coming down out of heaven from my God; and I will also write on him my new name."

7) 3:21 "To him who *overcomes*, I will give the right to sit with me on my throne, just as I overcame and sat down with my Father on his throne" (NIV, emphasis added).

The overcoming believers in their final destiny will: (a) eat from the tree of life, (b) receive the crown of life and will not be hurt at all by the second death, (c) eat the hidden manna and receive a white stone with a new name written on it, (d) have authority over the nations just as Jesus received authority from the Father and Jesus will give them the morning star, (e) Jesus will acknowledge their name before the Father and his angels and will never blot out their names from the book of life, (f) they will be a pillar in the temple of God and will never leave it, and (g) Jesus will give them the right to sit with him on his throne, just as Jesus overcame and sat down with his Father on his throne.

Thus, for believers Jesus is the model and whatever happened to Jesus after he overcame death in his resurrection as the firstborn from the dead (1:5) will happen to them in their final destiny. However, the unbelievers who do not trust in Christ will have the opposite as their final destiny and by implication will be hurt by the "second death" (2:11) and will not have their names written in the book of life (3:5). ACUTE summarizes that, "Those who refuse to worship God and the Lamb will meet the 'second death' in a fiery lake of burning sulphur. There worshippers of the beast will be tormented, with smoke rising forever, and the devil, beast and false prophet will be tormented forever" (cf. Rev 14:9–11; 20:7–15).[39] By contrast, in Revelation 5:9–10, the Lamb (Jesus) is worshipped by the heavenly chorus as the universal redeemer of those who believed in him with a song: "you were slain, and with your blood you purchased men for God from every tribe and language and people and nation. You have made them to be a kingdom and priests to serve our God, and they will reign on the earth" (NIV).

Referring to Revelation 6:9–11, which speaks of the believers who have died and are still awaiting resurrection in their temporary intermediate state, N. T. Wright comments,

> They are waiting and resting 'under the altar', longing for God's eventual victory over evil. They are told to rest a little longer, until the full number of their fellow-Christians have been killed as they were killed. This strange little scene only makes sense if we grant the Jewish, more specifically the Pharisaic, viewpoint that those who have died in the righteous cause *will be* raised in the future, on the day when the creator judges the world at last, but that they *have not been* raised just yet. This is also the right way to read the description of the martyrs in 7.14–17, unless indeed this is an anticipation of the vision in chapters 21 and 22. This, too, is the appropriate explanation for the interjected note in 14.13, where the voice from heaven tells the seer to write this: 'Blessed are the dead who die in the Lord.' The Spirit, he says, affirms this, 'because they rest from their labours, and their

---

39. ACUTE, *Nature of Hell*, 50.

deeds follow them.' This should not be taken as a statement of their final destiny (some kind of endless 'rest'), but only of their temporary abode. The same is true for those who are summoned to come up to heaven, and who are taken there on a cloud in full view of their enemies (11:12). We are right to assume that, in the larger drama of the book as a whole, the events of the last three chapters will see all these people enter upon a new life.[40]

Forty years ago, Oscar Cullmann argued strongly against those who claim that the resurrection of the body happens immediately after a person's death and noted,

> All these images express simply a special proximity to Christ, in which those dying in Christ before the end find themselves. They are "with Christ" or "in paradise" or "in Abraham's bosom" or, according to Rev 6:9, "under the altar." All these are simply various images of special nearness to God. But the most usual image for Paul is: "They are asleep." It would be difficult to dispute that the New Testament reckons with such an interim time for the dead, as well as for the living, although any sort of speculation upon the state of the dead in this interim period is lacking here.[41]

Thus, for believers, the intermediate state is a temporary conscious disembodied state in the nearer presence of the Lord awaiting full resurrection of their bodies. But the time *will* come for God to judge the dead, to reward the faithful believers of the Lord and "for destroying those who destroy the earth" (Rev 11:18; cf. Rev 19 for more details).

Finally, we will look at the last three chapters of Revelation and, as we begin to consider chapter 20, we are immediately drawn into the millennial debate. For the limited purpose of this chapter we will stay clear of that debate. It is enough to mention that three major views are held by responsible biblical scholars.[42] One indisputable truth in chapter 20 is that God is in control. In the end, Satan is bound and eventually punished but faithful believers are rewarded and blessed. More important for our study, some of the righteous

---

40. Wright, *Resurrection of the Son of God*, 471.
41. Oscar Cullmann, "Immortality of the Soul or Resurrection of the Dead?," in *Immortality and Resurrection*, ed. Krister Stendahl (New York, NY: Macmillan, 1965), 39.
42. Most hold either the *pre-millennial* or *a-millennial* view; a very few hold to a *post-millennial* view.

believers will be resurrected in an "initial resurrection" (mentioned twice in Rev 20:5–6). Following this, the rest of the righteous, those whose names are in the book of life, will be raised (along with the unrighteous) in the general resurrection (Rev 20:12–15). Here N. T. Wright helpfully looks for the author's intended meaning:

> It is conceivable that he thought of this 'first resurrection' in physical terms, locating the righteous in an embodied heavenly world (perhaps in the new Jerusalem which would eventually appear on earth, as in chapter 21), though few modern interpreters have gone this route. Classic 'pre-millennial' interpretation understands the passage in terms of a future period of a literal thousand years in which some or all of the righteous will rise and rule the world with Christ. In an effort to counteract this, it is often proposed that 'the first resurrection' is simply a way of describing the passage through death, into a blessed intermediate state, of all the righteous; but if that was what the writer meant it seems that he has not made it clear (not that that would be unusual in Revelation). Perhaps the most damaging objection to this view arises from the meaning of 'resurrection' throughout the literature we have studied, pagan, Jewish and Christian: however much death itself is to be re-evaluated in the light of Jesus' own death and resurrection, to use the word 'resurrection' to *refer* to death in an attempt to invest it with a new meaning seems to me to strain usage well beyond breaking point. In addition, verse 4 seems to envisage two stages: first, the martyrs are killed; then, at a later stage, they come to life. Collapsing these two into one (though, again, all things are possible with the kind of imagery we find in Revelation) seems implausible.[43]

This being the case, the initial resurrection seems to best fit with the literal thousand-year reign with Christ for some of the righteous who have been martyred for their Christian faith. At the same time, others have pointed out that there is no other evidence in the Scripture for this idea of initial resurrection for martyrs.[44] No one can be sure of the exact meaning here and perhaps Wright makes the best case in his following comments:

---

43. Wright, *Resurrection of the Son of God*, 474.
44. Cf. Trites, "Witness and the Resurrection," 285.

We can, however, suggest that there is some analogy in the concept of an *anticipated* resurrection, as in Romans 6, Colossians 3 and elsewhere. There, as we saw, the baptized believer, whose current life is based on the past event of Jesus' death and resurrection, and whose body will be raised in the future, is in a sense already "raised with the Messiah."

This metaphorical use of "resurrection" language to denote the believer's present status seems to me a partial parallel at least to the use in Revelation 20:4 of "the first resurrection" to denote a new life that these particular "souls" are given, based on Jesus' resurrection and anticipating the full bodily resurrection still to come. Thus, though the usage is very strange, it can be understood as a bold extension of categories already being tried out within early Christianity, rather than an abandonment of normal Jewish and Christian language.[45]

However, for the unrighteous (or the unbeliever), it seems clear that there is no possibility of initial resurrection but that the opposite of Revelation 20:6 is true for them. They will have no escape from the "second death" and will be raised in the general resurrection to be judged in 20:12–15. Because their names will not be found written in the book of life (verse 15), they will be thrown into the lake of fire along with *death* and *Hades* (verse 14) and this lake of fire is the "second death." If this is the same as the lake of burning sulphur in verse10 where the devil, the beast and the false prophet are thrown, they will suffer there forever, *eternally*. It is also mentioned that the unrighteous will be consigned to the fiery lake of burning sulphur (21:8) and the unrighteous are kept *outside* the New Jerusalem (Rev 21:27; 22:15).

In Revelation 21 and 22, we see the majestic imagery of what the *post-resurrection life* will be for the believers. For example, God creates a new heaven and a new earth for them to dwell there *eternally* in the New Jerusalem, the Holy City, which will be coming down from heaven with the glory of God (21:1, 2, 10, 11). There will be no temple in the city "because the Lord God Almighty and the Lamb are its temple" (21:22) and "God is with men, and he will live with them. They will be his people, and God himself will be with them and be their God. He will wipe every tear from their eyes. There will be no more death or mourning or crying or pain, for the old order of things has passed away" (21:3–4 NIV). There will be the river of water of

---

45. Wright, *Resurrection of the Son of God*, 475.

life and the tree of life yielding its fruit every month (22:1–2) and all who have washed their robes (*implied* by the blood of the Lamb), the righteous or the believers, will have the right to the tree of life (*implied* eternal life) and will be permitted to enter through the gates into the city (22:14). The Book of Revelation is Apocalyptic literature with symbolic pictures of the final destiny and generally scholars are not certain as to the message. Even the more conservative scholars are not unanimous about how to interpret the symbolic expressions found in chapters 21 and 22. However, following the overall thrust of the author's intention, it can be safely concluded that, in the grand finale of the book, the author, using great imagery, is urging the believers to be faithful and wait with eager expectation for the coming of the Lord Jesus Christ and his promised blessed hereafter.

Summary and Implications

In the letters of Paul, it is the centrality of the theme of resurrection that permeates all of the letters but most importantly in 1 Thessalonians 4:13–5:11, 1 Corinthians 15 and 2 Corinthians 4:7–5:10. A Pharisee prior to his conversion, Paul would have believed in bodily resurrection from the dead and, therefore understood Christ's resurrection from that perspective and applied that belief to the future resurrection of the believers. Paul was convinced of Christ's bodily resurrection and expected the same for believers. According to Paul, when believers die they are consciously present in the spirit with Christ in a temporary intermediate state until their bodies are raised up by Christ at his return and are transformed. Thus, for Paul, there is a continuity as well as discontinuity between the resurrected body and the physical body of a believer. The believers' transformation will include the revivification of the material body at the resurrection. There may have been some development in Paul's thought in his letters regarding the resurrection of believers within the progressive nature of God's revelation but his underlying theology of the resurrection of the body for those who believe in Christ remains constant.

Like John, Paul does not deal with *Hades* and *Gehenna* but does refer to other terms closely related to unbelievers' final destiny such as the term, *death*. For Paul, death is not merely physical or bodily death but also death of any relationship between God and humans, as death *reigned* through one man Adam (Romans 5:17) and no one can escape that destiny. But God himself has made a provision of grace through one man Jesus, who has *conquered* death and can reestablish that relationship. Paul also speaks of God's *wrath* and righteous *judgment*. In 2 Thessalonians 1:6–10, Paul foretells the coming judgment and wrath of God on the unbelievers. Paul also states that the unbelievers' final destiny will be the exact opposite of that of believers when Jesus returns. Thus, for Paul, if the believers will be raised from the dead, be transformed and have *eternal life* when Christ returns, then the unbelievers will face *everlasting destruction* (and separation) from the presence of the Lord and from the glory of his power.

In the Book of Revelation, we see God is going to judge the kingdoms of this world and establish his rule and as a result there are two different destinies one for the righteous and the other for the unrighteous. As with the Gospels and Paul's letters, the message is clear. Believers no longer need fear God's judgment or the punishment of *death* and *Hades,* because of the risen Jesus, who, having conquered death, has the keys of *death* and *Hades.* In the seven letters to the seven churches in Asia Minor, the same message is given to the believers about their final destiny by the risen Jesus, as he exhorts them to be "overcomers." Symbolic language in the Book of Revelation describes the reward for overcoming believers in their final destiny. They will eat from the tree of life, receive the crown of life and will not be hurt at all by the second death. They will have authority over the nations just as Jesus received authority from the Father and Jesus will give them the morning star. Jesus will never blot their names out of the book of life, but will acknowledge their name before the Father and his angels. They will be pillars in the temple of God and will never leave it, and Jesus will give them the right to sit with him on his throne, just as Jesus overcame and sat down with his Father on his throne. In spite of the symbolism, we can safely conclude that these are powerful descriptions of the believers' blessed hereafter at Christ's return.

As far as the unbelievers' final destiny is concerned, as they refuse to worship God and the Lamb, they will meet the "second death" in a fiery lake of burning sulphur where worshippers of the beast will be tormented, with smoke rising forever, and the devil, beast and false prophet will also be tormented forever (Rev 14:9–11; 20:7–15). However, the Lamb (Jesus) who was slain will redeem many people from every tribe, language, ethnic group and nation with his shed blood (5:9–10). Revelation 6:9–11 seems to suggest that believers who have died are resting "under the altar" in the presence of God in a temporary intermediate state and are awaiting full bodily resurrection.

In the final three chapters of Revelation, God is in control, Satan is bound and eventually punished (along with the unbelievers) and the believers are rewarded and blessed. In chapter 20 there is a possibility of an initial resurrection for some believers, perhaps those who were martyrs because of their faith, whereas the rest of the believers will be resurrected in the general resurrection along with the unrighteous even though, ultimately, all believers will be rewarded and blessed. But the unrighteous unbelievers after their resurrection will face God's judgment and will have no escape from the fiery furnace of "second death" where they will suffer *eternally*. In chapters 21 and 22, believers' *post-resurrection life* in the presence of God in the heavenly city is described symbolically. In conclusion, the believers are urged to be faithful and wait with expectancy for the return of the Lord Jesus Christ.

We have seen in the New Testament that "State-after-Death" is a critical component of God's universal mission to rescue humanity from a destiny that is without hope to a living alternative through Jesus Christ. We found that, in spite of the pluralistic religious contexts of the Greco-Roman world of the New Testament, this hopeful message of "State-after-Death" which God revealed to his people was quite *dissimilar* to the surrounding views, mainly because of the death and the resurrection of the Lord Jesus Christ. We shall now carry the study forward in history to review how the Apostolic Fathers and the Apologists communicated on death and after-death to the early church.

9

State-after-Death for the Apostolic Fathers

Having looked at the Old and New Testaments, the main source of Christian theology for the "State-after-Death," we will now consider the thinking on this issue within the early church by reviewing a selection of authoritative texts written by church theologians of the Ante-Nicene period that speak of the final destiny of both the believer and the unbeliever. N. T. Wright notes,

> The remarkable rise of the early church, and its progress through the second century of its existence, is a huge and sprawling story, too vast to even summarize here. Others have laboured and I have entered into their labour. As we should expect, granted its origins and environment, the church developed ways of talking about all kinds of subjects, including *life after death*, which sometimes reflected the sharp precision of most of the New Testament and sometimes did not.[1]

Whereas Wright, in his study of early church, was concerned primarily about the theme of the future hope and resurrection from the dead for the believer, I will also search for belief about unbelievers' destiny after death. Thus, following in Wright's footsteps, I too will enter the hard labor of these scholars on early church history for this chapter and the next. My task is to find out the early church's view of "State-after-Death" as the church began its life in the midst of a pluralistic Greco-Roman religious world. In this chapter, with the help of selected texts of the *Apostolic Fathers,* I will look at the theme

---

1. Wright, *Resurrection of the Son of God*, 480 (emphasis added).

of resurrection from the dead and subsequent eternal life for believers as well as the punishment of unbelievers.

The Apostolic Fathers

In working from a vast array of early texts of the *Apostolic Fathers*, I will follow N. T. Wright's study[2] as a road map for the theme of resurrection and the final destiny of unbelievers. I will quote mainly from *The Ante-Nicene Fathers: Translations of the Writings of the Fathers down to A. D. 325*, edited by Alexander Roberts and James Donaldson (Grand Rapids, MI: Eerdmans, 1979), Reprint, 10 vols. (Original: Edinburgh, UK: T. & T. Clark, 1867). I will look first at the "First Letter of Clement to the Corinthians," in short *1 Clement*.

Resurrection from the Dead

1 Clement is an early church letter and was composed around 95 or 96[3] CE by Clement of the Church of Rome. Probably, Clement was the presiding presbyter or bishop (the two titles were interchangeable) in a group of presbyters or bishops in that church.[4] This is very close to the dating of the New Testament canonical texts, perhaps, even earlier than some of them. Wright notes that, "Clement articulates a doctrine of resurrection not far removed from the New Testament."[5] *1 Clement* 5 says this about the after-death state for Peter and Paul:

> But not to dwell upon ancient examples, let us come to the most recent spiritual heroes . . . Let us set before our eyes the . . . apostles. Peter . . . suffered martyrdom, departed to *the place of glory* due to him . . . Paul also obtained the reward of patient

---

2. Ibid., 480–552.
3. Holmes (*The Apostolic Fathers*, ed. J. B. Lightfoot and trans. J. R. Harmer [Grand Rapids, MI: Baker, 1989], 25) refers to this as the widespread agreed date and gives some reasons for its validity. He also refers to the dissenting opinions about the date in his footnote 4 (Ibid).
4. Chadwick (*The Early Church*, vol. 1 of The Pelican History of the Church [Middlesex, UK: Penguin, 1967], 41, 46, 49–50); Frend (*The Rise of Christianity* [Philadelphia, PA: Fortress, 1984], 130) and Holmes (*Apostolic Fathers*, 24) contend that the office of a single monarchical bishop did not start at that time in Rome but a team of leadership was the norm. Also, the interchangeable use of the title presbyter or bishop is found even in *1 Clement* 44:1–6.
5. Wright, *Resurrection of the Son of God*, 481.

endurance, . . . suffered martyrdom . . . Thus was he removed from the world, and went into *the holy place*, having proved . . . a striking example of patience.[6]

According to *1 Clement*, Peter went after his death to *the place of glory* and Paul went to *the holy place*. We see further, in *1 Clement* 6:1–2, that a great multitude of the elect, both men and women, who joined the apostles in their example and suffered and died, as martyrs, and "received a noble reward." *1 Clement* 35 states that "Life in immortality" is a gift of God for those who wait for Him. *1 Clement* 44:5 says, "Blessed are those presbyters who, having finished their course before now, have obtained a fruitful and perfect departure [from this world]; for they have no fear lest anyone deprive them of the place now appointed them."[7] Finally, in *1 Clement* 50:3–4 it says,

> All the generations from Adam even unto this day have passed away; but those who, through the grace of God, have been made perfect in love, now possess a place among the godly, and shall be made manifest at the revelation of the kingdom of Christ. For it is written, "Enter into thy secret chambers for a little time, until my wrath and fury pass away; and I will remember a propitious day, and will raise you up out of your graves."[8]

Charles E. Hill argues concerning the above words, *contra* J. A. Fischer and Otto Knoch, that the temporary intermediate resting place for Peter, Paul, other martyrs and every other redeemed saint is not in *Hades* but in heaven.[9] Hill notes, "If this text leaves us in doubt as to the location . . . it at least gives us one important principle. For Clement all the elect dead have gone to the same place."[10] Hill argues that Peter's "State-after-Death," the "place of glory," could not be a locality in *Hades* "if we may accept Polycarp's expansion (Phil 9:2)."[11] Also, referring to Paul's departure to "the holy place," Hill notes,

> The assertion that Clement held to an interim existence in Hades for the just irretrievably flounders at the words "he was taken

---

6. Clement, "The First Epistle of Clement," in *The Ante-Nicene Fathers: Translations of the Writings of the Fathers down to A.D. 325,* vol. 1, eds. and trans. A. Roberts and J. Donaldson (Grand Rapids, MI: Eerdmans, 1979), 6 (emphasis added).
7. Ibid., 17.
8. Ibid., 18.
9. Charles E. Hill, *Regnum Caelorum: Patterns of Millennial Thought in Early Christianity,* (Grand Rapids, MI: Eerdmans, 2001), 78–83.
10. Ibid., 80.
11. Ibid., 82.

up to the holy place" (5.7). "The holy place" to which Paul has been taken up, especially as is indicated by the use of the article, can hardly refer to Hades and would seem to be appropriate for nothing but the heavenly sanctuary.[12]

These references in *1 Clement* not only show that the temporary intermediate place for the righteous is in heaven but also, as we have seen explicitly quoted above in *1 Clement* 50:3–4, they will be bodily raised from the dead at the return of Christ. N. T. Wright points out that Clement "not only believes in final resurrection; he mounts various arguments to show that it is not as unreasonable a thing to believe as one might suppose."[13] As in the New Testament, *1 Clement* teaches that the future resurrection of the disciples is based on the resurrection of the Lord Jesus,[14] and that this was what convinced the apostles to proclaim that the kingdom of God was at hand, according to *1 Clement* 42:1–3,

> The apostles have preached the Gospel to us from the Lord Jesus Christ; Jesus Christ [has done so] from God. Christ therefore was sent forth by God, and the apostles by Christ. Both these appointments, then, were made in an orderly way, according to the will of God. Having therefore received their orders, and *being fully assured by the resurrection of our Lord Jesus Christ*, and established in the word of God, with full assurance of the Holy Ghost, they went forth proclaiming that the kingdom of God was at hand.[15]

---

12. Ibid.

13. Wright, *Resurrection of the Son of God*, 482. Wright (Ibid., 482–483) refers to Clement's imagery of the seeds and the phoenix bird and three biblical passages that present the truth of future resurrection of the believers. Caroline W. Bynum (*The Resurrection of the Body in Western Christianity, 200–1336* [New York, NY: Columbia University Press, 1995], 24; also Perkins, *Resurrection*, 337) look at the same imagery that Clement used and acknowledge that his text and others from early church "depend in their resurrection imagery on Pauline metaphors of seeds and first fruits" but contends that "they do not mean at all what Paul means." I don't see why Bynum would come to that conclusion as Clement was most probably a disciple of the apostles (Sparks, *The Apostolic Fathers* [Nashville, TN: Thomas Nelson, 1978], 16). I think Wright (*Resurrection of the Son of God*, 483 fn 15) is correct in suspecting that Bynum (*Resurrection of the Body*, 3–6) has a faulty understanding of Paul.

14. For Dewart (*Death and Resurrection*, Message of the Fathers of the Church Series, No. 22 [Wilmington, DE: Michael Glazier, 1986], 40), "although referring to Christ as 'first fruits' the letter does not link the resurrection of the Christian directly with that of Christ, but instead makes use of analogies from nature in arguing for the resurrection of the just". Isn't 'first fruits' an analogy from nature? What comes after 'first fruits'? Jesus' resurrection is linked as 'first fruits' of a future resurrection (of the just) in *1 Clement* 24:1.

15. Clement, "First Epistle of Clement," 16 (emphasis added).

We strongly agree with N. T. Wright that "Clement thus stands as an early witness to a continuing creative development of the tradition, without in any obvious way deviating from the lines laid down in most of the New Testament."[16]

It is generally accepted that *2 Clement* was probably written in the first half of second century CE.[17] It is not a letter nor was it written by Clement of Rome. It is the oldest surviving Christian sermon for exhortation (probably by an anonymous presbyter) and may have been either preached at Corinth or sent there for some purpose.[18] *2 Clement* begins by referring to Jesus Christ as the "Judge of the living and the dead" (1:1), that "he saved us when we were perishing" (1:4), and also that he promised us "rest in the coming kingdom and eternal life" (5:5).[19] For the purpose of this chapter, it does have several references to the resurrection. We will quote here the most important passage for our consideration, *2 Clement* 9:1–6 in which the denial of the judgment and the resurrection of the flesh are rejected:

> 9. And let none of you say that this flesh is not judged and does not rise again. (2) Understand this: In what state were you saved? In what state did you recover your sight, if it was not while you were in this flesh? (3) We must, therefore, guard the flesh as a temple of God. (4) For just as you were called in the flesh, so you will come[20] in the flesh. (5) If Christ, the Lord who saved us, became flesh (even though he was originally spirit) and in that state called us, so also we will receive our reward in this flesh. (6) Therefore let us love one another, that we all may enter into the kingdom of God.[21]

2 Clement's argument is that, if the believers themselves were in the flesh when they were saved, and if Christ himself, who saved them, became flesh to save them, then it is logical to accept that the believers will receive their future reward in the flesh. Here, Wright helpfully comments,

---

16. Wright, *Resurrection of the Son of God*, 483.
17. J. B. Lightfoot, *The Apostolic Fathers*, reprint (Grand Rapids, MI: Baker, 1980), 43.
18. Holmes, *Apostolic Fathers*, 65.
19. Ibid., 68, 70.
20. Wright correctly inserts here "[i.e. rise again]" (*Resurrection of the Son of God*, 484) and earlier refers to this passage as "anticipating Tertullian's stress on the resurrection, not simply of the body, but of the *flesh*" (Ibid., 483).
21. Holmes, *Apostolic Fathers*, 72.

Clearly the author had either not pondered deeply on Paul's subtle distinction between 'flesh' and 'body', or had a polemical axe to grind which made it necessary for him to use 'flesh' and not just 'body'. Equally, there is no question but that he intended to affirm what Paul affirmed in 1 Corinthians 6, namely, that the continuity between the present body and the future one gave substance, via the Temple-image, to ethical endeavor in the present time. Likewise, he stresses that the agency by which the resurrection will happen is the Holy Spirit. Though this writer does not develop the picture further, and, perhaps surprisingly, does not mention the resurrection of Jesus himself, he clearly belongs in the same world of thought here as 1 Clement and the canonical writers.[22]

Thus, while Perkins notes that, "2 Clement is not primarily interested in defending the teaching of resurrection,"[23] we find Hill asserting that, "It is evident, moreover, that the author of *2 Clement* was not slack in upholding a traditional doctrine of the future resurrection of the body (see 9:1; 14:5; 19:3)."[24] Again, agreeing with Wright and Hill, we conclude that the author of *2 Clement* does belong to the same world of thought as the New Testament writers and the writer of *1 Clement*.

Ignatius (ca. 30–107 CE)[25] of Antioch wrote seven letters within a period of a very few weeks under intensely stressful conditions as he was taken to Rome from Syria by a Roman band of soldiers to face a martyr's execution during the reign of Trajan [98–117 CE].[26] Wright notes that, "Among the many concerns expressed . . . in his letters . . . the resurrection, of believers and especially of Jesus, is one of the anchor-points to which he repeatedly

---

22. Wright, *Resurrection of the Son of God*, 484.
23. Perkins, *Resurrection*, 337.
24. Hill, *Regnum Caelorum*, 100.
25. Roberts and Donaldson (*Ante-Nicene Fathers*, vol. 1, 45) note: "[AD 30–107.] The seductive myth which represents [Ignatius] as the little child whom the Lord placed in the midst of his apostles (St. Matt. xviii. 2) indicates at least the period when he may . . . have been born. That he and Polycarp were fellow-disciples under St. John, is a tradition by no means inconsistent with anything in the Epistles of either." Wright (*Resurrection of the Son of God*, 484) dates Ignatius's death c. 107, Frend (*Rise of Christianity*, 124) c. 107/108; but Roberts & Donaldson (*Ante-Nicene Fathers*, vol. 1, 48) c.107 or 116.
26. David E. Aune, *The Cultic Setting of Realized Eschatology in Early Christianity*, Supplements to Novum Testamentum, No. 28 (Leiden, Netherlands: E. J. Brill, 1972), 136; Holmes, *Apostolic Fathers*, 79–82.

returns."[27] In his letters, Ignatius strongly affirmed the humanity, passion and resurrection of Jesus. In this he takes his stand against the docetic teaching that Jesus was not truly human (in the flesh) but only appeared to be so. Ignatius also affirmed the resurrection of the believers in Jesus, as is seen in his letter to the Trallians, chapter 9 (shorter version):

> Jesus Christ, who was descended from David, and was also of Mary; who was truly born, and did eat and drink. He was truly persecuted under Pontius Pilate; He was truly crucified, and [truly] died, in the sight of beings in heaven, and on earth, and under the earth. He was also truly raised from the dead, His Father quickening Him, even as after the same manner His Father will so raise up us who believe in Him by Christ Jesus, apart from whom we do not possess the true life.[28]

Aune comments that, "Ignatius frequently expressed the gospel in terms of traditional creedal formulae which contain . . . the Incarnation, Passion and Resurrection of Jesus . . . The anti-heretical context of many of these creedal statements shows that they were used to stress the historical reality of the gospel events in opposition to docetism."[29] As in *2 Clement* (and Tertullian), Ignatius puts stress on the resurrection of the flesh as is illustrated in his letter to Smyrnaeans, chapter 3 (shorter version):

> For I know that after His resurrection also He was still possessed of flesh, and I believe that He is so now. When . . . He came to those who were with Peter, He said to them, "Lay hold, handle Me, and see that I am not an incorporeal spirit." And immediately they touched Him, and believed, being convinced both by His flesh and spirit. For this cause also they despised death, and were found its conquerors. And after his resurrection He did eat and drink with them, as being possessed of flesh, although spiritually He was united to the Father.[30]

---

27. Wright, *Resurrection of the Son of God*, 484.
28. Ignatius, "The Epistles of Ignatius," in *The Ante-Nicene Fathers: Translations of the Writings of the Fathers down to A.D. 325*, vol. 1, eds. and trans. A. Roberts and J. Donaldson, reprint (Grand Rapids, MI: Eerdmans, 1979), 70.
29. Aune, *Cultic Setting*, 139. Aune helpfully gives a list of references from all of his letters in his footnotes 2–3.
30. Ignatius, "Epistles of Ignatius," 87.

In Smyrnaeans chapter 2, Ignatius teaches that those who do not believe in Jesus' humanity or in his (passion and) resurrection, will themselves become bodiless evil spirits:

> Now, He suffered all these things for our sakes, that we might be saved. And He suffered truly, even as also He truly raised up Himself, not, as certain unbelievers maintain, that He only seemed to suffer, as they themselves only seem to be [Christians]. And as they believe, so shall it happen unto them, when they shall be divested of their bodies, and be mere evil spirits (shorter version, *Smyr. 2*).[31]

In Smyrnaeans chapter 5, he emphasizes their dangerous errors, but for believers, he says there is to be a future resurrection and that Christ's bodily passion is proof for their own resurrection (shorter version, *Smyr. 5*):

> Some ignorantly deny Him, or rather have been denied by Him, being the advocates of death rather than of the truth. These persons neither have the prophets . . . , nor the law of Moses, nor the Gospel . . . nor the sufferings we have individually endured. For they think also the same thing regarding us . . . not confessing that He was [truly] possessed of a body? But he who does not acknowledge this, has in fact altogether denied Him, being enveloped in death . . . Yea . . . until they repent and return to [a true belief in] Christ's passion, which is our resurrection.[32]

Finally, in the concluding salutations of his letter to the Smyrnaeans 12:2, Ignatius confirms his belief in Christ's bodily passion and resurrection with these words: "I salute your most worthy bishop, and your very venerable presbytery, and your deacons, my fellow-servants, and all of you individually, as well as generally, *in the name of Jesus Christ, and in His flesh and blood, in His passion and resurrection, both corporeal and spiritual,* in union with God and you."[33] Thus, it is clear that Ignatius sincerely believes in and is following the New Testament[34] perspective with respect to bodily resurrection from the

---

31. Ibid.
32. Ibid., 88.
33. Ibid., 92 (emphasis added).
34. Frend (*Rise of Christianity*, 135) notes that "sound doctrine" found in the sub-apostolic writings of Ignatius and others mainly comes from the Gospels and Paul's letters, and that "Ignatius is influenced through and through by John and Paul."

dead. N. T. Wright notes that Ignatius used the term "flesh" here as in Luke 24:39 as opposed to 1 Corinthians 15:50[35] and comments,

> Ignatius . . . , like Clement, has developed some ideas in new ways and has used different terminology. He does not make the distinction, clear in Paul and implicit elsewhere, between the nature of the crucified body and that of the risen one. His apologetic concern was for continuity, not discontinuity. The closing greeting of the letter to the Smyrnaeans emphasizes where his heart lay.[36]

Hill[37] cogently shows that Ignatius' most characteristic use of an unusual phrase, "to attain God," means that, like Clement, Ignatius taught that the believers attain "an intermediate-state blessing, entered, temporally, immediately upon death and, spatially, in God's presence in heaven"[38] before attaining final resurrection of the body at Christ's coming.

Like Ignatius, Polycarp (c. 69–155)[39] is one of the notable personalities of the post-apostolic period. When his friend and mentor, Ignatius, sent him one of his letters, Polycarp was then bishop of Smyrna in Asia Minor and, several decades later, died (c. 155–160) as a martyr at the age of eighty-six.[40] Polycarp sent a letter to the Philippians and Roberts & Donaldson affirm its authenticity:

> It is abundantly established by external testimony, and is also supported by the internal evidence. Irenaeus says (*Adv. Haer.*, iii. 3): "There is extant an Epistle of Polycarp written to the Philippians, most satisfactory, from which those that have a mind to do so may learn the character of his faith," etc. This passage is embodied by Eusebius in his *Ecclesiastical History* (iv. 14); and in another place the same writer refers to the Epistle before us as an undoubted production of Polycarp (*Hist. Eccl.*, iii. 36). Other ancient testimonies . . . easily be added, but are superfluous, inasmuch as there is a general consent among scholars at the

---

35. Wright, *Resurrection of the Son of God*, 486fn32.
36. Ibid., 485–486.
37. Hill, *Regnum Caelorum*, 85–90.
38. Ibid., 87.
39. Wright, *Resurrection of the Son of God*, 486; also Roberts and Donaldson, *Ante-Nicene Fathers*, vol. 1, 31 [AD 65–100–155].
40. Holmes, *Apostolic Fathers*, 119.

present day that we have in this letter an authentic production of the renowned Bishop of Smyrna.[41]

Polycarp's letter is completely in line with the New Testament, judged by the "astonishing amount of direct and indirect quotation from the New Testament; Matthew, Luke, and John, Acts, the letters to the Galatians, Thessalonians, Corinthians, Ephesians, Philippians, Colossians, Romans, the Pastorals, 1 Peter particularly, and 1 and 2 John are all used."[42] According to Polycarp's disciple, Irenaeus, "'Polycarp was instructed by the apostles, and was brought into contact with many who had seen Christ' (*Adv. Haer.*, iii. 3; Euseb. *Hist. Eccl.*, iv. 14)."[43] Irenaeus (and Eusebius) asserted that Polycarp was a disciple of Apostle John.[44]

However, our main interest here is to understand Polycarp's view of resurrection from the dead. We see continuity with the New Testament in Polycarp's *Philippians* 1:2, "our *Lord Jesus Christ, who for our sins suffered even unto death,* [but] '*whom God raised from the dead, having loosed the bands of the grave*'" and in 2:1, 2 "'believed in *Him who raised up our Lord Jesus Christ from the dead,* and gave Him glory . . . He comes *as the Judge of the living and the dead.* His blood will God require of those who do not believe in Him. But *He who raised Him up from the dead will raise up us also, if we do His will.*"[45] We also see in his *Philippians* 5:2 "If we please Him in this present world, we shall receive also the future world, according as He has promised to us that *He will raise us again from the dead,* and that if we live worthily of Him, 'we shall also reign together with Him,' *provided only we believe.*"[46] Polycarp believed not only that Jesus was truly raised from the dead, but also that believers in Jesus Christ will be raised from the dead, even as Christ was raised.

Like Ignatius (and the Apostle John), Polycarp strongly argued against the docetic heresy that denied the true humanity of Jesus, rebuking those, "whosoever perverts the oracles of the Lord to his own lusts, and says that

---

41. Roberts and Donaldson, *Ante-Nicene Fathers*, vol. 1, 31–32.
42. Frend, *Rise of Christianity*, 135. Holmes (*Apostolic Fathers*, 119–120) cites W. R. Schoedel's (*Polycarp, Martyrdom of Polycarp, Fragments of Papias*, The Apostolic Fathers, vol. 5 [London: Thomas Nelson, 1967], 4–5) note that it "reflects more or less direct contact" with Psalms, Proverbs, Isaiah, Jeremiah, Ezekiel and New Testament books mentioned here.
43. Roberts and Donaldson, *Ante-Nicene Fathers*, vol. 1, 32.
44. Holmes, *Apostolic Fathers*, 119; Sparks, *Apostolic Fathers*, 123.
45. Polycard, "The Epistle of Polycarp," in *The Ante-Nicene Fathers: Translations of the Writings of the Fathers down to A.D. 325*, vol. 1, eds. and trans. A. Roberts and J. Donaldson (Grand Rapids, MI: Eerdmans, 1979), 33 (emphasis added).
46. Ibid., 34 (emphasis added).

there is neither a resurrection nor a judgment, he is the first-born of Satan."[47] We learn from Irenaeus that Marcion, who denied the resurrection of the body, was similarly rebuked by Polycarp, "And Polycarp himself replied to Marcion, who met him on one occasion, and said, 'Dost thou know me?' 'I do know thee, the first-born of Satan.'"[48] To those critics of Polycarp who sneer at Polycarp for his lack of creativity and contend that he has no new theological insights, Jack Sparks responds, "We can be glad he was the way he was. Through Polycarp we have not only a link with the earliest days of Christianity, but a faithful transmission of apostolic doctrine as well. No, he was not creative. He was a loyal disciple of Christ and the apostles."[49]

N. T. Wright also shows from Polycarp's *Philippians* 9[50] that, similar to Paul, Polycarp points to an intermediate state before the final state of resurrection life,

> Polycarp also, rather after the manner of Clement, speaks of the intermediate state of the martyrs. Believers must be fully persuaded that Ignatius, Zosimus and Rufus, others of their own church, and of course Paul himself and the other apostles, did not "run in vain" (Polycarp again quotes Paul's letter to the Philippians, here from 2:16), but in faith and righteousness, "and that they are with the Lord" (*para to kyrio*), with whom they suffered, having now gone to the "place they have deserved" (*eis ton opheilomenon autois topon*). We see here the very cautious early Christian attempts to speak of the immediate life after death, in terms similar to Paul's in the first chapter of Philippians, while emphasizing also the importance of the final state, the resurrection life which will be given after this state of "life after death."[51]

The account of the martyrdom of Polycarp in the letter supposedly from the Church of Smyrna, highlights both the future resurrection and the present heavenly intermediate state for martyrs of Christ, without clear distinction between these two states. For example, the resurrection is highlighted in that letter by Polycarp's prayer before he is led to execution by fire,

---

47. *Phil.* 7:1 in Polycarp, "Epistle of Polycarp," 34.
48. *Adv. Haer.* Bk. III:4, in Roberts and Donaldson, *Ante-Nicene Fathers*, vol. 1, 416.
49. Sparks, *Apostolic Fathers*, 124.
50. Cf. Polycard, "Epistle of Polycarp," 35.
51. Wright, *Resurrection of the Son of God*, 486–487.

> O Lord God Almighty, the Father of thy beloved and blessed Son Jesus Christ ... I give Thee thanks that Thou hast counted me, worthy of this day and this hour, that I should have a part in the number of Thy martyrs, in the cup of thy Christ, *to the resurrection of eternal life, both of soul and body, through the incorruption [imparted] by the Holy Ghost.*[52]

But the letter also speaks of the immediate and glorious heavenly life of martyrs like Polycarp, as a reward, perhaps to encourage others preparing for martyrdom at that time:

> But when the adversary of the race of the righteous, the envious, malicious, and wicked one, perceived the impressive nature of his martyrdom, and [considered] the blameless life he had ... and how he was now crowned with the wreath of immortality, having beyond dispute received his reward.[53]

> This, then, is the account of the blessed Polycarp, who, being the twelfth that was martyred in Smyrna ... yet occupies a place of his own in the memory of all men, insomuch that he is everywhere spoken of by the heathen themselves. He was not merely an illustrious teacher, but also a pre-eminent martyr, whose martyrdom all desire to imitate, as having been altogether consistent with the gospel of Christ. For, having through patience overcome the unjust governor, and *thus acquired the crown of immortality, he now, with the apostles and all the righteous [in heaven], rejoicingly glorifies God, even the Father,* and blesses our Lord Jesus Christ, the Saviour of our souls, the Governor of our bodies, and the Shepherd of the Catholic Church throughout the world.[54]

Wright notes that the letter "insists, against the charges of Jews and pagans, that there remains a huge distinction between the Christian attitude to Christ ... whom the Christians worshipped as a son of God, and the Christian love for the martyrs as his disciples and imitators."[55]

---

52. *Martyrdom of Polycarp* 14:1, 2 in Roberts and Donaldson, *Ante-Nicene Fathers*, vol. 1, 42 (emphasis added).

53. *Mt. Pol.* 17:1, 2 in Roberts and Donaldson, *Ante-Nicene Fathers*, vol. 1, 42.

54. *Mt. Pol.* 19 in Roberts and Donaldson, *Ante-Nicene Fathers*, vol. 1, 43 (emphasis added).

55. Wright, *Resurrection of the Son of God*, 488. Cf. *Mt. Pol.* 17 in Roberts and Donaldson,

The next important document of the early church is *Didache*. This full but short text was found included in a manuscript discovered by Bryennios in 1873 and published in 1883.[56] For our purpose, the future resurrection of the dead is mentioned in the final chapter (chapter 16) of *Didache*:

> 1. Watch for your life's sake. Let not your lamps be quenched, nor your loins unloosed; but be ye ready, for ye know not the hour in which our Lord cometh. 2. But often shall ye come together, seeking the things which are befitting to your souls: for the whole time of your faith will not profit you, if ye be not made perfect in the last time.
>
> 3. For in the last days false prophets and corrupters shall be multiplied, and the sheep shall be turned into wolves, and love shall be turned into hate; 4. for when lawlessness increaseth, they shall hate and persecute and betray one another, and then shall appear the world-deceiver as Son of God, and shall do signs and wonders, and the earth shall be delivered into his hands, and he shall do iniquitous things which have never yet come to pass since the beginning. 5. Then shall the creation of men come into the fire of trial, and many shall be made to stumble and shall perish; but they that endure in their faith shall be saved from under the curse itself. 6. *And then shall appear the signs of the truth; first, the sign of an out-spreading in heaven; then the sign of the sound of the trumpet; and the third, the resurrection of the dead*; 7. *yet not of all, but as it is said: The Lord shall come and all His saints with Him.* 8. Then shall the world see the Lord coming upon the clouds of heaven.[57]

It seems the author or authors of *Didache* in this passage are heavily dependent on the gospel of Matthew, who wrote about signs of the end times (chapter 24), as well as on the resurrection theme from 1 Corinthians 15:52 and 1 Thessalonians 4:16 (also from the Old Testament prophecy in Zech 14:5 and

---

Ante-Nicene Fathers, vol. 1, 42–43.

56. Holmes, *Apostolic Fathers*, 145. For Holmes, a "wide range of dates, extending from before AD 50 to the third century or later, has been proposed . . . difficult by a lack of hard evidence . . . may have been put into its present form as late as 150, though a date considerably closer to the end of the first century seems more probable" (Ibid., 146).

57. Alexander Roberts and James Donaldson, eds., *The Ante-Nicene Fathers: Translations of the Writings of the Fathers down to A.D. 325,* Reprint in CCEL CD-ROM 2000 (Grand Rapids, MI: Eerdmans, 1999), VII (emphasis added).

Dan 7:13). Wright notes, "That it [*Didache*] affirms the resurrection, as part of a theology of a coming kingdom of god, means that, though the doctrine is not central to the document... it is another witness to the same theology that we find in Clement, Ignatius, Polycarp and... the New Testament itself."[58] No matter when it was written, the view given on the resurrection of the dead is in line with the New Testament.

As with the *Didache,* a wide range of dates has been proposed by scholars for the *Letter of Barnabas* roughly sometime "after the destruction of the temple in Jerusalem in AD 70 (16:3–5) but before the city was rebuilt by Hadrian following the revolt of AD 132–135."[59] This anonymous letter was most probably written by "an Alexandrian Jew of the times of Trajan and Hadrian" named Barnabas (often confused with the apostle) but "was attributed to St. Barnabas, by those who supposed that apostle to be the author of the Epistle to the Hebrews, and who discovered similarities in the plan and purpose of the two works."[60] This letter gives an allegorical interpretation of the Old Testament and its prophecies to show that "Christians are the true and intended heirs of God's covenant" and this kind of interpretation was dominant in the early and mediaeval church.[61]

We see the theme of life after death and judgment right away in *Barnabas* 1:6, 7:

> Well then, there are three basic doctrines of the Lord: *the hope of life, which is the beginning and end of our faith; righteousness, which is the beginning and the end of judgment*; and love shown in gladness and rejoicing, the testimony of righteous works. *For the Master has made known to us through the prophets things past and things present, and has given us a foretaste of things to come.*[62]

We also see the theme of resurrection from the dead in *Barnabas* 5:

> He being Lord of all the world, to whom God said at the foundation of the world, "Let us make man after our image, and after our likeness," understand how it was that He endured to suffer at the hand of men . . . And He (since it behoved Him to appear in flesh), *that He might abolish death, and reveal the*

---

58. Wright, *Resurrection of the Son of God*, 489.
59. Holmes, *Apostolic Fathers*, 160.
60. Roberts and Donaldson, *Ante-Nicene Fathers*, vol. 1, 133.
61. Holmes, *Apostolic Fathers*, 159–160.
62. Ibid., 162 (emphasis added).

> *resurrection from the dead*, endured . . . in order that He might fulfill the promise made unto the fathers, and by preparing a new people for Himself, might show, while He dwelt on earth, that He, *when He has raised mankind*, will also judge them.[63]

The letter follows through in *Barnabas* 5:10–12 and elsewhere to argue against Docetism (which denied that Jesus' humanity was real) and argues for the importance of Jesus coming in the flesh. It refers in 6:10–19 to the promise of a new land of milk and honey for believers but acknowledges that while this has not yet happened, it will happen in the future and "he has told us when it will be: when we ourselves have been made perfect, and so become heirs of the Lord's covenant."[64]

Barnabas 15 emphasizes the importance of Jesus' resurrection from the dead on the first day of the new week, which inaugurated a new Sabbath and the beginning of another world signifying a true eschatological rest:

> Further, He says to them, "Your new moons and your Sabbath I cannot endure." Ye perceive how He speaks: Your present Sabbaths are not acceptable to Me, but that is which I have made, [namely this,] when, giving rest to all things, I shall make a beginning of the eighth day, that is, a beginning of another world. Wherefore, also, we keep the eighth day with joyfulness, the day also on which Jesus rose again from the dead. And when He had manifested Himself, He ascended into the heavens.[65]

Finally, it ends urging the believers to live according to the Lord's commandments by highlighting the importance of resurrection for the righteous in chapter 21 (Conclusion):

> It is well, therefore, that he who has learned the judgments of the Lord, as many as have been written, should walk in them. For he who keepeth these shall be glorified in the kingdom of God; but he who chooseth other things shall be destroyed with his works. On this account there will be a *resurrection*, on this account a *retribution* . . . For the day is at hand on which all things shall perish with the evil [one]. The Lord is near, and His reward. Again, and yet again, I beseech you: be good lawgivers to one

---

63. Roberts and Donaldson, *Ante-Nicene Fathers*, vol. 1, 139 (emphasis added).
64. Holmes, *Apostolic Fathers*, 170.
65. Roberts and Donaldson, *Ante-Nicene Fathers*, vol. 1, 147.

another; continue faithful counsellors of one another; take away from among you all hypocrisy. And may God, who ruleth over all the world, give to you wisdom, intelligence, understanding, knowledge of His judgments, with patience. And be ye taught of God, inquiring diligently what the Lord asks from you; and do it that ye maybe safe in the day of judgment.[66]

I tend to agree with Wright that though the exposition here is of quite a different order than the New Testament, the letter attempts to present "the early theology of new creation and new covenant" in a different context where "the resurrection, both of Jesus and of Christians, as an important, though not very developed, strand within it."[67]

Another early church document, *Shepherd of Hermas*, was written before Irenaeus (ca. 175) since Irenaeus refers to it, although the Muratorian Canon claims that Hermas wrote it in Rome while his brother Pius was serving as the bishop of Rome (140–154 CE).[68] This document has a set of visions, commandments and similitudes (or parables) but it is mostly about the possibility of repentance after post-baptismal sin and has a detailed analyses of different levels and kinds of good and bad behavior.[69] Hill notes that, "Hermas envisions a time of unprecedented and final tribulation . . . closely bound up with the last judgment . . . that an appeal to it implies a dire and urgent warning to those who have lapsed for their speedy repentance."[70] Hill also gives a commentary on the possible reference to the theme of resurrection in *Shepherd of Hermas*,

> As to the doctrine of the bodily resurrection in Hermas, Pernveden says that it has been "replaced by the belief that upon the death of the body, the saved soul directly enters the kingdom of God." "Replaced," however, is not the right word. It should be remembered first of all that Hermas's principal image for the church is the tower. This image, for all its complaisance, is understandably not well equipped to accommodate the added

---

66. Ibid., 149 (emphasis added).
67. Wright, *Resurrection of the Son of God*, 491.
68. Holmes, *Apostolic Fathers*, 191; Sparks, *Apostolic Fathers*, 156. Roberts and Donaldson (*Ante-Nicene Fathers*, 1999, vol. II) date it AD 160. Wright (*Resurrection of the Son of God*, 491) dates it around CE 150 and notes that it was considered part of New Testament by Irenaeus, Clement of Alexandria and Tertullian.
69. Cf. Wright, *Resurrection of the Son of God*, 491.
70. Hill, *Regnum Caelorum*, 92–93.

jolt of the notion of resurrection. We are never told what happens to the tower when the Lord of the tower returns because we always leave the tower allegory before the Lord's advent. Under another image the righteous are like trees waiting to blossom in the summer/world to come (Sim. 4). This presentation is very conducive to the hope of a transformation of some kind.

More importantly, a future existence for the body is demanded by Sim.5.6.7: "For all flesh in which the holy Spirit has dwelled, when found undefiled and spotless, will receive a reward." In the context, the attention has moved from the reward due to the flesh of Christ for its faithful service to a reward for Christians in the flesh, and this must be an eschatological reward. The Christian must keep his flesh undefiled, "so that the Spirit that dwells in it may bear witness to it and your flesh may be justified (δικαιωθῃ). Beware, lest it enter your heart that this flesh of yours is mortal (φθαρτην) and you misuse it in some defilement . . . " (5.7.1). "By δικαιουσθαι the judgment naturally is meant," and this requires that the somatic nature, along with the spiritual, has more than a temporary significance. "For both [i.e., flesh and Spirit] belong together and neither can be defiled without the other" (5.7.4). *The near silence of Hermas on the resurrection is thus due to the accepted and uncontroverted place that the doctrine had with Hermas and his readers.*[71]

Hence, Hill concludes that the absence of discussion about believers' future bodily resurrection in *Shepherd* is due to the fact that it was already assumed by both Hermas and the readers to whom *Shepherd* was addressed.[72]

Papias (70–155) the bishop of Hieropolis, a city of Phrygia, was a contemporary of Polycarp, the bishop of Smyrna. Many fragments of Papias' teachings and writings appear in later writers, such as Irenaeus and Eusebius. These writers say that Papias died as a martyr in about 163 CE or about when

---

71. Ibid., 93–94 (emphasis added).
72. Wright (*Resurrection of the Son of God,* 492) also aptly responds to those who suggest that *Hermas* and *Martyrdom of Polycarp* seem to infer that "the righteous dead become angels" and shows that in none of these references does "the author *identify* the dead with angels" but only says "that they are in company of angels" and that most probably Hermas was not interested in the question that is being asked by present day scholars.

Polycarp suffered martyrdom while this is questioned by others.[73] Eusebius says this about Papias in the *Church History of Eusebius,*

> 11. The same writer [Papias] gives also other accounts which he says came to him through unwritten tradition, certain strange parables and teachings of the Saviour, and some other more mythical things.
>
> 12. *To these belong his statement that there will be a period of some thousand years after the resurrection of the dead, and that the kingdom of Christ will be set up in material form on this very earth.* I suppose he got these ideas through a misunderstanding of the apostolic accounts, not perceiving that the things said by them were spoken mystically in figures.
>
> 13. For he appears to have been of very limited understanding, as one can see from his discourses. but it was due to him that so many of the Church Fathers after him adopted a like opinion, urging in their own support the antiquity of the man; as for instance Irenaeus and anyone else that may have proclaimed similar views.[74]

Eusebius claims that Papias misunderstood what the apostles said "mystically in figures" and was of "very limited understanding." Eusebius does acknowledge, however, that many church fathers like Irenaeus and others followed Papias' millennial view. Jerome (ca. 342–420) also attests that Papias' millennial view was "followed by Irenaeus, Apollinarius, and others, who say that after the resurrection the Lord will reign in the flesh with the saints."[75] Hence, I would agree with Wright that Papias can be referred to "as an extra witness, along with Clement and Ignatius, for a robustly physical view of the final time of salvation, for the world as well as for righteous human beings."[76]

---

73. Roberts and Donaldson, *Ante-Nicene Fathers,* vol. 1, 151. Wright (*Resurrection of the Son of God,* 492) dates Papias c. 60–130 CE and Holmes (*Apostolic Fathers,* 307) thinks that he probably published his five volume *Expositions of the Sayings of the Lord* within a decade or so of 130 CE but neither has a reliable year of his death even though they both note that Papias was a contemporary of Polycarp.

74. Pamphilus Eusebius, "Church History of Eusebius," in *The Nicene and Post-Nicene Fathers,* Series II, vol. 1, eds. Philip Schaff and Henry Wace. Reprint in CCEL CD-ROM 2000. (Grand Rapids, MI: Eerdmans, 1999), Bk. III, chapter 39 (emphasis added).

75. Holmes, *Apostolic Fathers,* 319.

76. Wright, *Resurrection of the Son of God,* 493.

The final document of the Apostolic Fathers that we will examine is the *Epistle to Diognetus* (ca. 150)[77] which we include here more out of "tradition than logic" for it is more appropriately part of Apologists, such as Justin Martyr and others (which I will consider in the next chapter). The *Epistle to Diognetus* was more an "apology in epistolary form" written to the outside pagan unbelievers in response to their specific questions about "the nature and significance of the Christian faith."[78] According to Wright, this *Epistle* does not "belong with Clement, Ignatius and Polycarp when it comes to thinking about the Christian hope . . . it has nothing to say about it (nor about the resurrection of Jesus)."[79] The nearest the *Epistle to Diognetus* comes to mentioning a physical body which may relate to its resurrection is in chapter 6 where it deals with "The Relation of Christians to the World":

> To sum up all in one word – what the soul is in the body, that are Christians in the world. The soul is dispersed through all the members of the body, and Christians are scattered through all the cities of the world. The soul dwells in the body, yet is not of the body; and Christians dwell in the world, yet are not of the world. The invisible soul is guarded by the visible body, and Christians are known indeed to be in the world, but their godliness remains invisible. The flesh hates the soul, and wars against it, though itself suffering no injury, because it is prevented from enjoying pleasures; the world also hates the Christians, though in nowise injured, because they abjure pleasures. *The soul loves the flesh that hates it, and [loves also] the members*; Christians likewise love those that hate them. *The soul is imprisoned in the body, yet preserves that very body*; and Christians are confined in the world as in a prison, and yet they are the preservers of the world. *The immortal soul dwells in a mortal tabernacle; and Christians dwell as sojourners in corruptible [bodies], looking for an incorruptible dwelling in the heavens.*[80]

It seems the writer held the contemporary pagan view of an immortal soul imprisoned in physical body, yet he writes that the soul loves the body and

---

77. Frend (*Rise of Christianity*, 236, 261fn.24) notes c. 150 or "a relatively early date, not later than A.D. 150." Hill (*Regnum Caelorum*, 102fn.1) notes "from around 150 or slightly earlier." Roberts and Donaldson, *Ante-Nicene Fathers*, vol. 1, 23 note [AD 130].
78. Holmes, *Apostolic Fathers*, 291–292.
79. Wright, *Resurrection of the Son of God*, 493.
80. Roberts and Donaldson, *Ante-Nicene Fathers*, vol. 1, 27 (emphasis added).

preserves it while waiting for the incorruptible in the heavens. Referring to the *Epistle to Diognetus,* Hill notes,

> It is not difficult to surmise that, to this author, death for those who have loved God means elevation of the soul to obtain life and enter that incorruptible kingdom of heaven ... When Christ comes again, he shall come as judge (7:6). It should be said that there is no certain reference in this work to the doctrine of the bodily resurrection, though there is no evidence that it was doubted.[81]

I tend to agree with Wright, who finds in the *Epistle to Diognetus,* "a moderate Platonic statement, not seeing an incorruptible body as a gift from heaven but seeing the immortal soul awaiting a complete immortality, away from the corruptible material world, as a gift which will be enjoyed in heaven itself."[82]

Our next topic is the unbelievers' "State-after-Death" in selected texts of the *Apostolic Fathers* of the early church.

The Destiny of Unbelievers after Death

In this section, I will consider the *Apostolic Fathers'* understanding of ultimate punishment. We find ample references to the biblical passages about God's ultimate punishment for the unrighteous and unbelievers but little detail about that punishment in these early documents. *1 Clement* 8:2 quotes Ezekiel, "As I live, saith the Lord, I desire not the death of the sinner, but rather his repentance" (Ezek 33:11), and *1 Clement* 8:4 quotes Isaiah 1:16–20, "And if ye be willing and obey Me, ye shall eat the good of the land; but if ye refuse, and will not hearken unto Me, the sword shall devour you, for the mouth of the Lord hath spoken these things."[83] In *1 Clement* 11:1, "On account of his hospitality and godliness, Lot was saved out of Sodom when all the country round was punished by means of fire and brimstone, the Lord thus making it manifest that He does not forsake those that hope in Him, but gives up such as depart from Him to punishment and torture."[84]

1 Clement 20:5 says that, God is in total control and even "the incomprehensible depth of the abysses and the indescribable judgments (or punishments perhaps) of the underworld are constrained by [his] . . .

---

81. Hill, *Regnum Caelorum*, 103.
82. Wright, *Resurrection of the Son of God*, 494.
83. Clement, "First Epistle of Clement," 7.
84. Ibid., 8.

ordinances."[85] Finally, in 51:4, there is a reference to the inhabitants of *Hades*, as those who rebelled against Moses, that their hearts were hardened and they were condemned (cf. Num 16:33), "For they went down alive into Hades, and death swallowed them up."[86] Although, there is not much detail about the nature of punishment in *Hades*, *1 Clement* is in line with the Bible and affirms its view of ultimate punishment.

However, in *2 Clement*, there is somewhat more clarity as it closely follows the New Testament perspective of *eternal punishment*. *2 Clement* refers to the unrighteous as "those who are perishing" and those whom Christ came to save (2:5–7). It states that the Lord will throw "out" those who do not keep his commandments and call them "evildoers" (4:5). It quotes Jesus telling Peter not to fear those, "who, though they kill you, are not able to do anything else to you, but fear him who, after you are dead, has power to cast soul and body into the flames of hell" (5:4); also saying, "if we disobey his commandments, then nothing will save us from *eternal punishment*" (6:7). It quotes Isaiah 66:24 and Mark 9:48 to show the nature of the punishment, that "*their worm will not die and their fire will not be quenched*" (7:6). It repeats again the final destiny of the unbelievers or the ungodly when Jesus returns in glory and judges them (17:5–6) and punishes them "with dreadful torments in unquenchable fire" (17:7).[87]

Ignatius of Antioch (ca. 30–107) in his letter to the Ephesians in 20:2 refers to the partaking of the bread in the Holy Communion of the Lord's Supper as "the medicine of immortality, the antidote we take in order not to die but to live forever in Jesus Christ."[88] Here it seems Ignatius is thinking about Jesus' teaching in John 6:25–59 and, like Jesus, he is comparing eternal life and death. This does not mean that Ignatius would have understood "death" as a total extinction or that he denied eternal torment for the ungodly after death. As we have noted before, Ignatius mentored his younger friend Polycarp (ca. 69–155) of Smyrna and they both died a martyr's death, separately, about fifty years apart. Though Polycarp in his letter to the Philippians did not mention much about the final destiny of the unbelievers, he does explicitly state what he thinks about them in chapter 7:

> "For whosoever does not confess that Jesus Christ has come in the flesh, is antichrist;" and whosoever does not confess the

---

85. Holmes, *Apostolic Fathers*, 40, cf. 28:1.
86. Clement, "First Epistle of Clement," 19.
87. Holmes, *Apostolic Fathers*, 69, 70, 71, 77 (emphasis added).
88. Ibid., 93.

> testimony of the cross, is of the devil; and whosoever perverts the oracles of the Lord to his own lusts, and says that there is neither a resurrection nor a judgment, he is the first-born of Satan. Wherefore, forsaking the vanity of many, and their false doctrines, let us return to the word which has been handed down to us from the beginning; "watching unto prayer," and persevering in fasting; beseeching in our supplications the all-seeing God.[89]

We have noted before that Polycarp quoted liberally from the New Testament in this letter and what he says is in line with the New Testament. As a loyal disciple of Christ and the apostles, he believed in the eternal punishment of unbelievers, whom he referred to as antichrist, devil and first-born of Satan above. This is affirmed indirectly by the account of his martyrdom written by (his flock) the Church at Smyrna of which he was the bishop, prior to his death. This is what is recorded in chapter 2 of *Martyrdom of Polycarp* about how martyrs do escape eternal punishment in the fire that will never be quenched and are saved to eternal life:

> And, looking to the grace of Christ, they despised all the torments of this world, redeeming themselves *from eternal punishment* by [the suffering of] a single hour. For this reason the fire of their savage executioners appeared cool to them. For they kept before their view escape *from that fire which is eternal and never shall be quenched*, and looked forward with the eyes of their heart to those good things which are laid up for such as endure; things "which ear hath not heard, nor eye seen, neither have entered into the heart of man," but were revealed by the Lord to them.[90]

The *Letter of Barnabas* (ca. 70–135) speaks in chapter 4 of judgment to come (with references to the Old and New Testament) and how believers must behave to escape from being thrust out of the kingdom:

> As much as in us lies, let us meditate upon the fear of God, and let us keep His commandments, that we may rejoice in His ordinances. *The Lord will judge the world without respect of persons*. Each will receive as he has done . . . *Take heed, lest* resting

---

89. Polycarp, "Epistle of Polycarp," 34.
90. *Martyrdom of Polycarp*, in Roberts and Donaldson, *Ante-Nicene Fathers*, vol. 1, 39 (emphasis added).

at our ease, as those who are the called [of God], we should fall asleep in our sins, and *the wicked prince, acquiring power over us, should thrust us away from the kingdom of the Lord* . . . that after so great signs and wonders were wrought in Israel, they were thus [at length] abandoned. Let us beware lest we be found [fulfilling that saying], as it is written, "Many are called, but few are chosen."[91]

There is further elaboration in *Barnabas* chapters 20 and 21 that there is eternal death with/and punishment and retribution for the ungodly:

But the way of darkness is crooked, and full of cursing; for *it is the way of eternal death with punishment* [or "and punishment" Holmes 1989:186], *in which way are the things that destroy the soul*, viz., idolatry, over-confidence, the arrogance of power, hypocrisy, double-heartedness, adultery, murder, rapine, haughtiness, transgression, deceit, malice, self-sufficiency, poisoning, magic, avarice, want of the fear of God . . .

It is well, therefore, that he who has learned the judgments of the Lord . . . should walk in them. For he who keepeth these shall be glorified in the kingdom of God; but *he who chooseth other things shall be destroyed with his works. On this account there will be a resurrection, on this account a retribution.*[92]

In the *Epistle to Diognetus* (ca. 150) the writer ridicules certain arrogant pagan philosophers' view of God as fire in 8:2 in this way, "Or do you accept the empty and nonsensical statements of those pretentious philosophers, some of whom said that God was fire (the very thing they are headed for, they call God!)."[93] Thus, according to the *Epistle to Diognetus*, these philosophers are heading to that fire of punishment which they refer to as God. However, it gives a more explicit reference to the punishment in the eternal fire as opposed to true life in heaven in 10:7b, 8:

when you realize what the true life in heaven is, when you despise the apparent death here on earth, when you fear the real death, which is reserved for those *who will be condemned to the eternal fire which will punish to the very end* those delivered to it. (8)

---

91. Roberts and Donaldson, *Ante-Nicene Fathers*, vol. 1, 139 (emphasis added).
92. Ibid., 149 (emphasis added).
93. Holmes, *Apostolic Fathers*, 301.

> Then you will admire those who for righteousness' sake *endure the transitory fire*, and you will consider them blessed, *when you comprehend the other fire.*[94]

Here it is clearly asserted that punishment for the unrighteous is eternal in nature in *the eternal fire* and this eternal fire is also compared in its intensity or degree with the earthly fire which is of very short duration. Some righteous people did endure this earthly fire and died as martyrs because they understood the eternal fire to be far worse in terms of its intensity and length of time.

Summary and Implications

As we perused these early church documents of selected *Apostolic Fathers* we found that in the face of hostile, pagan, Platonic and Gnostic doctrines of *immortality* and ensuing *transmigration of soul* (that was even making its way into the church), the early church stood firm in their convictions concerning resurrection and eternal life for believers in Jesus Christ. The pagan view that *"when you are dead that's the end,"* assailed the Christian teaching, along with strong opposition from some Jewish groups like the Sadducees and others in their pluralistic contexts, but the Apostolic Fathers did not depart from Jesus' teaching about the future bodily resurrection of the dead and eternal life for believers at the final end. Thus, we find in the selected documents of the *Apostolic Fathers* overwhelming support for the biblical hope of the future bodily resurrection of the dead and eternal life for believers at the Second Coming of our Lord Jesus Christ in the midst of the pluralistic religious contexts of their time.

But that good news of the biblical perspective of "State-after-Death," affirmed by the stalwarts of the early church, is only half the story. Along with that good news, there is the bad news of the "State-after-Death" which awaits unbelievers. As opposed to the pagan understanding of duality of material body and immaterial pre-existent soul and ensuing disparaging of material body and the world, the fathers confessed that God created humankind as a unity. They affirmed that the body needs to be reunited with the soul at the final judgment both for rewards and punishment. We also found overwhelming consensus that *everlasting* conscious punishment awaits unbelievers at the final judgment when Christ returns.

---

94. Ibid., 303–304 (emphasis added).

10

State-after-Death in the Apologists

As we studied resurrection from the dead including the believers' "State-after-Death" in documents of the Apostolic Fathers, we found ample evidence for unquestioned confidence in the biblical promise of future bodily resurrection and eternal life. Along with that positive hope for believers in Jesus, in our study of unbelievers' destiny after death, there was clear affirmation of God's judgment and eternal punishment for unbelievers. I will now continue this study, in selected documents of the Apologists of second and early third century CE, to further understand the early church's perspectives on this subject.

The Apologists

The Apologists were second century Christians who firmly defended the uniqueness of their faith in the pluralistic context of pagan Greeks, hostile Jews and powerful Roman authorities.[1] Hagglund notes, "To these men Christianity was the only true philosophy, a perfect replacement for the philosophy of the Greeks and the religion of the Jews, which could do no more than present unsatisfactory answers to man's searching questions."[2] We shall begin by considering the theme of resurrection in the writings of Justin Martyr (ca. 100–165).[3]

---

1. Frend, *Rise of Christianity*, 234.
2. Bengt Hagglund, *History of Theology*, trans. Gene J. Lund (St. Louis, MO: Concordia Publishing House, 1968), 25.
3. Cf. Wright, *Resurrection of the Son of God*, 500.

Resurrection from the Dead

Justin was a Gentile, born in Samaria, and trained as a philosopher before his conversion to Christianity. After his conversion in his pluralistic religious context, he "acted as an evangelist, taking every opportunity to proclaim the gospel as the only safe and certain philosophy, the only way to salvation."[4] N. T. Wright sums up Justin Martyr's attitude with the following statement: "It was not that the rest of the world was simply wrong, and the Christians simply right; the rest of the world was looking at signposts and clues, and the Christians had found the goal to which they led."[5] Because of a general rejection of the Christian belief in the resurrection among the pagan populace, Justin dealt with the topic extensively in his writings. We will review briefly the main points of his arguments.

In his *Apology I* chapter 8, Justin refers to the righteous who may be willing to die as martyrs, "impelled by the desire of the eternal and pure life, [they] seek the abode that is with God." As for the unbeliever, Christ will judge "the wicked in the same bodies united again to their spirits which are now to undergo everlasting punishment."[6] These statements would definitely confirm his belief in the resurrection of the body for judgment and punishment. Further, in his *Apology I* chapter 18 (see also chapters 21 and 22), Justin employs various arguments, citing some of their own practices and beliefs,[7] to convince the pagans of the validity of bodily resurrection and concludes, "we expect to receive again our own bodies, though they be dead and cast into the earth, for we maintain that with God nothing is impossible."[8] Again, in his *Apology I* chapter 19, "that it is not impossible that the bodies of men, after they have been dissolved, and like seeds resolved into earth, should in God's appointed time rise again and put on incorruption"[9] In *Apology I* chapter 52, Justin refers to the future resurrection of bodies at Christ's second coming:

---

4. Roberts and Donaldson, *Ante-Nicene Fathers*, vol. 1, 160.
5. Wright, *Resurrection of the Son of God*, 500.
6. Martyr Justin, "The Writings of Justin," in *The Ante-Nicene Fathers: Translations of the Writings of the Fathers down to A.D. 325*, vol. 1, eds. and trans. A. Roberts and J. Donaldson, Reprint (Grand Rapids, MI: Eerdmans, 1979), 165.
7. "Justin is not identifying belief in resurrection with this kind of position, merely suggesting it as a stepping-stone towards the truth (21–2)" (Wright, *Resurrection of the Son of God*, 501) and so it is applicable for pluralistic contexts.
8. Justin, "Writings of Justin," 169.
9. Ibid. Wright (*Resurrection of the Son of God*, 501) sees here an echo of John 12 and 1 Corinthians 15 and notes that in *Apology I* Chapter 45 Justin is following Paul in 1 Corinthians 15 in quoting Psalms 110 as a prophecy for Christ's resurrection.

For the prophets have proclaimed two advents of His: the one, that which is already past, ... but the second, when, according to prophecy, He shall come from heaven with glory, accompanied by His angelic host, *when also He shall raise the bodies of all men who have lived, and shall clothe those of the worthy with immortality, and shall send those of the wicked, endued with eternal sensibility, into everlasting fire with the wicked devils.* And that these things also have been foretold as yet to be, we will prove. By Ezekiel the prophet it was said: "Joint shall be joined to joint, and bone to bone, and flesh shall grow again; and every knee shall bow to the Lord, and every tongue shall confess Him."[10]

The same view of future resurrection and judgment at Christ's Second Coming is taken up in Justin's *Dialogue with Trypho*. In chapter 45, the final resurrection of the dead is assumed in questions and answers about the final destiny of those who lived righteous lives according to the Law of Moses. In chapter 80, Justin admits that there are some differences of views among *true* Christians about the millennial reign of Christ, but he regards those who deny the particular doctrine of resurrection as *not* Christians,

For I choose to follow not men or men's doctrines, but God and the doctrines [delivered] by Him. For if you have fallen in with *some who are called Christians, but who do not admit this [truth], and venture to blaspheme the God of Abraham, and the God of Isaac, and the God of Jacob; who say there is no resurrection of the dead, and that their souls, when they die, are taken to heaven; do not imagine that they are Christians,* even as one, if he would rightly consider it, would not admit that the Sadducees, or similar sects of Genistae, Meristae, Galilaeans, Hellenists, Pharisees, Baptists, are Jews (do not hear me impatiently when I tell you what I think), but are [only] called Jews and *children of Abraham, worshipping God with the lips, as God Himself declared, but the heart was far from Him.*[11]

---

10. Justin, "Writings of Justin," 180 (emphasis added).

11. Ibid., 239 (emphasis added). Here Justin adds, "But I and others, who are right-minded Christians on all points, are assured that there will be a resurrection of the dead, and a thousand years in Jerusalem, which will then be built, adorned, and enlarged, [as] the prophets Ezekiel and Isaiah and others declare" and continues in chapter 81 about this thousand years before the general/eternal resurrection and judgment of all people. As I have noted above that Justin accepts differences of opinions among *true* Christians about end times, I think here his

N. T. Wright correctly notes concerning this passage of Justin that, "He seems unaware of any who take the further drastic step of retaining the language of 'resurrection' while using it to denote a spiritual experience in the present life."[12] It is clear that Justin believes in a literal bodily resurrection of the dead at Jesus' Second Coming.

There are other references to the resurrection in Justin's *Dialogue with Trypho* as in chapter 106. Referring to Psalm 22 Justin says concerning Jesus that, "The remainder of the Psalm makes it manifest that He knew His Father would grant to Him all things which He asked, and would raise Him from the dead."[13] In chapter 107, he discusses Jesus' reference to the "sign of Jonah" and that it proclaims Jesus would rise again on the third day. In chapter 108 he addresses the Jews:

> yet you not only have not repented, after you learned that He rose from the dead, but, as I said before you have sent chosen and ordained men throughout all the world to proclaim that a godless and lawless heresy had sprung from one Jesus, a Galilaean deceiver, whom we crucified, but his disciples stole him by night from the tomb, where he was laid when unfastened from the cross, and now deceive men by asserting that he has risen from the dead and ascended to heaven.[14]

In chapter 113, comparing Joshua with Jesus, Justin wrote: "For the former gave them a temporary inheritance, (as) he was neither Christ who is God, nor the Son of God; but the latter, after the holy resurrection, shall give us the eternal possession."[15]

Finally, Justin's treatise on the resurrection,[16] though not preserved entirely, deals at length with the objections raised at that time regarding the "resurrection of the flesh." Also, there was the threat of Docetism which proposed that Jesus only "appeared" to have come in the flesh, while his true

---

emphasis is more on the true belief of bodily resurrection from the dead and he would *not* consider them to be non-Christians who believe in a literal bodily resurrection from the dead like Jesus and yet believe in the symbolic interpretation of 'a thousand years in Jerusalem' that he refers to (also cf. Hill, *Regnum Caelorum*, 25–27).

12. Wright, *Resurrection of the Son of God*, 501. David Jenkins, the former bishop of Durham, Church of England (N. T. Wright is the present bishop of Durham) denied Jesus' literal *bodily* resurrection, yet claimed to believe in spiritual resurrection.

13. Justin, "Writings of Justin," 252.

14. Ibid., 253.

15. Ibid., 255.

16. Ibid., 294–299.

nature was "spiritual." Other arguments arose which attempted to prove that "flesh" was not important for resurrection and salvation. Justin argued, in chapter 7, that the body is important in God's sight because when God created man and woman in his own image, he made them "fleshly" or "of flesh."[17] In chapter 9, he argued that Jesus was raised from the dead "in the flesh" in which he suffered and ascended to heaven "in the flesh."[18] Thus Justin is very much in line with the New Testament as far as the concept of the resurrection of the body is concerned. N. T. Wright helpfully concludes,

> Justin thus stands foursquare with the New Testament, not only on the continuity between the present and future bodies (for which, unlike Paul, he uses the term 'flesh'), but also on the difference between them (the members may not have the same function in the future life as they do now, and deformities will be healed). He offers no theory about an intermediate state, but . . . we may assume he would think in terms of continuity of soul while awaiting renewal of body. He has no doubts that Jesus himself was bodily raised . . . Martyred roughly a hundred years after Paul, he shows every sign of having absorbed essentially the same view of this topic, and of defending it, at more length than Paul had ever done, within the swirling currents of pagan philosophy.[19]

Another Apologist, probably a younger contemporary of Justin, Athenagoras deals with similar issues in his writings.[20] Athenagoras was an Athenian philosopher who became a Christian and wrote his *Apology* (or Embassy as he calls it) for the Christians to the Emperors Marcus Aurelius Anoninus and Lucius Aurelius Commodus about 177 CE. His other surviving work is his treatise on *The Resurrection of the Dead* produced somewhat later than his *Apology*.[21] In chapter 31 of his *Apology*, he expresses what Christians

---

17. Ibid., 297.
18. Ibid., 298.
19. Wright, *Resurrection of the Son of God*, 503.
20. Ibid.
21. A. Roberts and J. Donaldson, *The Ante-Nicene Fathers: Translations of the Writings of the Fathers down to A.D. 325*, vol. 2, Reprint (Grand Rapids, MI: Eerdmans, 1979b), 127. Athenagoras was a future fruit of Paul's ministry in the pluralistic context of Athens (Acts 17:16–34). Roberts and Donaldson (Ibid., 125) note that, "In Athenagoras, whose very name is a retrospect, we discover a remote result of St. Paul's speech on Mars Hill. The apostle had cast his bread upon the waters of Ilissus and Cephisus to find it after many days. 'When they heard of the resurrection of the dead, some mocked,' but here comes a philosopher, from the Athenian *agora*, a convert to St. Paul's argument in his Epistle to the Corinthians, confessing

believed about the after-death state at that time and how that affected their earthly living:

> For if we believed that we should live only the present life, then we might be suspected of sinning, through being enslaved to flesh and blood, or overmastered by gain or carnal desire; but since we know that God is witness to what we think and . . . say both by night and by day, and that He, being Himself light, sees all things in our heart, we are persuaded that when we are removed from the present life we shall live another life, better than the present one, and heavenly, not earthly (since we shall abide near God, and with God, free from all change or suffering in the soul, not as flesh, even though we shall have flesh, but as heavenly spirit), or, falling with the rest, a worse one and in fire; for God has not made us as sheep or beasts of burden, a mere by-work, and that we should perish and be annihilated. On these grounds it is not likely that we should wish to do evil, or deliver ourselves over to the great Judge to be punished.[22]

Here he points to the expected "State-after-Death" for believers in the presence of God in heaven without any suffering, even though they continue to have physical body. In chapter 36 of his *Apology*, he counters the charge of cannibalism[23] against Christians by pointing to the fact that their belief in the resurrection of the body nullifies such thinking:

'the unknown God,' demolishing the marble mob of deities that so 'stirred the apostle's spirit within him,' and teaching alike the Platonist and the Stoic to sit at the feet of Jesus. 'Dionysius the Areopagite, and the woman named Damaris,' are no longer to be despised as the scanty first-fruits of Attica. They too have found a voice in this splendid trophy of the gospel; and, 'being dead, they yet speak' through him." This note is important for mission theology in pluralistic contexts.

22. Athenagoras, "Writings of Athenagoras," in *The Ante-Nicene Fathers: Translations of the Writings of the Fathers down to A.D. 325*, vol. 2, eds. and trans. A. Roberts and J. Donaldson (Grand Rapids, MI: Eerdmans, 1979), 146.

23. In chapter 35, he mentions about this charge, "What man of sound mind, therefore, will affirm, while such is our character, that we are murderers? For we cannot eat human flesh till we have killed some one. The former charge, therefore, being false, if any one should ask them in regard to the second, whether they have seen what they assert, not one of them would be so barefaced as to say that he had . . . For when they know that we cannot endure even to see a man put to death, though justly; who of them can accuse us of murder or cannibalism?" (Athenagoras, "Writings of Athenagoras," 147). I think partaking of the Lord's Supper was taken by some outsiders to believe that Christians eat human flesh and blood and hence the charge of cannibalism.

> Who, then, that believes in a resurrection, would make himself into a tomb for bodies that will rise again? For it is not the part of the same persons to believe that our bodies will rise again, and to eat them as if they would not; and to think that the earth will give back the bodies held by it, but that those which a man has entombed in himself will not be demanded back. On the contrary, it is reasonable to suppose, that those who think they shall have no account to give of the present life ... and that there is no resurrection, but calculate on the soul perishing with the body, and being as it were quenched in it, will refrain from no deed of daring; but as for those who are persuaded that nothing will escape the scrutiny of God, but that even the body which has ministered to the irrational impulses of the soul, and to its desires, will be punished along with it, it is not likely that they will commit even the smallest sin.[24]

In his treatise on *The Resurrection of the Dead*,[25] Athenagoras explains at length the importance of the future bodily resurrection and the final judgment. In chapter 1 of *The Resurrection of the Dead* he begins by defending the truth of the resurrection before his substantive arguments in the next chapters:

> And, therefore, from regard to greater utility, I myself sometimes place arguments in defence of the truth before those concerning the truth; and on the present occasion it appears to me, looking at the requirements of the case, not without advantage to follow the same method in treating of the resurrection. For in regard to this subject also we find some utterly disbelieving, and some others doubting, and even among those who have accepted the first principles some who are as much at a loss what to believe as those who doubt; the most unaccountable thing of all being, that they are in this state of mind without having any ground whatsoever in the matters themselves for their disbelief, or finding it possible

---

24. Athenagoras, "Writings of Athenagoras," 147–148.
25. Hill (*Regnum Caelorum*, 107) cites R. M. Grant ("Athenagoras or Pseudo-Athenagoras," *Harvard Theological Review* 47, no. 2 [1954]: 121–129) questioning Athenagoras' authorship for *the Resurrection of the Dead*, but L. W. Barnard ("The Authenticity of Athenagoras' *De Resurrectione*," *Studia Patristica* 15 [1984]: 39–49) and B. Pouderon (*Athénagore d'Athènes, philosophe chrétien* [Paris: Beauchesne, 1989]) affirm it.

> to assign any reasonable cause why they disbelieve or experience any perplexity.[26]

He continues to show, in chapters 2, 3 and 9, that resurrection, though impossible for humans, is not impossible for God. Since God is our creator he can also raise us up from the dead. He also argues in chapter 15 that the resurrection is based in the human nature itself. Since humans were created by God, composed of a body and an immortal soul together in harmony, so at the end, the body and soul are to be united again in resurrection to maintain that harmony.

Finally, Athenagoras concludes, in chapters 24–25, by arguing from the humans' chief end (or purpose in life) which is different from that of beasts and cattle because they possess an immortal soul and rational judgment. He argues that this end is *not* simply "freedom from pain" *nor* "happiness of soul separated from body" but,

> it is absolutely necessary that the end of a man's being should appear in some reconstitution of the two together, and of the same living being. And as this follows of necessity, there must by all means be a resurrection of the bodies which are dead, or even entirely dissolved, and the same men must be formed anew.[27]

For our pluralistic contexts, N. T. Wright is correct in noting that this conclusion rules out theories like transmigration of souls and disembodied final state for humans.[28] Thus, Athenagoras with others, such as, Justin Martyr, Ignatius of Antioch and Clement of Rome is in line with the New Testament teachings of a bodily resurrection in the end.

Theophilus of Antioch was born a pagan but became a Christian through careful study of the Scriptures. He went on to become the bishop of Antioch in CE 168 and died in about 181 or 188.[29] His sole surviving work of the

---

26. Athenagoras, "Writings of Athenagoras," 149–150.
27. Athenagoras, "Writings of Athenagoras," 162. The Editor of Athenagoras (Ibid) makes an interesting remark at the end of chapter 25 of *the Resurrection of the Dead* in a footnote, "This concluding chapter is of itself a masterpiece, and comforts my own soul unspeakably, as proving that this life is very precious, if only directed to the end from which we are created. Blest be Athenagoras for completing what St. Paul began on the Areopagus, and for giving us 'beauty for ashes' out of the gardens of Plato. Now we find what power there was in the apostle's word, when he preached to the Athenians, 'Jesus and the resurrection'" (Ibid). This note is important for us as we follow Paul's example of doing theology in a pluralistic context, such as Athens.
28. Wright, *Resurrection of the Son of God*, 505.
29. Roberts and Donaldson, *Ante-Nicene Fathers*, vol. 2, 88.

second half of the Second Century, addressed to one Autolycus, shows that Theophilus was an apologist just as Justin and Athenagoras.[30] For this study, I quote from his Book 1 chapters 7 and 8 to show that his view on resurrection is in line with the New Testament, especially with Paul's 1 Corinthians 15:

> *When thou shalt have put off the mortal, and put on incorruption, then shalt thou see God worthily. For God will raise thy flesh immortal with thy soul; and then, having become immortal, thou shalt see the Immortal, if now you believe on Him; and then you shall know that you have spoken unjustly against Him.*
>
> *But you do not believe that the dead are raised. When the resurrection shall take place, then you will believe, whether you will or no; and your faith shall be reckoned for unbelief, unless you believe now. And why do you not believe? Do you not know that faith is the leading principle in all matters? For what husbandman can reap, unless he first trust his seed to the earth? . . . For first He created you out of nothing, and brought you into existence (for if your father was not, nor your mother, much more were you yourself at one time not in being), and formed you out of a small and moist substance, even out of the least drop, which at one time had itself no being; and God introduced you into this life. Moreover, you believe that the images made by men are gods, and do great things; and can you not believe that the God who made you is able also to make you afterwards?*[31]

Theophilus, in his pluralistic pagan context, is another follower of Pauline tradition and "does not use 'resurrection' language metaphorically, whether with concrete or abstract referent, but always literally, referring concretely to the future embodiment of those who, in the present, believe and follow the way of righteousness."[32]

In considering other great Apologists' (e.g. Irenaeus, Tertullian and Minucius Felix) documents of Second and Third Century on resurrection, Bynum notes,

---

30. Wright, *Resurrection of the Son of God*, 506.
31. Theophilus, "Writings of Theophilus," in *The Ante-Nicene Fathers: Translations of the Writings of the Fathers down to A.D. 325,* vol. 2, eds. and trans. A. Roberts and J. Donaldson (Grand Rapids, MI: Eerdmans, 1979), 91 (emphasis added).
32. Wright, *Resurrection of the Son of God*, 508.

> Scholars have always viewed [them] ... as driven by a powerful need to assert the palpable fleshly quality of the body that will be rewarded or punished at the end of time ... [they] employ metaphors that suggest, as did ... Athenagoras and Theophilus, that the resurrection body is exactly the same material body ... material continuity ... for identity.[33]

There is a dispute among scholars whether Tertullian borrowed from Minucius Felix or the other way around and based on the answer to that question, Minucius' treatise *Octavius* could be from CE 166 or about 210.[34] It is a supposed dialogue between the anti-Christian Caecilius and the Christian Octavius. In Minucius Felix's *Octavius*, Caecilus brings the following pluralistic arguments against the Christians and their view of the resurrection of the body in chapters 5 and 11:

> Man, and every animal which is born, inspired with life, and nourished, is as a voluntary concretion of the elements, into which again man and every animal is divided, resolved, and dissipated. So all things flow back again into their source, and are turned again into themselves, without any artificer, or judge, or creator.[35]
>
> "And, not content with this wild opinion, they add to it ... they say that they will rise again after death, and ashes, and dust; and with I know not what confidence, they believe by turns in one another's lies: you would think that they had already lived again ... Deceived by this error, they promise to themselves, as being good, a blessed and perpetual life after their death; ... Yet I should be glad to be informed whether or no you rise again with bodies; and if so, with what bodies – whether with the same or with renewed bodies? Without a body? Then, as far as I know, there will neither be mind, nor soul, nor life. With the same body? But this has already been previously destroyed. With another body? Then it is a new man who is born, not the former one restored; and yet so long a time has passed away, innumerable

---

33. Bynum, *Resurrection of the Body*, 34.

34. A. Roberts and J. Donaldson, *The Ante-Nicene Fathers: Translations of the Writings of the Fathers down to A.D. 325*, vol. 4, Reprint (Grand Rapids, MI: Eerdmans, 1979c), 170.

35. Felix Minucius, "The Octavius of Minucius Felix," in *The Ante-Nicene Fathers: Translations of the Writings of the Fathers down to A.D. 325*, vol. 4, eds. and trans. A. Roberts and J. Donaldson (Grand Rapids, MI: Eerdmans, 1979), 175.

ages have flowed by, and what single individual has returned from the dead either by the fate of Protesilaus, with permission to sojourn even for a few hours, or that we might believe it for an example? All such figments of an unhealthy belief, and vain sources of comfort, with which deceiving poets have trifled in the sweetness of their verse, have been disgracefully remoulded by you, believing undoubtingly[36] on your God.[37]

However, the Christian Octavius responds to Caecilus in chapter 34 by showing that there is going to be a future judgment of this world along with resurrection from the dead and that even their ancient philosophers support that opinion:

> You observe that philosophers dispute of the same things that we are saying, not that we are following up their tracks, but that they, from the divine announcements of the prophets, imitated the shadow of the corrupted truth. Thus also the most illustrious of the wise men, Pythagoras first, and Plato chiefly, have delivered the doctrine of resurrection with a corrupt and divided faith; for they will have it, that the bodies being dissolved, the souls alone both abide for ever, and very often pass into other new bodies. To these things they add also this, by way of misrepresenting the truth, that the souls of men return into cattle, birds, and beasts. Assuredly such an opinion as that is not worthy of a philosopher's inquiry, but of the ribaldry of a buffoon. But for our argument it is sufficient, that even in this your wise men do in some measure harmonize with us.[38]

Even though the philosophers were wrong in misrepresenting the truth of resurrection in the form of *transmigration of souls* (or reincarnation) from one body to another, yet, in a way, they actually do support what Christians believe. Octavius responds further about the plausibility of the Christian claim of resurrection of the body:

> But who is so foolish or so brutish as to dare to deny that man, as he could first of all be formed by God, so can again be re-

---

36. Or "by your credulity into the service of your God" in G. H. Rendall's translation of Minacius in *Tertullian and Minacius Felix*, Loeb C. L. (Cambridge, MA: Harvard U. P., 1931; reprint 1960), 345.
37. Minucius, "Octavius of Minucius Felix," 178–179.
38. Ibid., 194.

formed; . . . and as from nothing it was possible for him to be born, so from nothing it may be possible for him to be restored? Moreover, it is more difficult to begin that which is not, than to repeat that which has been. Do you think that, if anything is withdrawn from our feeble eyes, it perishes to God? Every body, whether it is dried up into dust, or is dissolved into moisture, or is compressed into ashes, or is attenuated into smoke, is withdrawn from us, but it is reserved for God in the custody of the elements. Nor, as you believe, do we fear any loss from sepulture, but we adopt the ancient and better custom of burying in the earth. See, therefore, how for our consolation all nature suggests a future resurrection. The sun sinks down and arises, the stars pass away and return, the flowers die and revive again, after their wintry decay the shrubs resume their leaves, seeds do not flourish again unless they are rotted: thus the body in the sepulchre is like the trees which in winter hide their verdure with a deceptive dryness. Why are you in haste for it to revive and return, while the winter is still raw? We must wait also for the springtime of the body.[39]

Thus, for Octavius, because symbolically it is still winter (the body is in the grave) as the resurrection has not taken place yet, so we must wait for God's spring-time for the body. Wright summarizes Minucius' *Octavius*,

> We find, then, the same simple schema as in the other apologists. There is to be a future resurrection, awaited in conscious rest by those at present dead, and the evidence is not the resurrection of Jesus himself, but the plentiful witness of the natural world. Though some might suppose this a shift away from the secure foundations laid in the New Testament, the motive is not merely the desire to tie the doctrine to things familiar to any reader, but also to demonstrate that Christianity, so far from being a strange superstition, is rooted in the one world made by the creator god.[40]

Again, whether Minucius Felix borrowed from Tertullian or the other way around, it is certain that Tertullian was as good an apologist as the others were and is considered the founding father of Latin Christianity, of North African

---

39. Ibid.
40. Wright, *Resurrection of the Son of God*, 509.

(Carthage) branch of Latin Christianity.[41] According to Wright,[42] Tertullian was born in about 160, became a Christian (from pagan background)[43] in his thirties in the last decade of 200 and died in about 225. In chapter 18 of *Apology*, Tertullian makes a short but clear statement on the final destiny of humans in the hand of God, the creator and sustainer of this universe and of people,

> seeing that, when this age reaches its full end, He will sit as Judge, and *His worshippers He will repay with life eternal*, and the profane He will condemn to fire as perpetual and unceasing; *for the dead every man of them from the beginning, shall be raised, refashioned and reviewed, that their deserts of either kind, good or evil, may be adjudged*. Yes! We too in our day laughed at this. We are from among yourselves. Christians are made, not born.[44]

However, Tertullian deals at length on the subject of resurrection in his work on *The Resurrection of the Flesh*.[45] In chapter 1, Tertullian shows the inconsistencies of contrary beliefs and practices of pagans about "State-after-Death" – either "when you are dead that's the end" or "the transmigration of soul" (very similar to the present day views in the pluralistic context) which are in contrast to the Christian faith on the resurrection of the dead:

> *The resurrection of the dead is the Christian's trust*. By it we are believers. To the belief of this (article of the faith) truth compels us – that truth which God reveals, *but the crowd derides, which supposes that nothing will survive after death. And yet they do honour to their dead . . . with the daintiest banquets which the seasons can produce, on the presumption that those whom they declare to be incapable of all perception still retain an appetite . . .* especially when it burns up its dead with harshest inhumanity, only to pamper them immediately afterwards . . . *But the wise, too, join with the vulgar crowd in their opinion sometimes. There*

---

41. Frend, *Rise of Christianity*, 339, 348ff.
42. Wright, *Resurrection of the Son of God*, 510.
43. A. Roberts and J. Donaldson, *The Ante-Nicene Fathers: Translations of the Writings of the Fathers down to A.D. 325*, vol. 3, Reprint (Grand Rapids, MI: Eerdmans, 1978), 3.
44. Quote from G. H. Rendall's translation of Tertullian and Minucius Felix, *Apology: De Spectaculis. Octavius*, Loeb Classical Library (Cambridge, MA: Harvard University Press, 1931; reprint 1960), 91 (emphasis added).
45. Tertullian, "Writings of Tertullian," in *The Ante-Nicene Fathers: Translations of the Writings of the Fathers down to A.D. 325*, vol. 3, eds. and trans. A. Roberts and J. Donaldson (Grand Rapids, MI: Eerdmans, 1978), 545–594.

> *is nothing after death, according to the school of Epicurus. After death all things come to an end, even death itself, says Seneca to like effect. It is satisfactory, however, that the no less important . . . Pythagoras and Empedocles, and the Plantonists, take the contrary view, and declare the soul to be immortal; affirming, moreover, in a way which most nearly approaches (to our own doctrine), that the soul actually returns into bodies, although not the same bodies, and not even those of human beings invariably: thus Euphorbus is supposed to have passed into Phythagoras, and Homer into a peacock. They firmly pronounced the soul's renewal to be in a body, (deeming it) more tolerable to change the quality (of the corporeal state) than to deny it wholly: they at least knocked at the door of truth, although they entered not. Thus the world, with all its errors, does not ignore the resurrection of the dead.*[46]

In chapters 2–4, Tertullian also rebukes those who claimed to be Christians within the church or were on its fringes at that time yet who join hands with the Sadducees and the pagan philosophers to deny the teaching of the resurrection of the body. They considered the soul more important than the body and denied that Christ had real flesh (body), before or after his death and resurrection. In chapter 3, he chides them (whom he calls heretics) for being influenced by and following the pagans in denying the resurrection of the flesh. He calls them to base their beliefs on the Scriptures alone:

> But when they say, "What has undergone death is dead," and, "Enjoy life whilst you live," and, "After death all things come to an end, even death itself;" then I must remember both that "the heart of man is ashes," according to the estimate of God, and that the very "wisdom of the world is foolishness," (as the inspired word) pronounces it to be. Then, if even the heretic seeks refuge in the depraved thoughts of the vulgar, or the imaginations of the world, I must say to him: Part company with the heathen, O heretic! for although you are all agreed in imagining a God, yet while you do so in the name of Christ, so long as you deem yourself a Christian, you are a different man from a heathen: give him back his own views of things, since he does not himself learn from yours. Why lean upon a blind guide, if you have eyes of

---

46. Ibid., 545 (emphasis added).

your own? Why be clothed by one who is naked, if you have put on Christ? Why use the shield of another, when the apostle gives you armour of your own? *It would be better for him to learn from you to acknowledge the resurrection of the flesh, than for you from him to deny it*; because if Christians must needs deny it, it would be sufficient if they did so from their own knowledge, without any instruction from the ignorant multitude. *He, therefore, will not be a Christian who shall deny this doctrine which is confessed by Christians; denying it, moreover, on grounds which are adopted by a man who is not a Christian. Take away, indeed, from the heretics the wisdom which they share with the heathen, and let them support their inquiries from the Scriptures alone: they will then be unable to keep their ground.*[47]

Tertullian continues to argue in chapter 6, like other Apologists, that the excellence of flesh should be judged based on the greatness of its Creator God rather than the lowliness of its materials and reminds that even the Word (Christ) who was God became flesh.[48] In chapter 10, he notes, that although the Apostle Paul disparages the flesh in some of his statements, "yet in these and similar assertions which he makes, it is not the *substance* of the flesh, but its *actions*, which are censured."[49] In chapters 14–17, he argues that the body needs to be reunited with the soul to face the final judgment as they took part in actions together in this life and so must be rewarded or punished together in the end in the final judgment.[50]

Tertullian continues again to counter the heretics in chapter 18 that the Scriptures assert the resurrection of the body and not just the soul. In chapter 19, he points out that the heretics interpret the phrase "the resurrection of the dead" as a moral change in this life and some even think it means the escape of the soul from the body itself.[51] In chapter 20, he challenges their figurative interpretations and contends that, "But, in truth, all are not figures, but there are also literal statements; nor are all shadows, but there are bodies too: so that we have prophecies about the Lord Himself even, which are clearer than

---

47. Ibid., 547 (emphasis added).
48. Ibid., 549–550.
49. Ibid., 552. In this connection, Wright (*Resurrection of the Son of God*, 511) comments, "We see here, as in Irenaeus, that some were starting to quote Paul in a direction Paul himself rules out."
50. Tertullian, "Writings of Tertullian," 554–557.
51. Ibid., 557–559.

the day. For it was not figuratively that the Virgin conceived in her womb; nor in a trope did she bear Emmanuel, that is, Jesus, God with us" and so the figurative sense is based on literal reality.[52] In chapter 21, Tertullian argues the resurrection of the dead is not a figurative sense of something else and further notes the improbability of its figurative sense since that would not persuade non-Christians to accept the Christian faith,

> Then arises the improbability that the very mystery on which our trust wholly rests, on which also our instruction entirely depends, should have the appearance of being ambiguously announced and obscurely propounded, inasmuch as the hope of the resurrection, unless it be clearly set forth on the sides both of punishment and reward, would fail to persuade any to embrace a religion like ours, exposed as it is to public detestation and the imputation of hostility to others.[53]

In chapter 22, he argues that the Scriptures forbid us to claim that resurrection has already taken place or that it occurs immediately at death since it only happens at the end of the world at the Day of the Lord and that is still in the future. He ridicules heretics: "*He*, of course, has already quitted the grave of his own corpse – although he is even now liable to fevers and ulcers; he, too, has already trodden down his enemies – although he has even now to struggle with the powers of the world . . . he is already a king – although he even now owes to Caesar the things which are Caesar's."[54]

From chapter 23 onwards Tertullian deals with Scriptural passages from Pauline letters and others of the New Testament to show that even though some passages refer to a present spiritual resurrection of believers (in the mind), still they point forward to a future bodily resurrection when Christ will return. He looks at Ezekiel 37 and other related Old Testament passages in chapters 28–31, and then turns to Jesus' teachings and works in chapters 33–38. He shows that these passages all point to a resurrection of the body at the end and not simply a new life for the soul. In chapters 39–55, he continues to deal with relevant passages from Acts and Paul to show that it is the evil deed of the flesh that is condemned and not its substance. In chapter 51, he argues that Jesus is in heaven now, in God's right hand, in "flesh and blood," as "man yet God," which guarantees that there is going to be a bodily

---

52. Ibid., 559.
53. Ibid., 560.
54. Ibid., 561.

resurrection.⁵⁵ Of course the body will change to become incorruptible but that does not mean destruction of the substance, "the substance *of the flesh* will still be preserved safe."⁵⁶

The last judgment and its awards can only be possible with the identity of the raised body with the present one and the bodies will be perfectly restored in the resurrection so that the believers will enjoy everlasting joy and peace.⁵⁷ According to Tertullian (chapters 59–60), our essential physical identity and all the basic characteristics of our bodies will be retained and our humanity will be preserved unimpaired. This is because it is God's design to keep our body and soul together at the resurrection for his judgment so that, "they will be yet preserved for judgment, 'that every one may receive the things done in his body.' For the judgment-seat of God requires that man be kept entire."⁵⁸

Therefore, Tertullian follows the broad New Testament teachings of bodily resurrection and correctly interprets Paul on this, as opposed to those who interpreted Paul in terms of Gnosticism. N. T. Wright, citing Bynum, notes this about the father of Latin theology, "He is at this point, in fact, a close ally of one of the great fathers of Greek theology, Irenaeus, bishop of Lyons for the last two decades of the second century. The two of them, in complementary ways, brought together 'an extravagantly materialistic notion of the resurrection body' and an equivalent emphasis, too, on 'radical change.'"⁵⁹ Next, we will study Irenaeus.

Irenaeus (ca. 130–200)⁶⁰ joined as a presbyter with Pothnius, the first bishop of Lyons, as both of them were fellow students under Polycarp, bishop of Smyrna. When the persecution of 177 broke out Irenaeus was sent to Rome, but came back to Lyons to find out that Pothnius had died as a martyr during the persecution. Irenaeus then succeeded Pothnius as the bishop of Lyons.⁶¹ N. T. Wright's comment below is illuminating if we relate Irenaeus' works correctly to today's pluralistic contexts:

> Thus when he wrote about the heresies he observed in and alongside the church, not least to do with death and the Christian hope, these were not merely ideas to play with; nor were they,

---

55. Ibid., 579, 584.
56. Ibid., 588.
57. Ibid., 589–590.
58. Ibid., 591–594.
59. Wright, *Resurrection of the Son of God*, 513; Bynum, *Resurrection of the Body*, 38.
60. Frend (*Rise of Christianity*, 244) and Wright (*Resurrection of the Son of God*, 513); Roberts and Donaldson (*Ante-Nicene Fathers*, vol. 1, 309) CE 120–202.
61. Roberts and Donaldson, *Ante-Nicene Fathers*, vol. 1, 309.

as is sometimes suggested, ideas in the service of a comfortable, bourgeois church existence. For Irenaeus, theology and exegesis were part of the task of equipping the church for its dangerous and difficult witness against both pagan empire and pagan culture. The views he attacked were, in his view, ways of getting off the hook, ways of avoiding the real challenge of the gospel at every level.[62]

As soon as he began his ministry as the bishop of Lyons, Irenaeus faced the onslaught of false teachings of the Valentinian Gnostic movement and responded with his five books *Against Heresies* (ca. 180–185) which also "provide the classic statement of orthodoxy in the primitive Greek-speaking church."[63] Roberts and Donaldson summarize the contents of the five books of Irenaeus' *Against Heresies*:

> The *first* of these contains a minute description of the tenets of the various heretical sects, with occasional brief remarks in illustration of their absurdity, and in confirmation of the truth to which they were opposed. In his *second* book, Irenaeus proceeds to a more complete demolition of those heresies which he has already explained, and argues at great length against them, *on grounds principally of reason. The three remaining books set forth more directly the true doctrines of revelation,* as being in utter antagonism to the views held by the Gnostic teachers. *In the course of this argument, many passages of Scripture are quoted and commented on; many interesting statements are made, bearing on the rule of faith; and much important light is shed on the doctrines, held, as well as the practices observed, by the Church of the second century.*[64]

---

62. Wright, *Resurrection of the Son of God*, 513. Cf. Ibid., 549.

63. Frend, *Rise of Christianity*, 244. Roberts and Donaldson (*Ante-Nicene Fathers*, vol. 1, 309) point out the ancient Greek Church's contribution to Rome: "But let it be noted here, that, so far from being 'the mother and mistress' of even the Western Churches, Rome herself is a mission of the Greeks; Southern Gaul is evangelized from Asia Minor, and Lyons checks the heretical tendencies of the Bishop at Rome. Ante-Nicene Christianity, and indeed the Church herself, appears in Greek costume which lasts through the synodical period; and Latin Christianity, when it begins to appear, is African, and not Roman. It is strange that those who have recorded this great historical fact have so little perceived its bearings upon Roman pretensions in the Middle Ages and modern times."

64. Roberts and Donaldson, *Ante-Nicene Fathers*, vol. 1, 311 (emphasis added).

For Irenaeus, in the end, Christianity is based on revelation and the fact that "the Bible alone had authority" and provides theological proofs to refute false doctrines.[65]

In Book II chapter 29 of *Against Heresies*, Irenaeus refutes heretical views about the final destiny of soul and body, and notes the contradictions of these views in 29:1,

> For . . . when they declare that like will be gathered to like, spiritual things to spiritual, while material things continue among those that are material, they do in fact contradict themselves, inasmuch as they no longer maintain that souls pass, on account of their nature, into the intermediate place to those substances which are similar to themselves, but [that they do so] on account of the deeds done [in the body], since they affirm that those of the righteous do pass [into that abode], but those of the impious continue in the fire.[66]

But Irenaeus like Tertullian continues in Book II chapter 29:2 to show that God will raise the bodies at the end for judgment and both body and soul will be joined together for recompense:

> Either, therefore, all souls will of necessity pass into the intermediate place, and there will never be a judgment; or bodies, too, which have participated in righteousness, will attain to the place of enjoyment, along with the souls which have in like manner participated, if indeed righteousness is powerful enough to bring thither those substances which have participated in it. And then the doctrine concerning the resurrection of bodies which we believe, will emerge true and certain [from their system]; since, [as we hold,] God, when He resuscitates our mortal bodies which preserved righteousness, will render them incorruptible and immortal.[67]

---

65. Frend, *Rise of Christianity*, 244–245.
66. Irenaeus, "Irenaeus against Heresies," in *The Ante-Nicene Fathers: Translations of the Writings of the Fathers down to A.D. 325*, vol. 1, eds. and trans. A. Roberts and J. Donaldson, Reprint (Grand Rapids, MI: Eerdmans, 1979), 402.
67. Ibid., 403.

In Book II chapter 33, Irenaeus points out the absurdity of the pagan teaching of transmigration[68] of souls as the souls do not remember anything that happened in their previous state of existence and argues that,

> For if they were sent forth with this object, that they should have experience of every kind of action, they must of necessity retain a remembrance of those things which have been previously accomplished, that they might fill up those in which they were still deficient, and not by always hovering, without intermission, round the same pursuits, spend their labour wretchedly in vain . . . and especially as they came [into the world] for this very purpose.[69]

In Book II chapter 33:5, he argues that God does not lack resources to bestow on each individual body its own distinct soul but rather, in his appropriate time, he will do exactly that and reward the righteous and punish the unrighteous:

> And therefore, when the number [fixed upon] is completed, [that number] which He had predetermined in His own counsel, all those who have been enrolled for life [eternal] shall rise again, having their own bodies, and having also their own souls, and their own spirits, in which they had pleased God. Those, on the other hand, who are worthy of punishment, shall go away into it, they too having their own souls and their own bodies, in which they stood apart from the grace of God. Both classes shall then cease from any longer begetting and being begotten, from marrying and being given in marriage; so that the number of mankind, corresponding to the fore-ordination of God, being completed, may fully realize the scheme formed by the Father.[70]

In Book II chapter 34:1, Irenaeus refers to Christ's teaching in Luke 16, the story of the rich man and Lazarus, and shows that after death the disembodied souls continue to exist in the intermediate state without transmigrating to other bodies. These souls remember the deeds done in embodied state before

---

68. Roberts and Donaldson (*Ante-Nicene Fathers*, vol. 1, 410, footnote 1) and Frend (*Rise of Christianity*, 244) point out that Irenaeus was wrong in Book II 33:2 in his assertion that Plato originated the doctrine of metempsychosis, probably confusing him with Pythagoras.

69. Irenaeus, "Irenaeus against Heresies,"409.

70. Ibid., 411. Wright (*Resurrection of the Son of God*, 514) comments on this that Irenaeus is drawing on Jesus' response to the Sadducees that the life after death is a different sort of life than the present one with births and marriages.

death, recognizing each other after death in that intermediate state and "that each class [of souls] receives a habitation such as it has deserved, even before the judgment."[71] Irenaeus points out in Book II chapter 34:4 that "the soul herself is not life, but partakes in that life bestowed upon her by God". Similarly, "When God ... bestows life and perpetual duration, it comes to pass that even souls which did not previously exist should henceforth endure [for ever], since God has both willed that they should exist, and should continue in existence."[72]

After dealing with the issues of who is the true God and how the church can know for certain that she is faithful to the original message in Books III and IV of *Against Heresies*, Irenaeus again deals with the issue of the resurrection, this time extensively, in Book V.[73] In Book V chapter 3, he argues that the power and glory of God will be manifest in the weakness of the human flesh just as the body will participate in the resurrection and immortality. God will confer upon it the enjoyment of immortality just as he grants it the present short life in common with the soul.[74] In Book V chapter 4, Irenaeus contends that those who invented another "God the Father," besides the Creator of this world, are deceived as they show this "God the Father" to be feeble and useless or else envious and malignant, unable or unwilling to grant external life to our physical bodies to raise them up.[75]

In Book V chapter 5, Irenaeus points out that, the long earthly life of the ancients, the translation of Enoch and of Elijah with their own physical bodies, and the preservation of Jonah and Shadrach, Meshach, and Abednego in the midst of extreme danger, are clear evidences that nothing is impossible for God and that he can raise up our physical bodies to eternal life.[76] In Book V chapter 6, he writes, "Now the soul and the spirit are certainly a *part* of the man, but certainly not *the* man; for the perfect man consists in the commingling and the union of the soul receiving the spirit of the Father, and the admixture of that fleshly nature which was moulded after the image of God." Those whom the Apostle Paul refers to as "spiritual" are spiritual "because they partake of the Spirit, and not because their flesh has been

---

71. Irenaeus, "Irenaeus against Heresies,"411.
72. Ibid., 412.
73. Wright, *Resurrection of the Son of God*, 514.
74. Irenaeus, "Irenaeus against Heresies," 529.
75. Ibid., 530.
76. Ibid., 530–531.

stripped off and taken away" or they became purely spiritual without the body.[77]

In Book V chapter 7, he writes just as Christ rose in human flesh, so we too will rise since the resurrection promised to us is not referred to spirits naturally immortal but to physical bodies naturally mortal.[78] In Book V chapter 9, Irenaeus argues that the heretics misuse the Apostle Paul's words in 1 Corinthians 15:50 "flesh and blood cannot inherit the kingdom of God." This is because the heretics claim that Paul means God's handiwork (or material creation) is not saved. Nevertheless, for Irenaeus, Paul here means those people (flesh and blood) who do not have in themselves the Spirit of God which alone saves and forms eternal life.[79] In Book V chapter 13, Irenaeus shows the fact that Christ raised Lazarus and the daughter of Jairus, is ample proof of future bodily resurrection:

> As, therefore, those who were healed were made whole in those members which had in times past been afflicted; and the dead rose in the identical bodies, their limbs and bodies receiving health, and that life which was granted by the Lord, who prefigures eternal things by temporal, and shows that it is He who is Himself able to extend both healing and life to His handiwork, that His words concerning its [future] resurrection may also be believed; so also at the end, when the Lord utters His voice "by the last trumpet," the dead shall be raised, as He Himself declares: "The hour shall come, in which all the dead which are in the tombs shall hear the voice of the Son of man, and shall come forth; those that have done good to the resurrection of life, and those that have done evil to the resurrection of judgment."[80]

Thus by referring to, "Flesh and blood cannot inherit the kingdom of God" the heretics are "taking two expressions of Paul's, without having perceived the apostle's meaning, or examined critically the force of the terms, but keeping fast hold of the mere expressions by themselves, they die in consequence of their influence . . . overturning as far as in them lies the entire dispensation of God."[81] Irenaeus argues further from 1 Corinthians 15 that, "For then,

---

77. Ibid., 531–532.
78. Ibid., 532–533.
79. Ibid., 534–535.
80. Irenaeus, "Irenaeus against Heresies," 539.
81. Ibid., 540.

indeed, shall death be truly vanquished, when that flesh which is held down by it shall go forth from under its dominion" and also, from Philippians 3:29ff and 2 Corinthians 5:4, that the body which is mortal will be swallowed up with life.[82]

In Book V chapter 31, again the preservation of human physical bodies is confirmed by the resurrection and ascension of Christ and that after physical death the souls of the believers are and will be in a state of expectation during the intermediate period until that time when they receive their perfect and consummated glory.[83] Thus, for Irenaeus, a bodily resurrection will take place in a renewed world and it is not merely a continual existence of the immortal soul in heaven. Wright notes,

> But there is no question of the position he [Irenaeus] took, or of the basic position he was most concerned to oppose. *The bodily resurrection, both of Jesus and of humans in the future, was not an isolated doctrine for Irenaeus.* It was linked in a thousand ways to the doctrines of the good creator, of the Word as truly incarnate, and the church and its canonical scriptures as the repositories of the true teaching of Jesus – in other words, to the central themes of his work.[84]

In summary, Irenaeus, like his predecessors, believed in the bodily resurrection of Jesus and the future resurrection of believers and unbelievers alike at the return of Jesus. While the believers will enjoy eternal life with God, the unbelievers will be in dire trouble.

The Destiny of Unbelievers after Death

In his *Apology I* chapter 8, the Apologist Justin Martyr (ca. 100–165), who ministered as an evangelist in a pluralistic context, even uses Plato's reference to punishment of the wicked to persuade his hearers that Christ will punish the wicked with *everlasting punishment* and not just for a period of a thousand years as Plato says:

> This, then, to speak shortly, is what we expect and have learned from Christ, and teach. And Plato, in like manner, used to say that Rhadamanthus and Minos would punish the wicked who

---

82. Ibid.
83. Ibid., 560.
84. Wright, *Resurrection of the Son of God*, 517 (emphasis added).

> came before them; and we say that the same thing will be done, but at the hand of Christ, and *upon the wicked in the same bodies united again to their spirits which are now to undergo everlasting punishment; and not only, as Plato said, for a period of a thousand years.*[85]

Justin mentions *everlasting punishment* again, in *Apology I* chapter 12, to show why those who believe in this view are careful about their actions and help promote peace:

> And more than all other men are we your helpers and allies in promoting peace, seeing that we hold this view, that it is alike impossible for the wicked, the covetous, the conspirator, and for the virtuous, to escape the notice of God, and that each man goes to everlasting punishment or salvation according to the value of his actions. For if all men knew this, no one would choose wickedness even for a little, knowing that he goes to the everlasting punishment of fire; but would by all means restrain himself, and adorn himself with virtue, that he might obtain the good gifts of God, and escape the punishments.[86]

In *Apology I* chapter 16, he refers to Jesus' sayings in the gospels of Matthew and Luke that there will be wailing and gnashing of teeth for the wicked in the everlasting fire:

> And many will say unto Me, Lord, Lord, have we not eaten and drunk in Thy name, and done wonders? And then will I say unto them, *Depart from Me, ye workers of iniquity*. Then shall there be *wailing and gnashing of teeth*, when the righteous shall shine as the sun, and *the wicked are sent into everlasting fire*.[87]

In *Apology I* chapter 18, again he speaks about eternal punishment for the wicked: "But since sensation remains to all who have ever lived, and *eternal punishment is laid up (i.e., for the wicked)*, see that ye neglect not to be convinced, and to hold as your belief, that these things are true."[88] In *Apology I* chapter 19, Justin Martyr refers to Jesus' saying about hell for the wicked:

---

85. Justin, "Writings of Justin," 165 (emphasis added).
86. Ibid., 166.
87. Ibid., 168 (emphasis added).
88. Ibid., 169 (emphasis added).

"Fear not them that kill you, and after that can do no more; but fear Him who after death is able to cast both soul and body into hell." And hell is a place where those are to be punished who have lived wickedly, and who do not believe that those things which God has taught us by Christ will come to pass.[89]

In *Apology I* chapter 45, Justin Martyr says, "all who unjustly hate us, and do not repent, brings eternal punishment by fire."[90] In *Apology I* chapter 52, Justin repeats what kind of punishment it will be for the wicked:

> He shall come from heaven with glory, accompanied by His angelic host, when also He shall raise the bodies of all men who have lived, and shall clothe those of the worthy with immortality, and *shall send those of the wicked, endued with eternal sensibility, into everlasting fire with the wicked devils*. And that these things also have been foretold as yet to be . . . And in *what kind of sensation and punishment the wicked are to be*, hear from what was said in like manner with reference to this; it is as follows: *"Their worm shall not rest, and their fire shall not be quenched;" and then shall they repent, when it profits them not.*[91]

In all of these references, Justin Martyr is consistent with the New Testament and repeatedly affirms the truth of the everlasting punishment. Justin has one statement in *Apology II* chapter 7:1 in which he refers to God delaying the final "destruction of the whole world, by which the wicked angels and demons and men shall cease to exist." This is a single reference compared to all the other references from him that support everlasting punishment. The intent of this passage is to show why the present world is being preserved by God rather than to show how long the punishment will last after God's judgment. Justin follows this through by comparing the final judgment with the flood during Noah's time with the words, "but the fire of judgment would descend and utterly dissolve all things, even as formerly the flood left no one but him only with his family who is by us called Noah, and by you Deucalion."[92]

However, in chapter 5 of Justin's *Dialogue with Trypho*, in his discussion with Trypho the Jew, Justin points out that it is the Platonists who claim that the soul is immortal and then argues:

---

89. Ibid.
90. Ibid., 178.
91. Ibid., 180 (emphasis added).
92. Ibid., 190.

> "But I do not say, indeed, that all souls die; for that were truly a piece of good fortune to the evil. What then? *The souls of the pious remain in a better place, while those of the unjust and wicked are in a worse, waiting for the time of judgment. Thus some which have appeared worthy of God never die; but others are punished so long as God wills them to exist and to be punished.*
>
> . . . *For those things which exist after God, or shall at any time exist, these have the nature of decay, and are such as may be blotted out and cease to exist;* for God alone is unbegotten and incorruptible, and therefore He is God, but all other things after Him are created and corruptible. *For this reason souls both die and are punished: since, if they were unbegotten, they would neither sin, nor be filled with folly, nor be cowardly.*[93]

Here Justin is countering the 'Platonists' idea of immortality of all souls. According to ACUTE, Justin's student, Tatian, later argued against these Platonists to prove that all souls are mortal and subject to death.[94] Contrary to the Platonists, the Bible does not say that souls by nature are immortal, only that Christ or God is immortal (1 Tim 6:16). However, it is plausible that here Justin is giving a sequence for the wicked, that they must die, followed by punishment.

Furthermore, in *Dialogue with Trypho*, Justin refers to the everlasting punishment a couple of times which would suggest that he believed in everlasting punishment for unbelievers.[95] For example, in chapter 44 of *Dialogue with Trypho*, he notes:

---

93. Ibid., 197 (emphasis added).
94. ACUTE, *Nature of Hell*, 61.
95. It is noteworthy that in Chap. 82 of *Dialogue with Trypho*, following the Old Testament and Jesus Christ, Justin responds to his contemporary false theology: "And just as there were false prophets contemporaneous with your holy prophets, so are there now many false teachers amongst us, of whom our Lord forewarned us to beware; so that in no respect are we deficient, since we know that He foreknew all that would happen to us after His resurrection from the dead and ascension to heaven. For He said we would be put to death, and hated for His name's sake; and *that many false prophets and false Christs would appear in His name, and deceive many*: and so has it come about. *For many have taught godless, blasphemous, and unholy doctrines, forging them in His name; have taught, too, and even yet are teaching, those things which proceed from the unclean spirit of the devil, and which were put into their hearts. Therefore we are most anxious that you be persuaded not to be misled by such persons*, since we know that every one who can speak the truth, and yet speaks it not, shall be judged by God, as God testified by Ezekiel, when He said, 'I have made thee a watchman to the house of Judah. If the sinner sin, and thou warn him not, he himself shall die in his sin; but his blood will I require at thine hand. But if thou warn him, thou shalt be innocent.' And on this account we are, through fear, very earnest in desiring to converse [with men] according to the Scriptures, but not from

And in Isaiah . . . He spake thus: "The Lord God said, they shall both go forth and look on the members [of the bodies] of the men that have transgressed. *For their worm shall not die, and their fire shall not be quenched, and they shall be a gazing-stock to all flesh.*" So that it becomes you to eradicate this hope from your souls, and hasten to know in what way forgiveness of sins, and a hope of inheriting the promised good things, shall be yours. But there is no other [way] than this,-to become acquainted with this Christ, to be washed in the fountain spoken of by Isaiah for the remission of sins.[96]

Again, in chapter 45 of *Dialogue with Trypho*, he notes about unceasing punishment:

> by this dispensation, the serpent that sinned from the beginning, and the angels like him, may be destroyed, and that death may be contemned, and for ever quit, at the second coming of the Christ Himself, those who believe in Him and live acceptably, – and be no more: *when some are sent to be punished unceasingly into judgment and condemnation of fire*; but others shall exist in freedom from suffering, from corruption, and from grief, and in immortality.[97]

I find enough evidence, therefore, in Justin's *Dialogue with Trypho* to conclude that he believed in everlasting punishment for the unbelievers and that his true intentions were in line with the New Testament teachings.

Next, Athenagoras in his *Apology* chapter 31, expresses his belief that in a "State-after-Death," God is going to judge and punish some, and comments concerning the final destiny of believers and unbelievers:

> *For if we believed that we should live only the present life, then we might be suspected of sinning, through being enslaved to flesh and blood, or overmastered by gain or carnal desire; but since we know that God is witness to what we think and what we say both by*

---

love of money, or of glory, or of pleasure. For no man can convict us of any of these [vices]. No more do we wish to live like the rulers of your people, whom God reproaches when He says, 'Your rulers are companions of thieves, lovers of bribes, followers of the rewards.' Now, if you know certain amongst us to be of this sort, do not for their sakes blaspheme the Scriptures and Christ, and do not assiduously strive to give falsified interpretations" (Justin, "Writings of Justin," 240).

96. Justin, "Writings of Justin," 217 (emphasis added).
97. Ibid. (Emphasis added).

> *night and by day, and that He, being Himself light, sees all things in our heart, we are persuaded that when we are removed from the present life we shall live another life*, better than the present one, and heavenly, not earthly (since we shall abide near God, and with God, free from all change or suffering in the soul, not as flesh, even though we shall have flesh, but as heavenly spirit), or, *falling with the rest, a worse one and in fire; for God has not made us as sheep or beasts of burden, a mere by-work, and that we should perish and be annihilated. On these grounds it is not likely that we should wish to do evil, or deliver ourselves over to the great Judge to be punished.*[98]

Athenagoras had begun his argument that, if he believed that there is no existence after death (or when you are dead that's the end), then he might be suspected of sin because then there is no question of being judged after death. Nevertheless, because he knows God is watching and will ultimately judge one day (in a "State-after-Death") and punish some, it keeps him from sinning and, instead, he has hope of a life beyond this life. Thus, here Athenagoras is intently arguing against the pagan belief in annihilation at death.

In another Apologist, Minucius Felix's *Octavius*, anti-Christian Caecilus brings arguments against Christians in chapter 5. Questioning their fear of God as their creator or judge, he tries to show that God is not involved with humans because they die and return to dust from whence they came, and by this proposes that this life is all there is or "when you are dead that's the end,"

> what ground is there for religion, for terror and superstitious dread?[99] Man, and every animal which is born, inspired with life, and nourished, is as a voluntary concretion of the elements, into which again man and every animal is divided, resolved, and dissipated. So all things flow back again into their source, and are turned again into themselves, without any artificer, or judge, or creator.[100]

In chapters 10 and 11 of Minucius Felix's *Octavius*, anti-Christian Caecilus argues vehemently against the Christian view of God and his judgment and eternal punishment:

---

98. Athenagoras, "Writings of Athenagoras," 146 (emphasis added).
99. This first line is from G. H. Rendall's translation of Tertullian and Minucius Felix, *Apology: De Spectaculis. Octavius*, 325.
100. Minucius, "Octavius of Minucius Felix," 175.

> But the Christians, moreover, what wonders, what monstrosities do they feign! – that *he who is their God*, whom they can neither show nor behold, *inquires diligently into the character of all, the acts of all, and, in fine, into their words and secret thoughts; that he runs about everywhere, and is everywhere present* . . . What! because they threaten conflagration to the whole world, and to the universe itself, with all its stars, are they meditating its destruction? – as if either the eternal order constituted by the divine laws of nature would be disturbed, or the league of all the elements would be broken up, and the heavenly structure dissolved, and that fabric in which it is contained and bound together would be overthrown.
>
> And, not content with this wild opinion, they add to it and associate with it old women's fables: they say that they will rise again after death, and ashes, and dust; and with I know not what confidence, they believe by turns in one another's lies: you would think that they had already lived again . . . Deceived by this error, they promise to themselves, as being good, a blessed and perpetual life after their death; *to others, as being unrighteous, eternal punishment.*[101]

The Christian Octavius firmly responds to these arguments of Caecilus in chapter 34. First, he shows that there is going to be a future judgment and destruction of this world and that even their ancient philosophers support that position:

> Further, in respect of the burning up of the world, it is a vulgar error not to believe either that fire will fall upon it in an unforeseen way, or that the world will be destroyed by it. For who of wise men doubts, who is ignorant, that all things which have had a beginning perish, all things which are made come to an end? [T]he springs shall pass away into the power of fire. The Stoics have a constant belief that . . . all this world will take fire; and the Epicureans have the very same opinion concerning the conflagration of the elements and the destruction of the world. Plato speaks, saying that parts of the world are now inundated, and are now burnt up by alternate changes; and although he says

---

101. Ibid., 178–179 (emphasis added).

that the world itself is constructed perpetual and indissoluble, yet he adds that to God Himself, the only artificer, it is both dissoluble and mortal. Thus it is no wonder if that mass be destroyed by Him by whom it was reared. You observe that philosophers dispute of the same . . . we are saying, not that we are following up their tracks, but that they, from the divine announcements of the prophets, imitated the shadow of the corrupted truth.[102]

Then Octavius, in chapter 34, refers to some who prefer annihilation after death as their punishment instead of resurrection and then punishment:

And I am not ignorant that many, in the consciousness of what they deserve, rather desire than believe that they shall be nothing after death; for they would prefer to be altogether extinguished, rather than to be restored for the purpose of punishment. And their error also is enhanced, both by the liberty granted them in this life, and by God's very great patience, whose judgment, the more tardy it is, is so much the more just.[103]

Yet, by referring to the writings of the learned pagan poets and prophets and by using the natural analogies of lightning in the sky and fires of volcanoes, Octavius continues to argue for the veracity of eternal punishment for the wicked in chapter 35:

And yet men are admonished in the books and poems of the most learned poets of that fiery river, and of the heat flowing in manifold turns from the Stygian marsh, – things which, *prepared for eternal torments*, and known to them by the information of demons and from the oracles of their prophets . . . even king Jupiter himself swears religiously by the parching banks and the black abyss; for, with foreknowledge of the punishment destined to him, with his worshippers, he shudders. *Nor is there either measure or termination to these torments. There the intelligent fire burns the limbs and restores them, feeds on them and nourishes them.* As the fires of the thunderbolts strike upon the bodies, and do not consume them; as the fires of Mount Aetna and of Mount Vesuvius, and of burning where, glow, but are not wasted; so that penal fire is not fed by the waste of those who burn, but

---

102. Ibid., 194.
103. Ibid.

is nourished by the unexhausted eating away of their bodies. But that they who know not God are deservedly tormented as impious, as unrighteous persons, no one except a profane man hesitates to believe, since it is not less wicked to be ignorant of, than to offend the Parent of all, and the Lord of all.[104]

Commenting on Octavius' view on the eternal punishment, Bynum notes that, "Just as there are volcanoes and lightning bolts that burn without consuming, so bodies can perdure through the conflagration that ends the world; they can even survive eternally in the fires of hell . . . what the risen body triumphs over even in hell (if eternal punishment can be called a triumph) is feeding or being consumed by fire."[105] Thus, for Minucius Felix's *Octavius*, the unbelievers do not have the option of annihilation as their ultimate destiny, but a conscious eternal torment in the fires of hell after their bodily resurrection.

In the writings of Tertullian (ca. 160–225), we find "one of the earliest surviving accounts of the view" of eternal conscious punishment for the unbelievers in hell.[106] In chapter 18 of his *Apology*, Tertullian makes a short remark on the final destiny of unbelievers in the fire that is unending by the hand of God the Judge,

> seeing that, *when this age reaches its full end, He will sit as Judge*, and His worshippers He will repay with life eternal, and *the profane He will condemn to fire as perpetual and unceasing; for the dead every man of them from the beginning, shall be raised, refashioned and reviewed, that their deserts of either kind, good or evil, may be adjudged.* Yes! We too in our day laughed at this. We are from among yourselves. Christians are made, not born (Emphasis mine).[107]

However, we find in his work on *The Resurrection of the Flesh*, in chapter 35, Tertullian responds more at length to those who use Jesus' reference to destruction of body and soul in hell in Matthew 10:28 to propose annihilation rather than eternal conscious punishment for the unbelievers:

---

104. Ibid., 195 (emphasis added).
105. Bynum, *Resurrection of the Body*, 35.
106. ACUTE, *Nature of Hell*, 53.
107. Quote from G. H. Rendall's translation of Tertullian and Minucius Felix, *Apology: De Spectaculis. Octavius.* 91; for Roberts and Donaldson's translation see vol. 3 of *The Ante-Nicene Fathers*, 32.

> If, therefore, any one shall violently suppose that the destruction of the soul and the flesh in hell amounts to a final annihilation of the two substances, and not to their penal treatment (as if they were to be consumed, not punished), let him recollect that the fire of hell is eternal – expressly announced as an everlasting penalty; and let him then admit that it is from this circumstance that this never-ending "killing" is more formidable than a merely human murder, which is only temporal.[108]

Tertullian goes on to show that the punishment of annihilation at some point for unbelievers makes the final bodily resurrection of the unbelievers futile:

> Since, then, the body after the resurrection has to be killed by God in hell along with the soul, we surely have sufficient information in this fact respecting both the issues *which await it*, namely the resurrection of the flesh, and its eternal "killing." Else it would be most absurd if the flesh should be raised up and destined to "the killing in hell," in order to be put an end to, when it might suffer such an annihilation (more directly) if not raised again at all. A pretty paradox, to be sure, that an essence must be refitted with life, in order that it may receive that annihilation which has already in fact accrued to it![109]

Next, Irenaeus (ca. 130–200) in his *Against Heresies* Book II chapter 32:1 quotes Christ's teachings about the final end of the righteous and the unrighteous and points to everlasting punishment for the unrighteous:

> And, again, if there were really no such thing as good and evil, but certain things were deemed righteous, and certain others unrighteous, in human opinion only, He never would have expressed Himself thus in His teaching: "The righteous shall shine forth as the sun in the kingdom of their Father;" but *He shall send the unrighteous, and those who do not the works of righteousness,* "into everlasting fire, where their worm shall not die, and the fire shall not be quenched."[110]

In Book II chapter 33:5, Irenaeus argues that God will bestow to each individual body its own soul at the final resurrection and reward the righteous

---

108. Tertullian, "Writings of Tertullian," 570.
109. Ibid., 571.
110. Irenaeus, "Irenaeus against Heresies," 408 (emphasis added).

with eternal life. God also will punish the unrighteous along with their soul and body without the possibility of marriage or procreation, implying the eternality of existence in punishment:

> And therefore, when the number [fixed upon] is completed, [that number] which He had predetermined in His own counsel, all those who have been enrolled for life [eternal] shall rise again, having their own bodies, and having also their own souls, and their own spirits, in which they had pleased God. *Those, on the other hand, who are worthy of punishment, shall go away into it, they too having their own souls and their own bodies, in which they stood apart from the grace of God.* Both classes shall then cease from any longer begetting and being begotten, from marrying and being given in marriage; so that the number of mankind, corresponding to the fore-ordination of God, being completed, may fully realize the scheme formed by the Father.[111]

Thus, like Tertullian, Irenaeus follows the New Testament teaching of conscious eternal punishment for the unbelievers after the Parousia and the final resurrection.

Finally, we must give a brief overview of the great thinker and theologian Origen (ca. 185–254) of Alexandria. Origen, along with Clement of the same city, seems to have borrowed more from some kind of Platonic philosophy than others. In order to contextualize his theology in relation to Platonic philosophy, he was judged to have gone too far. Because of this the church disapproved of him and tended to discount him. Wright notes that, "His doctrine of *apokatastasis*, a restoration or return of all things to their place of primal origin [very much akin to Hindu-Buddhist concept of the ultimate end], was so strong that he even seems to have held that the devil would be saved. [Thus] following severe attacks by Augustine, he was condemned by the Council of Constantinople in AD 543."[112] ACUTE summarizes this doctrine:

> Origen's restitutionism proposed that human souls pre-existed their earthly form, had fallen from a heavenly realm into an earthly existence as part of their punishment, and would ultimately be released into eternal bliss. Although he accepted that this process would take some time, he saw it unfolding

---

111. Ibid., 411 (emphasis added).
112. Wright, *Resurrection of the Son of God*, 518–519.

through a succession of lives experienced in different universes. Lacking biblical support for this doctrine, Origen looked to Neoplatonist philosophy, and its conviction that the soul is the essential element of human anthropology. From this point of view, such a succession of lives seemed plausible. Although it is unclear whether Origen believed on these grounds that there would be more than one *incarnation* for human beings, this is at least a plausible inference to be drawn from his theology.[113]

Bynum thinks that Origen tried to tread "a middle way between . . . Jews, millenarian Christians, and pagans who [he thought] understood bodily resurrection as the reanimation of dead flesh and . . . Gnostics and Hellenists who [he thought] denied any kind of ultimate reality either to resurrection or to body."[114] Origen also believed that our body in heaven will be "a spiritual and luminous one" and not the earthly body as this body changes everyday like a river and is in a continual flux.[115] But as far as final punishment of the unrighteous is concerned, Daley points out that for both Origen and Clement of Alexandria "all punishment is ultimately medicinal and educational" and they both had "strong conviction that all human souls will ultimately be saved, and will be united to God forever in loving contemplation."[116] Thus, in essence, Origen was a Universalist and to him it would not, in the final analysis, matter whether one is a believer, since all will be saved in the end and will enjoy eternal bliss. However, in our study of all the other early church perspectives, we found that the overwhelming consensus is that everlasting conscious punishment awaits unrighteous unbelievers at the final judgment when Christ comes again.

Summary and Implications

To sum it up, in this selective study of the *Apologists*' perspectives about "State-after-Death," we found continuity of beliefs in the early church with what both the Old Testament and the New Testament teach. We found that

---

113. ACUTE, *Nature of Hell*, 12. Daley (*The Hope of the Early Church* [Cambridge, UK: Cambridge University Press, 1991], 58), "Although Origen . . . regarded the reincarnation of souls . . . a theoretical possibility . . . endless cycle of alternating falls and redemptions is almost certainly foreign to his thought."
114. Bynum, *Resurrection of the Body*, 64.
115. Ibid.
116. Daley, *Hope of the Early Church*, 58.

the *Apologists* were confronted with hostile, Platonic and Gnostic doctrines of *immortality,* ideas of *transmigration of soul* and other pagan views including total annihilation at death. There was also strong opposition from Jewish groups such as Sadducees and others in the pluralistic contexts of the early church. With all of this, these stalwarts of Christian faith affirmed the biblical teaching of future bodily resurrection of the dead and subsequent eternal life for believers. The early church Fathers argued for the unity of body and soul as an intrinsic characteristic of humans who are bearers of God's image.

As opposed to the pagan understanding of the duality of material body and immaterial pre-existent soul and the consequent disparagement of the material body and the world, the Apologists confessed that God created humankind as a unity. They affirmed that the body needs to be reunited with the soul at the final judgment both for reward and punishment. We also found there was consensus that everlasting conscious punishment awaits unbelievers at the final judgment when Christ returns and some, like Tertullian, even argued that the punishment of annihilation at some point after death makes the final bodily resurrection of the unbelievers futile. However, Origen's teaching was an exception to that overall rule.

Conclusions

We have explored here important components of an alternative model (compared to John Hick) for a global Christian theology of "State-after-Death." We did this by investigating three non-Christian religious perspectives, reviewing current scholars, looking into biblical insights and gathering perspectives from the early church Fathers. In the Introduction, we noted that urban societies are increasingly multi-cultural and multi-religious, concluding that the Christian church can no longer avoid interacting with people who hold other religious perspectives. We saw that "State-after-Death" is a critical topic in these other faiths as well as a major component of God's mission to rescue humankind from a hopeless destiny, calling them to eternal life as communicated in the Bible. Hence, what happens at and after death is an important and fruitful area of conversation with people of other faiths.

We have learned from experience and from such thinkers as Paul D. Devanandan and others that dialogue is a first step for any kind of communication of the gospel in pluralistic contexts. This dialogue needs to occur in interpersonal conversations rather than in large public events. John Hick and Hans Küng served well in taking global pluralistic contexts seriously, respecting "other" religions and allowing them to inform the conversation in pluralistic contexts, although they proved less than exemplary through their lack of adherence to the Scriptures. Indeed, God's missionary people, the Christian church, will need to engage in conversation with people of other faiths and learn more about their beliefs in order to articulate the gospel in relation to other faiths. However, we recognize, as Stephen Neill showed, that Christians do not easily find partners in dialogue from other faiths who are sincere, open-minded and willing, and that if such a partner is found, the faith of the Christian will be severely tested, yet purified, modified and strengthened.[1] In this study, we seek to offer some new directions toward a theology of "State-after-Death" which Christians may use to *effectively* communicate the gospel in pluralistic contexts.

To be truly Christian, Christian theology must first and foremost be rooted in the Christian Scripture, which is given to us by special revelation as the unique gospel of Jesus Christ. In our conversation with people of other

---

1. Neill, *Salvation Tomorrow*, 42.

faiths, we must be securely rooted in the Bible, as were Bonhoeffer, Kraemer and Neill, and in contrast to Hick and Küng. In approaching Scripture, I have highlighted the essential three-dimensional hermeneutical model: the priority of authorial intention, the metacritical perspective and the constructive use of biblical narratives in hermeneutics. Any attempt to engage people of other faiths apart from a firm grounding in Scriptures will result in *ineffective* communication of the Christian gospel in pluralistic contexts.

Following are some suggestions and recommendations leading to a missiological approach to "State-after-Death" for the communication of the gospel of Jesus Christ among representatives of Secular, Hindu, and Muslim views. We have found that the universal reality of death makes "State-after-Death" an important topic for discussion among people of other faiths. Interpersonal dialogue is the *first* step for effective communication of the gospel to those of other faiths. Conversations with individuals from the main religious perspectives should explore some of the following points.

First, in order to communicate the gospel effectively to present day Secular Humanists, the primary hurdle is to communicate that something happens after death. The Modern Secular perspective has its roots in Classical Greek philosophy which says that biological life is all there is and when that life ends there is nothing more. The Greco-Roman world during the early church period, had the same perspective which led to a state of hopelessness. As a result they also accepted the so-called contrasting view of "transmigration of souls." Conversation about "State-after-Death" is less threatening and existentially more real to a Secular Humanist than the question of whether or not God exists. Only if people accept the possibility of existence after death can they consider the possibility of some form of accountability for one's life after death to a higher supernatural power (or judgment of God). Yet, God's inevitable judgment is critical to the Christian gospel. Christians should discuss the truth of final judgment and also of God's forgiveness and offer of eternal life through the death and resurrection of Jesus Christ.

One weakness of the Modern Secular no-life-after-death theory is that it provides no hope for a large majority of the human race who do not live this life in comfort. Bonhoeffer points out another weakness of the notion that "death is the final end," in that, no one knows when they are going to die and hence are afraid of death. This perspective can push people to, in frantic defiance, try to get as much as possible out of this life in a short period of time. Such people could destroy their lives before their time. It would be hard for us as Christians to engage in conversation when people are living such fast-paced lives and have no room to think about "State-after-Death." However, when these Secular Humanists fail to squeeze the best out of this life in a short period of time, that may lead to despair. This is where we as Christians have an opportunity for conversation.

Some of those in their hopelessness, may seek an alternative to annihilation in some form of reincarnation with no accountability to God. Instead of a philosophy of despair and denial of death, some Secularists even believe in a general heaven. In such cases, Christians need to be available among them to hold conversations about judgment to come and also about God's forgiveness and offer of eternal life through Jesus Christ. Christians themselves though need to take care that they are rooted in the Christian faith and not swayed by the delusion of this Modern Secular perspective in their day-to-day lives. Aldwinckle has shown how many Christians in the church, influenced by the Modern Secular perspective, promote "an exclusively this-worldly version of the Christian faith" with no thought for "State-after-Death." He rightly argues that it is not a case of "either-or" but "both-and."[2] I would add that it is only when we are truly assured of eternal life in Jesus Christ then we can live this life fearlessly in service for God and his created humanity.

Second, in discussing "State-after-Death" as part of our communication of the gospel to *Hindus, Buddhists and others* who believe in some form of more than one life on earth, the first hurdle would be to persuade them to believe in one life on earth. There is no point in talking about judgment after death and punishment for sins, if they expect to escape judgment and punishment by repetitive cycles of life. Even if they ignore the prospect of death in their day-to-day lives, Hindus and Buddhists do recognize death as an existential reality and admit that their views about "State-after-Death" influence their present living. While Hindus and Buddhists generally find it easy and non-threatening to talk about what they believe may happen after death, Christians must keep in mind that such perspectives of "State-after-Death" are closely related to their views of God as impersonal ultimate Reality. However, they may find talking about what happens after death easier than comparing which view of God or the ultimate Reality is more plausible.

Christians could raise questions with Hindus about exactly what dimension of an individual's human person is subject to the deterministic consequences of *Karma*. Is it only the so-called "subtle body" that faces the consequences of actions from the past life into the next in the cycle of

---

2. Aldwinckle, *Death in the Secular City*, 23.

rebirth? Or, after-death, does the whole being of an individual person face the full consequence of actions done in one's life? Perhaps this is why many urban Hindus, vying to succeed in the fast pace of today, leave little time for practising the three religious ways of escape from the cycle of rebirth. These Hindus have more or less accepted, in practice, the Modern Secular notion that death is the end of all existence. Some serious Hindus and Buddhists may see the cycle of rebirth as a form of judgment and punishment of their deeds (*Karma*) rather than a second chance and may strive to escape that cycle of rebirth. Motivated by this, they will seek some form of salvation by meditation, good deeds or sincere devotion to a personal deity or Buddha. In our conversation, we may be able to persuade them to understand how Jesus Christ has secured our salvation by his death and that we do not have to strive to save ourselves with our own good works but instead trust in Christ's death and resurrection for our salvation.

We ourselves need to be alert that in our conversations we do not shift from *Christocentric* to *Theocentric*, or even to *Ultimate-Reality centered*, as John Hick did. We need to be sure we believe in a "State-after-Death" that leads to eternal life through Jesus Christ in the presence of God who is *personal* and *wholly other* than his creation. Also, by eternal life, we do not mean eternally being merged into some impersonal ultimate Reality. These are important distinctions between Christianity and other faiths.

In our conversation with Hindus and Buddhists who see the many second chances of multiple lives as a better option than the one life on earth of Christian faith, we need to talk about Jesus' own teaching and predictions about resurrection, and the historicity of his own bodily resurrection and his visible ascension to heaven after one life on earth. We need to share not only the good news and promise of eternal life with God for believers according to the Christian gospel but also the judgment of God and consequent punishment if we reject the gospel of Jesus Christ in this life. In the past, some Christians have used this argument effectively: If the Hindu perspective of "State-after-Death" is true, then the Christians have nothing to worry about because they too will be saved in the end. However, if the biblical Christian perspective of "State-after-Death" is true, Christians, Hindus, Buddhists and everyone else need to come to God in fear and trembling, repent of their sins and accept forgiveness through Jesus as their Savior.

Third, since the *Muslim* views of judgment, future resurrection of the dead, and heaven and hell as reward and punishment, are in many ways similar to Jewish and Christian perspectives of "State-after-Death," these themes are less threatening as a start-up conversation with Muslims. Usually the topics of the deity of Jesus Christ, his crucifixion, and the doctrine of the Trinity can be less fruitful in initial conversations. Some Muslims who choose suicide as part of terrorism, believe God will reward them for their "courageous" acts. Their expected "State-after-Death" in paradise appears far better than their present life, so in that sense suicide is not a selfless act.

Muslims, in general, fear the judgment of God and believe their final destiny depends entirely on their individual good works. In conversation, we may challenge their vague assurance of salvation or confidence in someone's power to intercede for them. Some sincere Muslims, under the burden of a religion of works and current fundamentalism and extremism, may feel disillusioned and seek the truth of the gospel. Therefore, Christians should be available in pluralistic contexts to befriend them and share the promise of the assured "State-after-Death" of the Christian gospel.

Fourth, in order for *Christians* to engage competently in conversations with people of other faiths, they must first know the Scriptures and experience deep personal faith and relationship with the Living God enough to not be swayed by other faith perspectives. Christians must understand that there are differences between various unbelievers, and must be trained to discern what an individual believes in order to effectively communicate gospel truth. Christians must also know and understand what other faiths believe about "State-after-Death" as it is one of the major tenets of belief that influences their present life. Christians must know the key points of conversation about "State-after-Death" which might prove fruitful in communicating the gospel message to unbelievers. Preachers must include "State-after-Death" as an important part of the unique message of the gospel of Jesus Christ in a pluralistic society.

Fifth, we further recommend comparative study of symbols and figurative language used in the Book of Revelation Chapter 21 with the language used in Hindu and Muslim scriptures to depict the blessed hereafter for the righteous. Due to limited scope of this dissertation, I was not able to make this comparative study of this subject further. One of the dimensions of the hermeneutical method proposed here was the constructive use of the narratives of Scripture, including metaphors, for the communication of the gospel. This symbolism might yield additional connecting points for fruitful and effective conversation with people of other faiths.

Sixth, we suggest further study of Hick and Küng, to refine the model of theology for "State-after-Death" held by the Global Christian Church. It seems Küng still holds to the uniqueness of Christian faith and tradition to some extent in comparison to the other world faiths. But, according to Hick, Jesus Christ had no business coming to this world to die on the cross for the sins of the world. Hick questions why the Christian church exists and questions preaching the Christian gospel to people of other faiths. This is Hick's challenge to us through his exclusivistic theory of Pluralism. He wants us to reject the gospel in favor of his new Buddhistic gospel, in effect denying the uniqueness of the Lamb of God who came to take away the sins of the world.

However, it seems Küng does not want to openly deny the particularity of Christian truth, however vague that is in his case, to sacrifice it on the altar of the religion of world unity. Küng's position is in tension and he is striving to walk the middle ground. If he is reticent to communicate the unique gospel of Jesus Christ to people of other faiths, then he reminds us of Jesus' saying, "He who is not with me is against me, and he who does not gather with me scatters" (Matt 12:30; Luke 11:23).

Finally, let us return to the first paragraph of the background of this study and reconsider the memorial service in which I preached from the narrative of Lazarus' resurrection in John 11. If I were asked to take the same service now, after completing this study, I would present the message quite differently from what I did then. First, I would give a longer Introduction on the possibilities of where the departed loved one might be after death, according to pluralistic religious and secular perspectives. My hearers must see that I take their and others' perspectives about ultimate destiny quite seriously even if these viewpoints are not held by the people who were present at that memorial service. If some present held these perspectives, they would also recognize my interest in their viewpoints and that I care about them as people.

Next, I would sensitively reason to show the pointlessness and the inconsistencies of some of these perspectives. I would point to the hopelessness of these non-Christian views of the deceased person's "State-after-Death." I would discuss in order: (1) "when you are dead that's the end," (2) reincarnation and rebirth, and (3) one life on earth and then face the judgment of God with no or little assurance of deliverance in the ultimate destiny. I would also deal with the inconsistency of universalism, which claims all will be well for the whole of humanity in the end by pointing only to God's benevolence and mercy and neglecting his justice and righteous wrath.

In the end, I would point to Jesus, who (a) through his response to the Sadducees, (b) through his predictions of his own death and resurrection, (c) through raising Lazarus and others, and (d) through his own death and resurrection proves the validity and hope of the Christian gospel.

Bibliography

ACUTE (Evangelical Alliance's Commission on Unity and Truth among Evangelicals). *The Nature of Hell*. Carlisle, UK: Paternoster/ACUTE, 2000.

Adiswarananda, Swami. "Hinduism." In *Encounters with Eternity: Religious Views of Death and Life After-Death*, edited by Christopher J. Johnson and Marsha G. McGee, 157–183. New York, NY: Philosophical Library, 1986.

Aldwinckle, Russell. *Death in the Secular City*. London: George Allen & Unwin Ltd, 1972.

Al-Qahtani, Saeed Ali. *The Supreme Triumph and the Evident Loss*. Riyadh, Saudi Arabia: IIPH, 1999.

Andersen, Francis I. *Job: An Introduction and Commentary*. Tyndale Old Testament Commentaries, No. 13. London: InterVarsity, 1976.

Anderson, Bernhard W. *Out of the Depths: The Psalms Speak for Us Today*. Philadelphia, PA: The Westminster Press, 1983.

Anderson, Gerald H. "Theology of Religions and Missiology: A Time of Testing." In *The Good News of the Kingdom: Mission Theology for the Third Millennium*, edited by Charles Van Engen, Dean S. Gilliland and Paul Pierson, 200–208. Maryknoll, NY: Orbis Books, 1993.

Athenagoras. "Writings of Athenagoras." In *The Ante-Nicene Fathers: Translations of the Writings of the Fathers down to A.D. 325*. vol. 2, edited and translated by A. Roberts and J. Donaldson, 129–162. Grand Rapids, MI: Eerdmans, 1979. (First published: Edinburgh, UK: T. & T. Clark, 1867.)

Atkinson, Basil F. C. *Life and Immortality: An Examination of the Nature and Meaning of Life and Death as They are Revealed in the Scriptures*. Taunton, UK: E. Goodman, n.d.

Aune, David E. *The Cultic Setting of Realized Eschatology in Early Christianity*. Supplements to Novum Testamentum, No. 28. Leiden, Netherlands: E. J. Brill, 1972.

Bacik, James J. "Hans Küng." In *A New Handbook of Christian Theologians*, edited by Donald W. Musser and Joseph L. Price, 261–270. Nashville, TN: Abingdon, 1996.

Bailey, Lloyd R. *Biblical Perspective on Death*. Philadelphia, PA: Fortress Press, 1979.

Baldwin, Joyce G. *Daniel: An Introduction and Commentary*. Tyndale Old Testament Commentaries, No. 21. Leicester, UK: InterVarsity, 1978.

Barnard, L. W. "The Authenticity of Athenagoras' De Resurrectione." *Studia Patristica* 15 (1984): 39–49.

Bayer, Hans F. "Predictions of Jesus' Passion and Resurrection." In *Dictionary of Jesus and the Gospels*, edited by Joel B. Green, Scot McKnight and I. Howard Marshall, 630–633. Downers Grove, IL: InterVarsity, 1992.

Bietenhard, Hans. "Hell, Gehenna." In *The New International Dictionary of New Testament Theology*. vol. 2, edited by Colin Brown, 208–209. Grand Rapids, MI: Zondervan, 1986. (Original: Grand Rapids, MI: Zondervan, 1976.)

Blenkinsopp, Joseph. *Ezekiel*. Interpretation: A Bible Commentary for Teaching and Preaching. Louisville, KY: John Knox Press, 1990.

Block, Daniel I. *The Book of Ezekiel: Chapters 25–48*. The New International Commentary on the Old Testament, No. 26. Grand Rapids, MI: Eerdmans, 1998.

Bobo, Truett E. "The Intermediate State." PhD dissertation, Fuller Theological Seminary, 1978.

Bonhoeffer, Dietrich. *Letters and Papers from Prison*. Translated by Eberhard Bethge. London: Collins, Fontana, 1953.

———. *Life Together*. New York, NY: Harper & Row, 1954.

———. *Ethics*. Edited by E. Bethge. London: SCM, 1955.

———. *The Cost of Discipleship*. First paperback edition. Translated by R. H. Fuller. New York, NY: Macmillan, 1963. (Original: 1948).

———. "The Barmen Confession." In *A Testament to Freedom: The Essential Writings of Dietrich Bonhoeffer*, edited by G. B. Kelly and F. B. Nelson. San Francisco: HarperSanFrancisco, 1990.

Boring, M. Eugene. *Revelation*. Louisville: John Knox Press, 1989.

Bosch, David J. *Witness to the World: The Christian Mission in Theological Perspective*. Atlanta, GA: John Knox Press, 1980.

———. *Transforming Mission: Paradigm Shifts in Theology of Mission*. Maryknoll, NY: Orbis Books, 1991.

Bose, Bobby. "E. Stanley Jones: Doing theology in a pluralistic context." In *Footprints of God: A Narrative Theology of Mission*, edited by Charles Van Engen, Nancy Thomas and Robert Gallagher, 52–61. Monrovia, CA: MARC, 1999.

Boyd, Robin. *An Introduction to Indian Christian Theology*. Second edition. New Delhi, India: ISPCK, 1975.

Brown, Colin. "Resurrection." In *The New International Dictionary of New Testament Theology*, vol. 3, edited by Colin Brown, 259–305. Grand Rapids, MI: Zondervan, 1986. (Original: Grand Rapids, MI: Zondervan, 1978.)

Broyles, Craig C. *Psalms.* New International Biblical Commentary, No. 11. Peabody, MA: Hendrickson Publishers, 1999.

Burney, C. F. *Israel's Hope of Immortality.* Oxford, UK: Clarendon Press, 1909.

Bynum, Caroline Walker. *The Resurrection of the Body in Western Christianity, 200–1336.* New York, NY: Columbia University Press, 1995.

Carson, D. A. *The Gospel According To John.* Grand Rapids, MI: Eerdmans, 1991.

———. *The Gagging of God: Christianity Confronts Pluralism.* Grand Rapids, MI: Zondervan, 1996.

Chadwick, Henry. *The Early Church.* vol. 1 of The Pelican History of the Church. Middlesex, UK: Penguin, 1967.

Chandran, J. Russell. "Development of Christian Theology in India." In *Readings in Indian Christian Theology,* vol. 1, edited by R. S. Sugirtharajah and Cecil Hargreaves, 4–13. Delhi, India: ISPCK, 1993.

Chittick, William C. "'Your Sight Today is Piercing': The Muslim Understanding of Death And Afterlife." In *Death and Afterlife: Perspectives of World Religions,* edited by Hiroshi Obayashi, 125–139. Westport, CT: Greenwood Press, 1992.

Clement. "The First Epistle of Clement." In *The Ante-Nicene Fathers: Translations of the Writings of the Fathers down to A.D. 325,* vol. 1, edited and translated by A. Roberts and J. Donaldson, 5–21. Reprint. Grand Rapids, MI: Eerdmans, 1979. (Original: Edinburgh, UK: T. & T. Clark, 1867.)

Coward, Harold, ed. *Life after Death in World Religions.* Maryknoll, NY: Orbis Books, 1997.

Cox, Harvey. *The Secular City: Secularization and Urbanization.* Revised edition. New York, NY: Macmillan, 1966.

Cullmann, Oscar. "Immortality of the Soul or Resurrection of the Dead?" In *Immortality and Resurrection,* edited by Krister Stendahl, 9–53. New York, NY: Macmillan, 1965.

Craigie, Peter C. *Psalms 1–50.* Word Biblical Commentary, No. 19. Dallas, TX: Word Books, 1983.

Daley, Brian E. *The Hope of the Early Church.* Cambridge, UK: Cambridge University Press, 1991.

Devanandan, Paul David. *Christian Concern in Hinduism.* Bangalore, India: Christian Institute for the Study of Religion and Society, 1961.

———. *Christian Issues in Southern Asia.* New York, NY: Friendship Press, 1963.

———. *Preparation for Dialogue.* Bangalore, India: Christian Institute for the Study of Religion and Society, 1964.

Dewart, Joanne E. McWilliam. *Death and Resurrection.* Message of the Fathers of the Church Series, No. 22. Wilmington, DE: Michael Glazier, 1986.

Edgerton, Franklin, trans. *The Bhagavad Gita*. New York, NY: Harper & Row (Torchbooks), 1964.

Edwards, James R. *Romans*. New International Biblical Commentary, No. 6. Peabody, MA: Hendrickson Publishers, 1992.

El-Droubie, R. "Statements and Extracts: Islam." In *Living Faiths: Death*, edited by John Prickett, 92–101. London: Lutterworth Educational, 1980.

Eusebius, Pamphilus. "Church History of Eusebius." In *The Nicene and Post-Nicene Fathers*. Series II, vol. 1. Philip Schaff and Henry Wace, Eds. Reprint in CCEL CD-ROM 2000. Grand Rapids, MI: Eerdmans, 1999. (Original: Edinburgh, UK: T. & T. Clark.)

Evans, C. F. *Resurrection and the New Testament*. London: SCM Press Ltd, 1970.

Evans, Craig A. *Luke*. New International Biblical Commentary, No. 3. Peabody, MA: Hendrickson Publishers, 1990.

———. *Noncanonical Writings and New Testament Interpretation*. Peabody, MA: Hendrickson Publishers, 1992.

Fernando, Ajith. *Crucial Questions about Hell*. Eastbourne, UK: Kingsway, 1991.

Frend, W. H. C. *The Rise of Christianity*. Philadelphia, PA: Fortress, 1984.

Gandhi, Mohatma K. *Why Fear or Mourn Death?* New Delhi, India: Gandhi Peace Foundation, 1971.

Gillis, Chester. "John Harwood Hick." In *A New Handbook of Christian Theologians*, edited by Donald W. Musser and Joseph L. Price, 221–228. Nashville, TN: Abingdon, 1996.

Glenn, Alfred A. "Bonhoeffer, Dietrich." In *Dictionary of Christianity in America*, edited by Daniel G. Reid, Robert D. Linder, Bruce L. Shelley, and Harry S. Stout, 172–173. Downers Grove, IL: InterVarsity, 1990.

Grant, R. M. "Athenagoras or Pseudo-Athenagoras." *Harvard Theological Review* 47, no. 2 (1954): 121–129.

Grenz, Stanley J., and Roger E. Olson. *20th-Century Theology: God & the World in a Transitional Age*. Downers Grove, IL: InterVarsity, 1992.

Grudem, Wayne. *Systematic Theology*. Grand Rapids, MI: Zondervan, 1994.

Gualtieri, Antonio R. *The Vulture and the Bull: Religious Responses to Death*. Lanham Way, MD: University Press of America, 1984.

Hagglund, Bengt. *History of Theology*. Translated by Gene J. Lund. St. Louis, MO: Concordia Publishing House, 1968.

Hagner, Donald A. "Gospel, Kingdom, and Resurrection in the Synoptic Gospels." In *Life in the Face of Death: The Resurrection Message of the New Testament*, edited by Richard N. Longenecker, 99–121. Grand Rapids, MI: Eerdmans, 1998.

Harris, Murray J. *Raised Immortal: The Relation between Resurrection and Immortality in New Testament Teaching*. London: Marshall, Morgan & Scott, 1983.

———. "Death." In *New Dictionary of Theology*, edited by S. B. Ferguson, D. F. Wright, and J. I. Packer, 188. Downers Grove, IL: InterVarsity, 1988a.

———. "Resurrection, General." In *New Dictionary of Theology*, edited by S. B. Ferguson, D. F. Wright, and J. I. Packer, 581–582. Downers Grove, IL: InterVarsity, 1988b.

———. "Resurrection and Immortality in the Pauline Corpus." In *Life in the Face of Death: The Resurrection Message of the New Testament*, edited by Richard N. Longenecker, 147–170. Grand Rapids, MI: Eerdmans, 1998.

Hartley, John E. *Genesis*. New International Biblical Commentary, No. 1. Peabody, MA: Hendrickson Publishers, 2000.

Hedlund, Roger E. *Roots of the Great Debate in Mission: Mission in Historical and Theological Perspective*. Revised edition. Bangalore, India: Theological Book Trust, 1993.

Hendriksen, William. *I & II Thessalonians*. Edinburgh, UK: Banner of Truth Trust, 1955.

Hick, John. *Death and Eternal Life*. New York, NY: Harper & Row Publishers, 1976.

———. *Death and Eternal Life*. Louisville, KY: Westminster John Knox Press, 1994.

———. *The Fifth Dimension: An Exploration of the Spiritual Realm*. Oxford, England: Oneworld Publications, 1999.

———. *John Hick: An Autobiography*. Oxford, England: Oneworld Publications, 2002.

Hill, Charles E. *Regnum Caelorum: Patterns of Millennial Thought in Early Christianity*. Second edition. Grand Rapids, MI: Eerdmans, 2001.

Hoedemaker, Libertus A. "The Legacy of Hendrik Kraemer." *Occasional Bulletin from the Missionary Research Library* 4, no. 2 (1980): 60–64.

Holck, Frederick H. *Death and Eastern Thought: Understanding Death in Eastern Religions and Philosophies*. Nashville, TN: Abingdon Press, 1974.

Holmes, Michael W., ed. *The Apostolic Fathers*. Second edition. Translated by J. B. Lightfoot and J. R. Harmer. Grand Rapids, MI: Baker, 1989.

———. *The Apostolic Fathers: Greek Texts and English Translations*. Second edition. Translated by J. B. Lightfoot and J. R. Harmer. Grand Rapids, MI: Baker, 1992.

Hopkins, Thomas J. "Hindu Views of Death and Afterlife." In *Death and Afterlife: Perspectives of World Religions*, edited by Hiroshi Obayashi, 143–155. Westport, CT: Greenwood Press, 1992.

Hubbard, David Allan. *Hosea: An Introduction and Commentary.* Tyndale Old Testament Commentaries, No. 22a. Downers Grove, IL: InterVarsity, 1989.

Ignatius. "The Epistles of Ignatius." In *The Ante-Nicene Fathers: Translations of the Writings of the Fathers down to A.D. 325,* vol. 1, edited and translated by A. Roberts and J. Donaldson, 49–96. Reprint. Grand Rapids, MI: Eerdmans, 1979. (Original: Edinburgh, UK: T. & T. Clark, 1867.)

Irenaeus. "Irenaeus against Heresies." In *The Ante-Nicene Fathers: Translations of the Writings of the Fathers down to A.D. 325,* vol. 1, edited and translated by A. Roberts and J. Donaldson, 315–567. Reprint. Grand Rapids, MI: Eerdmans, 1979. (Original: Edinburgh, UK: T. & T. Clark, 1867.)

Jackson, Eleanor M. *God's Apprentice: The Autobiography of Bishop Stephen Neill.* London: Hodder & Stoughton, 1991.

———. "The Continuing Legacy of Stephen Neill." *International Bulletin of Missionary Research* 19, no. 2 (1995): 77–80.

Jeanrond, Werner G. "Hans Küng." In *The Modern Theologians: An Introduction to Christian Theology in the Twentieth Century.* Second edition. Edited by David F. Ford, 162–178. Oxford, UK: Blackwell, 1997.

Johnson, Christopher J., and Marsha G. McGee, eds. *Encounters with Eternity: Religious Views of Death and Life After-Death.* New York, NY: Philosophical Library, 1986.

Johnston, Philip S. *Shades of Sheol: Death and Afterlife in the Old Testament.* Downers Grove, IL: InterVarsity, 2002.

Justin, Martyr. "The Writings of Justin." In *The Ante-Nicene Fathers: Translations of the Writings of the Fathers down to A.D. 325,* vol. 1, edited and translated by A. Roberts and J. Donaldson, 163–302. Reprint. Grand Rapids, MI: Eerdmans, 1979. (Original: Edinburgh, UK: T. & T. Clark, 1867.)

Kassis, Hanna. "Islam." In *Life after Death in World Religions,* edited by Harold Coward, 48–65. Maryknoll, NY: Orbis Books, 1997.

Kidner, Derek. *Proverbs: An Introduction and Commentary.* Tyndale Old Testament Commentaries, No. 15. Downers Grove, IL: InterVarsity, 1964.

———. *Genesis: An Introduction and Commentary.* Tyndale Old Testament Commentaries. Leicester, UK: InterVarsity, 1967.

———. *Psalms 1–72: An Introduction and Commentary on Books I and II of the Psalms.* Tyndale Old Testament Commentaries, No. 14a. Leicester, UK: InterVarsity, 1973.

———. *Psalms 73–150: An Introduction and Commentary on Books III–IV of the Psalms.* Tyndale Old Testament Commentaries, No. 14b. Leicester, UK: InterVarsity, 1975.

———. *Love to the Loveless: The Message of Hosea*. The Bible Speaks Today. Downers Grove, IL: InterVarsity, 1981.

Kirk, J. Andrew. *What is Mission?: Theological Explorations*. Minneapolis, MN: Fortress, 2000. (Original: London: Darton, Longman & Todd, 1999).

Klein, William W., Craig L. Blomberg, and Robert L. Hubbard, Jr. *Introduction to Biblical Interpretation*. Dallas, TX: Word, 1993.

Kraemer, Hendrik. *The Christian Message in a Non-Christian World*. Grand Rapids, MI: Kregel Publications, 1938.

Kramer, Kenneth P. *The Sacred Art of Dying: How World Religions Understand Death*. New York, NY/Mahwah, NJ: Paulist Press, 1988.

Kreitzer, Larry J. "Resurrection." In *Dictionary of Paul and his Letters*, edited by Gerald F. Hawthorne, Ralph P. Martin and Daniel G. Reid, 805–812. Downers Grove, IL: InterVarsity, 1993.

Küng, Hans. *On Being a Christian*. Translated by Edward Quinn. Garden City, NY: Doubleday, 1976.

———. *Does God Exist?* Translated by Edward Quinn. Garden City, N.Y.: Doubleday, 1980.

———. *Eternal Life?* Translated by Edward Quinn. New York, NY: Doubleday, 1984.

———. "Is There One True Religion?" In *Christianity and Other Religions*, edited by John Hick and Brian Hebblethwaite, 118–145. Oxford, UK: Oneworld Publications, 2001.

———. *My Struggle for Freedom: Memoirs*. Translated by John Bowden. Grand Rapids, MI: Eerdmans, 2003.

Ladd, George Eldon. *I Believe in the Resurrection of Jesus*. Grand Rapids, MI: Eerdmans, 1975.

Lamb, Christopher. "The Legacy of Stephen Neill." *International Bulletin of Missionary Research* 11, no. 2 (1987): 62–66.

Lane, W. L. *The Gospel According to Mark*. NLC. Grand Rapids: Eerdmans, 1974.

Lee, Gary A. "Gehenna." In *The International Standard Bible Encyclopedia*, vol. 2, edited by Geoffrey W. Bromiley, 423. Grand Rapids, MI: Eerdmans, 1982.

Leibholz, G. "Memoir." In *The Cost of Discipleship*, edited by Dietrich Bonhoeffer and translated by R. H. Fuller, 11–35. First paperback edition. New York, NY: Macmillan, 1963. (Original: 1948).

Lenski, Richard C. H. *The Interpretation of St. John's Revelation*. Minneapolis, MN: Augsburg Publishing House, 1943.

Lightfoot, J. B., ed. and trans. *The Apostolic Fathers*. Reprint. Grand Rapids, MI: Baker, 1980. (Original: London, UK: Macmillan, 1891.)

Lincoln, Andrew T. "'I Am the Resurrection and the Life': The Resurrection Message of the Fourth Gospel." In *Life in the Face of Death: The Resurrection Message of the New Testament*, edited by Richard N. Longenecker, 99–121. Grand Rapids, MI: Eerdmans, 1998.

Longenecker, Richard N., ed. *Life in the Face of Death: The Resurrection Message of the New Testament*. Grand Rapids, MI: Eerdmans, 1998.

Marsh, Charles. "Dietrich Bonhoeffer." In *The Modern Theologians: An Introduction to Christian Theology in the Twentieth Century*, edited by David F. Ford, 37–51. Second edition. Oxford, UK: Blackwell Publishers, 1997.

Martin-Achard, Robert. *From Death to Life: A Study of the Development of the Doctrine of the Resurrection in the Old Testament*. Translated by John Penney Smith. Edinburgh and London: Oliver & Boyd Ltd, 1960.

Miller, Ed L., and Stanley J. Grenz. *Fortress Introduction to Contemporary Theologies*. Minneapolis, MN: Fortress Press, 1998.

Minucius Felix. "The Octavius of Minucius Felix." In *The Ante-Nicene Fathers: Translations of the Writings of the Fathers down to A.D. 325*, vol. 4, edited and translated by A. Roberts and J. Donaldson, 173–198. Reprint. Grand Rapids, MI: Eerdmans, 1979. (Original: Edinburgh, UK: T & T Clark, 1867.)

Murphy, Roland E., and Elizabeth Huwiler. *Proverbs, Ecclesiastes, Song of Songs*. New International Biblical Commentary, No. 12. Peabody, MA: Hendrickson Publishers, 1999.

Murphy, Roland E. *Proverbs*. Word Biblical Commentary, No. 22. Dallas, TX: Word Books, 1998.

Morey, Robert A. *Death and the Afterlife*. Minneapolis, MN: Bethany House Publishers, 1984.

Motyer, J. Alec. *The Prophecy of Isaiah*. Leicester, UK: InterVarsity, 1993.

Narayan, V., and S. N. Bharadwaj. "Statements and Extracts: Hinduism." In *Living Faiths: Death*, edited by John Prickett, 80–89. London: Lutterworth Educational, 1980.

Neill, Stephen Charles. *Creative Tension*. London: Edinburgh House Press, 1959.

———. *Men of Unity*. London: SCM Press Ltd, 1960.

———. *Salvation Tomorrow*. London: Lutterworth Press, 1976.

Neil, Stephen, Gerald H. Anderson, and John Goodwin, eds. *Concise Dictionary of the Christian World Mission*. Nashville, and New York, NY: Abingdon Press, 1971.

Netland, Harold. *Dissonant Voices*. Grand Rapids, MI: Eerdmans, 1991.

———. "Theology of Religions, Missiology, and Evangelicals." *Missiology: An International Review* 33, no. 2 (2005): 141–158.

Obayashi, Hiroshi, ed. *Death and Afterlife: Perspectives of World Religions.* Westport, CT: Greenwood Press, 1992.

Okholm, Dennis L., and Timothy R. Phillips, eds. *Four Views on Salvation in a Pluralistic World.* Grand Rapids, MI: Zondervan, 1996. (Original: *More than One Way?* Grand Rapids, MI: Zondervan, 1995.)

Osborne, Grant R. *The Resurrection Narratives: A Redactional Study.* Grand Rapids, MI: Baker, 1984.

———. *The Hermeneutical Spiral: A Comprehensive Introduction to Biblical Interpretation.* Downers Grove, IL: InterVarsity, 1991.

———. "Resurrection." In *Dictionary of Jesus and the Gospels,* eds. Joel B. Green, Scot McKnight and I. Howard Marshall, 673–688. Downers Grove, IL: InterVarsity, 1992.

O'Shaughnessy, Thomas, S. J. *Muhammad's Thoughts on Death.* Leiden, Holland: E. J. Brill, 1969.

Parrinder, Geoffrey. "Death in the World Faiths: Introduction." In *Living Faiths: Death,* edited by John Prickett, 3–20. London: Lutterworth Educational, 1980.

Perkins, Pheme. *Resurrection: New Testament Witness and Contemporary Reflection.* Garden City, NY: Doubleday & Co, 1984.

Philip, T. M. *The Encounter between Theology and Ideology: An Exploration into the Cummunicative Theology of M. M. Thomas.* Madras, India: CLS, 1986.

Philips, Abu Ameenah Bilal. *Funeral Rites in Islam.* Sharjah, U.A.E.: Dar Al Fatah, 1996.

Polycarp. "The Epistle of Polycarp." In *The Ante-Nicene Fathers: Translations of the Writings of the Fathers down to A.D. 325,* vol. 1, edited and translated by A. Roberts and J. Donaldson, 33–36. Reprint. Grand Rapids, MI: Eerdmans, 1979. (Original: Edinburgh, UK:T & T Clark, 1867.)

Pouderon, B. *Athénagore d'Athènes, philosophe chrétien.* Paris: Beauchesne, 1989.

Prabhavananda, Swami, and Frederick Manchester, trans. *The Upanishads: Breath of the Eternal.* New York, NY: Mentor Books, 1957.

Prickett, John, ed. *Living Faiths: Death.* London: Lutterworth Educational, 1980.

Ramachandra, Vinoth. *The Recovery of Mission.* Indian Edition Delhi, India: ISPCK, 1996.

Rambachan, Anantanand. "Hinduism." In *Life after Death in World Religions,* edited by Harold Coward, 66–86. Maryknoll, NY: Orbis Books, 1997.

Roberts, Alexander, and James Donaldson, eds. *The Ante-Nicene Fathers: Translations of the Writings of the Fathers down to A.D. 325,* vol. 3. Reprint. Grand Rapids, MI: Eerdmans, 1978. (Original: Edinburgh, UK: T. & T. Clark, 1867.)

———. *The Ante-Nicene Fathers: Translations of the Writings of the Fathers down to A.D. 325*. vol. 1. Reprint. Grand Rapids, MI: Eerdmans, 1979a. (Original: Edinburgh, UK: T. & T. Clark, 1867.)

———. *The Ante-Nicene Fathers: Translations of the Writings of the Fathers down to A.D. 325*. vol. 2. Reprint. Grand Rapids, MI: Eerdmans, 1979b. (Original: Edinburgh, UK: T. & T. Clark, 1867.)

———. *The Ante-Nicene Fathers: Translations of the Writings of the Fathers down to A.D. 325*. vol. 4. Reprint. Grand Rapids, MI: Eerdmans, 1979c. (Original: Edinburgh, UK: T. & T. Clark, 1867.)

———. *The Ante-Nicene Fathers: Translations of the Writings of the Fathers down to A.D. 325*. Reprint in CCEL CD-ROM 2000. Grand Rapids, MI: Eerdmans, 1999. (Original: Edinburgh, UK: T. & T. Clark, 1867.)

Schaff, Philip, and Henry Wace, eds. *The Nicene and Post-Nicene Fathers*. Series II. Reprint in CCEL CD-ROM 2000. Grand Rapids, MI: Eerdmans, 1999. (Original: Edinburgh, UK: T. & T. Clark, 1867.)

Schoedel, W. R. *Polycarp, Martyrdom of Polycarp, Fragments of Papias*. The Apostolic Fathers, vol. 5. London: Thomas Nelson, 1967.

Seale, M. S. "Islamic Society." In *Life after Death,* edited by Arnold Toynbee and Arthur Koestler, 123–131. New York, NY: McGraw-Hill Book Co, 1976.

Segal, Eliezer. "Judaism." In *Life after Death in World Religions*, edited by Harold Coward, 11–30. Maryknoll, NY: Orbis Books, 1997.

Smith, C. Ryder. *The Bible Doctrine of the Hereafter*. London: The Epworth Press, 1958.

Smith, Jane Idleman, and Yvonne Yazbeck Haddad. *Islamic Understanding of Death and Resurrection*. New York, NY: State University of New York Press, 1983.

Smith, Jane Idleman. "Islam." In *Encounters with Eternity: Religious Views of Death and Life After-Death*, edited by Christopher J. Johnson and Marsha G. McGee, 185–203. New York, NY: Philosophical Library, 1986.

Sparks, Jack N., ed. *The Apostolic Fathers*. Nashville, TN: Thomas Nelson, 1978.

Spronk, Klaas. *Beatific Afterlife in Ancient Israel and in the Ancient Near East*. Kevelaer, Germany: Butzon and Bercker; Neukirchen-Vluyn: Neukirchener Verlag, 1986.

Sumithra, Sunand. *Christian Theologies from an Indian Perspective*. Bangalore, India: Theological Book Trust, 1995.

Stuart, Douglas K. "Sheol." In *The International Standard Bible Encyclopedia*, vol. 4, edited by Geoffrey W. Bromiley, 472. Grand Rapids, MI: Eerdmans, 1988.

Tertullian and Minucius Felix. *Apology: De Spectaculis. Octavius.* Translated by G. H. Rendall. Loeb Classical Library. Cambridge, MA: Harvard University Press, 1931; reprint 1960.

———. "Writings of Tertullian." In *The Ante-Nicene Fathers: Translations of the Writings of the Fathers down to A.D. 325,* vol. 3, edited and translated by A. Roberts and J. Donaldson, 17–718. Reprint. Grand Rapids, MI: Eerdmans, 1978. (Original: Edinburgh, UK: T. & T. Clark, 1867.)

Theophilus. "Writings of Theophilus." In *The Ante-Nicene Fathers: Translations of the Writings of the Fathers down to A.D. 325,* vol. 2, edited and translated by A. Roberts and J. Donaldson, 89–121. Reprint. Grand Rapids, MI: Eerdmans, 1979. (Original: Edinburgh, UK: T. & T. Clark, 1867.)

Thiselton, Anthony C. *The Two Horizons.* Exeter, UK: The Paternoster Press, 1980.

———. "Hermeneutics." In *New Dictionary of Theology*, edited by Sinclair B. Ferguson, David F. Wright, and J. I. Packer, 293–297. Downers Grove, IL: InterVarsity, 1988.

———. *New Horizons in Hermeneutics.* Grand Rapids, MI: Zondervan, 1992.

———. *Interpreting God and the Postmodern Self.* Grand Rapids, MI: Eerdmans, 1995.

———. "Biblical Theology and Hermeneutics." In *The Modern Theologians*, edited by David F. Ford, 520–537. Malden, MA: Blackwell, 1997.

Thomas, Jacob. *Ethics of World Community: Contribution of Dr. M.M. Thomas based on Indian Reality.* Calcutta, India: Punthi Pustak, 1993.

Thomas, M. M. *The Christian Response to the Asian Revolution.* Bangalore, India: CISRS, 1966.

———. *The Acknowledged Christ of the Indian Renaissance.* London: SCM, 1969.

———. "Spirituality for Combat." In *Roots of the Great Debate in Mission: Mission in Historical and Theological Perspective,* edited by Roger Hedlund, 355–373. Revised edition. Bangalore, India: Theological Book Trust, 1993a.

———. "The Secular Ideologies of India and the Secular Meaning of Christ." In *Readings in Indian Christian Theology,* vol. 1, edited by R. S. Sugirtharajah and Cecil Hargreaves, 93–101. Delhi, India: ISPCK, 1993b.

Thomas, M. M. and P. T. Thomas. *Towards an Indian Christian Theology.* Tiruvalla, India: Christava Sahitya Samithi, 1998.

Thomson, Marianne Meye. "John, Gospel of." In *Dictionary of Jesus and the Gospels,* edited by Joel B. Green, Scot McKnight and I. Howard Marshall, 368–383. Downers Grove, IL: InterVarsity, 1992.

Toynbee, Arnold, and Arthur Koestler, eds. *Life after Death.* New York, NY: McGraw-Hill Book Company, 1976.

Trites, Allison A. "Witness and the Resurrection in the Apocalypse of John." In *Life in the Face of Death: The Resurrection Message of the New Testament*, edited by Richard N. Longenecker, 270–288. Grand Rapids, MI: Eerdmans, 1998.

Tromp, Nicholas J. *Primitive Conceptions of Death and the Nether World in the Old Testament*. Rome: Pontifical Biblical Institute, 1969.

Van Engen, Charles E. *Mission on the Way: Issues in Mission Theology*. Grand Rapids, MI: Baker, 1996.

Vanhoozer, Kevin J. *Biblical Narrative in the Philosophy of Paul Ricoeur*. Cambridge, UK: Cambridge University Press, 1990.

———. *Is There a Meaning in This Text?: The Bible, the Reader, and the Morality of Literary Knowledge*. Grand Rapids, MI: Zondervan, 1998.

Verkuyl, Johannes. *Contemporary Missiology*. Edited and translated by Dale Cooper. Grand Rapids, MI: Eerdmans, 1978.

Wall, Robert W. *Revelation*. New International Biblical Commentary, No. 18. Peabody, MA: Hendrickson Publishers, 1991.

Webb, Barry. *The Message of Isaiah: On Eagle's Wings*. The Bible Speaks Today. Leicester, UK: InterVarsity, 1996.

Webster, John B. "Bonhoeffer, Dietrich." In *New Dictionary of Theology*, edited by Sinclair B. Ferguson, David F. Wright, and J. I. Packer, 107–108. Downers Grove, IL: InterVarsity, 1988.

Wietzke, Joachim. *P. D. Devanandan*. Bangalore, India: The Christian Literature Society, 1983.

Wilckens, Ulrich. *Resurrection*. Translated by A. M. Stewert. Atlanta, GA: John Knox Press, 1978.

Williams, David J. *1 and 2 Thessalonians*. New International Biblical Commentary, No. 12. Peabody, MA: Hendrickson Publishers, 1992.

Wright, Christopher J. H. *Deuteronomy*. New International Biblical Commentary, No. 4. Peabody, MA: Hendrickson Publishers, 1996.

———. *The Message of Ezekiel: A New Heart and a New Spirit*. The Bible Speaks Today. Downers Grove, IL: InterVarsity, 2001.

Wright, N. T. Interview in *The Christian Century* (18 December 2002): 28–31.

———. *The Resurrection of the Son of God*. Christian Origins and the Question of God, No. 3. Minneapolis, MN: Fortress Press, 2003.

Zain, Abdul Qadir Ahmad. *Save from Hell-Fire*. Buraydah, Kingdom of Saudi Arabia: Foreigners Guidance Center in Al-Qasseem, 1995.

Index

A

Abraham, 41, 119, 172, 194, 202–204, 211, 216, 230, 255, 261, 293
absolutism, 90
accountability, 35, 47, 50, 328, 329
ACUTE, 178, 214, 218, 228, 230, 231, 233, 260, 316, 323, 333
Adam, 26, 28, 31, 34, 172, 173, 177, 186, 199, 201, 251, 254, 255, 258, 264, 269
Adiswarananda, Swami, iv, 16, 21, 22, 49, 333
Agony, 31, 34, 229, 230
Aldwinckle, Russell, 44, 45, 47, 52, 59, 329, 333
Allah, 26, 51
Allegorical, 138, 139, 158, 280
Al-Qahtani, Saeed Ali, iv, 36, 37, 333
Altar, 260, 261, 265, 332
Amsterdam, Holland, 83, 94
Anagogical, 139
Andersen Francis I., 196–198, 333
Anderson, Gerald H., ii, 2, 3, 55, 190, 333, 340
Anderson, Bernhard W., 333
angel, 26, 30, 33, 35, 170
angels, 25, 27–29, 33, 35, 37, 50, 256, 259, 265, 283, 315, 317
anthropomorphic, 73, 106
Apocalypse, 212, 258, 344
Apologist, 295, 299, 302, 313, 318
Apologists, ii, 266, 285, 291, 299, 302, 305, 324, 325
Apostolic, 266–268, 285, 286, 290, 291, 337, 339, 342
Aryan, 57
ascension, 224, 240, 313, 316, 330
Asian, ii, 24, 67, 68, 69, 94, 95, 258, 343
Assumption, xv, 38, 60, 67, 74, 105–107, 177, 230
Assyria, 205, 213
Athenagoras, iv, 295–300, 317, 318, 333, 334, 336
Atkinson, Basil, 182, 333
Aune, David E., 272, 273, 333
authorial, 157, 159–165, 169–171, 189, 218, 245, 328

B

Babylonian, 121, 175, 219
Bailey, Lloyd R., 180, 221
Bangalore, 64, 94
Barmen, 57, 334
Barth, Karl, 56, 60, 61, 65, 66, 68, 87, 114, 115, 141, 189,
Bayer, Hans F., 223–225
Bengal, 74
Bethel, 63, 187
Bietenhard, Hans, 230, 231, 334
Blenkinsopp, Joseph, 208–210, 334
Blomberg, Craig L., 133, 339
bodily resurrection, 125, 198, 208, 210, 212, 214, 241, 242, 247, 248, 250, 263–265, 274, 282, 283, 286, 290–292, 294, 297, 298, 306, 307, 312, 313, 321, 322, 324, 325, 330
Bonhoeffer, Dietrich, 6, 47, 52, 56–64, 91, 328, 334, 336, 339, 340, 344
Boyd, Robin, 64–66, 69, 72, 73, 95, 96, 98, 102, 334
bridge, 28, 35, 36, 223
Brown, Colin, 120, 121, 219–221, 225, 226, 231, 334
Buddhist, 5, 24, 42, 105, 111–113, 323
Bultmann, Rudolph, 137, 141–144, 250

C

Calvin, 139
Chadwick, Henry, 268, 335
Chandran, J. Russell, 96, 97, 335
chasm, 229, 230
Christ-centered, 58, 94
Christianity, ii, iv, xvi, 12, 24, 29, 30, 58, 61, 65, 68–70, 75, 81, 87–89, 93, 97, 98, 103, 105, 106, 109, 116, 117, 128, 219, 233, 263, 277, 291, 292, 302, 303, 308, 309, 330
Christology, 58, 59, 104, 137
Clement, 138, 268–273, 275, 277, 280, 282, 284–287, 298, 323, 324, 335
Communion, 21, 72, 188–190, 197, 199
community, 4, 27, 48, 58, 59, 61, 70–72, 86, 96, 99, 101, 102, 115, 121, 142, 145, 147, 158, 167, 169
Confucianism, 46, 52
conscious, 9, 20, 34, 72, 112, 121, 144, 147, 212, 219, 261, 290, 302, 321, 323–325
context-relative, 147, 148, 151, 167
contextualization, 71, 91, 132, 134, 135, 169
continuity, 2, 119, 125, 174, 199, 217, 221, 222, 229, 241, 252, 264, 272, 275, 276, 295, 300, 324
conversion, 70, 75, 84, 123, 127, 166, 169, 170, 247, 264, 292
Corinth, 247, 249, 250, 271
cosmic, 27, 50, 70, 71, 113, 142, 158
covenant, 79, 120, 166, 220, 253, 280–282
Coward, Harold, 11–13, 19, 24, 29, 174, 335, 338, 341, 342
Cox, Harvey, 43, 335
creation, 26, 37, 70–72, 79, 80, 98, 100, 124, 159, 162, 166, 180, 211, 253, 255, 279, 282, 312, 330
creed, 66, 67, 74
cross-cultural, 67, 74
Cullmann, Oscar, 261, 335

culture, xvii, 2, 43, 44, 66, 67, 74, 87, 96, 99, 105, 116, 121, 133, 135, 164, 167, 175, 227, 308

D

darkness, 31, 38, 62, 80, 83, 119, 180, 182, 199, 233, 289
Day of Judgment, 27, 28, 29, 33, 35, 36, 41, 51, 238
Day of Resurrection, 25, 27, 29, 32, 35, 38, 50
deductive, 135
dehumanization, 99, 129
demonic, 66, 98
Dewart, Joanne E. McWilliam, iv, 222, 270, 335
dialogue, ii, iii, xv, 15, 68, 69, 74, 81, 82, 92, 95, 96, 102, 116, 129, 145, 146, 237, 242, 300, 327, 328
discontinuity, 65, 90, 91, 221, 222, 241, 251, 252, 264, 275
disembodied, 180, 261, 298, 310
disobedience, 173, 174, 199, 201, 254, 255
Droubie, el-, R. *See* El-Droubie.
Dutch, 56, 84, 85

E

Eastern, 24, 28, 42, 46, 52, 84, 175, 176, 178, 179, 199, 337
ecumenical, 56, 60, 76, 94, 97, 116
Edgerton, Franklin, 17, 18, 336
Egypt, 175, 213
El-Droubie, R., 30, 31, 336
Elijah, 185–188, 199, 202, 204, 209, 311
Elisha, 186, 187, 209
enemy, 11, 188, 255
Enoch, 185–188, 194, 199, 202, 204, 217, 311
Epicurean, 45, 52
eschatology, 25, 30, 31, 117, 157, 189, 195, 235, 236, 249, 253
eternal death, 26, 289
ethics, 61, 97, 98, 158, 159

Eusebius, 275, 276, 283, 284, 336
Evangelical, v, 55, 57, 169, 228, 333
evangelism, v, 61, 69, 71–73, 78, 82, 91, 93, 97, 98, 102, 169
evil deeds, 22, 27, 38, 48, 51
exegesis, 118, 132, 134, 197, 206, 220, 241, 308
existential, 48, 142, 143, 164, 329
extinction, 45, 105, 220, 287
Ezekiel, 119, 120, 182, 206, 208–212, 216, 276, 286, 293, 306, 316, 334, 344

F

fellowship, 70, 72, 73, 83, 93, 102, 127, 185, 188, 193, 199, 215
Fernando, Ajith, iv, 231, 336
fiction, 154–156, 168
forgiveness, 30, 51, 70, 89, 97, 98, 170, 317, 328, 329, 330

G

Gabriel, 33, 104
Gadamer, 134, 135, 143–148, 150, 153, 157
Galilee, 228, 239, 240
garden, 34, 37–41, 50, 51, 172, 227
gardens, 27, 32, 35, 40, 298
Gehenna, 28, 37, 39, 40, 218, 219, 228–233, 240, 242, 246, 254, 264, 334, 339
genre, 136, 151
gentile, 70, 170, 292
Gentiles, 78, 79, 228
German, 56–58, 60, 93, 164, 188
Germany, 56–58, 60, 61, 342
Gestapo, 57
Gillis, Chester, 103, 104, 336
global, i, iii, iv, xvi, xvii, 3, 5, 6, 24, 42, 43, 56, 60, 86, 93, 110, 111, 113, 116, 170, 216, 242, 327
globalization, 42
good deeds, 12, 23, 36–38, 49–51, 330

grace, 61, 89, 97, 114, 174, 255, 264, 269, 288, 310, 323
grave, 25, 29, 30–35, 38, 50, 105, 174, 180, 182, 190, 276, 302, 306
Greco-Roman, 24, 44, 217, 241, 242, 266, 267, 328
Grenz, Stanley J., 56–62, 64, 117, 118, 336, 340
Grudem, Wayne, 222, 247, 252, 336

H

Hades, 178, 217–219, 228–233, 240–242, 246, 254, 258, 259, 263–265, 269, 270, 287
Hagglund, Bengt, 291, 336
hell, 21, 22, 25, 32–41, 51, 105, 111–113, 117, 127, 128, 180, 181, 217, 228, 231, 248, 287, 314, 315, 321, 322, 330
Hellenism, 75
Hendriksen, William, 247, 337
hermeneutical spiral, 136
Hick, John, iii, 5, 6, 43, 46, 47, 52, 56, 93, 103–113, 117, 119, 122, 126–129, 327, 328, 330–332, 337, 339
Hindu, i, ii, iii, iv, xv, xvi, xvii, 1, 3–6, 10–13, 16, 19–24, 42, 48–50, 66, 68, 69, 75, 95, 96, 103, 105, 111–113, 216, 243, 323, 328, 330, 331, 337
Hinduism, ii, 10–13, 16, 17, 19, 21–24, 48, 49, 64–66, 68–70, 89, 95, 103, 333, 335, 340, 341;
teachings & traditions, i, ii, iii, iv, xiii, xiv, xv, 1, 3–6, 10–13, 16, 19, 20–24, 42, 48–50, 66, 68, 69, 75, 95, 96, 103, 105, 111–113, 216, 243, 323, 328, 330, 331, 337
historical-critical, 118, 123, 139, 164
Hitler, 57, 58, 60
holistic, 78

Holmes, Michael W., 268, 271, 272, 275, 276, 279–282, 284, 285, 287, 289, 337
Horeb, 120, 121, 172, 220
Hosea, 120, 205–208, 216, 246, 254, 338, 339
Hubbard, David A., 207, 338
humanistic, 5, 47, 52, 59
humanization, 96, 97, 99, 101, 102

I

Ignatius, 272–277, 280, 284, 285, 287, 298, 338
image, 39, 101, 106, 134, 135, 251, 261, 272, 280–283, 295, 311, 325
immortality, 13, 14, 16, 17, 19, 22, 46, 173, 189, 195, 237, 252, 269, 278, 286, 287, 290, 293, 311, 315–317, 325
India, i, ii, iv, v, 6, 11, 12, 56, 64–66, 68, 69, 72–74, 76, 81, 82, 85, 92–96, 107, 111, 334–337, 341–344
Indian Christian, 64, 94, 95, 334, 335, 343
inductive, 135, 169
infallible, 119, 125, 127
inter-disciplinary, 5, 110
intermediate state, 30, 35, 241, 248, 260–262, 264, 265, 277, 295, 310, 311
International Missionary Council, 76
intertestamental, 121, 217–219, 230
InterVarsity Christian Fellowship, 75
Irenaeus, iv, 208, 275–277, 282–284, 299, 305, 307–313, 322, 323, 338
Isaac, 119, 172, 194, 202–204, 293
Isaiah, 119, 120, 174, 178, 180, 182, 190, 208, 212–216, 232, 276, 286, 287, 293, 317, 340, 344
Islam, ii, 12, 24–28, 30–39, 50, 51, 68, 106, 119, 336, 338, 341, 342
Islamic, iv, 24, 25, 28, 30–35, 39, 41, 51, 126, 342

J

Jacob, 119, 172, 184, 293, 343
Jerusalem, 33, 85, 86, 90, 213, 223, 227, 231, 236, 239, 240, 251, 259, 262, 263, 280, 293, 294
Jewish, 5, 24, 38, 57, 120, 121, 123, 126, 138, 166, 170, 177, 201, 210, 217, 219, 226, 232, 236, 241, 247–250, 253, 260, 262, 263, 290, 325, 330
Job, 179–184, 190, 196–199, 252, 333
Jordan, 187
Josephus, 226
Judaism, 12, 24, 30, 80, 81, 106, 198, 205, 208, 247, 248, 342
Justin, Martyr, 208, 285, 291, 292, 298, 313–315

K

karma, 96
Kassis, Hanna, iv, 28–30
Kidner, Derek, 189, 190, 193–195, 202, 206, 207,
Kirk, J. Andrew, 3, 4
Klein, William W., 133, 339
knowledge, 10, 21–23, 26, 31, 33, 49, 50, 87, 88, 105, 137, 140, 144, 150, 159, 160, 172, 209, 210, 282, 305
Koran. *See also* Quran, 68, 119
Kraemer, Hendrik, iii, 6, 56, 65, 66, 68, 83–91, 328, 337
Küng, Hans, iii, iv, 6, 56, 93, 114–129, 327, 328, 331–333, 338, 339

L

Ladd, George Eldon, 233, 248, 250–252,
Lamb, Christopher, 75, 339
last day, 37, 205, 236
Lazarus, 225, 228–230, 236–238, 242, 310, 312, 332
Leibholz, 60, 339

Liberal, 84
liberation, 11, 15, 20, 21, 23, 73, 96, 97, 99, 162
Lightfoot, J. B., 337, 339
literacy, 73
literary, 133, 146, 148, 155, 156, 158–160, 169, 212
Longenecker, Richard N., 9, 10, 43, 46, 52, 220, 249, 251, 254, 336, 337, 340
love, xix, 25, 63, 87, 89, 94, 115, 129, 166, 167, 202, 225, 227, 269, 271, 278–280, 285, 317
Luther, 114, 139

M

Madras, 64, 85, 86, 90
Marsh, Charles, 56–58, 340
Mar Thoma, 93, 94
Martin-Achard, Robert, 172, 173, 175, 178, 186, 188–193, 196–198, 202, 205, 206, 208, 213, 215, 216, 340
materialism, 85
Maya, 64, 65, 69
metacritical, 147–150, 152, 153, 156, 164–168, 170, 171, 203, 218, 245, 328
metaphor, 153–155, 207, 233
methodology, ii, 6, 95, 131, 134, 145, 158
militant, xvi, 86, 90
millennial, 261, 262, 284, 293
missiology, xvii, 2, 5, 85, 166, 170
missionary, xvi, 1, 3, 6, 70, 74–79, 84–91, 129, 327
mission theology, xv, 3, 55, 56, 73, 76, 77, 79, 85, 93, 296
modern, iv, 2, 9, 43–45, 60, 66, 69, 73, 81, 92, 95, 96, 102, 103, 105, 118, 148, 157, 158, 163, 166, 184, 210, 262, 308
Molech, 231
monism, 75, 90

monotheism, 176
mortality, 113, 252
Moses, 41, 119–121, 166, 172, 203–205, 220, 274, 287, 293
Motyer, J. Alec, 213, 214, 340
Muhammad, 25, 26, 29, 31–33, 35–38, 41, 42, 51, 52, 205, 341
Muslim, Muslims: teachings & traditions, i, ii, iii, xv, xvi, xvii, 1, 3–6, 10, 24, 26, 28–31, 34, 36, 37, 39, 40, 42, 48, 50, 51, 105, 106, 216, 243, 328, 330, 331, 335
myth, 143, 176, 272

N

narrative, 11, 124, 143, 147, 153–156, 161, 165, 168–170, 180, 184, 187, 202, 234, 237, 248, 253, 332
nation-building, 65, 69
nations, 27, 50, 79, 80, 174, 211, 214, 215, 228, 259, 265
Naturalism, 105
Nazi, 57, 58, 60, 63
Nazism, 58
Neill, Stephen Charles, 56, 74–83, 91, 92, 327, 328, 340
Netland, Harold, 3, 23, 55, 340
new creation, 70–72, 282
New York, 57, 65, 85, 94,
Noah, 186, 315
non-Christian, xvi, 4, 48, 65, 68, 71, 81, 86–90, 129, 327, 332

O

Obayashi, Hiroshi, 24, 25, 341
obedience, 3, 37, 61–64, 91, 204, 255
objective reality, 6
Okholm, Dennis L., 105, 106, 341
Origen, 138, 139, 323–325
original sin, 100
other faiths, ii, v, xvii, 1, 2, 3, 7, 24, 58, 65, 69–72, 74, 75, 77, 79–82, 87, 88, 90–92, 97, 102, 103, 111,

113, 118, 122, 128–130, 327, 328, 330–332

P

paganism, 247, 249
pain, 31, 33, 34, 149, 263, 298
paradigm, 3, 42, 45, 141, 144
paradise, 25, 27, 32, 36–39, 51, 101, 123, 259, 261, 331
Parrinder, Geoffrey, 12, 24, 26, 27, 30, 31, 37, 38, 341
Passover, 209
Perkins, Pheme, 246, 272, 341
Persian, 120, 121, 212, 217, 219, 220
personal God, 19
Pharisee, 246, 264
Philips, Abu Ameenah Bilal, 31, 106, 341
philosopher, 150, 292, 295, 301
philosophy, xvii, 10, 11, 45, 53, 64, 76, 97, 103–105, 110, 111, 114, 132, 138, 148, 149, 158, 160, 173, 249, 291, 292, 295, 323, 324, 328, 329
physical body, 19, 20, 48–50, 52, 62, 64, 73, 76, 97, 101, 105, 125, 174, 185, 187, 188, 197, 199, 222, 238, 240–242, 251, 252, 255, 262, 264, 284, 285, 296, 307, 311–313
physical death, 62, 64, 101, 174, 188, 199, 238, 240, 242, 313
pit, 174, 177, 178, 180, 191
Plato, 173, 298, 301, 310, 313, 314, 319
pluralism, 2, 4, 6, 55, 58, 61, 76, 80, 81, 88, 91, 93, 105, 107, 113, 116, 129, 149, 166, 167, 171
pluralist, 6, 56, 129, 149
pneuma, 251
politics, 61, 99, 102, 148, 159
Polycarp, 269, 272, 275–278, 280, 283, 284, 285, 287, 288, 307, 341
Polytheism, 176
positivism, 45
post-Christian, 78
Post-Modern, 42

Prabhavananda, Swami, 14, 20, 341
pre-understanding, 135, 137, 145
Prickett, John, 12, 24, 336, 341
propaganda, 70
propositional, 170
Protestant, iii, iv, 55, 114, 133

Q

Qahtani, al-, Saeed Ali. *See* Al-Qahtani.
Quran. *See also* Koran, 33

R

Ramachandra, Vinoth, 107, 170
Rambachan, Anantanand, 19, 20, 22, 48, 341
reader, iii, xvii, 95, 133, 134, 136, 137, 141, 142, 145, 146, 155, 158–162, 164, 168, 169, 210, 302
realized eschatology, 235, 236, 249
redemption, 98, 100, 101, 211, 249
Reformed, 84, 112, 159
Reich, 57, 58
reincarnation, 32, 47, 48, 50, 53, 74, 111, 113, 116, 126, 127, 301, 324, 329, 332
relativism, 85, 90, 91, 106, 128, 146, 158
religion, ii, iii, xvi, 5, 9, 10, 29, 42, 43, 48, 58, 66–68, 70, 73, 74, 87, 89, 90, 105–108, 110, 112, 116, 128, 174, 233, 291, 306, 318, 331, 332
religious freedom, 73, 128
religious leaders, 9, 68
Renaissance, 46, 95, 96, 343
renewal, 67, 153, 207, 209, 211, 253, 295, 304
repentance, 61, 205, 206, 282, 286
responsibility, 49, 50, 63, 72, 77, 86, 91, 101, 116, 142, 159
rest, 29, 34, 47, 75, 90, 122, 174, 180, 186, 187, 211, 239, 260–262, 266, 271, 281, 292, 296, 302, 315, 318
ritual, 14
Roberts, Alexander, 268, 341, 308

Roman Catholic, iv, 6, 26, 55, 56, 93, 115, 116
Rome, 114, 115, 138, 268, 271, 272, 282, 298, 307, 308, 344
rural, 73

S

sacrifice, 14, 21, 62, 63, 76, 79, 202, 203, 231, 332
Sadducee, 121
Samuel, 120, 180, 203–205, 216
Sankaracharya, 16
Satan, 30, 229, 261, 265, 277, 288
Saudi Arabia, 24, 333, 344
Saul, King, 180
Schleiermacher, 139, 140, 141, 144
Scotland, 74
Seale, 28, 34–37, 39–41, 342
second death, 10, 230, 259, 260, 263, 265, 266
secular, iv, xvi, 1, 2, 4, 10, 59, 60, 62, 69, 77, 95, 96, 102, 332
Secularism, 5, 42, 43, 70
secularization, 43
Segal, Eliezer, iv, 174, 342
Self, the, 13–23, 48–50, 68, 343
self-sacrifice, 62, 63
Semitic religions, 11, 24
shade, 36, 40, 180
signpost, 253
sleep, 16, 22, 32, 120, 214, 215, 219, 248
Smith, Jane Idleman, 27, 28, 30, 32–34, 38, 39, 342
Smith, C. Ryder, 191, 192, 342
social, 1, 18, 44, 70, 73, 83, 84, 91, 94, 97–99, 102, 129, 139, 140, 142, 147–150, 152, 163, 167, 182, 190
Socialism, 60
Sparks, Jack, 277, 342
spiritual body, 222, 251, 252
Spronk, Klaas, 189, 342
Stoics, Stoicism, 46, 52, 138, 249, 296, 319
Student Christian Movement, 75, 93, 94

subjective reality, 6
suffering, 34, 50, 62, 63, 94, 102, 191, 193, 197, 253, 285, 288, 296, 317, 318
Sumithra, Sunand, iv, 64–66, 68, 93–96, 100–103, 342
supernatural, 46, 106, 174, 175, 328
Switzerland, 85, 114
symbol, 101
syncretism, 85, 89, 90, 91, 128
synoptic, 122, 219, 222, 233
synthesis, 128, 155
Systematic Theology, 56, 336

T

temple, 193, 224, 235, 237, 242, 259, 260, 263, 265, 271, 280
Tertullian, 208, 271, 273, 282, 299, 300–307, 309, 321–323, 325, 343
textual, 135, 136, 152, 157, 160, 170, 192, 197, 246
theologian, 6, 38, 51, 56, 85, 90, 93, 95, 114, 115, 117, 129, 131, 148, 323
theologizing, 99, 103, 117
theology of religions, ii, xv, xvi, 2, 3, 5, 55, 66
Theophilus, 298–300, 343
Theosophy, 103, 105, 111
Thessalonica, 247
Thiselton, Anthony C., 131–135, 137–157, 165–168, 249, 343
Thomas, M. M., iii, 6, 56, 70, 93–103, 129, 343
tolerance, 69, 89, 128, 129, 141, 148
torment, 29, 33, 39, 50, 229, 230–233, 240, 287, 321
Toynbee, Arnold, 45, 52, 343
transcendent, 61, 62, 105, 143, 207
trans-contextual, 148, 150, 165–167, 171, 207, 218, 245
transfiguration, 224, 228
transmigration of soul, 290, 303, 325
typological, 139

U

Ugarit, 175
ultimate reality, 43, 105, 112, 324
underworld, 35, 127, 176–180, 184, 190, 191, 199, 230, 286
unity, 26, 60, 68, 72, 82, 83, 89, 92, 101, 112, 128, 129, 155, 290, 325, 332
universal, v, 1, 2, 4, 9, 10, 43, 88, 89, 127, 144, 149, 150, 167, 169, 173, 199, 215, 216, 260, 266, 328
unquenchable, 232, 233, 287
urban, 1, 2, 42, 43, 47, 49, 51, 52, 73, 327, 330

V

Verkuyl, Johannes, 83–85, 95, 344

W

Webb, Barry, 213, 344
Western, iv, 2, 24, 42, 44–47, 52, 77, 79, 87, 308, 335
Wilckens, Ulrich, 225, 226, 344
wine, 37, 40, 69
wisdom, 17, 21, 24, 144–147, 158, 187, 190, 191, 202, 249, 282, 304, 305
women, i, 12, 36, 37, 83, 123, 227, 239, 241, 269, 319
World Council of Churches, 64, 94
World War, 85, 103
worship, 36, 41, 78, 82, 174, 199, 202, 213, 260, 265
wrath, 174, 233, 247, 255, 256, 264, 265, 269, 332

Z

Zain, Abdul Qadir Ahmad, iv, 24, 29, 344
Zoroastrianism, 219

Langham Literature and its imprints are a ministry of Langham Partnership.

Langham Partnership is a global fellowship working in pursuit of the vision God entrusted to its founder John Stott –

> *to facilitate the growth of the church in maturity and Christ-likeness through raising the standards of biblical preaching and teaching.*

Our vision is to see churches in the majority world equipped for mission and growing to maturity in Christ through the ministry of pastors and leaders who believe, teach and live by the Word of God.

Our mission is to strengthen the ministry of the Word of God through:
- nurturing national movements for biblical preaching
- fostering the creation and distribution of evangelical literature
- enhancing evangelical theological education

especially in countries where churches are under-resourced.

Our ministry

Langham Preaching partners with national leaders to nurture indigenous biblical preaching movements for pastors and lay preachers all around the world. With the support of a team of trainers from many countries, a multi-level programme of seminars provides practical training, and is followed by a programme for training local facilitators. Local preachers' groups and national and regional networks ensure continuity and ongoing development, seeking to build vigorous movements committed to Bible exposition.

Langham Literature provides majority world preachers, scholars and seminary libraries with evangelical books and electronic resources through publishing and distribution, grants and discounts. The programme also fosters the creation of indigenous evangelical books in many languages, through writer's grants, strengthening local evangelical publishing houses, and investment in major regional literature projects, such as one volume Bible commentaries like *The Africa Bible Commentary* and *The South Asia Bible Commentary*.

Langham Scholars provides financial support for evangelical doctoral students from the majority world so that, when they return home, they may train pastors and other Christian leaders with sound, biblical and theological teaching. This programme equips those who equip others. Langham Scholars also works in partnership with majority world seminaries in strengthening evangelical theological education. A growing number of Langham Scholars study in high quality doctoral programmes in the majority world itself. As well as teaching the next generation of pastors, graduated Langham Scholars exercise significant influence through their writing and leadership.

To learn more about Langham Partnership and the work we do visit **langham.org**

www.ingramcontent.com/pod-product-compliance
Lightning Source LLC
Chambersburg PA
CBHW050330230426

43663CB00010B/1804